THE NEW SCIENCE OF AGEING

Edited by Alan Walker

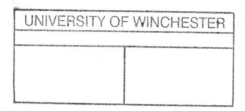

First published in Great Britain in 2014 by

Policy Press
University of Bristol
6th Floor
Howard House
Queen's Avenue
Clifton
Bristol BS8 1SD
UK
Tel +44 (0)117 331 5020
Fax +44 (0)117 331 5367
e-mail pp-info@bristol.ac.uk
www.policypress.co.uk

North American office:
Policy Press
c/o The University of Chicago Press
1427 East 60th Street
Chicago, IL 60637, USA
t: +1 773 702 7700
f: +1 773-702-9756
e:sales@press.uchicago.edu
www.press.uchicago.edu

British Library Cataloguing in Publication Data
A catalogue record for this book is available from the British Library

Library of Congress Cataloging-in-Publication Data
A catalog record for this book has been requested

ISBN 978 1 44731 467 7 paperback
ISBN 978 1 44731 466 0 hardcover

Cover design by Policy Press
Front cover images: wwwistock.com
Printed and bound in Great Britain by CMP, Poole
Policy Press use environmentally responsible print partners

Contents

List of tables and figures   iv

Acknowledgements   v

List of contributors   vii

one   Towards a new science of ageing   1
       Alan Walker

two   Understanding ageing: biological and social perspectives   25
       Lynne S. Cox, Penelope A. Mason, Mark C. Bagley, David Steinsaltz,
       Aneta Stefanovska, Alan Bernjak, Peter V.E. McClintock,
       Anna C. Phillips, Jane Upton, Joanna E. Latimer and Terence Davis

three   Understanding and transforming ageing through the arts   77
       Michael Murray, David Amigoni, Miriam Bernard, Amanda
       Crummett, Anna Goulding, Lucy Munro, Andrew Newman,
       Jill Rezzano, Michelle Rickett, Philip Tew and Lorna Warren

four   Maintaining health and well-being: overcoming barriers   113
       to healthy ageing
       Sara Arber, Ann Bowling, Andrea Creech, Myanna Duncan,
       Anna Goulding, Diane Gyi, Susan Hallam, Cheryl Haslam,
       Aadil Kazi, Liz Lloyd, Janet Lord, MAP2030 team,
       Mike Murphy, Andrew Newman, Anna C. Phillips,
       Ricardo Twumasi and Jane Upton

five   Food environments: from home to hospital   155
       Janice L. Thompson, Sheila Peace, Arlene Astell,
       Paula Moynihan and Alastair Macdonald

six   Participation and social connectivity   181
       Penny Vera-Sanso, Armando Barrientos, Leela Damodaran,
       Kenneth Gilhooly, Anna Goulding, Catherine Hennessy, Robin Means,
       Michael Murray, Andrew Newman, Wendy Olphert, Jatinder Sandhu,
       Philip Tew, Janice L. Thompson, Christina Victor and Nigel Walford

seven   Design for living in later life   209
       Mike Timmins, Alastair Macdonald, Constantinos Maganaris,
       Cheryl Haslam, Diane Gyi, Eleanor van den Heuvel,
       Irene di Giulio, Jane McCann, Martin Maguire, Sheila Peace
       and John Percival

eight   A new policy perspective on ageing   241
       Alan Walker

References   261

Appendix: NDA Programme project team members   309

Index   317

List of tables and figures

Tables

1.1	Research Council initiatives on ageing	14
1.2	Cross-Research Council initiatives on ageing	14
1.3	Distribution of investigators across Research Council domains in three ageing research programmes (%)	19
4.1	Population aged 65 and over and 85 and over, and growth in period 2010–35, UK	115
7.1	NDA projects contributing to this chapter	214
7.2	Aspects of the design process	214
7.3	Processes for involvement of users with the designer	233

Figures

2.1	Assessing processes of ageing from cells through tissues to organ systems	26
2.2	Ageing as a risk factor for age-related disease	32
2.3	Mortality rates plotted on a logarithmic scale, various human populations	35
2.4	Compression of morbidity and the increase in healthspan	39
2.5	Biological pathways that affect ageing	40
2.6	Proposed effects of senescent cells on tissue pathology	49
2.7	The cardiovascular system	51
2.8	Heart rate variability decreases with age, but the amplitude of blood flow pulsation increases	54
2.9A	Schematic representation of a neuron, consisting of the cell body (soma), the dendrites that surround it, the axon and the nerve ending with synapses	57
2.9B	Averaged cross-section of the brain as imaged by MRI	57
2.9C	A sketch of the local structure of the brain	57
2.9D	White matter volume does not appreciably change with age in either males (upper line) or females (lower line)	57
2.9E	By contrast, the volume of grey matter decreases significantly with age	57
2.10	Immune cells and ageing	61
4.1	Examples of @ work cards	143
6.1	A 'traditional' style network map with the participant at the centre	200
6.2	A textual network list	200
7.1	Communicating with older people	230
8.1	The cycle of well-being	252

Acknowledgements

The preparation of a volume such as this requires an unusually high level of collaboration across projects and disciplines. The aspiration to create an integrated multi-disciplinary approach to key gerontological topics is very difficult to achieve even when, due to the resources available to the New Dynamics of Ageing (NDA) Programme, it is possible to enable potential co-authors to sit together in the same room. The ideal of a sustained symposium as the engine of co-production between disciplines is simply not feasible. As well as time and material resources, such an endeavour is impossible without the enthusiasm of the participants. I am pleased to say that we had this in abundance, even from researchers in disciplines that generally frown upon (or worse) book chapters. So, first, thanks go to all of those who contributed to this book. Your commitments to the NDA Programme and to this joint project are appreciated greatly.

Such a major programme as the NDA takes a great deal of effort to realise. The essential element is funding and, therefore, the contributions of the five Research Councils (the Arts and Humanities Research Council – AHRC; the Biotechnology and Biological Sciences Research Council – BBSRC; the Engineering and Physical Sciences Research Council – EPSRC; the Economic and Social Research Council – ESRC; and the Medical Research Council – MRC) cannot be underestimated. On behalf of all of the NDA researchers, I very gratefully acknowledge this funding. The key players who backed the idea from the outset and put in the detailed work necessary to secure funding for it were Joy Todd and Ros Rouse from the ESRC, and Peter Hedges and Kedar Pandya from the EPSRC. Joy's support over the life of the Programme has been important to its success. Then there are those who took part in Commissioning Panels, and in the New Dynamics of Nutrition IDEAS Factory and those who provided peer reviews of the many proposals. The NDA Advisory Committee, chaired by Sally Greengross and Anthea Tinker, was a superb and much valued source of support. Other members were Alan Beazley, Alan Blackwell, Chris Carey, Mark Gorman, Tessa Harding, David Leon, Angela McCullagh, Bronagh Miskelly, Naina Patel, Chris Phillipson and Jim Soulsby. Previous members include: Keith Bright, Paul Cann, Steve Cook, Rachel Kyrs, Janet Lord and Tony Martin. Special mention must be made of Anthea, whose wise advice, clear judgement, enthusiasm and friendship could always be relied upon.

The Older Persons Reference Group, while rightly challenging at times, was also an essential ingredient in this Programme's success. Led by Mary Sinfield, its current members include: John Barry, Mary Brown, Cynthia Conrad, Jim Harding, Anthony Hill, John Jeffrey, Savita Katbamna, Teresa Lefort, Irene Richards, Elsie Richardson, Elizabeth Sclater, Harbhajan Singh and Brian Todd. Previous members include: Diane Andrews, John Appleyard, Bob Bell, Brian Booker, Tony Carter, John Christie, Janet Cullup, Iris Dodds, Christine Hamilton, David Hart, Shirley Heselton, Pauline Richards, Norman Richards, Barbara Shillabeer, Diane Smeeton, Steve Thornett, Stephen Townsend and Urmilla Tanna.

The NDA Programme has had three ESRC liaison officers, Joy Todd, Andrew Stafford and Chiaki Beis. In Sheffield it has had three administrators, Marg Walker, Karen Tsui and Sarah Howson. My thanks go to all of these colleagues who contributed substantially to the NDA Programme and my apologies to those inadvertently overlooked.

Lastly, thanks go to those engaged in the final production process: Sarah Howson, Rhonda Martin, Natalija Jarosenko, Rachel Kaye and Adele Blinston at Sheffield; Isobel Bainton at Policy Press; the anonymous Policy Press reader who provided helpful comments; and especially Alan Blackwell who volunteered to read all of the chapters and who provided detailed and very constructive feedback. Of those involved in the production process, Sarah Howson's contribution was phenomenal. She badgered and coaxed contributors with determination and diplomacy, set and re-set deadlines, took on a wide range of technical tasks in the preparation of the manuscript and oversaw the whole process with incredible fortitude. My special thanks to her.

Alan Walker
University of Sheffield

List of contributors

David Amigoni, Professor of Victorian Literature, Keele University

Sara Arber, Professor of Sociology, University of Surrey

Arlene Astell, Professor of Health Services Research, University of Sheffield

Mark C. Bagley, Professor of Organic Chemistry, University of Sussex

Armando Barrientos, Professor in Poverty and Social Justice, University of Manchester

Miriam Bernard, Professor of Social Gerontology, Keele University

Alan Bernjak, Research Associate, University of Sheffield

Ann Bowling, Professor of Health Sciences, University of Southampton

Lynne S. Cox, Associate Professor in Biochemistry, University of Oxford

Andrea Creech, Senior Lecturer in Education, Institute of Education

Amanda Crummett, Research Associate, Keele University

Leela Damodaran, Professor of Digital Inclusion and Participation, Loughborough University

Terence Davis, Research Fellow in Biogerontology, Cardiff University

Irene di Giulio, Research Associate, University College London

Myanna Duncan, Research Associate, Loughborough University

Kenneth Gilhooly, Research Professor in Quantitative Gerontology, Brunel University

Anna Goulding, Research Associate, Newcastle University

Diane Gyi, Reader in Health Ergonomics and Design, Loughborough University

Susan Hallam, Professor of Education, Institute of Education

Cheryl Haslam, Professor of Health Psychology, Loughborough University

Catherine Hennessy, Professor of Public Health and Ageing, Plymouth University

Aadil Kazi, Research Associate, Loughborough University

Joanna E. Latimer, Professor of Sociology, Cardiff University School of Social Sciences

Liz Lloyd, Reader in Social Gerontology, University of Bristol

Janet Lord, Professor of Immune Cell Biology, University of Birmingham

Alastair Macdonald, Senior Researcher, Glasgow School of Art

Jane McCann, Visiting Professor, University of South Wales

Peter V.E. McClintock, Emeritus Professor of Physics, Lancaster University

Constantinos Maganaris, Professor of Musculoskeletal Biomechanics, Liverpool John Moores University

Martin Maguire, Lecturer, Loughborough University

Penelope A. Mason, Research Associate, University of Oxford

Robin Means, Professor of Health and Social Care, University of the West of England

Paula Moynihan, Professor of Nutrition and Oral Health, Newcastle University

Lucy Munro, Lecturer in Shakespeare and Early Modern Drama, King's College London

Mike Murphy, Professor of Demography, London School of Economics and Political Science

Michael Murray, Professor of Psychology, Keele University

Andrew Newman, Senior Lecturer, Newcastle University

Wendy Olphert, Senior Research Fellow, Loughborough University

Sheila Peace, Professor of Social Gerontology, The Open University

John Percival, Research Associate, Centre for Academic Primary Care NIHR, School for Primary Care Research, School of Social & Community Medicine, University of Bristol

Anna C. Phillips, Reader in Behavioural Medicine, University of Birmingham

Jill Rezzano, Head of Education, New Vic Theatre, Newcastle-under-Lyme

Michelle Rickett, Research Associate, Keele University

Jatinder Sandhu, Researcher, Nottingham Trent University

Aneta Stefanovska, Professor of Biomedical Physics, Lancaster University

David Steinsaltz, Lecturer in Statistics, University of Oxford

Philip Tew, Professor of English (Post-1990 Literature); Director of the Brunel Centre for Contemporary Writing, Brunel University

Janice L. Thompson, Professor of Public Health Nutrition and Exercise, University of Birmingham

Mike Timmins, Consultant, Design for Ageing Well Project

Ricardo Twumasi, Research Associate, Loughborough University

Jane Upton, Research Fellow, University of Birmingham

Eleanor van den Heuvel, Research Fellow, Brunel University

Penny Vera-Sanso, Senior Lecturer in Development Studies and Social Anthropology, Birkbeck, University of London

Christina Victor, Professor of Gerontology and Public Health, Brunel University

Nigel Walford, Professor of Applied GIS, Kingston University London

Alan Walker, Professor of Social Policy and Social Gerontology, University of Sheffield and Director of the New Dynamics of Ageing Research Programme

Lorna Warren, Senior Lecturer in Social Policy, University of Sheffield

ONE

Towards a new science of ageing

Alan Walker

This book and the series it launches arises from a unique collaboration between more than 200 researchers and the widest possible range of non-academic stakeholders in the field of ageing research. The nine-year New Dynamics of Ageing (NDA) Research Programme was funded by five UK Research Councils covering the arts and humanities, biological sciences, engineering, social sciences and medical research. It therefore brought together researchers from every major discipline with an interest in ageing. This was intentional because the NDA Programme was the UK's first major research initiative in the ageing field to attempt to embrace all of the relevant disciplines. The primary intention of this chapter is to outline the objectives and contents of the Programme, as an essential backcloth to the subsequent chapters.

This chapter also identifies significant changes taking place in the field of gerontological science. It is not claimed that these stem directly from the NDA Programme but, rather, that the Programme was both a reflection of the shifting scientific context as well as a source of further stimulation to the changes already under way. The key elements of this emergent new science of ageing are multi-disciplinarity, user engagement and knowledge exchange. The life course perspective and an increasing recognition of inequalities and diversities in ageing are also important aspects of the new approach.

Finally, this chapter explains the process that produced this book and introduces the main chapters.

The starting point is the NDA Programme.

The New Dynamics of Ageing Research Programme

The NDA Programme was the first of its kind: a multi-disciplinary collaboration between five UK Research Councils. At the beginning, in April 2005, there were four Research Councils behind the programme: the Economic and Social Research Council (ESRC), the

Biotechnology and Biological Sciences Research Council (BBSRC), the Engineering and Physical Sciences Research Council (EPSRC) and the Medical Research Council (MRC). A year later the Arts and Humanities Research Council (AHRC) joined in as a co-funder of the Programme. Later, in 2008, the Canadian Institute of Aging (part of the Canadian Institutes of Health Research) also became a co-funding partner in the Programme as 10 new projects were linked to existing UK ones.

The NDA Programme was established with the aims of understanding the new dynamics of ageing, the various influences shaping them and their implications for individuals and society. It had five specific objectives:

- to explore the ways in which individual ageing is subject to different influences over the life course;
- to understand the dynamic ways in which the meaning and experience of ageing are currently changing and becoming more diverse;
- to encourage and support the development of innovative inter-disciplinary research groups and methods;
- to provide a sound evidence base for policy and practice (including the development of prototype systems, procedures and devices) so that research contributes to well-being and quality of life; and
- to promote new opportunities for UK science to link with researchers in the European Union (EU) and beyond.

The NDA Programme consisted of two substantive research themes – ageing well across the life course and ageing and its environments – with eight subthemes:

- active ageing
- autonomy and independence
- later life transitions
- the oldest old
- resources for ageing
- locality, place and participation
- the built and technological environment
- the global dynamics of ageing

The multi-faceted and lengthy commissioning process produced a total of 35 projects (excluding the Canadian ones), each of which lasted anywhere between 18 months and 4 years, with the majority spanning 2 to 3 years. These projects fell into two broad groups. On the one hand there were 11 large collaborative research projects. Those multi-disciplinary and multi-work package collaborations (involving disciplines under at least two of the participatory Research Councils) could be said to represent the essence of the NDA Programme. On the other hand there were 24 smaller-scale programme projects which included a few that were not multi-disciplinary (see below). There follows a list of these projects, with the names and affiliations of the principal investigators (PIs) and, in brackets, their completion dates.

Collaborative research projects

- SomnIA: Optimising quality of sleep among older people in the community and care homes: An integrated approach – Sara Arber, University of Surrey (May 2011).
- NANA: Novel assessment of nutrition and ageing – Arlene Astell, St Andrews University (March 2013).
- SUS-IT: Sustaining IT use by older people to promote autonomy and independence – Leela Damodaran, Loughborough University (September 2012).
- Working Late: Strategies to enhance productive and healthy environments for the older workers – Cheryl Haslam, Loughborough University (March 2013).
- Grey and pleasant land? An inter-disciplinary exploration of the connectivity of older people in rural civic society – Catherine Hennessey, University of Plymouth (March 2012).
- HALCyon Project: Healthy ageing across the life course – Diana Kuh, Medical Research Council (March 2014).
- Design for Ageing Well: Improving quality of life for the ageing population using a technology enabled garment system – Jane McCann, Newport School of Art, Media & Design (April 2012).
- mappmal: Multi-disciplinary approaches to develop prototype for the prevention of malnutrition in older people: Products, places, people and procedures – Paula Moynihan, Newcastle University (April 2012).
- MAP2030: Modelling needs and resources of older people to 2030 – Michael Murphy, London School of Economics and Political Science, (June 2010).
- MINA: Migration, nutrition and ageing across the life course in Bangladeshi families: A transnational perspective – Janice Thompson, University of Bristol (November 2011).

- TACT3: Tackling ageing continence through theory, tools and technology – Eleanor van den Heuvel, Brunel University (April 2012).

Programme projects

- Ageing and biology: A combined genetic and small molecule approach to studying the role of p38/MK2 stress signaling pathway in human premature ageing syndrome – Mark C. Bagley, Cardiff University (December 2012).
- Ageing, well-being and development: A comparative study of Brazil and South Africa – Armando Barrientos, University of Manchester (June 2011).
- Ages and stages: The place of theatre in representations and recollections of ageing – Miriam Bernard, Keele University (July 2012) (follow-on funding August 2012-July 2013).
- Longitudinal data: Transitions, choices and health at older ages: life course analyses of longitudinal data – David Blane, Imperial College London (December 2009).
- Quality of life: Psychometric testing of the multidimensional older people's quality of life (OPQoL) questionnaire and the causal model of QoL underpinning it – Ann Bowling, University College London (March 2009) (follow-on funding October 2010-September 2011).
- Cell ageing: Towards understanding the biological drivers of cellular ageing – Lynne Cox, University of Oxford (September 2012).
- Financial abuse: Detecting and preventing financial abuse: An examination of decision-making by managers and professionals – Mary Gilhooly, Brunel University (March 2011) (follow-on Knowledge Transfer Grant September 2011-August 2012).
- Music for life: Promoting social engagement and well-being in older people through participation in musical activities – Susan Hallam, Institute of Education (January 2011) (follow-on funding September 2011-December 2012).
- Dignity in care: Maintaining dignity in later life: A longitudinal qualitative study of older people's experiences of supportive care – Liz Lloyd, University of Bristol (June 2011).
- Stress and immunity: Synergistic effects of physical and psychological stress upon immunosenescence – Janet Lord, University of Birmingham (December 2012).
- Envision: Innovation in envisioning dynamic biomechanical data to inform healthcare and design practice – Alastair Macdonald, Glasgow School of Art (January 2009).

- Safety on stairs (SOS): Biomechanical and sensory constraints of step and stair negotiation in old age – Constantinos Maganaris, Manchester Metropolitan University (February 2014).
- Mobility and ageing: New metrics for exploring the relationship between mobility and successful ageing – Lynn McInnes, Northumbria University (December 2009).
- CALL-ME: Promoting independence and social engagement among older people in disadvantaged communities – Michael Murray, Keele University (February 2011).
- Art and identity: Contemporary visual art and identity construction – Well-being amongst older people – Andrew Newman, Newcastle University (October 2011) (follow-on funding January 2012-January 2013).
- Kitchen living: Transitions in Kitchen Living (TiKL) – Sheila Peace, Open University (November 2011).
- OPUS: Older People's Use of Unfamiliar Space – Judith Phillips, University of Wales (April 2010).
- Cardiovascular ageing: Dynamics of cardiovascular ageing – Aneta Stefanovska, Lancaster University (March 2012).
- Longitudinal ageing: Trajectories of senescence through Markov models – David Steinsaltz, University of Oxford (June 2012).
- Ageing and fiction: Fiction and the cultural mediation of ageing – Philip Tew, Brunel University (May 2012) (follow-on funding September 2012-July 2013).
- Poverty in India: Ageing, poverty and neoliberalism in urban South India – Penny Vera-Sanso, Birkbeck, University of London (April 2010).
- South Asian: Families and caring in South Asian communities – Christina Victor, University of Reading (June 2011).
- Look at me! Representing self – Representing ageing – Lorna Warren, University of Sheffield (November 2011).
- Landscapes: Landscapes of cross-generational engagement – Peter Wright, Sheffield Hallam University (December 2010).

Commissioning the NDA Programme

It is obvious that such a large and complex multi-disciplinary programme would have a complicated commissioning process. Four or five Research Councils had not previously collaborated in this way and, before the first call for project proposals could be issued, they had to agree a common set of commissioning and funding criteria. Because each Council had its own set of rules, covering everything from initial eligibility to what specific items could be claimed within budgets, this was a protracted process. In the end a common–sense version of the musketeers' code was adopted: if one Council allowed it, all would. (It is easy to underestimate the labour involved in such negotiations by Research Council staff and, in the end, they did a superb job.)

The first call for proposals was published in April 2005. Following a two–stage application process and two commissioning panels, in October 2005 and April 2006, only two collaborative research projects (CRPs) were funded. This disappointing outcome was made worse by the fact that the two CRPs were predominantly in the social sciences. Given that the first stage of commissioning had brought forward nearly 300 expressions of interest and involved compulsory attendance at one of two workshops aimed at grouping them into topic areas, there was a predictably adverse reaction from many of those involved. Thus the Programme's reputation suffered an initial set back and the adverse effect on the context in which it operated was longer lasting.

The Research Councils' response was creative and, as well as streamlining the commissioning process, a new initiative was launched: preparatory networks. These were designed to enable researchers to meet together and prepare NDA applications. Funding of up to £20,000 was available for each network for up to 12 months. In September 2006 a commissioning panel funded 11 networks (out of 33 applications). In June 2007 12 programme projects were funded. In early 2008 the second round of CRP applications was shortlisted and this included 10 of the 11 preparatory networks.

Then an IDEAS Factory on the New Dynamics of Nutrition took place, involving 20 participants selected from a total of 90 outline proposals. The week–long IDEAS Factory (or 'creative sandpit') comprised a mixture of research stimulation events and presentations, as well as time devoted to preparing applications, with a commissioning panel as the final stage. Additional funding from EPSRC enabled three of the CRP proposals from the sandpit to be supported.

The third set of CRPs commissioned, in June 2008, saw six funded from a shortlist of 11. Five of these had started life as preparatory networks so this initiative proved to be successful, and was later adopted by the Lifelong Health and Wellbeing (LLHW) joint Council Programme.

The final stage of NDA commissioning, from 2008–09, added a further 12 programme projects. Special efforts were made in this last round to stimulate interest among under-represented disciplines in the arts and humanities and biological sciences. As a result, these disciplines were strongly represented in both the 40 short-listed applications (out of 189) and the final 12. Also, although it was not obligatory for programme project applicants to create multi-disciplinary teams, the majority (two-thirds) spanned at least two Research Councils and one in six covered three of them.

The Canadian NDA

As mentioned earlier, a partnership was formed with the Canadian Institutes of Health Research (CIHR) which enabled Canadian researchers to bid for funds to link themselves to NDA research teams. Two commissioning rounds were carried out, in 2008 and 2009, which produced the 10 linked projects shown below. It should also be noted that the CIHR applications were peer reviewed by NDA commissioning panel members, which indicates both the high level of trust generated between the CHIR and the NDA Programme and the flexibility open to the former.

- Health and creative ageing: Theatre as a pathway to healthy ageing – Janet Fast, University of Alberta.
  This project is linked to the NDA project 'Ages and stages: The place of theatre in representations and recollections of ageing' led by Miriam Bernard, Keele University (2012).
- How do catastrophic events by modulating the immune response lead to frailty? – Tamàs Fülöp, Université de Sherbrooke.
  This project is linked to the NDA project 'Synergistic effects of physical and psychological stress upon immunosenescence' led by Janet Lord, University of Birmingham (2012).
- Working late: Strategies to enhance productive and healthy environments for the older workforce – the Canadian context – Lan Gien, Memorial University of Newfoundland.
  This project is linked to the NDA project 'Working Late: Strategies to enhance productive and healthy environments for the older workers' led by Cheryl Haslam, Loughborough University (2013).
- Interactive analysis of functional and cognitive change across the IALSA (Integrative Analysis of Longitudinal Studies of Aging) (Canada) and HALCyon (UK) longitudinal research networks – Scott Hofer, University of Victoria.
  This project is linked to the NDA project 'HALCyon Project: Healthy ageing across the life course' led by Diana Kuh, Medical Research Council (2014).

- Developing and validation of a questionnaire to measure the psychological impact of   assistive technologies for continence in elderly individuals – Jeffrey W. Jutai, University of Ottawa.
  This project is linked to the NDA project 'TACT3: Tackling ageing continence through theory, tools and technology' led by Eleanor van den Heuvel, Brunel University (2012).
- Connectivity of older adults in rural communities: Health in context – Norah Keating, University of Alberta.
  This project is linked to the NDA project 'Grey and pleasant land? An inter-disciplinary exploration of the connectivity of older people in rural civic society' led by Catherine Hennessey, Plymouth University (2012).
- Effects of normal and impaired cognitive function on stair descent mobility for older adults – Bradford J. McFadyen, Université Laval.
  This project is linked to the NDA project 'Safety on stairs (SOS): Biomechanical and sensory constraints of step and stair negotiation in old age' led by Costantinos Maganaris, Manchester Metropolitan University (2013).
- The extension of the COACH prompting system to nutrition-related activities among older adults – Alex Mihailidis, University of Toronto.
  This project is linked to the NDA project 'NANA: Novel assessment of nutrition and ageing' led by Arlene Astell, St Andrews University (2013).
- Sustaining information technology use by older adults to promote autonomy and independence: Newfoundland and Labrador cohort – Wendy Young, Memorial University of Newfoundland.
  This project is linked to the NDA project 'SUS-IT: Sustaining IT use by older people to promote autonomy and independence' led by Leela Damodaran, Loughborough University (2012).
- Improving continence across continents, an RCT of continence promotion intervention for older women in the community – Cara Tannenbaum, Université de Montréal.
  This project is linked to the NDA project 'TACT3: Tackling ageing continence through theory, tools and technology' led by Eleanor van den Heuvel, Brunel University (2012).

Elements of a new science of ageing

The NDA Programme may be seen as a manifestation of a significant shift in the field of gerontology, among both scientists and research funders. It was, on the one hand, a reflection of change and, on the other, a further impetus to a continuing development process. What is the nature of this paradigm shift and what explains its occurrence?

First of all, pressures for change came from within the scientific community and externally. Over the last two decades the focus of gerontological research has mirrored the transformation in longevity. An emphasis on extending life expectancy and reducing premature mortality, in the developed world, was appropriate when death rates from infectious diseases were high. With falling death rates, even in late old age, the emphasis has shifted towards ensuring quality of life in the extended years – healthy life expectancy, not just life expectancy (FUTURAGE, 2011). The World Health Organization (WHO) captured this sea change when it said that years have been added to life, and now we must add life to those years. Thus, both science and public policy have been in tune about this new research agenda.

Within science there have been important developments in the understanding of ageing: broadly, a transition from an adherence to chronology as the key indicator of age to a range of other markers, stretching from the biological to the social. Most importantly, the now common acceptance of limitation of function or capability as one common biological aspect of old age, or senescence, rather than in terms of disease or chronology, has had a major impact on the scientific research agenda. For example, it has led to the adoption of a life course perspective which places later life loss of function (and its prevention) in the context of earlier stages of life including childhood. This shift in emphasis from old age and older people to continuous ageing has been aided by the expansion of longitudinal data sets such as the English Longitudinal Study of Ageing. It must be emphasised that loss of function is only one characteristic of old age and it is not necessarily the defining one. Some gerontologists argue that this loss of function should be termed 'senescence' rather than old age, but this does not avoid the risk of negative attribution because it is merely a synonym for old age. Some older people suffer from chronic conditions that dominate their lives, but that is disability rather than old age. The assumption that loss of function is inevitable in old age is widespread, among policy makers, in popular culture and even among gerontologists. Not surprisingly, therefore, this belief is very common among older people themselves: 'What can I expect at my age?' The new science of ageing seeks to question this assumption of the inevitability of decline: while ageing, old age and senescence are inevitable, at least for the foreseeable future, as far as the bulk of the lifelong ageing process is concerned, loss of function and capability are not. If this idea can be more widely accepted, its effects would be transformational (see Chapter Eight, this volume).

There has also been a parallel expansion of definitions and conceptions of age and ageing which include biological, cultural, social and technological conceptions. Perhaps the biggest shift in scientific emphasis has been the growth of multi-disciplinary research. Because this was a central feature of the NDA Programme, it will be discussed at length below. At this stage it should be noted that research funders, notably the UK Research Councils, have been key actors in the growth of multi-disciplinary science in the field of ageing.

Pressures external to science have also been influential in the development of new approaches. Two leading examples require mention. First of all, the subjects of gerontology, older people, have recently begun to press for a closer involvement in all stages of the research process (Barnes and Walker, 1996). This pressure led to the creation of the NDA Older People's Reference Group (OPRG), which, in turn, further encouraged the advocates of older people's involvement. The OPRG was an independent standing reference group which carried out various tasks including advising the director, advising and taking part in projects and representing the Programme at conferences and other events. It compromised around 20 older people, drawn from local forums, who had experience of or an interest in research. Second, the funders of research have, over the past 5-10 years, placed more or less continuously increasing emphasis on the impact of research on society. This is hardly surprising, but, as public resources have come under heavier and heavier scrutiny, the pressures on funders, especially Research Councils, have become greater and greater. As a result the knowledge exchange and communications expectations placed on researchers have also risen exponentially. Scientists have had to respond to this new context and, some willingly, others less so, have adapted their methods and how they tackle the research process.

What all this amounts to, I contend, is a paradigm shift in the gerontological research agenda. It is not a scientific revolution (Kuhn, 1962) because the assumptions and methods of gerontology have not been transformed uniformly, but rather, an uneven evolution in response to changes in science and society. Inevitably some disciplines are in the vanguard of these changes, partly because they cannot avoid them, but more often, for positive reasons, such as the pursuit of richer understandings of ageing and later life, and to fulfil moral beliefs such as the human right of older people to full citizenship in research as well as everyday life (Walker, 2009). Social gerontologists are notably in this position, whereas those working in the biological sciences are less likely to feel the external pressures. The paradigm shift did not commence with the NDA Programme but, when the proper independent evaluations have been carried out, I am certain that it will be shown to have made a significant contribution to it.

So, to summarise, the new science of ageing consists of an increase in the prevalence of multi-disciplinary research (see below); a greater than previous emphasis on life course influences; the common use of the person–environment perspective which places the older or ageing person in a social, economic and physical context; a closer engagement with research end users, including older people; and an increased emphasis on knowledge exchange. This is not to suggest that gerontology has reached a point of perfection in this paradigm shift – far from it. As noted already, progress is patchy across both disciplines and aspects of the research process (which, of course, questions the use of the term 'paradigm shift'). Moreover there are still essential elements that are poorly represented, including multi-disciplinary theorising and age-related inequalities, to which I return in Chapter Eight.

Importance of multi-disciplinarity

On the face of it, the case of multi-disciplinary ageing research should not need to be made: people do not age in disciplinary boxes, and surely a combination of them is required to understand the various aspects of the ageing process? It looks like a no-brainer, on paper at least. In practice, however, there are some formidable barriers blocking multi-disciplinarity, let alone the more advanced goal of inter-disciplinarity. Bruun, Hakkinen and Klein (2005) identify seven such barriers:

- *Structural:* the organisation of science and associated incentives.
- *Knowledge:* lack of familiarity with other disciplines and a vision of their potential contributions.
- *Cultural:* accepted disciplinary understandings, practices, values and language.
- *Epistemological:* disciplinary specific world views.
- *Methodological:* theories and words of enquiry.
- *Psychological:* attitudes and disciplinary identity.
- *Reception:* lack of understanding of the value of multi-disciplinary research by non-scientific audiences.

In similar vein, participants in the workshops organised by the UK National Collaboration on Ageing Research (NCAR) pinpointed a number of these barriers, but highlighted in particular a perceived inflexibility on the part of the Research Councils to support multi- and inter-disciplinary approaches.

Examples of perceived barriers to inter-disciplinarity in research on ageing

- The RAE (Research Assessment Exercise) (now REF, Research Excellence Framework) process through which the quality of academic departments is rated in the UK is based on criteria that are a significant disincentive to inter-disciplinary research collaboration.
- Multi-disciplinary research is typically complex and more time-consuming to orchestrate than single discipline research. Pressures to obtain funding work against developing inter-disciplinary partnerships.
- Ideological differences between academic disciplines which maintain preferences and status distinctions in approaches to knowledge (for example, the implied superiority of approaches based on the experimental paradigm versus phenomenological approaches; the devaluation of interdisciplinary research as a 'pseudo-discipline') are an important barrier to cross-disciplinary working.
- The lack of specific funding designated for inter-disciplinary research, the paucity of inter-disciplinary academic programmes and of opportunities for multi-disciplinary 'cross-training' of established scientists are all additional barriers to this type of research.
- The current peer review system for research proposals in which referees are perceived as often unqualified to assess submissions outside of their own disciplines is inadequate for evaluating complex interdisciplinary study protocols.
- The current structure of Research Council funding is perceived to be risk-aversive in relation to inter-disciplinary proposals with traditional methodologies (for example, randomised controlled trials or RCTs) being favoured to the exclusion of other innovative approaches (for example, mixed qualitative/quantitative methods) required for examining complex research questions related to ageing.
- Research funders are typically unwilling to cover the costs of coordination necessitated by inter-disciplinary collaboration.

Source: Hennessy and Walker (2011)

Despite these barriers, the case for multi- and inter-disciplinary research in the ageing field has been building for some time, from the bottom up, among scientists (Clair and Allman, 2000; Alkema and Alley, 2006). This case derives from the fact that ageing is a multi-dimensional developmental process and therefore requires multiple disciplines, methods and documents of analysis to comprehend it (Huyck, 2003; Settersten, 2003). Combinations of scientists have responded to the obvious need to approach ageing in a multi-disciplinary way, and have successfully surmounted the barriers facing them. The field of environmental gerontology is a case in point (Kendig, 2003). Building on a social-ecological or a person–environment perspective, it typically embraces a wide range of disciplines such as psychology, sociology, health sciences, clinical science, planning, architecture and design (Bronfenbrenner, 1979; Wahl and Iwarsson, 2007). Longitudinal studies of ageing have, for obvious reasons, proved to be major stimulators of multi-disciplinary science. One exemplar is the Nun Study on ageing and Alzheimer's disease among members of a Catholic religious order in the US, which brought together methods and analyses of a wide range of disciplines including neuroscience, psycholinguistics, food science, genetics, dentistry and informatics (Riley and Snowden, 2000; Snowden et al, 1996, 2007; Stein et al, 2007).

UK multi-disciplinary research initiatives

In common with other countries, such as the US (Hodes, 2003), the case for multi-disciplinary research on ageing has been advanced, top down, in the UK by government and the Research Councils. The government's Technology Foresight Initiative (1994/95) and EQUAL (Extend Quality Life) Initiative (1995) were important stimuli for research in ageing. Four of the Research Councils – BBSRC, EPSRC, ESRC and MRC – responded by prioritising ageing as a research topic, including the promotion of specific initiatives which contained elements of multi-disciplinarity (see Table 1.1).

The multi-disciplinary priority in ageing research became more explicit in the late 1990s with the establishment of Age Net (1997-2000). Age Net aimed to 'stimulate multi-disciplinary and multi-sector research partnerships relevant to academia, industry and the National Health Service which would have a beneficial outcome for the health and quality of life of older people.' It was funded by the MRC with government, non-governmental organisation (NGO) and industry partners. During its short life, Age Net convened a series of themed workshops which brought together researchers, users of research findings and policy makers. It also performed the valuable task of producing an inventory of more than 50 existing longitudinal data sets on ageing in the UK with the potential for multi-disciplinary

Table 1.1: Research Council initiatives on ageing

BBSRC	*The Science of Ageing (SAGE) Programme* (1998–2001) focused on normal ageing including cellular senescence, biochemistry of stress, ageing in biological systems and the ageing population and evolution. *The Experimental Research on Ageing (ERA) Programme* (2001–07) supported research on the basic biology of normal ageing including genetic and other dietary, pharmaceutical and environmental factors affecting ageing.
EPSRC	*The EQUAL Programme* (1997–2013) supported four cycles of funding for research in the areas of the built environment, universal design, rehabilitation and prolonging independence in old age.
ESRC	*The Growing Older Programme* (1999–2005) investigated older people's quality of life (QoL) in six areas: defining and measuring QoL; inequalities in QoL; technology and the built environment; healthy and active ageing; family and support networks; and participation and activity in later life.
MRC	The MRC research portfolio on ageing includes basic and clinical studies on healthy ageing and on the causes, prevention and treatment of a wide range of conditions that affect older people. *The MRC-led Integrated Approaches to Healthy Ageing Programme* was a government LINK scheme to promote collaboration between academia and industry.

Source: Hennessy and Walker (2011)

Table 1.2: Cross-Research Council initiatives on ageing

MRC, EPSRC, ESRC, BBSRC	*National Collaboration on Ageing Research (NCAR)* (2001–04) aimed to develop consensus among researchers/research end users regarding priorities for inter-disciplinary research collaboration and the means and methods for reducing barriers to this collaboration; it worked with the sponsoring Research Councils to develop innovations in the joint sponsorship and funding of inter-disciplinary research on ageing.
EPSRC, BBSRC	*Strategic Promotion of Ageing Research Capacity (SPARC)* (2005–09) was established to stimulate ageing research through showcasing the latest research findings from design, engineering and biology; lobbying policy makers regarding the application of research in needs of older people; and providing pump-priming funds for newcomers to ageing research.
ESRC, EPSRC, MRC, BBSRC, AHRC	*The New Dynamics of Ageing (NDA) Programme* (2005–14) encouraged and supported the development of innovative multi-disciplinary research groups and methods to advance the understanding of the dynamic forces which influence ageing well and to provide a sound evidence base for policy and practice relevant to older people's quality of life.
MRC, BBSRC, EPSRC, ESRC	*Lifelong Health and Wellbeing (LLHW)* (2007–) was developed to strengthen multi-disciplinary and collaborative research into lifelong health and well-being within the UK in the areas of the ageing brain, frailty and health-related quality of life.

Source: Hennessy and Walker (2011)

secondary analysis (Huppert et al, 2000a). The groundwork done by Age Net helped to prepare the way for several subsequent initiatives taken by the Research Councils to promote multi-disciplinary ageing research (see Table 1.2).

The first of these Research Council partnerships was the NCAR, which was specifically created to generate a cross-Council approach to ageing research and to encourage multi-disciplinary applications to the Research Councils (Walker and Hennessy, 2002). As such, the NCAR was not a research funding programme, but was rather intended as a vehicle for facilitating the structural and intellectual collaboration on which subsequent cross-Council funding streams for ageing research were to be based. The objectives of the NCAR included:

- *stimulating new multi-disciplinary research groups in the field of ageing* through working with existing ageing research networks (that is, the EPSRC's EQUAL network and the ESRC's Growing Older Programme) and fostering new networks via scientific workshops and consultations with researchers in the field of ageing;
- *promoting coordination among the research funding bodies* through working with the Cross-Council Coordination Committee on Ageing Research comprised of members from the sponsoring Research Councils, and participating in a Funders' Forum for Research on Ageing and Older People with representation from the Research Councils, the Department of Health and various UK research charities with interest or commitment to research on ageing or age-associated disease. These activities were aimed at identifying areas where joint working could have the maximum impact and reducing the organisational barriers to inter-disciplinary working through the development of joint strategies for sponsoring and funding research on ageing;
- *encouraging stronger links between research and policy and practice in the ageing field* through consultation with research end users including government bodies, NGOs and charities with interests relevant to ageing and older people;
- *developing the European dimension of ageing research in the UK* through participation in and leadership of the European Research Area on Ageing (ERA-AGE) project (2004–09) funded by the European Commission to conduct parallel research development activities with European partners in nine countries (Geyer, 2005).

Since the conclusion of NCAR in 2004, the Research Councils have launched the three major co-sponsored research programmes outlined in Table 1.2 – SPARC, NDA and LLHW. Collectively these initiatives provide broad coverage of topics relevant to the conditions, influences and supports for quality of later life, and actively encourage work at the intersection of disciplines in these areas.

NDA approach to multi-disciplinarity

As noted previously, the NDA Programme was established, in large part, to promote multi-disciplinary research on ageing. The five Research Councils supporting it were explicit in their intention to encourage, by the tried and tested mechanism of the carrot of research funding, scientists from a wide range of disciplines to collaborate. This addressed in the most direct way the problem of lack of funding identified by NCAR workshops with scientists.

In what specific ways was multi-disciplinarity supported by the Programme? First of all, in the early stages of commissioning, it was stipulated that applications must cross the boundaries of at least two of the funding Research Councils. This stipulation proved to be challenging to the research communities and, in any case, it had to be dropped for the final round of commissioning to try and ensure a reasonable spread of projects across the five Research Councils. None the less, as noted earlier, the last round of commissioning, for programme projects, did secure a high level of multi-disciplinary applications. Contrary to claims made elsewhere (Lansley, 2013) this suggests that the research community was not well prepared for multi-disciplinary ageing research but, rather, had to learn the ropes. Efforts were made to reach out to potential applicants, following the announcement of a call for proposals, by holding special introductory workshops to explain the key aspects of the NDA Programme and the nuts and bolts of how to make applications. Fifteen of these NDA research stimulation workshops were held, with three of them being devoted to the arts and humanities as the relative newcomers to the field.

Second, in order to address directly the feedback from researchers in the NCAR workshops and following the first round of NDA commissioning, that a principle barrier to multi-disciplinary collaboration was the lack of resources required to support the development of contacts between different disciplines, the Research Council took the bold step of providing seed-corn money to incubate research partnerships. In 2006 the NDA funded 11 preparatory networks for periods of up to one year to give scientists the modest support they asked for in order to plan project applications by, for example, enlisting team members, creating contacts with research and users, scoping facilities and conducting literature reviews (Klein, 1990; Tait and Lyall, 2001).

Each preparatory network was funded up to £20,000 and, apart from observing the rules with regard to the appropriate expenditure of their grant, the only stipulation was that an application had to be made in response to the second call for CRPs in the autumn of 2007. In practice, the networks used the seed-corn funding to do a wide variety of creative things, such as literature reviews, holding away days and sandpits, identifying data sets for secondary analysis, forming reference groups of older people and supporting regular meetings of the network. All 11 of the networks submitted a proposal to the second CRP open call, 10 of which were short-listed. That call for proposals led to the award of six major projects, following the usual commissioning panels and full peer review process, five of which were from preparatory networks. Moreover, the other alpha-rated but unfunded applications were all from these networks.

In terms of their hit rate alone, the novel preparatory networks initiative must be judged a success but, more importantly, they all matured into highly successful NDA projects based on the reports of the preparatory network coordinators. Hennessy and Walker (2011) identify five specific benefits of this innovation: the facilitation of new multi-disciplinary collaborations, the expansion of research capacity, organic growth in networks, an expansion of individual research portfolios and the embedding of user engagement within research plans (the preparatory networks comprised over 130 academic participants, 80 from non-academic research user organisations and groups). In addition to these benefits, the preparatory network innovation allowed the NDA director a great deal of latitude to influence the shape of the networks and their research agendas; history will judge whether or not this was beneficial! For now if can be concluded that the preparatory networks were highly successful in promoting multi-disciplinary collaborations. They did what it said on the tin.

The third way in which the Programme promoted multi-disciplinarity was by capacity building. This took two main forms. First of all, the bi-annual Programme meetings had formed presentations on multi-disciplinarity, shared experiences and knowledge between projects, and allowed researchers at all stages of their careers to discuss together the challenges of such collaborations. There was a lot of learning from the 'talent in the room' whereby successful projects explained the secrets of their success. Towards the end of the programme researchers worked in thematic groups which sponsored all disciplines, one tangible result of which is the chapters in this book. Second, a specific objective of the

NDA Programme was to build capacity among early career researchers, and the chief mechanisms to fulfil this, apart from Programme meetings, was a series of a dozen workshops and mini conferences geared specifically to PhD and post-doctoral researchers. Three of these were mounted in collaboration with the British Society of Gerontology's Early Career Researchers in Ageing group and one with KT-EQUAL. Altogether 42 post-doctoral researchers and 25 PhD students were trained within the NDA Programme, so it contributed significantly to the coming generations of researchers on ageing.

There is little doubt that the NDA Programme boosted multi-disciplinary ageing research in the UK and, in partnership with CIHR, in Canada too, albeit to a more modest extent. But multi-disciplinarity should not be regarded as an end in itself; the key issue is, was this approach necessary and beneficial to the research endeavour? Did it lead to findings and societal impact that could not have been produced by single disciplinary researchers pursuing their own private agendas? The answer to these questions is an emphatic yes. The evidence is legion and all available publically in the form of the 35 NDA findings documents, the programme summary and this volume (as well as subsequent ones). Pick any of the CRPs and you will see the fruits of the multi-disciplinarity at work. The rest of this book has examples a plenty, so here is just one for now. It would have been impossible for the Hospitalfoodie device to have been produced without collaboration between nutritionists, health service researchers, clinicians, psychologists, computer scientists and graphic designers, and also a wide range of non-academic research users. As indicated previously, there were some NDA projects that were not multi-disciplinary or which comprised only cognate disciplines, but they were a minority. Thus, even relatively small-scale projects, such as 'Transitions in Kitchen Living', required input from at least five disciplines, ranging from gerontology to ergonomics, to achieve its research objectives.

A diversion

Despite the considerable amount of evidence to the contrary, the multi-disciplinary nature of the NDA Programme has been called into question. In an article which extols the virtues of the EQUAL Programme, by the one-time director of the EQUAL network, the multi-disciplinarity of the NDA was rated as only modest (Lansley, 2013). I have addressed at length the flimsy nature of the evidence behind this false claim (see Walker, 2013; www.newdynamics.group. shef.ac.uk/assets/files/Multidisciplinarity%20Rejoinder.pdf), but it is important here to reiterate two elements of that rebuttal. First of all, the claim was based on a complete misunderstanding of the NDA Programme. As pointed out earlier, there were some NDA projects that were not multi-disciplinary. This is because the research questions they tackled did not require a variety of disciplines to answer them. But this does not mean, as claimed, that the multi-disciplinary power of the programme was diminished. This is because those few projects functioned within the context of a multi-disciplinary research environment, a fact that is completely ignored by the offending article. The Programme was multi-disciplinary, but not every project within it.

Second, some highly spurious data are adduced to support the central assertion of multi-disciplinary superiority for the EQUAL Programme. These data consist of the 'home' Research Councils of the PIs of the projects within the three programmes being compared. Although seriously doubting the validity of this exercise and the reliability of the data employed in the original table, Table 1.3 presents a re-working of them to show the 'home' Research Councils of all researchers engaged in the projects and not only those of the PIs. As can be seen, the NDA Programme has the flattest, most even distribution of the three. EQUAL was dominated by the EPSRC and performed below the NDA in terms of disciplinary spread.

Table 1.3: Distribution of investigators across Research Council domains in three ageing research programmes (%)

Programme	Research Councils						
	AHRC	**BBSRC**	**EPSRC**	**ESRC**	**MRC/Health**	**Total**	**Number**
EQUAL	6.8	3.4	54.8	13.0	21.8	100	146
LLHW	3.7	8.1	8.7	18.1	42.4	100	160
NDA	10.6	13.5	15.00	33.8	27.1	100	207

Source: Derived from Lansley (2013, p 10)

Table 1.3 raises at least one further question: is it simply the case that the lead Research Council for each cross-Council Programme ends up with the most projects? This would appear to be the case. Perhaps the lead Council communicates best and resonates most clearly with its own constituency when calls for proposals are issued. Perhaps a factor as basic as the language and terminology contained within call documents has an influential impact. In the case of the NDA Programme, however, the largest contributor to its budget, in fact, was the EPSRC (even though the ESRC was the designated administrative lead). It is a considerable tribute to that Research Council that it was less concerned with funding research projects within its own domain and much more focused on promoting the best possible and most practically useful research regardless of the 'home domains' issue. This commitment was demonstrated fully in the New Dynamics of Nutrition sandpit which EPSRC funded and which supported mostly non-EPSRC researchers.

A related issue concerns the role of social gerontology in multi-disciplinary research. The social sciences are clearly central to the development of a new science of ageing. While they cannot be the sole contributors, it is a social model of ageing, rather than a biological or chronological one, that is the main engine of the emerging new model discussed earlier. Also, in terms of methods, it is arguable that the social sciences are essential contributors to the new science of ageing. These methods – ranging from secondary analysis of longitudinal data sets to focus groups – are often the thread that links different disciplines in a multi-disciplinary collaboration.

Introducing the book

The chapters in this volume all derive from research conducted under the NDA Programme. The 49 authors and associate authors consist of all the NDA PIs on the NDA projects and many of their co-researchers (a full list is in the Appendix, p 309). The volume is unique because rather than the very familiar format of similar books which are divided into disciplines, this one is avowedly multi-disciplinary. To achieve this outcome NDA meetings were used to, first, refine the proposed themes of the volume, and then to enable the authors to plan and begin writing their collective chapters. Given the wide disciplinary spread of the programme this was a challenging process, and inevitably, some fared more successfully than others in combining their approaches. This is the first attempt to break the mould of gerontological scholarship, and it is a tribute to the skill as well as the commitment of its authors. Together they have produced a unique introduction to the new multi-disciplinary science of ageing.

Chapter Two focuses chiefly on the basic biology of ageing. This consideration is prefaced by insights into the social construction of age which emphasises that what biologists or biogerontologists understand as ageing, cell senescence, is only one manifestation of a complex phenomenon. In everyday life ageing is often attributed to chronology and appearance. So, for example, people may be discriminated against in the labour market from the age of 50 regardless of their biological status. There is a connection, however, between cell senescence and social perceptions of ageing, and that is, loss of functional capacity. Following this contextual preface the authors provide an authoritative overview of the biology of ageing – from theories of ageing processes, to measurement, to the idea of normal ageing. For all non-biologists this expert summary should be required reading. The chapter then considers what might be done to modulate cellular ageing, such as calorie restriction, inhibiting stress and supplementing the immune system. Again, this is a highly authoritative summary of the latest research evidence. Finally, the authors discuss the ethics of interventions in the ageing process.

Chapter Three focuses on narratives of ageing and, specifically, how in telling and sharing different types of stories, older people can begin to both reflect on their lives and explore new opportunities. This concern with how older people represent themselves, and are represented by others, is a relatively new one in gerontology. This is surprising because images of old age and especially ageing bodies have such a powerful and largely negative impact on social attitudes to older people. The NDA authors are not content to simply describe such social representations in narratives, but they also seek to challenge the dominant ones by developing transformative narratives, for example, through participation in a range of arts-related activities including reading, art appreciation, community arts and photography. In five path-breaking NDA projects older people actively engaged with the dominant cultural narratives of ageing, which tend to exclude, and began to explore more positive and personally enriching ones which demonstrate creativity and opened up numerous new possibilities for them. In several projects it was possible to see distinct counter-narratives of ageing.

Chapter Four considers the various aspects of health and well-being in later life that were studied by 14 different NDA projects. This very broad and varied portfolio is distilled expertly into two main components. Following discussion of some of the key concepts in this field, including quality of life and subjective well-being, the chapter concentrates on the barriers to healthy ageing and good quality of life in old age. These include economic barriers, physiological ones (with reduced immunity and poor sleep as examples), limits to mobility, barriers to paid employment and psychosocial barriers. The second half of the chapter considers interventions to support well-being and healthy ageing. Drawing on the extensive testing of models and trialling of innovations by the NDA projects, the authors concentrate on six different types of intervention: financial, pharmacological, physical (exercise), environmental (blue light and OWL), community music making and engagement with art. The enormous potential of these interventions to transform the quality of later life is truly impressive, and should be required reading for all national and local policy makers and practitioners with responsibilities regarding older people. The chapter concludes by pinpointing the challenges for policy in this field, such as the deficit model of ageing and how to change public perceptions of old age. The authors pose a sharp question to policy makers: is it more economical, in the long run, to promote health and well-being in currently 'well' older people in preference to meeting the costs of more intense care that may be required without this provision?

Chapter Five concentrates on food and nutrition, drawing on four diverse NDA projects with this common theme. The authors emphasise the critical importance of nutrition to well-being in later life and the danger that malnutrition poses. Following a brief description of the projects on which the chapter is based, the discussion focuses on four essential issues: biographical experiences with food and their impact in old age; lifestyle including physical, social and family contexts; health and well-being; and the loss of independence. Under each of these headings key research findings are reported. Taken as a whole, the chapter provides deep insights into the many faceted roles that food plays in old age, coupled with clear policy guidance on how to tackle the scourge of under-nutrition.

Chapter Six provides a comprehensive introduction to the major gerontological topic of participation and social connectivity based on 11 separate NDA projects. This extraordinary rich analysis benefits from both UK-based research and projects focused on three less developed countries: Brazil, India and South Africa. The chapter opens with a summary of the critical importance of participation to health and well-being in later life. Access is broken down into spatial, digital and institutional components, as well as those concerning social and political organisations. Like most other NDA researchers, the authors of this chapter are not content to analyse participation, but also want to challenge negative stereotypes of ageing and older people – such as declining participation. They do this with specific reference to rural community capital and the economic contribution of older people. The chapter demonstrates that older people do participate and are often tenacious in this but, at the same time, they are confronted with multiple barriers that prevent them from doing so which, in turn, create inequalities in the scope, extent and benefits from the participation. The authors' collective plea to policy makers focuses on cross-generational issues, social class and cultural participation, and ethnicity. The chapter concludes with a discussion of examples of how to improve meaningful participation in later life, which ranges from community arts to literature.

Chapter Seven concentrates on design. This topic was an important aspect of the NDA Programme and is a hugely under-represented one in gerontology. The chapter derives from six NDA projects, ranging from virtual images to step and stair negotiations, to clothing design and manufacture. As with the previous chapters the disciplinary mix is very broad (textile designers; electrical, mechanical and biomedical engineers; specialists in muscle mechanics; design experts for health and social care; ergonomists; and social gerontologists). The authors were driven by practical everyday questions, such as how can wearable technology be developed, how can falls be prevented and how can industry learn from older workers to facilitate healthy behaviour and good design? The chapter kicks off with a discussion of the aspects of ageing that are critical to the design process, such as inclusion, staying active, feeling connected and empowerment. It then considers designer competencies and interactions with user groups. The latter is exemplified with reference to two specific projects, 'Design for Ageing Well' and 'Transitions in Kitchen Living'. The chapter ends with an enlightening discussion of synergy across the six projects, despite their very different research emphases and disciplinary contributors.

The concluding chapter (Chapter Eight) assesses the contribution of this multi-disciplinary symposium, and then outlines the new policy approach that is required to accompany the new scientific one advanced in this volume.

TWO

Understanding ageing: biological and social perspectives

Lynne S. Cox, Penelope A. Mason, Mark C. Bagley, David Steinsaltz, Aneta Stefanovska, Alan Bernjak, Peter V.E. McClintock, Anna C. Phillips, Jane Upton, Joanna E. Latimer and Terence Davis

Introduction

In this chapter, we discuss how social and biological studies of ageing can converge to provide a meaningful framework for progress in both understanding ageing and dealing with it in a positive manner. We start by discussing the meaning of the term 'ageing' and how it is in part defined by social context, and then, how psychosocial factors have an impact on both perception and the biological reality of ageing. From a theoretical perspective, we assess how ageing might have evolved, and how it is measured. The biological impacts of ageing are then described, moving from individual cells through tissues to major organ systems (immune, cardiovascular and nervous systems) (see Figure 2.1). What causes individual cells of the body to age is dealt with at both a cellular and molecular level, and we further discuss how studies of both extremely long-lived and short-lived humans have contributed significantly not only to our understanding of the biological processes of ageing, but also to the possibility of developing therapies to deal with the problems that cause greatest loss of quality of life in older age. We end by assessing the ethical case for intervening in those biological processes underpinning the development of those illnesses that so undermine health in later life.

Given the enormous scope and breadth of material that is covered, and the wide differences in perspectives and language used by the diverse disciplines that contribute to this chapter, we have tried to avoid jargon terms wherever possible, and provide simple definitions of unavoidable terminology as notes at the end of the chapter to assist the reader not specialist in that particular field.

Figure 2.1: Assessing processes of ageing from cells through tissues to organ systems

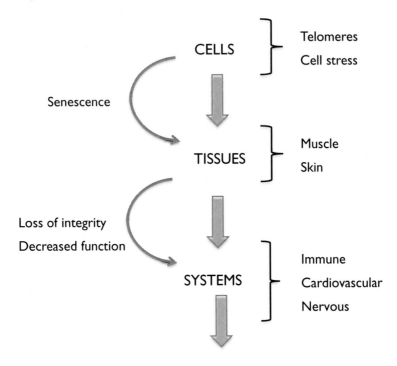

Not 'what' is ageing, but 'how'?

In order to study ageing in any meaningful way, we need to understand how the term 'ageing' is being used. To biologists, it can mean damage to molecules of the cell, and to cells of the tissue; to the physiologist, alterations in organ function; to the clinician, increased frailty and accumulation of diverse diseases. For the older person, ageing is felt and experienced, with changes in physical abilities and social activities and status having both positive and negative effects on the quality of their later life. Ageing is thus not so much a thing, but rather multi-dimensional, underpinned by complex social and biological processes, made up of many different mechanisms. Kirkwood (2011), for example, suggests that around 200 mechanisms of biological ageing have already been identified. Critically, at the level of society, age is infrastructural to how society is organised. While there have been a range of social and health policies around pension schemes and health and social care that address the needs of older people, ageing as a complex biological and social process has, until relatively recently, been largely ignored on the political agenda. There has been an increased appreciation of the urgency of understanding the different ways in which people age, particularly in the context of the needs of, and contributions that can be made by, an ageing population.

In this book series that reports a range of studies of ageing, we are studying ageing, but from very different perspectives. For some, age is either a social construct or a purely biological phenomenon (most commonly experienced as a combination of diseases and disabilities that accumulate with time). In what follows, we offer the understanding of ageing as the combined effects of social and cultural as well as biological processes. Our questions include: How might the social and biological aspects interact to affect the lives of older people? Is ageing a diverse ('private') or a shared ('public') experience? Is it wholly negative in terms of personal experience, or are there positive aspects? Can the perception of ageing by the individual and by society be understood, and if necessary, transformed? What aspects of the experience of ageing can be modified at the social level, and what aspects are amenable to intervention at the biological and clinical level, all with the aim of enhancing the quality of later life? In this chapter we provide an overview of research on the biological basis of human ageing in the context of a social perspective, in an attempt to define the human experience of ageing.

Social constructs of ageing: 'long-lived humans – problems for society and biology?'

In this section, we explore the relationship between the need for biological understanding of ageing and social approaches to ageing and later life. Social gerontologists, such as Phillipson (1982), Townsend (1981) and Walker (1980), have been at pains to help us see that ageing is not simply a natural or normal phenomenon. This is not to suggest that ageing is solely an effect of a person's biography and the so-called lifestyle choices they make. Rather, the specificities of how someone ages are also to be understood as relational, constructed by complex interactions between social and cultural processes and social structures (Bazalgette et al, 2011).

Different social categories associated with chronological age are infrastructural to how society organises itself. While 'infant', 'child', 'adolescent' and 'adult' are each age-related social categories, they are not just biological or chronological phenomena. For example, the category 'child' and the period of life that we call 'childhood' are both fairly recent social phenomena that have only some basis in the developmental sciences. Aries (1962), for example, points to how in the *Age of reason* (Paine, 2011) a child was considered a small adult, while more recent theorists argue that childhood is either rapidly disappearing (Postman, 1994) or is becoming more and more ambiguous as children engage in, and mimic, adult activities (Lee, 2001). We can see this ambiguity over the division between adult and child in national variations in the age of consent, suffrage and criminal responsibility.

Similarly, old age is not simply a biological phenomenon, and like childhood, it has also been understood as in part a socially constructed phenomenon. For example, it has been understood as an effect of the institution of a retirement age (Walker, 1980; Phillipson, 1982). Retirement ages and statutory limits around pensionable age have enormous social, material and experiential consequences for older people: for example, statutory requirements can be seen as forcing people out of work and into a structural position in society in which they are no longer seen as productive or fully participant. Retirement age in the UK has itself become a movable feast. The move-ability of the appropriate time for retirement is connected more to economic and political pressure than to the need for people to stop work because they can no longer biologically or physiologically cope with it. In his later analysis of ageing in contemporary societies in which work and identity have become more fluid and precarious, Phillipson (1998) argues that growing older has become even more problematic. For example, with increases in longevity and improvements in mortality rates, people are living longer but not necessarily well, partly because an ageing identity is so precarious in societies that denigrate old age.

Recent theorising advocates a different approach to age structures that take account of demographic and cultural changes. This life course approach distinguishes between stages of later life as including 'young old', 'old old' and 'oldest old' (Neugarten, 1974). More recently terminology has been adopted that reflects this shift to distinguish the third from the fourth age, with a growing emphasis on extending the third age by staying younger and active for longer. These developments are characterised as a contemporary 'anti-ageing' culture (Gilleard and Higgs, 2000), including policy drives for positive ageing because they promote the image of the third age as an extension of youthfulness, productivity and activity.

Becoming 'old old', or in the fourth age, is constituted almost entirely in negative terms. For example, medicine imagines ageing in terms of a deficit model (Latimer, 2011). In this model, becoming old is constructed as a time of loss – of function, health and status.

Governmental programmes promoting positive ageing are also problematic. This is for two reasons: first, because in associating ageing well with the extension of youthfulness, activity and productivity, they devalue those people who are unable to maintain their productivity, activity and youthfulness – they get marked as ageing badly; and second, because it narrows the parameters of what health and well-being may look like in later life. This creates a real tension:

> The strategies [that promote positive ageing] therefore provide an opportunity to improve the situation of older people in society by drawing attention to the negative effects of age discrimination and exclusion from opportunities to participate. However, some aspects of the underlying concepts of active, productive and positive ageing remain questionable. Without a broadening of these concepts there is a risk that the frail old may be further marginalised. It may be only the active old who benefit. (Davey and Glasgow, 2006, p 26)

Thus, from a social perspective, there are important and deeply problematic issues around the relationship between age and identity that have both material and personal consequences for individuals and their families, and which may interact with biological processes of ageing. In recent times this problematic relationship can be seen in the proliferation of 'anti-ageing' marketing and the huge emphasis on health and anti-ageing products and lifestyles. This culture of anti-ageing generates a tension, where anti-ageing strategies reinforce negative attitudes to growing older, and to older people themselves, especially in some of our key institutions, such as healthcare and medicine (Oliver, 2008). Alongside a growing cultural and market preoccupation with a 'war on age', this reinforces the dominant cultural view that devalues old age and older people (Vincent, 2006).

So there are a number of issues that require consideration in the context of advances in gerontology and biogerontology. There are practical and economic imperatives that result from an ageing population, including how the bio-physiological effects of ageing are unevenly distributed; socio-economic inequalities produce health inequalities *particularly* in later life. Questions also arise as to how to ensure ageing science is used to *support*, not undermine, later life. The question is, how can ageing biology offer knowledge and understanding to improve the quality of ageing lives in a cultural context that demonises and devalues ageing as some kind of monster, a dragon that is to be heroically overcome by science and technology (Bostrom, 2005)? That is, is biogerontology intrinsically 'anti-ageing', paradoxically undermining the very group of people it seeks to support?

The research undertaken by Latimer as a part of the New Dynamics of Ageing (NDA) study 'Biology and ageing' (Bagley et al, 2011; Latimer et al, 2011) has identified this tension as both expressed by and debated in the field of ageing science. While there is no doubt that biological ageing is demonstrable, and may be the greatest risk factor for chronic illnesses of later life, ageing itself is also deeply socially and culturally constructed – what is perceived as ageing inside the biology of ageing is itself prefigured. For example, in studies of ageing cells discussed later, they are recognisable as those whose appearance changes in ways that indicate a loss of vitality and reproductive capacity. These senescent cells are problematic because they appear to serve no useful function but do not die. Parallels have been drawn between these aged cells and older people themselves seen in relation to what the British anthropologist Mary Douglas (1996) calls the social body – ageing cells, like older people, clog up the body, and create the conditions that may underpin the development of disease. Like older people themselves, those that are no longer reproductive are not just obsolete: in not dying off, they take up valuable resources and create problematic conditions for the body (social and individual) to operate. These cells are not described as of any value. Since biogerontologists view ageing as a progressive biological deficit, it has been argued that older people may be seen in the same way, but this could not be further from the truth. However, the fact that such parallels exist in people's minds, and even in the literature, entangles the new biology of ageing in a relationship between ageing, the body and regimes of value that configure and may be seen to devalue ageing. However, we strongly distance ourselves from this view: the parallels are false and misleading, unnecessarily creating tension between biogerontologists and social gerontologists.

Thus, how ageing science is caught in the contemporary relationship between ageing, the body and regimes of value is very complex: it is potentially both constructive of new ways of thinking about ageing, but also at risk of reinforcing negative ideas about what it is to grow and be old. This is particularly of concern when some scientists insist on refiguring ageing as a disease (see, for example, de Grey, 2005).

What the rest of this chapter explores is that while ageing is many things, it is not in and of itself a disease. Rather, ageing emerges as the effects of complex biosocial phenomena. The objective is to distinguish between biological processes that are inevitable and those that are effects. The research presented illuminates the mechanisms through which human organisms age, and identifies the conditions through which diseases can accumulate in an ageing body, and how the ageing process itself under these conditions is correlated with the incidence of diseases of old age. But, and critically, what this research on biological theories and mechanisms of ageing has the potential to do is help us to understand the complexity of ageing as a process in which biological age may not be the same as chronological age, and which may be malleable.

Biological realities of ageing

Despite these modulations of behaviour and reported health being dependent on perceptions of ageing, there are certain inescapable realities about ageing of the body. Biologically, ageing is defined as a gradual loss of function with chronological time, with increasing probability of death. Despite recent claims to the contrary that very old people may have stopped ageing (Rose, 2011), there are no documented cases of escape from mortality, so this definition of ageing applies to all, irrespective of whether they age 'well' or 'badly'. Although certain individuals and even populations appear to age well, retaining health and vigour up until death as centenarians, for example, Okinawa Japanese and Ashkenazi Jews in New York (see Willcox et al, 2008; Rajpathak et al, 2011), for the majority of people, biological ageing is not greeted with enthusiasm. Strehler has defined five characteristics of ageing under the acronym CUPID: *C*umulative, *U*niversal, *P*rogressive, *I*nherent and *D*eleterious (Strehler, 1959; Arking, 2006). Shakespeare captured this most eloquently in Jaques' speech on the seven ages of man from *As you like it*:

> The sixth age shifts
>> Into the lean and slipper'd pantaloon,
>> With spectacles on nose and pouch on side,
>> His youthful hose, well saved, a world too wide
>> For his shrunk shank; and his big manly voice,
>> Turning again toward childish treble, pipes
>> And whistles in his sound. Last scene of all,
>> That ends this strange eventful history,
>> Is second childishness and mere oblivion,
>> Sans teeth, sans eyes, sans taste, sans everything.

This demonstrates an astute appreciation of some biological aspects of ageing – decline in visual acuity, muscle wasting (sarcopenia), decrease in lung capacity (possibly also breathlessness from chronic heart disease), age-related macular degeneration (AMD) and blindness, severe decrease in physical senses, culminating in senile dementia. Given this pessimistic appraisal of ageing, can anything be done to ameliorate the course of human ageing? Current medical care seeks to treat the distinct diseases associated with old age: atherosclerosis with statins, AMD with lucentis, and cancer with cytotoxic chemotherapeutics. Indeed, to date, this has been very much the preserve of the medical specialist, or even the geriatrician (see Figure 2.2), but little work has historically been done to discover and modulate the underlying cause(s) and to prevent the development of age-related diseases. To address these processes requires an understanding of why and how we age.

Figure 2.2: Ageing as a risk factor for age-related disease

Traditionally, research into age-related disease has taken place within disease-specific disciplines and research groups often largely under the category of geriatrics. These methodologies often fail to recognise and consider the role for the ageing process itself and consider the diseases present in older people to be similar to those present much earlier in life. Biogerontology, however, recognises that age-related diseases have a major underpinning risk factor — age itself. Thus, an improved understanding of the nature of the normal ageing process may open new avenues and opportunities for the development of interventions in age-related disease.

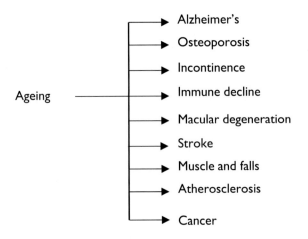

Source: Adapted from Bagley et al (2011)

Why we age: theories of ageing

Why do we need a theory of ageing? Nothing could seem more obvious than that human beings and animals, like cars and shoelaces, are strongest when they are young, then gradually wear out, becoming less functional, and eventually they are scrapped. (This intuitive non-theory is sometimes called the 'wear-and-tear' theory of ageing.) However, this analogy has limitations: the new shoelace is in the best condition it will ever be in. The new-born human, on the other hand, is small and weak, excessively susceptible to all manner of infections and injuries. George Williams, in 1957, summarised the conundrum thus: 'it is indeed remarkable that after a seemingly miraculous feat of morphogenesis a complex organism should be unable to perform the much simpler task of merely maintaining what is already formed.' Extensive accounts of current theories of ageing may be found in the following books: *The biology of ageing: observations and principles* (Arking, 2006) and *Handbook of theories of aging* (Bengtson et al, 2009). We briefly discuss the major biological theories of ageing below.

Evolutionary theories

Why should organisms that have evolved by natural selection tend to exhibit the failure of maintenance that is ageing? Either immortality is not optimal, or natural selection systematically fails to achieve optimality in this respect. The first possibility underlies Williams' proposal, now generally known as *antagonistic pleiotropy*. A mutant allele[1] with multiple ('pleiotropic') effects, increasing robustness in early life at the expense of later increased frailty, will be a net gain: in a dangerous world, far more individuals will receive the boost to early reproduction than will survive to pay the cost. Hence the mutation will become prevalent in the population. Peter Medawar's earlier notion of mutation accumulation is based on the second possibility: mutations causing late-life decay may accumulate in the genome even without any countervailing benefit, simply by entropy (Medawar, 1952). Such mutations will not be actively selected, but the force driving them out may be extremely weak, allowing significant accumulation.

All current evolutionary theories are variants of one or both of these. In the *disposable soma* theory, antagonism arises from the need for trade-offs within a fixed energy budget: more expenditure on maintaining the body for long life detracts from energy for immediate reproduction or growth (Kirkwood, 1977). Economists have applied mutation accumulation to trajectories of ageing, ciphering the cost of a death as the loss of parental investment up to that age, net of that individual's investment in the next generation. In broad strokes, these models seem to predict (Chu et al, 2008) something like the U-shaped pattern of mortality rates common to so many organisms (see the next section). In particular, the contribution of older people to the survival and success of their grandchildren has long been posited as an evolutionary explanation – familiarly called 'the grandmother effect' – for the unusually long lifespans of humans (Hawkes, 2004).

Mechanistic theories

A mechanistic theory of ageing aims to find a weak point in the general make-up of organisms – that is, what would be difficult or impossible to maintain indefinitely? Candidate mechanisms include telomere shortening, free radicals (and mitochondrial failure), DNA damage, protein misfolding, and cellular dys-differentiation, as discussed in more detail below. A few general principles may be extracted:

- *Error catastrophe:* the same biological machinery responsible for repair is itself subject to damage (and repair). This feedback can lead to a vicious circle of dysfunction.
- *Signalling incoherence:* complicated metazoans depend on complex and delicate signalling between cells, tissues, organs and organ systems. These signalling pathways inevitably drift away from their initial coherent state.
- *Immunological challenge:* rapid turnover of generations (particularly by sexual reproduction) allows complex organisms to stay ahead of their parasites and infectious microbes. Hence investment in reproduction over longevity favours survival of the species.
- *Cancer:* the same mechanisms that allow efficient cellular growth (for example, signalling and repair) may also be hijacked by tumours for lethally unrestrained growth and proliferation. Improving repair processes within cells may thus not actually improve the longevity of the organism.

Measuring ageing

From the perspectives of medicine and demography, ageing is most naturally identified with an organism's increasing susceptibility to death and disease, and decreasing fecundity. Age-specific susceptibility to death is measured by the mortality rate (force of mortality in demography). This may be estimated by the fraction of individuals aged x who die before they reach age $x+1$. The more general problem of estimating mortality rates, particularly in small populations, is a topic of survival analysis (Klein and Moeschberger, 2003).

When mortality rates are considered as a function of age, we see a U-shaped pattern with certain generic features apparent that are common to many (but by no means all) species:

- high mortality in early infancy, declining rapidly;
- rapid increase in mortality rate starting around the time of sexual maturity;
- steady exponential increase in mortality rate through most of mature life ('Gompertz mortality pattern');
- slowing and even reversal of the rate of increase at extremely advanced age ('mortality plateau').

In Figure 2.3 mortality rates are plotted on a logarithmic scale against age for two different UK periods (data from the Human Mortality Database), showing clearly the first three features above; however, mortality plateaux in humans are barely observable even by 100 years of age, requiring sophisticated statistical techniques to establish their presence in centenarians.

Figure 2.3: Mortality rates plotted on a logarithmic scale, various human populations

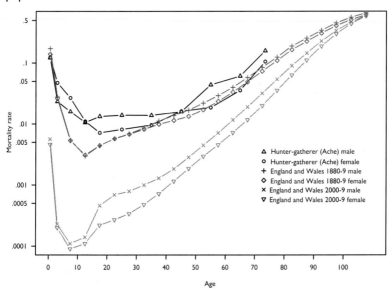

Source: Data from Hill and Hurtada (1996); England and Wales 1878-79 and 2000-09 data from Human Mortality Database (see www.mortality.org)

These regularities in mortality rates, which are reflected in patterns of incidences of individual diseases and disabilities, would seem to suggest a long inexorable slide into decrepitude and death. The truth is more complicated. While many measures of physiological and cognitive function show steady decline with age when averaged over the population (the cross-sectional measure), the development of any individual's capacity (the longitudinal measure) is more complicated, often showing long periods of stasis punctuated by rapid slumps (Arking, 2006).

The picture that emerges is one of a universal, persistent ageing process that is nonetheless, in crucial respects, random. The pace of age-related changes is known to be affected by conditions of birth and gestation: poor intrauterine nutrition is associated with short lifespan; low post-natal protein intake conversely extends lifespan (see Barnes and Ozanne, 2011). The pace of age-related change is also influenced by variables of social environment such as social class (for example, a 65-year-old man in Kensington will live on average nearly 23 more years, while his counterpart in Glasgow has less than 14 years remaining; see ONS, 2011b), and of course, by the cumulative accidents of ill health and disease. Even larger variation in the pace of ageing is found between regions of the world and across time. As shown in Figure 2.3, there has been an enormous decline in mid-life mortality rates in the UK since the 19th century, accompanied by an acceleration of age-related mortality in late life. Similar variation is seen in the age-specific incidence of disease and disability. This contrasts markedly with the Aché population of hunter-gathers who are prone to early mortality from accidents and disease (Hill and Hurtada, 1996). Hence the mortality trajectory in human populations is not fixed but can be altered markedly by interventions such as improved healthcare and medical treatment, together with public health improvements such as good housing and sanitation. While such interventions have had a marked impact on decreasing early and mid-life mortality in the West, there is no effect on extreme late-life mortality.

Focusing on a single time and place, the near-universality of age-related infirmity creates a semblance of immutability. It has been demonstrated how rapidly past attempts to posit an upper limit to life expectancy have been overtaken by events (Oeppen and Vaupel, 2002). Looking at a broader range of statistics suggests a far more plastic ageing process, more subject to amelioration and intervention. One response to this plasticity has been the concept of the 'social construction of ageing', which emphasises the role that society and social policies, such as retirement, play in defining people as 'old' (Walker, 1980). Some, however, have interpreted this as though older people suffer primarily from societal prejudice or disdain for their abilities. While this is clearly excessive – even the healthiest older person eventually suffers diminution of physical and mental capacities with advancing years, irrespective of expectations or prejudice – there is also a substantial body of research showing that expectations of inevitable decline can be self-fulfilling. One famous example is the study showing that merely inducing young people to think about words associated with older people causes them to walk more slowly (Bargh et al, 1996; but see Doyen et al, 2012, for challenging this interpretation). Conversely, immersing older men (over 70 years) in an environment in which they lived their young adult lives (the '1950s house' experiment) enhanced their mood, cognitive and physical abilities (Langer, 2009; Feinberg, 2010). In addition, different social structures in different countries, for example, Japan, and African cultures that value older people more than contemporary Western cultures, allowing greater freedom for older people to undertake activities that would not usually be deemed appropriate (Znaimer, 2013), allow older people more capability to 'age well'.

How can the biological basis of ageing be studied in humans?

Mortality is, of course, the most easily measurable end point of ageing, but mortality rates do not provide sufficient information on the ageing process prior to death. Population-wide studies of longitudinal ageing (that is, across the life course) have been conducted which measure a range of physiological features such as blood sugar levels, blood pressure, height, weight, and so on (for example, the Baltimore Longitudinal Study of Aging, www.grc.nia.nih.gov/branches/blsa/blsanew.htm). A major, perhaps anticipated, finding of such studies is the wide variation across populations, and the tiny contribution made to overall ageing by individual genes that act on single biochemical processes. The effect of multiple genes acting together is called polygenic.

In addition to genetic effects, there are environmental inputs that affect the rate and nature of biological ageing, such as chronic psychological stress and environmental pollutants (for example, cigarette smoke, ultraviolet light through sunbathing) (Nyunoya et al, 2006; Polefka et al, 2012). Cohort studies of people exposed to severe food restriction in the Second World War (the Dutch famine) discovered that under-nutrition in adolescence predisposes women to developing later-life diabetes and peripheral arterial disease (Portrait et al, 2011), while carer stress (see page 63, this volume) and raised stress hormone cortisol levels are associated with shortening of chromosome ends (Tomiyama et al, 2012), a key driver of cell ageing. These, possibly stochastic, influences from the environment (including diet), may affect gene expression to produce unpredictable outcomes; thus this highly polygenic nature makes the study of biological ageing a complex undertaking.

Narrowing down the number of genes critical to ageing

Although the idea of genes that cause ageing is widely discounted, there are certainly genes that prevent ageing processes, and when lost, result in premature ageing. Such genes give profound insights into the underlying causes of ageing, and optimism for the development of strategies to increase healthspan – the period of life essentially free of disease. Such 'compression of morbidity' (see Figure 2.4) would have major benefits for the ageing individual, but also huge social and financial benefits in terms of healthcare costs and the ability of older people to continue to contribute socially and economically to society. It is highly unlikely that compression of morbidity will lead to an increase in lifespan so significant that it will have social repercussions: preventing hip fractures by tackling frailty will indeed prevent premature death, but not death *per se*. Indeed, studies on more than 450 healthy older people (aged between 95 and 112 – 'super-centenarians') in a genetically similar population of Ashkenazi Jews in New York (The Longevity Genes Project, see www.einstein.yu.edu/centers/aging/longevity-genes-project) has shown that these people have a marked reduction in age-related disease burden compared with the general population, and live active and healthy lives until extreme old age, but they do die, usually in their 11th decade (Rajpathak et al, 2011). What is important is that they die 'of old age' before they succumb to life-limiting or life-threatening disease, and so have a much better quality of life than the majority of older people, and cost far less in healthcare terms to governmental or private health providers. Genetic analysis of these super-centenarians has identified a handful of genes that predispose to healthy old age. Perhaps unsurprisingly, one of the gene variants found in the healthy super-old is important in regulating cholesterol levels in the blood, promoting HDL ('good cholesterol'), while others have an impact on blood pressure, DNA repair and electrical insulation in the brain.

Figure 2.4: Compression of morbidity and the increase in healthspan

(a) Current situation of maximum lifespan and (for some) a significant period of morbidity (in black). (b) Immediate goals of geriatrics are to shrink the period of morbidity within the existing human lifespan by treating age-related disease; biogerontologists believe this may be better achieved by modulating the ageing process instead. A secondary effect is an increase in the median lifespan. (c) Possible effects of ameliorating the rate of human ageing is an increase in the total lifespan with a small period of morbidity (some would consider this an ideal scenario). (d) However, many fear that biogerontologists will simply extend both lifespan and the period of morbidity (undesirable outcome).

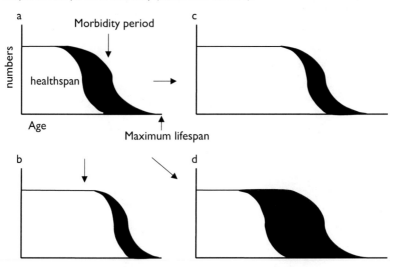

Perhaps surprisingly, there has been a major convergence of findings from ageing studies in organisms as diverse as brewer's yeast, tiny nematode worms, fruit flies, mice and humans. In all of these organisms, a central signalling axis appears critical in determining longevity: the insulin/insulin-like signalling pathway, and nutrient-sensing pathway, both of which converge on a central integrating hub called TORC (mTORC in mammals) (see Figure 2.5).

Mutations that block the action either of the the insulin receptor or of proteins that relay the signal (termed 'downstream' in the pathway) lead to increased longevity in worms and flies; similarly, mutation of a component downstream of mTORC1 in mice also increases lifespan. Since these pathways respond to insulin, a hormone produced after a meal to signal to the body that blood sugar levels are high, the overall response to nutrients may be critical in determining a cell's longevity. A direct way of studying this is to limit nutrient intake: in worms, mutation of a gene called *eat-2* diminishes the worm's ability to 'swallow' and so leads to decreased food intake; it also causes a remarkable extension

Figure 2.5: Biological pathways that affect ageing

Cells sense nutrients, hormones such as insulin and related growth factors (for example, IGF) when these factors bind to specific proteins that span the cell membrane. Binding of a factor on the outside of the cell subtly changes the receptor so that it can convey a signal inside the cell. The signal is passed chemically between proteins in a 'signalling cascade'. IIS and nutrient sensing both converge on the central coordinating hub, mTORC1. Stimulation of mTORC1 leads to protein manufacture and cell proliferation; conversely, inhibiting mTORC1 results in increased 'autophagy' where the cell clears debris and cellular components, utilising them for fuel, and in increased cell longevity. Remarkably, agents that inhibit mTORC1 (for example, rapamycin) not only affect cellular longevity but also enhance survival of the entire organism.

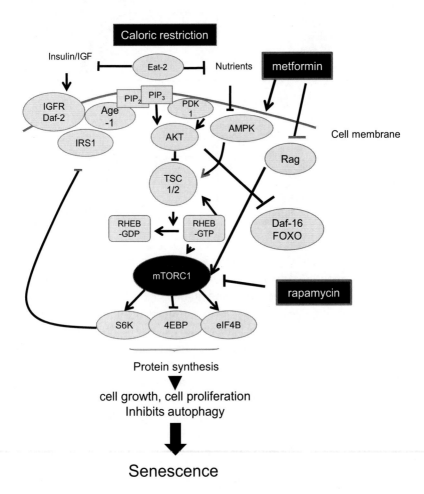

of lifespan (Lakowski and Hekimi, 1998) and, as far as is measurable, healthspan. Hence, cutting down on calories in worms is an anti-ageing strategy. This finding becomes of especial relevance if it is conserved in other species (see 'Modulating ageing' at the end of this chapter).

Premature human ageing diseases

Studying genes that help super-centenarians and model organisms to stay healthy is vitally important in understanding ageing. Another route to studying human ageing is to investigate diseases that look very much like normal ageing, but that happen over an accelerated time frame. Such diseases are called progerias, leading in many cases to lifespan shortening. The most studied progeroid syndromes are monogenic (that is, caused by loss of function of a single gene), simplifying analysis of the causes of ageing. An issue, however, is that progerias are not fully reflective of the whole ageing process, but are segmental – that is, they only have some of the clinical characteristics of normal ageing (Brown et al, 1985). The age-related symptoms that do occur can be more or less severe than in normal ageing, and not all tissues are affected. In addition, some patients manifest non-age-related symptoms. These issues have led to criticism that progerias are mere phenocopies of normal ageing, or even a blind alley, and should not be used as ageing models (Miller, 2004). However, it is the remarkable similarity of the premature ageing processes and pathologies that occur in progerias to normally aged individuals, and the very segmental nature of these syndromes making them tractable to analysis, that makes them so valuable to ageing studies (Kipling et al, 2004). Research effort into progerias has increased massively over the past two decades, with the expectation that identifying causative genes could support understanding of some of the mechanisms underlying normal ageing (Cox and Faragher, 2007).

Werner syndrome

The progeroid syndrome that perhaps most closely resembles normal ageing is Werner syndrome (WS). Although generally termed 'adult onset', WS individuals are small in stature and develop some of the clinical symptoms (for example, hoarse voice) in childhood; however, they are most commonly diagnosed post-puberty, when they fail to undergo the usual growth spurt of adolescence, and development of secondary sexual characteristics is limited. Indeed, the mean body mass of female (Japanese) WS patients is around 30 kg (Goto, 1997). In addition, patients develop type II diabetes, atherosclerosis ('hardening of the arteries'), cataracts, osteoporosis and non-healing ulcers; they also have a greatly elevated cancer risk with a median age of death of 47 (Martin et al, 1999; Kipling et al, 2004; Cox and Faragher, 2007), although this is increasing with improved cancer surveillance and therapy (Yokote and Saito, 2008). As well as ageing at the whole body level in a manner highly reminiscent of normal ageing, skin and white blood cells from WS individuals are far less able to divide than equivalent normal cells, entering an essentially irreversible state called cellular senescence. Even at the level of gene expression, the process where double-stranded DNA is opened up to make an RNA copy that is then decoded to make proteins – the main functional and structural components of the cell – WS cells appear much more similar to aged normal cells than to young cells of the same chronological age from non-WS donors (Kyng et al, 2003).

The only gene that is defective in WS is called WRN, and it encodes a protein with two enzyme activities: it unwinds double-stranded DNA (that is, it is a helicase) and it can sequentially cut free ends of DNA (it is an exonuclease). That loss of these two activities alone can lead to so many signs and diseases of normal ageing suggests that WRN plays a key role in keeping the cellular DNA healthy. A large body of research has now identified that WRN acts in many processes where DNA is vulnerable: during copying of the DNA (replication), cutting and rejoining (recombination), repair of damage, maintaining intact ends of chromosomes (telomeres – see below), and even during gene expression (reviewed in Cox and Faragher, 2007). Thus studying exactly how WRN acts in these various DNA transactions should illuminate critical processes that prevent cells from ageing prematurely – indeed, work to understand the changes in protein composition in cells when WRN is inactive is under way. Furthermore, model organisms such as flies and worms that carry mutation in their versions of the WRN genes (Lee et al, 2004; Cox et al, 2007) should provide ethical whole animal systems to test drugs that improve ageing outcomes. Such models and drugs are in early stages of development (Boubriak et al, 2009; Bagley et al, 2010; Mason et al, 2012).

Childhood-onset progeria

Hutchinson-Gilford progeria syndrome (HGPS) is a rare disorder associated with a characteristic aged appearance very early in life (Hutchinson, 1886; Gilford, 1904). Children born with HGPS typically appear normal at birth, but within a year they begin to display the effects of ageing. Initial symptoms include severe growth retardation and individuals are short in stature and below average weight. Clinical symptoms include alopecia, arteriosclerosis and atherosclerosis. By the age of 10 an affected child has a similar respiratory, cardiovascular and arthritic condition to a senior citizen, and as the disease progresses, there is an increased incidence of strokes and atherosclerosis (Debusk, 1972). In short, these children give the distinct impression of being many decades older than they actually are. The average age of death is 13, with at least 90 per cent of HGPS individuals dying from cardiovascular disease including atherosclerosis (Brown, 1992).

HGPS is caused by mutations in the LMNA gene that encodes the nuclear lamina component lamin A/C; this change results in a novel protein called progerin (Eriksson et al, 2003). Most patients carry the same genetic change that appears to arise as a spontaneous mutation; only one LMNA allele needs to be altered in order for disease to result – this is called a dominant genetic disease.

Nuclear lamins are proteins that form a stable but dynamic meshwork that supports the flexible nuclear envelope (Aebi et al, 1986). Unlike normal lamins, progerin protein remains in the membrane, making it 'brittle' and resulting in instability of the cell's nucleus and even chromosome breakage. This leads to cell death or premature senescence due to increased cell fragility, and many of the affected tissues, such as skin and vasculature, are under intense mechanical stress (Bridger and Kill, 2004; Dahl et al, 2006). The elevated rate of cell death and senescence in HGPS individuals is likely to lead to a loss of functional 'young' cells early in life compared to normal individuals, resulting in loss of renewal capacity, compromised tissue homeostasis and premature ageing (Bridger and Kill, 2004; Kipling et al, 2004). For example, smooth muscle cells are severely depleted in the arteries of HGPS individuals, and this depletion may play a role in the pathogenesis of accelerated atherosclerotic disease seen in HGPS (Stehbens et al, 2001). Interestingly, low amounts of progerin are found in normal cells (Cao et al, 2007), and although levels vary between individuals, they increase with age; age-related progerin accumulation in cells lining blood vessels (the endothelium) may play a role in the progression of atherosclerosis in normal human ageing.

Processes of normal ageing

In the preceding sections we considered how genes can affect ageing in those who live extremely long and healthy lives, and in those whose lifespans are shortened by mutation of critical genes. While lessons can be learned from both, we must also consider what constitutes the norm in ageing. We therefore discuss the 'normal' course of ageing in cells, tissues and organ systems ageing below.

Cell ageing

Ageing is associated with loss of function of many cells, tissues and organs of the body. Since every tissue and organ is made up of many billions or even trillions of cells, it is necessary to understand how cells age and what contribution old cells make to the tissue in which they lie in order to discover the impact of cell ageing on frailty and disability in the older human. Although until recently controversial, it is becoming increasingly accepted that cell ageing (also called replicative senescence) is a major player in organismal ageing. Various causes of cell ageing have been postulated. Below, we deal with two of the major types of cell senescence: replicative senescence and stress-induced senescence. It should be borne in mind that this distinction may be somewhat artificial, and that molecular mechanisms driving each are likely to show significant overlap.

Replicative senescence is caused by loss of telomeres

At conception, a human is a single cell, which divides more than 50 times over the lifetime, giving rise to greater than 10^{14} (100,000,000 million) cells.[2] In order to divide, a cell must duplicate its constituents including the genetic material – the DNA. DNA in each human cell is made up of about 3 billion bases, comprising letters of the genetic code, and is arranged in extremely long linear structures called chromosomes. Around 2 metres of DNA are packaged into each cell within the nucleus, requiring a high degree of structural organisation.

The ends of linear chromosomes are called telomeres, which are specialised nucleoprotein complexes made up of highly repeated short sequences of DNA bound by a number of different proteins. They function to cap the chromosome, much as the end of a bootlace prevents fraying. Every time the chromosomes are copied to pass on to a daughter cell at division, a small section of the telomere is lost (Olovnikov, 1973) – thus the telomere shortens, reflecting the number of divisions the cell has gone through and generating in essence a cellular clock that ticks with each division. Genetic damage, in particular oxidative stress, is a prominent driver of telomere erosion and hence accelerates the rate of cell ageing (von Zglinicki and Martin-Ruiz, 2005) – the 'clock' ticks faster and cells age more quickly. Eventually, critically short telomeres trigger a DNA damage response that results in the cells entering replicative senescence, an essentially irreversible state whereby no further cell division can occur (Hayflick and Moorhead, 1961). The presence of functional tumour suppressor[3] gene products, particularly a protein known as p53, is necessary for cells to recognise the DNA damage signal generated by eroding telomeres; cells can be made to override the mortality signal by removing p53 activity (Preto et al, 2004). It is vital to the survival of species that cells of the germ line that gives rise to eggs and sperm (and hence the next generation of organisms) avoid replicative senescence and mortality: they do this by expressing an enzyme called telomerase that replaces telomeric DNA and avoids triggering the counting mechanism of cell age.

Cell senescence is thought to be an important anti-cancer mechanism, preventing the proliferation of old cells that have presumably accumulated damage to DNA and other cellular components over time (Campisi, 2000). That the telomeric 'counting' mechanism is a critical barrier to cancer development is demonstrated by the finding that an early step in the development of many cancers is aberrant expression of the enzyme telomerase – this essentially resets the clock to zero at every cell division and makes cancer cells immortal.

Loss of telomeric DNA is thus a driver of cell senescence: it can also be usefully employed as a biomarker of biological (as opposed to chronological) ageing. Indeed, telomere length has been shown to gradually decline with age in many human tissues (Sahin and Depinho, 2012). The presence of shorter telomeres is a feature of many age-related conditions and diseases, including: immunosenescence, cardiovascular disease, sarcopenia, osteoporosis, osteoarthritis and skin ageing (von Zglinicki and Martin-Ruiz, 2005). Moreover, there are plausible mechanisms by which telomere attrition might contribute to these diseases. However, it is also possible that telomere length may primarily be a proxy for chronic stress exposure rather than a cause of illness (von Zglinicki and Martin-Ruiz, 2005). This may help explain environmentally induced differences in rates of ageing, such as those associated with caregiving stress (Epel et al, 2004; Damjanovic et al, 2007) and childhood adversity (Kananen et al, 2010; Tyrka et al, 2010).

Further evidence for a role of telomeres in ageing comes from individuals with mutations in components of the telomere maintenance system, for example, in dykeratosis congenita: these individuals have shortened telomeres and undergo premature ageing (Sahin and Depinho, 2012). Short telomeres have also been seen in individuals with the progeroid WS, ataxia telangiectasia and HGPS (Davis et al, 2009). Although there is an association between telomere length and ageing, however, the use of telomere length as a marker of biological ageing has been criticised, and evidence linking telomere length to functional decline is somewhat equivocal (Shiels, 2010; Mather et al, 2011).

The possible role for telomeres in the ageing of various tissues is discussed in more detail in the sections on tissue and organ system ageing, below.

Stress-induced premature senescence

In the context of biology and physiology, the term 'stress' is used to mean any adverse factor that has the potential to disrupt the correct functioning of a biological system – it is not synonymous with the generally understood use of the term stress in a psychosocial context (work stress, carer stress and so on, as described elsewhere in this chapter).

Cells encounter stress on exposure to agents such as ultraviolet radiation (for example, sunbathing) or chemicals (for example, cigarette smoke, alcohol, heavy metals), or damaging forms of oxygen (reactive oxygen species, or ROS, that are generated as a by-product of much cell metabolism). Similarly, an imbalance of nutrients, higher than optimal temperatures, changes in pH (a measure of acidity/alkalinity), perturbation of the cell membrane, disruption of protein and ion transport, or activation of genes that promote cancer development (oncogenes) can all result in cell stress, as can conflicting signals that 'tell' a cell to divide or die. Cells that suffer high levels of (or chronic) stress stop dividing transiently (this is known as cell cycle arrest); a more permanent state of arrest known as stress-induced senescence (Wang et al, 2002; Deng et al, 2004; Nyunoya et al, 2006) can then be triggered, probably through a feedback loop (Passos et al, 2010). In all these cases, this is termed stress-induced premature senescence (or telomere-independent senescence), although in most aspects the cells are remarkably similar to those undergoing replicative senescence, and indeed, the mechanism used to recognise general DNA damage and 'damage' at a short telomere may be identical. Cell stresses activate a signalling pathway based on a protein termed p38 MAP kinase that results in cessation of cell growth (Iwasa et al, 2003). The involvement of p38 in stress-induced premature senescence has suggested that p38 inhibition may provide a therapeutic possibility for modulating cellular senescence processes (see 'Modulating ageing', below).

Cellular senescence and organismal ageing

The gradual build-up of senescent cells during a human lifetime is believed to underlie many of the ageing pathologies (Ostler et al, 2000), although for many years it was disputed whether senescent cells actually accumulated during ageing. However, it is possible to show the presence of senescent cells in tissues by staining them blue with a dye for an age-specific marker (SA-beta-gal) (Dimri et al, 1995); in the skin of baboons, for example, the number of senescent cells increases with chronological age (Herbig et al, 2006). Over the last decade numerous studies have now reported senescent cells in various human tissues (reviewed in Davis and Kipling, 2006). That senescent cells may contribute to the ageing process has recently been demonstrated in mice by showing that the elimination of such cells, or the prevention of their build-up, slowed or even reversed the acquisition of age-related pathologies in several tissues, including fatty tissue, skeletal muscle, spleen, intestine, the nervous system and the eye (Baker et al, 2011; Jaskelioff et al, 2011). Thus, although it may not yet be formally proven, there is strong evidence supporting a link between the build-up of senescent cells and biological ageing processes.

Although senescence is an important anti-cancer mechanism (Campisi, 2000), limited cellular lifespan has two main drawbacks:

- during life, many human tissues require continuous turnover and repair, thus a limited division ability may eventually result in inability to repair damaged tissue;
- senescent cells are not merely passive, but adversely affect the surrounding cells and tissue.

Cells such as those lining the digestive tract, mucous membranes and blood vessels, as well as skin cells, are regularly lost (for example, by physical shearing), and are replaced by division of nearby cells. Likewise, cells of the immune system divide many times during an immune response. Such highly proliferative tissues are those most susceptible to senescence as they go through so many divisions that their telomeres become critically short. Unsurprisingly, these are the tissues that also show major degeneration with age. For example, many older people are immune-compromised and respond poorly to infections such as influenza – their immune systems are also less able to raise a protective response following vaccination. Such changes are termed 'immune senescence' (see 'immune system').

Once a cell has entered senescence, it shows marked changes, losing its usual functionality and gaining a secretory phenotype whereby enzymes (for example, metalloproteases such as collagenase) that degrade surrounding tissue and inflammatory mediators such as IL-6 and TNF-alpha are secreted locally and have major impacts on remodelling surrounding tissues (Campisi et al, 2011). A possible model for the effects of cellular senescence in tissue ageing is shown in Figure 2.6. Moreover, senescent cells may lead to their normal neighbours prematurely entering the senescence pathway – the so-called 'bystander effect' (Nelson et al, 2012). Not only does this tissue remodelling result in the obvious changes seen with ageing – skin wrinkling, for example – but it also causes more sinister changes that allow pre-cancerous cells to proliferate and invade surrounding tissues. Hence cell senescence is a two-edged sword: it prevents old, damaged and potentially cancerous cells from dividing, but it also creates an environment suitable for cancer spread (see Figure 2.6). The exponential increase in cancer incidence with age is almost certainly linked to both the accumulation of DNA damage over time (with concomitant activation of oncogenes and inactivation of tumour suppressor genes) and the damaging effects of large numbers of senescence cells in a tissue.

Tissue ageing

Since cells senesce in response to DNA damage or telomere attrition after a fixed number of cell divisions and adversely affect their environment, cell senescence is likely to contribute to the deterioration observed in many tissues as they age. It is often a combination of minor deficits in different tissues that leads to major clinical problems. For example, social isolation can lead to low mobility and consequent loss of muscle tone; vitamin D and calcium deficiency together with altered blood pH can lead to bone loss; muscle weakness and poor balance leads to falls; falls can result in hip fractures, and hip fractures can result in depression, weakened immune responses and death from infectious diseases such as pneumonia. Ageing of individual tissues cannot therefore be viewed in isolation, although it is useful to understand the changes that major tissues and organ systems undergo during normal ageing. In the following sections we provide summations of how

Figure 2.6: Proposed effects of senescent cells on tissue pathology

With ongoing human lifespan, cells become damaged and die, leading to increased cell division and turnover. This produces senescent cells via telomere erosion (telomere-dependent senescence). These senescent cells contribute to tissue ageing through their altered phenotype, such as the production of degradative enzymes and inflammatory molecules that damage tissue. In addition, a reduction of self-renewing cells results in a loss of tissue homeostasis in tissues that require division throughout life. The presence of the senescent cells can also stimulate the progression of cancer. Various stress processes may also contribute to the build-up of senescent cells in tissues (stress-induced premature senescence), a process that would synergise with telomere-dependent senescence. Key: light grey are normal young cells (a cross indicates cell death), dark grey are senescent cells, and white spiky are cancer cells.

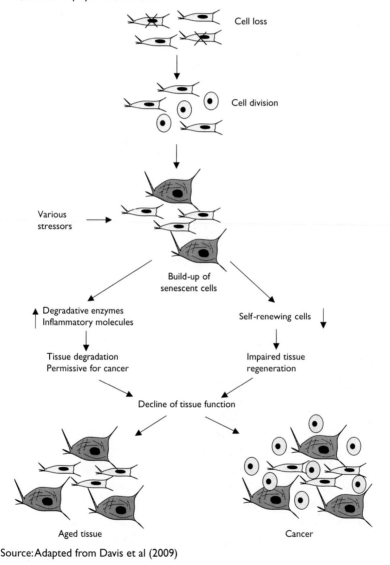

Source: Adapted from Davis et al (2009)

individual tissues may age; it should be noted, however, that this is not an exhaustive review of all human tissues, but reflects the individual NDA projects with which the authors are involved.

Sarcopenia (muscle wasting)

Sarcopenia is an almost universal feature of human ageing (Evans and Campbell, 1993; Lee et al, 2007) and, although regular exercise can delay or minimise muscle loss, it cannot prevent it (Lacour et al, 2002). Such muscle loss leads to problems with frailty and, together with loss of balance, results in a large number of falls in older people with often serious consequences such as hip fracture (see 'Physical body trauma', below). Muscle and nerve atrophy can also result in aspects of ageing such as urinary and faecal incontinence that are rarely acknowledged openly, but which cause great distress and loss of quality of later life. Thus, loss of muscle function (leading to falls and incontinence) provides the single biggest cause of institutionalisation of older people (Matsumoto and Inoue, 2007), as well as being a major contributor to social isolation, depression and concomitant morbidity.

Skin ageing

Skin deteriorates with age concomitant with an increase in the number of senescent cells, and this is likely to be a major contributor to poor wound healing and persistent venous ulcers that are a common feature of ageing, particularly in post-menopausal women (Emmerson and Hardman, 2012). Chronic venous insufficiency caused by immobility (for example, social isolation, frailty from sarcopenia) and/or poor cardiovascular circulation (see 'Ageing of the cardiovascular system') commonly lead to ulceration (Park-Lee and Caffrey, 2009). Current ulcer treatments appear almost medieval, using maggots to remove dead tissue to promote healing, together with, or instead of, physical abrasion (Jones, 2009). Infection is common and complicates treatment options – treatment failure can lead to amputation and permanent disability. Persistent ulcers are a major cause of social exclusion, immobility and consequent loss of muscle mass and other adverse health effects often requiring the institutionalisation of older people. Hence there is a pressing need for improved understanding of the causes of such poor healing and in developing novel therapies. Recent studies using ovarectomised female mice show the importance of oestrogen in promoting healing: molecular pathways mediated by oestrogen are starting to be deciphered, with experimental therapies in clinical trials to restore the oestrogen–sensitive pathways (Emmerson and Hardman, 2012).

Ageing of systems in the human body

Ageing of the cardiovascular system

Major age-related changes can be detected in the functionality of the cardiovascular system, which comprises the heart and lungs together with a closed system of tubes, the vasculature (in a typical adult human, the blood vessels making up the body's vasculature are longer than the circumference of the Earth). The vasculature consists of two distinct circulations: the pulmonary (to the lungs) and systemic (to the rest of the body) (see Figure 2.7). Oxygen is transported from the lungs to the rest of the body in the arteries, carbon dioxide is returned via veins to the lungs for exhalation, while nutrients are carried from the digestive tract to other cells, and waste products (for example, urea)

Figure 2.7: The cardiovascular system

The arteries (light grey) transport the blood from the heart, and the veins (dark grey) return it to the heart. There are two branches of the circulation, known as systemic and pulmonary. The pulmonary branch takes the blood to and from the lungs where it gets oxygenated. The systemic branch brings nutrients carried by the blood to the rest of the body. It is within the capillary network that the exchange of nutrients, oxygen and waste products of cellular metabolism takes place. All vessels are lined with endothelium and the larger vessels have an additional layer of smooth muscle on the outside. A cross-section through a human artery is shown on the right, with the smooth muscle and endothelium, as indicated: note that red blood cells fill the cavity (the fluid phase of the blood, plasma, is not shown). By contrast, the diameter of capillaries allows passage of a single blood cell at a time (not shown)

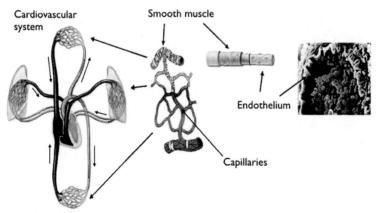

Source: After Seeley, Rod et al. *Anatomy and Physiology*, 7/e ©2006
ISBN:0072507470; McGraw Hill Higher Education, New York, 2006; reproduced with permission

are taken away from cells to their site of detoxification or excretion via the blood stream.

The main pumps in this system comprise the heart and the lungs (strictly, the muscles of the rib cage and the diaphragm, which are responsible for breathing). Both pumps are controlled by sophisticated regulatory mechanisms that, in a healthy human, maintain the continuous circulation of blood and oxygen to each cell of the body, even in sleep or unconsciousness. The two pumps interact with each other, contributing to the continuous variation in heart rate that is seen in healthy individuals, even when resting (see below).

Circulation plays a vital role in homeostasis, that is, keeping the body in a 'balanced' state. Hormones that signal changes in circumstances to which the body must respond (for example, the 'flight or fight' hormone adrenaline, or appetite regulators leptin and grehlin) circulate in the blood from their source to their site of action. The body's temperature control (thermoregulation) is also mediated via the circulation, as is the acid–base balance (pH) which is critical for both nerve and muscle function and for bone health. Since correct blood flow is essential to the maintenance of health for each cell of the body, changes that result either in decreased blood flow or that prevent a normal response to demand are likely to have deleterious effects on the body's ability to respond appropriately to changes in activity level.

The age-related reduction in cardiovascular functionality arises through several contributory mechanisms:

- reduced elasticity of the lungs resulting in reduced oxygen intake in each breathing cycle;
- thickening of the vessels' walls and a reduction in their elasticity leading to an increase in radius and, in addition, possible narrowing due to atherosclerotic plaques;
- possible increased blood pressure due to stiffening of the vessels (which can result from atherosclerosis);
- reduction in vasomotion (continuous movement of the vessels) due to endothelial and smooth muscle dysfunction;
- regulatory dysfunction in response to changing demand.

This progressive failure in the regulation of blood flow via the heart and lungs is an almost universal aspect of ageing. As well as contributing to increased frailty with age, the inability to thermoregulate (that is, lose/preserve heat via increased/decreased peripheral blood flow) is a major cause of death in older people during heat waves or cold spells, while poor physiological responses in older adults to lowered oxygen concentrations in the blood (hypoxia) is clinically dangerous below 95 per cent oxygen saturation. Failure of the blood to return to physiological norms following stress, that is, loss of homeostasis, is likely to be a major contributor to age-related morbidity. For example, low blood potassium interferes with proper nerve muscle activity and can result in loss of strength and falls, while low blood pH (that is, too acidic) leads to loss of bone mineralisation and susceptibility to fractures on falling. Falls, as discussed below, are not only an important reason for hospitalisation of older people, but they also account for a very high mortality rate through impacts on the immune system (see 'Physical body trauma').

These problems are not manifested in young adults, where the amount of blood pumped by the heart around the body is commensurate with need, and where any temporal perturbations in blood pressure, flow or composition are quickly returned to their homeostatic norms. At rest in a healthy young adult, the total blood volume of approximately 5 litres is circulated by the heart every minute, although this can quadruple during intense exercise. In young adults, the heart rate (HR) varies to compensate for the varying volume of blood within each cycle, that is, the amount of blood coming from the lungs to the left atrium of the heart. That is why lung function can, to some extent, control the heart rate. This process has been known for centuries as respiratory sinus arrhythmia (Hales, 1733), and is a major contributor to the continuously changing heart rate – a normal process in a healthy human known as heart rate variability (HRV) that plays an important role in cardiovascular control.

In fact, not only heart rate, but almost all physiological variables are in a state of continuous oscillation, and it can now be understood that it is these oscillations that provide the underlying mechanism of homeostasis: continual small adjustments of parameters to maintain the body in a balanced state. The heart and respiration rates also need to be able to respond to large changes in physiological need, for example, during exercise. The mean heart rate in a resting healthy young subject is about 60 beats/min and is subject to continuous, spontaneous, variations of approximately ± 20 per cent. Figure 2.8 shows the significant degree of variation in time between heart beats (RR) in a young subject, and how this variability is greatly diminished in older subjects. Most of the reduction in variability is attributable to a decrease in the respiration-induced modulation of the heart rate (Iatsenko et al, 2013), which is probably near zero at the end of life. Hence with ageing, the heart rate is much less responsive to the needs of the person – perhaps explaining the decrease in the exercise tolerance of older people. Indeed, on account of reduced elasticity of cardiac and vascular tissue, and hence decreased instantaneous regulation of cardiac output, exercise should be moderate rather than strenuous. However, every effort should be made to ventilate the lungs, for example, by moderate exercise or long walks, thus increasing the oxygenation of the blood which, in turn, improves the elastic properties of all tissues including those of the vessels and the heart, thereby reducing the usual effects of ageing. There is clear evidence that regular exercise can minimise the physiological effects of an otherwise sedentary lifestyle (Chodzko-Zajko et al, 2009).

Figure 2.8: Heart rate variability decreases with age, but the amplitude of blood flow pulsation increases

At rest, the heart contracts approximately once per second to pump the blood around the body. HR varies to match the needs of the body. In this way the RR interval between beats (upper panel, as registered by electrocardiogram [ECG]) continuously varies. Notably, the extent of this RR variability decreases with age. At the same time in normal ageing vessels gradually lose their elasticity and their radii increase, so that the amplitude of flow pulsations (A) in the capillary bed increases with age (bottom row). Atherosclerosis builds up a layer that may reduce the open radius, but there can still be increased flow on account of the loss of elasticity unless the effect of atherosclerosis dominates.

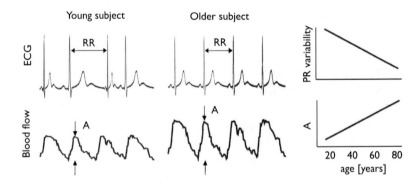

A much more recent addition to the understanding of the origin of HRV comes from the discovery of the functional role of the endothelium (the inner lining of the blood vessels). It is characterised by continuous oscillation in its contractile and electrical activity, which increases and decreases with time, enabling oxygen and nutrients to diffuse through a cell's membrane. The state of the endothelium, as well as that of the entire vasculature, is reflected in a larger or smaller resistance to blood flow, which is sensed mechanically by the heart. Consequently, the heart continuously adjusts its stroke volume (amount of blood pumped in each cycle) and/or heart rate. Where there is atherosclerotic plaque, this deposits on top of the endothelium and renders it less effective.

Elasticity of the blood vessel walls also has an impact on heart rate variability and blood pressure variations. So these are also affected by age. In particular, the reactivity of the smooth muscle cells covering the outer part of the larger vessels is reduced, as is the reactivity of the endothelial cells lining the vessels (Shiogai et al, 2010). A simple manifestation of this ageing mechanism is the increase in the amplitude of pulsation within each heart beat (see Figure 2.8). The overall effect is a decrease with age in ability to properly oxygenate tissues, leading to chronic tissue hypoxia. Notably, hypoxia not only leads to loss of function of cells or even cell death, but it can also favour the development of cancer in the older population.

Cellular senescence and heart disease

Vascular endothelial cells (those that line all blood vessels, including the arteries) have a finite lifespan and eventually senesce. Vascular cells harvested from atherosclerotic plaques show impaired growth in culture, and such cells develop senescence earlier than vascular cells from normal vessels (Kumazaki et al, 1993; Bennett et al, 1998). It has been demonstrated histologically that both vascular endothelial and smooth muscle cells from human atherosclerotic lesions exhibit the morphological features of cellular senescence (Ross et al, 1984; Burrig, 1991), suggesting the occurrence of vascular cell senescence in the body. In addition, senescent-like endothelial cells have been found in atherosclerotic plaques obtained from coronary arteries from individuals with heart disease, but not in areas from the same individuals where atherosclerotic plaques were minimal (Minamino et al, 2002). These data support a role for senescence of endothelial cells in vascular ageing in humans. Further support comes from the observation that smooth muscle cells are seriously depleted from the arteries of individuals with HGPS (Stehbens et al, 2001), with atherosclerotic diseases being the primary cause of death in such individuals.

Telomere shortening occurs in cells lining human blood vessels, and may be related to atherogenesis, with telomere lengths showing a strong inverse correlation with age. Interestingly, this telomere loss occurs faster in cardiac arteries than internal mammary arteries, suggesting that a high level of haemodynamic stress may lead to increased cell turnover (Chang and Harley, 1995; Aviv et al, 2001). Telomeres are also shorter in coronary arteries from individuals with heart disease than in healthy individuals (Ogami et al, 2004). As well as endothelial cells, myocytes (muscle cells) turnover and decline with advancing age (Olivetti et al, 1995; Kajstura et al, 1998), and the number of myocytes with short telomeres increases in the ageing heart (Kajstura et al, 2000). Likewise, telomere length is significantly reduced in cells of the failing heart compared with normal samples (Oh et al, 2003). These impairments are associated with ventricular dilatation and systolic dysfunction (Leri et al, 2003). All these data suggest that telomere shortening and increased cellular senescence with age could contribute to cardiac failure in older people.

Ageing of the nervous system

A major aspect of human ageing is the progressive deterioration in the performance of the neuronal system and the brain. The neuronal system comprises an enormous network of individual nerve cells (neurons) that act in sensory or motor roles. It extends throughout the entire body. Sensory neurons convey the responses to stimuli such as pressure, light, and so on, and carry them in the form of electrical signals (via waves of sodium and potassium ions crossing neuronal membranes). Signals are transmitted via bundles of neurons – the nerves – to be integrated by higher centres, in particular the spinal cord and the brain. Motor neurons convey signals from the brain or spinal cord to muscle cells to cause contraction. A highly simplified neuron is shown in Figure 2.9A: the cell body (soma) is usually located in the grey matter of the brain. The fatty deposits (myelin sheaths) around the axon serve as electrical insulation and contribute to the appearance of the white matter. Nerves with myelinated axons transmit signals relatively fast and are involved in conscious movements. There are also neurons whose axons do not have myelin sheaths, in which the nerve signals travel more slowly. Nerves with unmyelinated axons are involved in the regulation of the cardiovascular system and other organs in the body.

Physical changes in the brain associated with ageing can be measured in living subjects by magnetic resonance imaging (MRI), which reveals the structure of the brain including the volumes of the different kinds of tissues (see Figure 2.9B). The two most distinct structures in the brain are the grey and the white matter. The grey matter consists of neuronal cell bodies, dendrites (small branches around the neuronal cell body), unmyelinated axons, glial cells (astrocytes and oligodendrocytes) and capillaries. The white matter consists of glial cells, capillaries and myelinated axons. The glial cells bring nutrition from the blood vessels to the nerve cells and thus link the brain to the cardiovascular system.

Hence, dysfunction of the cardiovascular system inevitably has an impact on the brain.

Figures 2.9A–2.9E

Figure 2.9A: Schematic representation of a neuron, consisting of the cell body (soma), the dendrites that surround it, the axon and the nerve ending with synapses
Here, a myelinated axon is illustrated with a surrounding fatty sheath. Nerves with myelinated axons are involved in movements and they transmit fast, while those with axons that are unmyelinated transmit relatively slowly. The latter are involved in controlling cardiovascular function and the functions of other organs.
Figure 2.9B: Averaged cross-section of the brain as imaged by MRI
The volume of grey matter decreases with age. The coloured regions indicate areas with larger (black fringed with white) and smaller (white fringed with black) losses of grey matter with age.
Figure 2.9C: A sketch of the local structure of the brain
It consists of nerve cells including their axons (not shown), blood vessels and glial cells that provide the link between them. Glial cells consist mostly of astrocytes and bring nutrition to the nerve cells. In white matter the axons are myelinated, while grey matter contains unmyelinated axons.
Figure 2.9D: White matter volume does not appreciably change with age in either males (upper line) or females (lower line)
Figure 2.9E: By contrast, the volume of grey matter decreases significantly with age

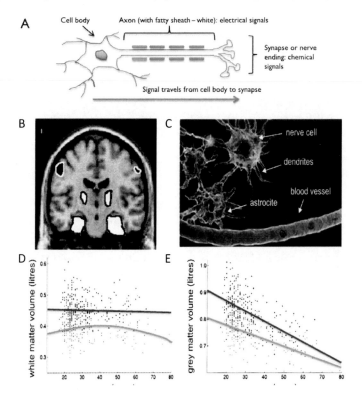

Source: Modified from Good et al (2001)

The effects of age on the grey and white matter were examined in 465 normal adults using MRI (Good et al, 2001). It was shown that the global volume of grey matter decreased linearly with age (Figure 2.9E), with a significantly steeper decline in males. Total white matter did not decline with age (Figure 2.9D), although variation could be seen locally, with some areas of relatively accelerated loss, and others where volume was preserved.

Like other capillaries, those in the brain are made of endothelium. Endothelial reactivity declines with age, and this plays an important role in the ageing of the brain. The reactivity is dependent on oxygen and its reduction may be associated with the hypoxia (a state with a lower level of oxygenation), which becomes pronounced in old age. That is probably one reason why physical exercise with particular emphasis on breathing is found to have a therapeutic effect on cognitive function (Chodzko-Zajko et al, 2009).

Endothelial dysfunction appears to be an underlying factor in states such as Alzheimer's disease. This is because endothelial reactivity is crucially involved in enabling neuronal function in the brain. Thus, the symptoms of both Alzheimer's disease and senile dementia can be ameliorated by moderate exercise. Maintaining endothelial health may reduce the likelihood of vascular accident such as those that result in strokes. Endothelial health is also dependent on diet and, in particular, on foods rich in antioxidants such as olive oil and red wine. Intensive research is in progress (Gates et al, 2009) discussing their effect on endothelial function and thus their potential contribution to healthy ageing.

The immune system

Older individuals are susceptible to many different infections and often experience reactivation of diseases acquired in childhood (for example, shingles) (Berger et al, 1981), suggesting that the immune system becomes less effective at tackling infectious diseases with age. Immune insufficiency may be overtly associated with at least one (pneumonia/influenza), if not more, of the top five causes of death in the population over 65 years of age (Aspinall and Andrew, 2000). How can this age-associated immune insufficiency come about?

The immune system comprises biological structures and processes that protect against diseases caused by infectious agents and aberrant changes to cells, for example, in cancer (immune surveillance is thought to clear the majority of tumours before they become of clinical significance). It uses a layered defence consisting both of simple physical barriers and chemical defences, together with an active cell-based pathogen recognition and destruction system. Physical barriers include the skin and mucus membranes such as the linings of the lungs, and body fluids such as saliva, breast milk, vaginal secretions and semen that contain numerous anti-pathogen peptides (small proteins) and enzymes (Hankiewicz and Swierczek, 1974; Boyton and Openshaw, 2002). Barriers present mostly passive mechanisms that will undergo wear and tear as individuals age.

If physical and basic chemical barriers are breached by pathogenic organisms (for example, on wounding, or if inadequate levels of peptides and enzymes exist), an active cell-based system of defence is triggered. Two types occur: innate and adaptive. The innate immune system is evolutionarily ancient and is not specifically tailored to individual pathogens, although it can deal effectively and rapidly with a wide range of infectious agents using chemical defences against molecular motifs present on many pathogens. Localised inflammation (swelling and reddening) of a damaged tissue in which the barrier has been breached results from, and provides a trigger for, further recruitment of immune cells (neutrophils) that can destroy the invading organism – often by producing toxic bursts of the gas nitric oxide. The immune system is based on various different types of white blood cells; some play a role specifically in pathogen recognition, others in killing, and yet others serve as a memory of the event for future protection. The adaptive immune system, by contrast to the innate system, responds specifically to a particular infectious agent by a process of molecular recognition via cell surface receptors on white blood cells called B and T lymphocytes, that bind with high affinity to small regions of protein (or other macromolecule) exposed on the pathogen surface or on cells infected by the pathogen. Humans have a maximum 'pool' of these cells that stays roughly the same size (similar cell numbers) in young and old people (Utsuyama and Hirokawa, 1987; Hulstaert et al, 1994). T lymphocytes are produced throughout life by an organ called the thymus, while B lymphocytes originate in the bone marrow.

When an individual encounters an infectious agent, the immune system responds by recognising molecules on the surface of the pathogen. Some cells have fairly general molecule recognition and trigger a process of engulfing and/or killing the infectious agent. Others have more specific receptors to recognise pathogens. These cells (the B and T lymphocytes) upon pathogen binding are stimulated to proliferate, giving rise to a cell lineage that then shows extensive division producing large cell numbers (Aspinall and Andrew, 2000). When the infection is over, most of these cells will die, leaving small numbers of memory cells, but with repeated infection these can be rapidly triggered for further division. These continued rounds of proliferation may lead to the accumulation of senescent (or near senescent) cells through telomere erosion (Effros and Pawelec, 1997).

As we age, the thymus atrophies, so reducing the number of new cell lineages that can be initiated when we encounter new infectious agents. The reason for this atrophy is not fully understood, but senescence of cells within the thymus has been proposed as a mechanism (Aspinall and Andrew, 2000). In addition, humans are repeatedly exposed to a few persistent infections, particularly varicella-zoster (chickenpox-shingles), Epstein Barr virus (EBV) and cytomegalovirus (CMV). These are often acquired during childhood, but become latent for long periods and establish lifelong persistence. Periodically, these are 'awakened', resulting in extensive turnover of existing immune cell populations, even if disease is subclinical (Akbar and Fletcher, 2005). It is thought that these two factors result in the 'pool' of immune cells being dominated largely by a few lineages with many cells having limited replicative capacity (summarised in Figure 2.10). Thus the observed reduced ability to fight new infections as we age may be due in part to the lessened ability to produce new immune cell types specific for the new infection, together with immunosenescence of existing cells within the pool. In addition, other types of cells that recognise pathogens and engulf them and produce killing chemicals to eliminate them may lose some of their abilities with ageing. For example, neutrophil cells, which help to kill off infections like pneumonia, can lose their capacity to travel towards sites of infection effectively, and can thus cause much tissue damage on the way as well as being less able to combat infections.

Stress in ageing

The immune system is regulated to prevent over-activity, and is suppressed by the glucocorticoid hormone cortisol, levels of which stay relatively constant across the life course. By contrast, factors that stimulate the immune system, in particular two compounds known as DHEA and DHEAS (serum dehydroepiandrosterone and its sulphated form, dehydroepiandrosterone-sulphate), peak during the third decade of life followed by a gradual decline to only 10-20 per cent by the age of 70 (Orentreich et al, 1984). This process, termed the adrenopause, occurs at similar rates in both sexes. Because cortisol production does not decline with age, glucocorticoid-induced immune suppressive effects dominate over the immune-enhancing effects of DHEAS. This raised serum cortisol:DHEAS ratio is associated with a higher incidence

Figure 2.10: Immune cells and ageing

In young individuals virus-specific lineages – in this case CMV – are present in high numbers together with other infection-specific lineages. With increasing age these CMV lineages expand as a result of CMV reactivation and become increasingly non-functional as they undergo telomere shortening (they may be close to senescence). In old age the build-up of the non-functional CMV lineage may reduce the space for the other lineages. Together these effects reduce the ability of older individuals to respond to both recurrent and new infections.

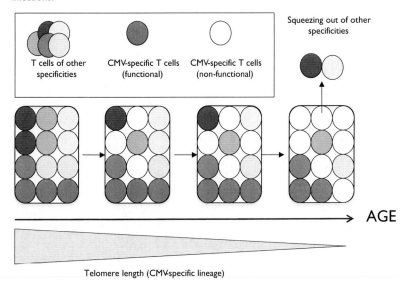

Source: Adapted from Akbar and Fletcher (2005)

of bacterial infections (Butcher et al, 2003). Cortisol is used clinically to treat inflammatory diseases, which occur more frequently in the older population. It also increases blood sugar and decreases bone formation, so has systemic effects beyond its impact on the immune system. Notably, cortisol levels rise and stay high in individuals experiencing chronic psychological stress.

Depression and immunity in older adults

Older adults appear to suffer higher rates of depression and depressive symptoms than younger adults (Bekesi et al, 2000). This is of particular importance, not only psychologically, but also because depression is associated with increased susceptibility to infectious disease and mortality (Kiecolt-Glaser and Glaser, 2002), and with reduced immune cell function that gets poorer across individuals as depressive symptom scores increase (Park et al, 2006). Remarkably, immune cell function returns to normal after patients recover from depression (Cruess et al, 2005). Adrenocortical steroid hormones can have a considerable impact on mood. Raised serum cortisol (the hormone that suppresses the immune system) is strongly associated with melancholic and psychotic depressive subtypes (Thomson and Craighead, 2008), and depression is associated with an increased cortisol:DHEAS ratio. The role of DHEA a regulator of mood is well documented. For example, it has been shown that DHEA replacement to increase DHEAS levels improves mood and well-being in patients receiving chronic glucocorticoid treatment (Nordmark et al, 2005; Brooke et al, 2006). Further, DHEA supplementation has been shown to improve minor and major depression in older individuals (Schmidt et al, 2005).

It has been suggested that major depressive disorder (MDD) can accelerate ageing (Wolkowitz et al, 2011). The incidence of depression is high among individuals with ageing-related illnesses (Heuser, 2002; Kiecolt-Glaser and Glaser, 2002; Chodosh et al, 2007) – but is this cause or effect (chronic illness *per se* is likely to have marked negative effects on mood)? Several underlying mechanisms have been proposed including allostatic load – the cumulative wear and tear on physiological systems from a lifetime of responding to stress (McEwen, 2000), the effects of cumulative psychological stress on cortisol levels (Sapolsky et al, 1986), and, more recently, telomere shortening as an index of biological ageing (Wolkowitz et al, 2011), all of which contribute to increased incidence of age-related diseases (Bauer, 2005; Blasco, 2005). Over the past few years, a number of studies have found associations between MDD and telomere length; those with long-term MDD have been reported to have shorter telomeres than non-depressed controls (Simon et al, 2006; Lung et al, 2007; Wikgren et al, 2012). MDD has also been associated with shorter telomere length in patients with certain disease conditions including coronary heart disease, although there was no relationship between MDD and the five-year change in telomere length (Hoen et al, 2011). Less is known about telomere length and symptoms of depression in the general population or patients without a clinical diagnosis of MDD.

Physical body trauma

Physical body trauma, such as hip fracture, can also be considered a chronic stressor, and is associated with decrements in immune function. For example, hip fracture in previously healthy adults aged over 65 is associated with a significant incidence (43 per cent) of bacterial infection (Butcher and Lord, 2004); this effect of trauma on infection rates was not observed in a younger fracture group, suggesting that this immune impact of stress is worsened by the presence of immunosenescence. Data from the NDA research on synergistic effects of hip fracture and depression on immunity in ageing (see Chapter Four, this volume) highlight the real need to develop effective interventions for depression to improve immune function as well as quality of life among these individuals.

Carer stress has an impact on the ageing immune system

Psychosocial stress has been associated with immune system changes in older populations (Graham et al, 2006). When considering the impact of stress on the process of ageing, a commonly used model is that of being a caregiver for a spouse with dementia or for another family member with a physical or intellectual disability. This is because stress can be defined as an environmental stimulus which puts us psychologically or physiologically out of homeostasis (Cannon, 1932; Selye and Fortier, 1949); caregiving is considered a chronic stressor and is highly distressing (Taylor et al, 2008). This source of chronic stress has been shown to have a variety of immunological decrements, including changes in immune cell counts, poorer latent virus control (that is, viruses that have lain dormant for years may reactivate), a reduced vaccination response, slower wound healing, and a weakened ability to kill virus-infected cells. The impact of caregiving stress on immunity has been shown to remain in some cases even when the caregiving role is over (Kiecolt-Glaser et al, 1996). Caregiver stress also has an impact on wound healing, and caregivers whose wounds were slower to heal than matched controls showed reduced production of the immune modulator IL-1β in response to stimulation, which is essential for initiating wound healing (Kiecolt-Glaser and Glaser, 1995).

The stress of caregiving has been studied in the context of stress management interventions where, following an eight-week intervention, more elderly caregivers registered a four-fold increased response to the influenza vaccine than non-intervention caregivers, although their response was still poorer than non-caregiver controls (Vedhara et al, 2002). Although the mechanisms of this effect are not yet fully understood, these data support the clinical utility of attempts to identify interventions to reduce stress in older people.

Caregiving stress has also been shown to accelerate telomere shortening; mothers of chronically ill children who were caregivers for a long period of time had shorter telomeres and lower telomerase activity than mothers who were caregivers for less time (Epel et al,

2004). In older dementia caregivers, telomeres were shorter compared to age-matched controls (Damjanovic et al, 2007), thus showing another pathway by which caregiving might accelerate cell ageing and immunosenescence. Shortened telomeres in white blood cells will limit their proliferative capacity and hence the ability to mount an effect adaptive immune response to pathogens (Akbar and Fletcher, 2005).

A common cause of biological ageing?

The science of biogerontology is gradually establishing a general definition of the causes and consequences of ageing. Combining the findings from human studies across populations with those from progerias and super-centenarians, and with basic research on model organisms as diverse as yeast, worms, flies and mice, has led to a new view of biological ageing. This emerging consensus suggests that the diverse manifestations of ageing may stem from a common cause: accumulation of damage to cellular and extracellular components that triggers a response leading to irreversible cell ageing, known as cellular senescence. A major consequence of cell senescence is a change in the functionality of a differentiated cell, leading often to loss of appropriate function as well as gain of a secretory activity that promotes loss of tissue integrity and inflammation. Thus old cells in a tissue recruit old neutrophils, and these act synergistically, causing more inflammation and more damage in a vicious cycle.

The growing appreciation that senescent cells may be at the heart of most, or indeed all, of the age-related changes in tissue and organ function lends optimism to the view that ageing can be modulated. If there is a common cause, then perhaps early intervention in this cause could modify the outcomes of human ageing.

Modulating ageing

The marked increase in human lifespan that has been observed almost globally over the past century can be accounted for in general by reduction or amelioration of disease (better sanitation to prevent disease transmission, preventive medicine, for example, vaccination programmes, and better healthcare if people succumb to disease, for example, bacterial infection or cancer). Further lifespan extension beyond these advances is likely to require more direct intervention in the ageing process or in diseases of ageing (which are, of course, likely to be a continuum rather than separate).

Attempts to modify molecular ageing at the cellular level have taken essentially two opposite approaches:

- Observe the whole organism effects of strategies that influence longevity, and then try to work out the cellular and biochemical details by which that strategy acts.
- Identify a cellular component that requires alteration and design or screen for a drug to modify (inhibit or activate) its function.

Caloric restriction

Biological analysis of genes that increase longevity and healthspan have indicated that moderating food intake by caloric restriction (CR) is likely to have beneficial consequences (see 'Narrowing down the number of genes critical to ageing', above), and this effect has been recapitulated in almost all animal models studies. For example (Colman et. al, 2009), young rats fed 40 per cent fewer total calories than rats fed *ad libitum* (that is, ate what they wanted) had increased lifespan and healthspan, although CR for prepubescent mammals tends to inhibit maximal growth and stunt the animals. Animals that start CR later in life (after the onset of adulthood) typically show much less dramatic effects from CR. The degree of CR is also important, with levels of 10 or 20 per cent CR showing much less marked effects on the rats' lifespan.

The effect of CR on humans is more difficult to extrapolate as no long-term rigorous experimentation has been reported. The most relevant studies are perhaps those conducted on Rhesus monkeys (Colman et al, 2009; Mattison et al, 2012), which suggest that CR with good nutrition does have significant effects on healthspan: monkeys show no signs of diabetes, coat is maintained, muscle and bone strength are those of chronologically younger *ad libitum* animals and tellingly, brain scans suggest that white and grey matter are preserved (reviewed in Cox and Mattison, 2009). This is of particular interest in terms of human ageing; perhaps the greatest fear associated with ageing is the loss of cognitive ability and the onset of age-related dementia. There is some conflict in the published literature over effects of CR on monkey lifespan (Colman et al, 2009; Mattison et al, 2012); it seems to depend on many factors including prior dietary exposure, current composition of the diet, genetic differences and pre-existing medical conditions. There may be some extension of lifespan, but it has not yet been shown as a robust outcome.

Limited research into adult human CR (20 per cent for two or more years) shows that body weight decreases, and many markers of heath such as blood pressure and cholesterol improve (Fontana et al, 2004; Meyer et al, 2006). However, the side effects of more extreme CR, such as lethargy, hunger, depression and possibly a reduced ability to fight infection (Sun et al, 2001; Gardner, 2005), suggest that widespread extreme CR is not a useful therapeutic strategy for humans. Presumably, too, these symptoms preclude an increase in healthspan as this must include a component of psychological well-being. Thus far it is suggested that in humans, moderate CR may well increase healthspan whether or not lifespan is also increased. (Of course, this only refers to specific maximal lifespan, as an increase in healthspan without the intervention of medicine will cause an increase in the average or population lifespan the same way that modern drugs have increased the average in the last century.)

CR may also be used as a direct therapy for many age-associated diseases. For example, many cancers increase in incidence with age. CR diets almost always reduce the amount of free glucose in the blood as they restrict carbohydrate intake. Most cancer cells rely on glycolysis (using glucose) for nutrition as they often have dysfunctional mitochondria (which can utilise a number of sources for energy production). Therefore, a diet low in glucose allows healthy normal cells to out-compete cancer cells at the level of energy production. One proof of principle of this is a mouse model for an aggressive brain cancer, glioblastoma multiforme, where mice fed a low-calorie ketogenic diet that restricts glucose have a better prognosis (Sherrington et al, 2008).

Regulating the TOR complex

Rapamycin, a macrolide antibiotic, inhibits the activity of the TOR complex, which is a master regulator in the insulin/IGF-signalling pathway (see Figure 2.5). In this way it has similar effects to CR, which also has an impact on TORC to cause many, if not most, of its effects on lifespan and healthspan. Remarkably, this single drug can extend lifespan in organisms as diverse as yeast and mice. Late-life administration to mice extended female (but not male) lifespan by a small but significant amount, which may equate to as much as an extra 10 years of life in humans (Harrison et al, 2009). In this study, no particular health benefits were observed, with the profile of disease and causes of death similar between the rapamycin and control groups. However, subsequent studies have shown strong health benefits in tackling serious disease of old age, notably dementia. In a mouse model of Alzheimer's disease, not only did rapamycin lead to significantly diminished levels of amyloid plaques and tangles, but it also improved cognitive performance

(Spilman et al, 2010). Rapamycin is currently licensed for use in the clinic as an immune-suppressive agent in transplant patients; however, at the doses used in the dementia and longevity experiments in mice, no adverse impacts on immunity to both bacterial and viral challenge were observed. This holds out hope that rapamycin may be usefully deployed at low doses in treatment of age-related disease. Notably, it also restores normal phenotype to cells from patients with severe HGPS (Cao et al, 2011): rapamycin is thus likely to be incorporated into clinical trials for progeria treatment in the near future. To enhance the beneficial effects of rapamycin while minimising unpleasant drug side effects, there is a large pharmacological drive to develop novel rapalogs[4] (paradoxically driven by the finding that TORC inhibition is a potential route to treating otherwise intractable cancers). Whether rapamycin and caloric restriction act through the same or related biochemical pathways is a topic under current research (see Cox, 2009) through analysis in model organisms and through drug studies in human cells. Other agents such as metformin (an anti-diabetic) is showing promise in altering aspects of TORC signalling indirectly by affecting nutrient sensing pathways; it also has a moderate but significant anti-cancer effect. Combining dugs that target different parts of biochemical pathways may be one approach to minimising side effects, although very early tests need to be carried out on human cell cultures and model organisms before it will be possible to determine additive or synergistic outcomes.

Inhibiting stress kinase signalling rejuvenates cells

Fibroblasts from the progeria WS have a very short replicative capacity compared to normal fibroblasts, and they have an aged phenotype, that is, they appear senescent (Davis et al, 2005). This rapid cell ageing may underlie some of the accelerated ageing seen in the syndrome. It was recently noted that treatment of these cells with a drug prevented this cell ageing and restored an almost normal cellular lifespan (Davis et al, 2005). This drug acts on the stress pathways within the cell, in particular p38 MAP kinase, the same pathways responsible for the production of inflammatory molecules such as TNF-alpha, which may be responsible for the incidence of inflammatory diseases associated with WS, such as atherosclerosis and type II diabetes. If so, such drugs may play a role in possible therapeutics for the syndrome (Davis and Kipling, 2006). The concept of using drug therapy to enhance both lifespan and healthspan in WS is supported by observations that the mean lifespan of WS individuals has been increased by some six years by the use of anti-diabetic drugs of the glitazone class and by good clinical monitoring and care (Yokote and Saito, 2008). In addition, as inflammatory conditions and cell ageing are part of normal ageing processes, it is possible to envisage the use of such drugs to alleviate aspects of the normal ageing process.

Telomerase reactivation

Since telomere shortening is a core mechanism in promoting cell senescence (see 'Replicative senescence is caused by loss of telomeres'), it has long been viewed as a possible target for intervention. In a proof of principle study, telomerase (the enzyme that adds ends back onto chromosomes) was activated in mice that had already developed signs of age-related tissue degradation and dysfunction (Jaskelioff et al, 2011). Remarkably, significant rejuvenation in a range of tissues was seen, strongly suggesting that telomerase reactivation is a viable route to regeneration (see Cox and Mason, 2010, for a commentary). Perhaps even more remarkably, no increased incidence of cancer was reported in the mice; however, parallel work by others shows that in a cancer-prone system (and we can consider older humans in this way), telomerase reactivation promotes aggressive tumour formation (Ding et al, 2012). Given that agents designed to activate telomerase are already available for sale online, such studies provide caveats for those considering telomerase reactivation as a useful strategy to increase healthspan and lifespan.

Preventing progerin accumulation

Can we also learn lessons from other progeroid syndromes that do not so closely match normal human ageing? For instance, will studies of severe childhood HGPS reveal strategies for treating not only progeria but also normal ageing?

As described above, altered lamin protein (progerin) is defective in HGPS; progerin is incorporated into the nuclear membrane rather than the lamina, resulting in cell death from nuclear fragility (Navarro et al, 2006). The lamins are normally processed by an enzyme that adds a fatty group called a farnesyl to the terminal part of the protein. This allows the lamin to be inserted into the nuclear membrane. The terminus of the protein is then removed by a second enzyme, allowing transfer of the lamin to the lamina (Corrigan et al, 2005). Progerin lacks the site for this second enzyme, so it remains in the membrane. This mechanism suggested a possible treatment for the defect in HGPS cells: namely, to prevent the first enzyme adding the farnesyl group to progerin.

This enzyme is called a farnesyltransferase, and it has been shown that farnesyltransferase inhibitors (FTIs) can restore the correct localisation of progerin and alleviate cellular HGPS symptoms (Scaffidi and Misteli, 2005). FTIs may therefore be used clinically to treat individuals with HGPS, and such clinical trials are currently under way (Mehta et al, 2010). Indeed, recent 'breaking news' indicates that FTIs can bring improvements in one or more areas of the condition in 28 children with HGPS, including improvements in arterial stiffness. This finding is of particular importance, as cardiovascular disease is the main cause of mortality (Gordon et al, 2012). It is too early, however, to determine whether FTI treatment will reduce the frequency of strokes or heart attacks in these individuals. In addition, as progerin is found in normal individuals and increases with age, and is also thought to be involved in the onset of atherosclerosis (Cao et al, 2007), it is possible that FTIs may find use as therapeutics for normal ageing. Note that the successful HGPS trial was a triple therapy including statins and bisphosphonates in addition to the FTI; statins are in common use in the general population to reduce cholesterol levels and bisphosphonates are used to treat osteoporosis in older people, so extension to 'normal' ageing trials may benefit from the fact that these drugs are already licensed.

Modulating the ageing immune system

Nutritional supplements such as DHEA can directly reverse the imbalance in cortisol: DHEAS (Allolio and Arlt, 2002) seen in older patients, particularly those suffering from hip fracture (Butcher et al, 2005), to restore immune function. Further, as noted earlier, DHEA administration has been shown to improve well-being, depressive symptoms and quality of life (Buvat, 2003; Nordmark et al, 2005) among older adults in some studies, although a Cochrane review showed the effect on well-being to be limited (meta-analysis was hampered by the fact that studies only administered DHEA for two weeks and used non-validated measures) (Huppert et al, 2000a). Well-being effects are not always accompanied by improvements in immune function (Abrams et al, 2007). However, others show improvements among hormonally insufficient patients (Coles et al, 2005), where the best effects are generally observed (Allolio and Arlt, 2002). DHEA tablets, classed as a nutritional supplement in the US, are cheap and actually available to buy over the counter and use without prescription in the US, but not in Europe. We note that doses of 200 mg per day have been used with minimum side effects (oily skin) in patients with a high cortisol:DHEAS ratio such as those with rheumatoid arthritis (Giltay et al, 1998).

Other interventions

Throughout the section above, we focused predominantly on exciting new advances in developing molecular interventions based on biological understanding of the biological ageing process; such therapies have the potential to improve healthspan in later life. However, there are already current regimes and holistic social and psychological interventions that are highly likely to be of benefit in healthspan and the well-being of the older population. Simple dietary interventions can help to protect the brain against age-related decline: for example, vitamin B helps to counter the adverse effects of homocysteine (de Jager et al, 2012). Falls are a major cause of morbidity and mortality in older people. Simply removing trip hazards from the home, improving lighting on stairs and increasing tread width are all likely to have major impacts in decreasing falls incidence. Increasing exercise and retraining older subjects specifically in core muscle strength and balance has a marked impact on preventing falls (Sherrington et al, 2008), while vitamin D and calcium administration has reduced hip fractures following falls (Avenell et al, 2009); since hip fractures have a high consequent mortality rate, this is a hugely important intervention. However, as with any intervention, it is important to monitor possible side effects and to determine strategies for minimising them, for example, administering vitamin D by injection rather than diet. These are all simple and generally cheap interventions that could be initiated at GP level, with exercise clinics set up to encourage participation by older people in a safe and pleasant environment, ensuring both compliance with the exercise regime and greater social inclusion, with knock-on mental health benefits. Management of stress in older people is also a field ripe for investigation, given the huge immune consequences of stress that lead to adverse health outcomes in older people. Management of the built environment and ensuring that homes and public spaces accommodate older people's needs should also improve quality of life and perception of ageing, factors that in turn have a positive impact on the course of biological ageing.

Ethics of intervening in ageing

Interventions into the human condition have been capable since time immemorial of altering life expectancy, although no intervention has yet been able to alter basic ageing processes, and maximum human lifespan has remained at approximately 120 years (Horrobin, 2006). However, recent advances in biogerontology suggest that it may be possible to extend this lifespan by altering the course of the ageing process itself, for example, by preventing the loss of muscle strength that is a major feature of ageing. If this is indeed possible, should we do so?

Some argue against life extension on the basis of the 'sanctity' of life, by which they mean its 'inviolability' due to a belief that it is simply 'un-natural' (Huhse, 1987). However, ethicists commonly accept the reasonableness of the human prerogative to combat both exogenous and endogenous diseases to prevent early death. Unless a clear reason exists as to why exogenous intervention in human lifespan differs fundamentally from that of intervention in disease, a position that denies the former but accepts the latter appears seriously inconsistent (Millar, 1988). The biogerontologists among us argue that no such clear reason exists (Kirkwood, 2001). Others will say that by arguing for life extension, this will lead to negative associations for older people, leading to increased social exclusion; however, it has been argued that biogerontology could actually do the exact opposite (Latimer et al, 2011).

A major concern of moralists and governments is that ageing research may inadvertently lead to major increases in lifespan and alter beyond recognition the structure of our societies. If intervention in ageing is successful, individuals will indeed live longer; however, biogerontologists would argue that this is already happening as, although maximum lifespan may not have changed, life expectancy has increased markedly through a combination of biomedical interventions and improvements in general living conditions (Bagley et al, 2011). The increasing fraction of the population living to later life should be a cause for celebration, and many (such as Moses Znaimer) argue powerfully for the positive contribution that older people bring to society (Znaimer, 2013).

Unfortunately, this great success story brings great challenges as, although many individuals do undergo what may be termed 'successful ageing', this is not a universal experience, for with older age comes a range of age-related diseases that can profoundly affect quality of life and lead to social exclusion on grounds of ill health (Science and Technology Committee, 2005). A shift to a population with a greater proportion of older individuals will also lead to an increase in overall health and social care costs. In addition, this shift is exacerbated by the diminishing proportion of working individuals contributing to state taxation, creating an increasing 'dependency ratio' within society. This 'dependency ratio' can lead directly to an unhelpful image of older people as a 'burden' or as a group of 'welfare consumers', leading to discrimination and social exclusion, all negative associations. UK pensioners are already included in government statistics as 'benefit claimants', inculcating negative attitudes and ignoring the contributions older people have made to society throughout their lives.

The biogerontologist seeks, by an understanding of the basic biology of ageing, together with the idea that it is the ageing process that leads to much of the age-related ill health, to intervene and postpone ageing itself. Using the example of muscle wasting above, it is likely that preventing muscle wasting and hence falls in an older person will prevent the inevitable hospitalisation for a broken femur, the ensuing pneumonia and high incidence of death after a prolonged period of ill health. The additional consequence will be an increase in average lifespan of the population and may indeed lead to an increase in the maximum human lifespan, although this is by no means inevitable. But in economic terms, prevention is far cheaper than treatment, for the consequences of age-related decline and the impact on quality of life for the individual is priceless. This economic and moral argument holds true for all of the other major age-related frailties – incontinence, blindness and ulcers, to name only three major causes of age-related institutionalisation. In addition, the increased 'healthspan' of individuals allows fuller participation in society as a whole that biogerontologists believe would help to remove many of the negative associations so often attached to older people (Latimer et al, 2011), a world view that is strongly promoted by pro-'active ageing' societies such as Zoomer Nation (Znaimer, 2013), together with both governmental and non-governmental bodies such as the charity sector and the US National Institute on Aging (Bagley et al, 2011). These bodies must be viewed as very distinct from a small fringe element of 'immortalist' groups (mainly in the US), and it is necessary to emphasise that biogerontology is not *immortality or your money back*, but a means of extending human healthspan.

We reiterate the overwhelming theme of this chapter: there is no bigger cause of death than ageing, and no greater disease and healthcare burdens than those resulting from biological ageing, yet it is current practice only to treat the symptoms of biological ageing, rather than the underlying cause. The personal and social costs of this attitude are enormous and increasing with an ageing population. Retaining good health into old age is a goal worth aiming for – an ageing but productive and engaged population is far better socially, politically and morally than a dependent, frail and suffering ageing population. Thus, not only do we believe that it is ethical to intervene in human ageing processes; it may be unethical not to do so.

Conclusion

We have shown in this chapter how the basic science of ageing is helping us to understand how ageing begins in the womb, and how its progress and character is deeply affected by biological stress, genetic diversity and accidents.

While the first revolution in ageing, effected by improvements in living conditions, medicine, diet and sanitation, means that we live longer, it has not ensured that we live longer well (Olshansky and Carnes, 2001). Indeed, one of the legitimations for understanding and developing ways to improve how bodies age in the 'realist' (Carnes and Olshansky, 2007) view of the purpose of ageing science is that from an evolutionary perspective, increased longevity in humans is actually unnatural. This is important because as suggested in the previous section, ethical arguments against interfering directly in the ageing process often rest on a notion that ageing is natural, and to interfere goes against nature in some way. Indeed, one of the most virulent debates amongst biogerontologists is over whether there is a limit to how long humans can live, or whether there is a bioclock that means we could (if our lives were accident and stress-free) be essentially immortal – like the 400-year-old clams found in the Atlantic ocean (Abele et al, 2008).

The new biologies suggest possibilities for changing how people age by contributing knowledge of ageing and the conditions necessary for people to age in such a way that they do, indeed, die of old age rather than suffer an old age of long-term and disabling illness. In the UK, it is estimated that the last 8-10 years of life (on average) are spent in a state of accumulating and worsening disease – the 'morbid period'. In this regard, the objective is not with the immortalists or the prolongevity movement – to extend life – but rather to 'add life to years'. Such compression of morbidity (see Figure 2.4) would have major social consequences, both in terms of improving the quality of later life, and in vast economic savings on nursing and social care. In much the same way as understandings from embryology and developmental science have helped illuminate the relationship between genotype, environment and the health and well-being of the child, so, too, the new biology of ageing may be able to help us understand better some aspects of the relationship between ageing, genetics, the environment and health in later life, and perhaps even to intervene to improve the perceived quality of later life. What it cannot do is define what counts as well-being or vitality in a philosophical sense.

What is important here is the extent to which biological understandings are translated into individual problems, and the extent to which they are translated as pertinent to social and community approaches to health and well-being. There needs to be policy debate over what to do here. It is not simply a matter of discovering the elixir of life, a remedy for ageing. Rather, it is a matter of understanding how societies and communities can support forms of education and living that help people age better. Here, concepts of social inclusion need to incorporate opportunities for ageing well, so that knowledge from the biology of ageing gets translated into giving access to activities and facilities that are pro-ageing (designed specifically to benefit an ageing population). Perhaps the most radical thing that we could do in terms of helping people to age well is build a swimming and sports centre at the end of every street, and give people free access to it. It seems ironic, that the very time in which we are beginning to understand the relationship between how people live, their genetic make-up and how they age, is occurring alongside the privatisation of community swimming pools and sports halls and the selling off of school playing fields.

Where we live, how we live and how we relate to aspects of our youth can have profound effects on the way that we age, not only psychologically, but also physically. In a landmark study, Langer transplanted men in their 70s and 80s away from their accustomed environment to one designed to recreate the appearance, sounds, smells and tastes of the 1950s (Feinberg, 2010, Langer, 2009). The men all showed improvements in physical and intellectual abilities: re-experiencing their youth had a rejuvenating effect.[5] Objective measures of cognitive abilities, hearing and eyesight complemented the anecdotal evidence that the men, some of whom had previously relied on walking sticks, even took part in a football game. Langer concluded that the way that ageing is thought of by the aged can markedly influence their biological ageing. Resilience in ageing is influenced by attitudes and perception – optimism, high self-esteem, social engagement and personal control were all cited as factors important in successful ageing (Lamond et al, 2008). While hard to disentangle confounding factors of cause and effect, it is notable that psychological and social factors appear to have such a marked impact on ageing well. This is explored further in Chapter Five (this volume) where the work of the NDA project 'Look at me!' is described.

Notes

[1] An allele is one copy of a gene – there are two copies of every gene, one inherited from the mother and one from the father. A *gene* can specify a certain trait, for example, eye colour, but the *allele* can be 'blue', 'brown' etc. Some alleles are dominant over others, for example, a person with one 'brown' and one 'blue' allele for eye colour has brown eyes. Genes are regions of chromosomal DNA that encode functional products. Each allele of a gene can vary slightly in the many hundred to thousands of nucleotide building blocks ('letters') that make up the DNA sequence. Minor variations in DNA sequence can have subtle but important consequences on the proteins that the genes encode.

[2] Cell division is exponential: one cell divides into two, the two into four, those four into eight and so on. The number of cells (n) is therefore related to the number of divisions (d) by the simple formula $n=2^d$. (Note: this is a simplification that does not take into account losses through damage or programmed cell death.)

[3] A tumour suppressor is a protein whose role is to actively prevent the formation of a tumour, and thus tumour-suppressor function is found to be lost through mutation in most human cancers.

[4] Drugs that mimic the effects of rapamycin.

[5] Academic references to this work are sparse; reports have been made recently in mainstream media, for example, see http://news.bbc.co.uk/1/hi/magazine/8498233.stm.

THREE

Understanding and transforming ageing through the arts

Michael Murray, David Amigoni, Miriam Bernard, Amanda Crummett, Anna Goulding, Lucy Munro, Andrew Newman, Jill Rezzano, Michelle Rickett, Philip Tew and Lorna Warren

Introduction

Ageing can be both understood and described as a storied process, part of what Holstein and Gubrium (2011, p 103) have described as 'the narrative quality of lives'. We hear and tell stories about growing old; we read and watch published and filmed stories about older people; we are surrounded by images of ageing with their implicit narratives. Such stories permeate our social world and shape our expectations about older people and about growing old ourselves. In this chapter we intend to explore this process further, drawing on research that has explored the character of the stories that older people tell about their lives and, in some cases, making the links to more formal narratives found in genres such as fiction and other representational practices, in collaborative artwork, in art galleries and the theatre. We are particularly interested in how dominant social representations of ageing (Moscovici, 2000) can be contested through a process of active narrative work, that is, engaging older people with representational processes at various levels as consumers of such narratives (as readers, as members of group interactions, as theatre goers, as social beings) and as producers of them (discursively, in interviews and groups, using diaries and through various forms of artistic expression). In highlighting such elements, we are interested in ways of challenging negative social representations of ageing through the active participation of older people in different art forms.

Both narrative making and narrative exchange are everyday processes of making sense of a changing world by which we provide a certain meaningful coherence to a series of events. Such narratives have a certain form and structure which can convey not only particular thoughts about those events, but also incorporate gestures, feelings and actions. As such, narratives can become not only descriptions of past events but plots for future actions. Freeman (2011) has described the phenomenon of 'narrative foreclosure' or the process by which we come to believe that life is over before it is physically ended. We stop developing initiatives and accept that decline and exclusion are inevitable. Public institutions often reinforce this narrative in their negative representations of ageing and in their exclusion of older people from a range of activities.

Narrative accounts are habitually and constantly exchanged and shared in everyday social interaction. Through this process they contribute to and draw on broader social representations about ways of living and the world in which we live (Murray, 2002). While these social representations can consist of abstract ideas and more detailed narrative accounts of particular issues, they can also include more organised social narratives of broader social phenomena about particular social categories and the relationships between those categories. For example, we can talk about the national story, or a locality's story, which includes details of the supposed major events in the history of a nation or locality, and how these events are connected and organised.

These social narratives shape our very understanding of past events, can influence how we interpret and situate current events and can set guidelines for future actions. Such contexts are complicated, since we are born into a complex of overlapping social categories (such as gender, ethnicity, nationality, locality, and so forth), each of which has its own particular variety of social narratives about which we learn as we develop as individuals (Hammack, 2012). Our human development can be characterised as a process of narrative engagement and exchange with members of our own and other social categories. We learn what is expected of us from the stories told about ourselves, our families, our communities and our broader social categories. As we develop, our membership of particular categories may change, and so too, may the details of their associated narratives.

Admittedly, the character of these social categories and narratives overlap and interpenetrate such that the narrative associated with old age in one culture will differ from that in another. Furthermore, social narratives are not fixed and can certainly be resisted or challenged variously. Such challenges can be in some ways as rather mundane matters of everyday resistance, deploying, for example, ridicule and silence. In addition, they can be more organised and subversive. De Fina and Georgakopoulou (2012, p 149) have recently noted that 'studies have increasingly stressed the need to shift attention away from more or less static reproduction of such master narratives towards the tellers' resistance and lack of compliance with them.' Resistance to dominant narratives can become organised. History is filled with examples of how groups of people have challenged expected social narratives and begun to assert an alternative narrative. Selbin (2010), among others, has argued that the movement for challenge is facilitated by the development of an oppositional narrative which promises new forms of social organisation.

Traditionally, social narratives of younger and older people are presented in a rather dichotomous fashion. Early life is often characterised as the age of potential, with life stories often crafted in terms of what will happen or plans for the future, of becoming. This is supposedly reflected in young people's greater interest, both in fiction and in fantasy. Conversely, later life is presented in terms of what has been, of past achievements or of disappointments. At best it is accounted as more a period of looking back as reflected in interest in memoirs, biographies and broader historical accounts. At worst it conforms to Shakespeare's famous seven ages of man speech found in *As you like it*, where death awaits after a period of inevitable debilitating decline. This general dichotomy casts younger people as agents of change, of life creators, while older people are cast as passive recipients of care.

Exploration of narratives typically privileges language as the medium through which stories are told and shared. However, people are increasingly storying themselves and being storied through visual media: we only have to consider the popularity of Facebook and the power of advertising, although the use of visual storying is also becoming more widespread among academics, including those looking at ageing (Phoenix, 2010). Soden (2011, p 85) has identified three broad, taken-for-granted 'fabulous narrations' or what in *Mythologies* Barthes (1972) termed myths, which Ylänne (2012, p 8) believes to be manifest in many images of ageing in popular media: (i) ageing as decline – mental and physical; (ii) ageing as synonymous with loss of power – sexual, economic and social; and (iii) a necessary attitude of resistance to ageing. The notion of 'critical narrativity' (Biggs, 2001) not only draws attention to such fabulous narrations; it highlights the importance of identifying 'counter-stories' or different perspectives on these myths.

In this chapter we are particularly concerned with exploring how in telling and sharing different types of story older people can begin to both reflect on their lives, and also to explore new opportunities (cf Hammack, 2012). We are interested in how older people represent themselves and are, in turn, represented through the many narratives they share. However, we are keen to go beyond that to explore ways of challenging dominant social representations of ageing by developing more activist narratives of ageing through participation in a range of arts activities. As Hepworth (2000, p 3) has stressed, with increasing longevity people are capably 'finding new images of positive meaning to life after 50.' To illustrate this process we consider a number of studies in which different art forms are used as a means of exploring the character of social narratives about growing older. We then go beyond that to consider how active involvement of older people in various art forms can provide an opportunity to develop an alternative personal and social narrative of ageing more generally.

Fiction, cultural narratives and self-reflection

Novels and other artistic products contribute to and reflect broader social representations of multiple phenomena, including that of ageing. As Hepworth (2000, p 5) comments: 'Fiction evidently adds a further dimension to our understanding of the quality of the ageing experience.' In everyday life we use literary concepts to convey experiences (for example, turning over a new page), so embedded are the concepts concerning such aesthetic acts in framing our social selves. The Fiction and Cultural Mediation of Ageing Project (FCMAP) was predicated on the concept that narrative animates social values, and was specifically concerned with how older people could understand ageing through the prism of both social and fictional narratives of ageing encountered in loosely structured frameworks (both individual and group), where such narratives become a catalyst for personal reflections in diary form on how one experiences later life in contemporary culture.

FCMAP combined mass observation diary keeping as a form of gathering qualitative in-depth social data, the use of the novel as a stimulus for reflection, and reading groups as a form of periodic social engagement which could animate the diary keeping and set a regular framework for individual reading, interpretation and thought. The central research focused on reactions to literary representation and the depictions of such fiction during that period. It also assessed social and personal attitudes in Britain towards ageing among older people, as mediated through a complex economy of fictional representation and also the respondents' narrative responses to these. Finally, the FCMAP team used the data gathered to explore the role of literary representations in shaping older people's self-understanding of ageing, and to inform a policy report (Bazalgette et al, 2011).

Eight reading groups met monthly, involving more than 80 volunteers who ranged in age from their early 60s to their 90s. The groups were located in different London district associations of the Third Age Trust or University of the Third Age (U3A). During 2009–10, all groups read nine nominated novels, although they could vary one of these nominated texts by selecting another drawn from a B-list.[1] These texts provided various contrasting and thought-provoking vantage points on later life. The volunteers kept diaries recording their responses to each book after reading it, and again after the group discussion. As Highmore (2002, p 34) explains: 'The attention to the details of everyday life (a form of sociological microscopy) means that the experiential, instead of being located in great events, is extended to the non-event-ness of the everyday.' The FCMAP team was committed to scholarship that 'gave voice' to the experiences of older people as well placing them as integral to the research process. The reading groups also formally mirror the narrative propensity found in the life-world narrative, and which provide a central, common human experience that Rubinstein (2002, p 141) tentatively suggests is an innate element for humans in relating and understanding their experiences:

> There are many cultural and individual formats or templates that render what may have been an amorphous chain of raw material into a culturally appropriate experience and, thereafter, a narrative. One critical cultural format is the propensity for stories to have beginnings, middles, and endings, and to be structured in other important ways as well. Getting closure on an experience is a key cultural and therapeutic motif.

Key to the project, both methodologically and structurally, was the active engagement of older people in an environment that diminished researcher influence and fostered more autonomous thinking. As seen in the resultant data, most non-academic people leading what they regard as their 'ordinary' lives do not obtain their views of ageing through matters such as demographics, statistics, academic research, or even, in most cases, any lived experience of older people. One participant noted: 'Certainly the perception of ageing has changed remarkably in the time [last 50–60 years] – 70 is the new 50, though not perhaps to those under 30.' Another group participant, reflecting on this change, noted:

> The present young and middle-aged seem to share interests inside as well as outside the home to a greater extent and definite roles are now rarely restricted to one sex. Also, as jobs are unlikely to be for life, and career changes common

and accepted, the perception of age-related ideas and behaviour might become more flexible for both men and women of that generation.

The same participant, reflecting on the first book encountered by all reading groups, David Lodge's *Deaf sentence* (2008), felt that it conveyed much of the negativity about growing old: 'He notes personal and domestic neglect, isolation, and general shrinking of interest in the outside world and apprehension and dislike of change.' In the novel, society would appear to still associate growing old primarily with such aspects as isolation and frailty. However, this literary representation of ageing might reflect the lives of some older people. As another reading group participant commented in her diary:

> Elderly people usually have less energy and ambition than younger people, so tend to socialise less and care less if society leaves them alone. (I suspect that sometimes people, esp men, who don't want to socialise – and these tend to be retired – are happy to live in such a mess that visiting their home is an embarrassing experience and a stressful one, for others.)

Jim Crace's novel *Arcadia* attracted much criticism. One participant stressed that ageing was not a fixed negative condition, but rather it depended on the person: 'Reading Crace has made me think old age isn't a problem, it's old people.' Another participant thought that this novel was prejudiced since it foregrounds 'the physical disabilities of the older characters [which] pepper the text ...', and which she proceeded to enumerate at length. She commented on the group discussion of the text: 'It was noted that Victor could not recall the faces of his mother or aunt. He more or less invented his own story. We are all prone to selective memory and build our own narratives.' Another participant said of a younger middle-aged employee whose view of Victor draws on a general view of the latter's age: 'A suggestion that Rook's view of Victor is somewhat like David Lodge's view of his father, with "old" used as image, "elderly" equated with "frail". Is the writer making a political statement?'

The group discussion stressed that real experiences run counter to the negative coordinates of the lives of Crace's characters. One participant said about the group discussions of the novel:

"There was some discussion about the opinion that older people can be creative and innovative. There are many examples of older writers having time to produce books and it was felt that women in particular are freed by age to be creative and productive."

Another said of these discussions: "It is interesting that the pains of ageing preoccupy us far less than the positives."

Few of the readers identified with Victor's isolation directly as an experience that defined their own lives. One remarked on changing social representations of ageing: "The author himself was in his early 40s, that is, middle-aged at the time! Maybe attitudes have changed since and the views it portrays are somewhat dated?"

Ageing could still be daunting. One diarist reflected:

> My auntie who had spells of dementia but at times seemed perfectly lucid, frequently told the mini-cab bringing her home from a hospital appointment to drop her off at her previous address, and was found wandering the streets. This was despite my frequent complaints to the hospital and instructions not to deliver her to any other address than that given on her notes.

But, as indicated implicitly here, the effects can be managed and minimised, and the individual could still retain their dignity. Moreover, overall ageing was regarded differently in contemporary culture, as offering ever more an active phase with great potential. As another diarist reflected, 'It's heartening to hear about 60-year-olds dancing. They reflect the attitude of older people today who want to continue to learn and do fresh things when they retire.' Another mused, 'How can we hang on to the identity we prefer and reject or ignore the one being thrust on us?' Active ageing and engagement characterised the generally positive perception of the diarists concerning their ambitions for later life.

The dynamic textual and real-life interaction of these groups was designed to encourage self-reflection, for, as Taylor (1991, p 58) emphasises, while rejecting monological perspectives of identity-formation:

> Human beings always have a sense of self, in the sense that they situate themselves somewhere in ethical space. Their sense of who they are is defined partly by some

identification of what are truly important issues, standards, goods or demands; and correlative to this, by some sense of where they stand relative to these and/or measure up on them.

Taylor, perhaps, might also have emphasised that although this assessment appears to be an individual one, it has a complex collective element, its parameters and very process being largely determined intersubjectively through narrative discursive structures and exchanges, deploying implicit comparators and modes of exchange in the acts of so doing. Taylor (1991, p 59) adds importantly, that 'we easily tend to see the human agent as primarily a subject of representations: representations first about the world outside; and second depictions of ends desired or feared', and that identity 'also places us in some social space' (p 63). The reader groups are part of that ongoing process, as mutative as ageing itself. The selected books were published during and reflecting on those years that constituted a very large part if not the entirety of the life experience of the people volunteering for the various strands. Among the key objectives two included the aim of making the insights revealed by the study available to stakeholders and policy makers, and to contribute to the field of critical and cultural gerontology in an innovative fashion.

Counter-narratives and community arts

Community arts are variously defined as the use of multiple forms of creative activities in community settings (for example, housing estates, community centres). They involve the active participation of and ongoing dialogue with individuals and groups, and are characterised by their experimental and inclusive nature. The aim of community arts is to involve people in developing and sharing their creative talents and through this, to promote confidence and greater social interaction among participants as well as drawing attention to particular social issues. As such, community arts can be both personally and socially transformative. Much of it has been directed at young people, and there has been less obvious concern about its potential in work with older people. One of the aims of the 'CALL-ME' project was to explore the potential role of community arts to transform the lives of older people through the development of counter-narratives of creativity and sociality.

Older residents of disadvantaged neighbourhoods often report social isolation and loneliness. The nature of this experience is dependent on their neighbourhood, the type of facilities and resources available, and their opportunity to access additional resources nearby. The 'CALL-ME' project adopted a participatory action design to both explore and challenge the character and extent of such social isolation. It took place in four disadvantaged urban neighbourhoods in Manchester. In each neighbourhood we developed with some older residents a community project. In one neighbourhood we developed an arts project, in two others a gardening project and in the fourth, a community exercise project. Throughout the project the researchers engaged in ongoing conversation with the participants as well as formal and informal individual and group interviews. In addition, we interviewed a sample of community stakeholders who worked in the neighbourhoods to further develop our understanding of the experience of growing old in an urban neighbourhood, and the challenges faced by those attempting to implement forms of community intervention.

In this section we focus on the community arts project, which took place in one of the neighbourhoods. Further details of this and the other projects are detailed elsewhere (Murray and Crummett, 2010). Initially there was a considerable amount of door stepping in the neighbourhood by the researchers to get to know some of the local residents and community workers. This was followed by a community meeting, where the idea of developing a project was introduced. Particular small resources for the project were sought from the local council and various community agencies. The aim was to have something concrete to show at the end of the project for an open house/exhibition.

A dozen older residents formed the core of this arts project which took place in the local community rooms. The project ran over one year and consisted of four subprojects, each lasting about 10 weeks, with weekly meetings lasting two hours. A community arts worker coordinated each subproject. The sessions were informal and encouraged the residents to develop a range of artworks including paintings, drawings, writings, craftwork and silk-screen prints. Since the project was held in the community rooms at the centre of the neighbourhood, it itself became a focus for wider social activity. Local residents who were not part of the core group would drop in and join in the conversation or ask advice about particular issues. The local community police officer and the housing support officer began to use the rooms as a base where they could have a cup of tea and meet residents informally.

At the close of each subproject there was an exhibition of the artwork in the community rooms to which local people and the media were invited. At one exhibition the central exhibit was a community map which included photographs of the area over the past 30 years. This provoked substantial discussion and was subsequently mounted on the wall of the community rooms (see Photo 3.1).

Photo 3.1: Community map

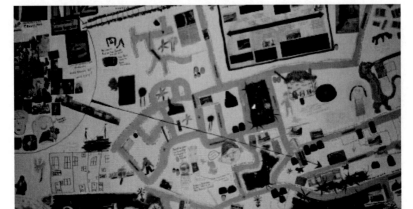

Photo taken by Amanda Crummett.

In another, we worked with local community artist Ian McKay to create a series of silk-screen prints. A selection of these was framed and put on display, and sweatshirts produced with one of the prints as the main image (see Photo 3.2).

Contact was made with the local primary school, and it was agreed to organise a collaborative art project around small 10cm × 10cm artworks (see Photo 3.3). The exhibitions attracted a large number of local residents as well as local councillors and officials, and some press representatives. Details of the exhibitions were carried in the local newspapers and also in community newsletters.

In the focus group at the close of the project, the older people were enthusiastic about the opportunity to participate in the arts activities, and also talked about the benefits to them personally and also to the wider community. Involvement in the projects gave them a sense of achievement. They were immensely proud of their artwork and of the exhibitions. When other residents visited the exhibition they were pleased to comment on the group's work. In this way they were challenging the idea of 'narrative foreclosure' for older people, especially those from disadvantaged communities. Some recalled that they had enjoyed artwork at school but had been discouraged by their teacher and had never had the opportunity subsequently. Others brought to the meetings some examples of their own craftwork, for example, embroidery or knitting. One brought samples of her poetry which she had written for certain local or family occasions. For a community map project the participants brought old photographs to the meetings which encouraged extensive recollection on how the community had changed and on their own lives.

Photo 3.2: Participants with silk screen sweatshirts

Photo taken by Amanda Crummett. (See www.mckayart.co.uk/M1211/m1211.html for more photos.)

During the project they explored different art forms and each drew different reactions from the other participants. Often they referred to other family members and how proud they would be of their achievements. For example, after a session of making pots from clay, Janet, who had lost her husband a few years earlier, said:

> "Mike would be very proud of me if he could see what I'm doing. I'm making these pots for Mike. I'll put plants and flowers in them for him, to remember him."

Photo 3.3: Small artworks with a local school

Photo taken by Amanda Crummet. (See http://westgorton10x10.wordpress.com/ for more examples.)

Ann said: "Had a lovely day – have achieved a lifelong ambition to mess with clay and make something." After the creative writing session, Monica said:

> "It was really good. I enjoyed it. It wasn't what I thought though. I thought that we would be doing fancy writing but we had to write a story. I wrote about my Fred – past and present. I wrote about the stories he tells me about growing up in Newby."

George really enjoyed the silk-screen printing. Afterwards, he said:

> "I could do what I wanted. I didn't have to constrain. I could experiment. All my work is the way I want to do it."

The structure of the project allowed the older people to explore different art forms in a non-threatening environment. Some of the art forms were more challenging than others, but all were enjoyable and promoted discussion.

Some of the group members were surprised at their own talents. As George said:

> "I didn't know what to expect because we've never had this before so I wasn't sure what to expect. I was surprised that we had so much talent. I mean there are certain people that

have astounded me. I mean Mary, her work has been very good, and Monica surprises me all the time."

Others reflected on the opportunity the art provided to escape from other everyday concerns:

"I used to think well I've got no time to take for me but now with this, it is time for me. You get lost in what you're doing and you've no time to think what's happening around you. Well, we're just here doing your project and just for a couple of hours you're in your own world doing what you want and nobody's there to interfere with it."

An important part of the artwork was the final product which they could admire and show to others. They talked about each other's work and supported each other. As George said:

"One of the main points is you can turn round or look at whatever it is and think and yes, I made that."

The artwork was a concrete expression of their abilities which they could talk about with others in the project or in the wider community. One of the women felt that other members of the community also had lots of abilities, but they did not express them because "they're a bit frightened, they think – I can't do that".

But there was also a broader social challenge. The participants felt that they were able to demonstrate to outside officials and others their talents that they felt had not been recognised. In publicly displaying their artwork at the end of each project they were challenging the perceived negative social representation of their community as being talentless.

Some referred not to the artwork but to the enhanced opportunity provided for social interaction and forming new friendships. For example, one man said:

"Why I'm happy is everyone is together, we enjoy what we're going....Yeh, that's the thing, that's the thing for me. I'm really not bothered about drawings and things like that. I'm more happier that people are together and enjoying that. I'll support that all the way because, as I say, if it gets people out like Monica and George and they enjoy it, I'm happy with that."

Some referred back to their early days in the area, and felt that the project was contributing to community building (for example, "It seems to be getting people together"; another added "I'm very pleased with everything that's happening for the community"). The project created a sense of identity and belonging.

The regular meetings and community artwork promoted a sense of group solidarity and discussion about other activities. During the course of the project these activities included a bus trip to the seaside (one of the older women had never been to the seaside before), a Christmas lunch in a local pub and a small market stall outside the community rooms to raise some funds for the project. The initial hesitancy and nervousness among some of the participants was replaced with a certain confidence in their ability and what they could do as a group:

> "I would love to go to the countryside, could we do that? Could we do that together? Oh yes, I would like that if we all went together in the countryside."

It is interesting to note the media representation of the project. While some described the project in rather non-committal terms, one newspaper made reference to the history of the estate and surprise that the residents were producing artwork. The participants in the project were very annoyed at this media representation, and felt that it reflected the broader outsider representation, which they were attempting to challenge through their artwork.

An important part of the community artwork was its participatory nature. The older people resented being told what to do. For example, at one early meeting of the project some council officials detailed their expectations. Although this was done in a low-key fashion, the older people felt uncomfortable. One of them subsequently told one of the research team that she felt she was being told what to do, and she added:

> "I'm really angry and so are other people. [...] They wanted to tell us how we had to do things. [...] Well they can stuff it. I'm going to get my big table out and we'll meet in my back kitchen. We don't want those people telling us what to do."

The older residents enjoyed making art together, but they did not want other people bossing them about. This brought back to many of them memories of officialdom and curtailment of their activities. In making art they were challenging those traditional restrictions, showing officialdom what they could do on their own when they had the opportunity. They were beginning to develop a new narrative of talent and potential.

Art galleries and identity

Art galleries form an important social institution in modern society. For example, from April 2011 to March 2012, 48.9 per cent of adults (in the UK) visited a museum or gallery (DCMS, 2012, p 19). Older people, particularly those with higher educational qualifications, make a significant audience for shows of avant-garde work shown in contemporary visual art galleries. The 'Contemporary visual art and identity construction – Well-being amongst older people' project was concerned with exploring older people's reactions to contemporary visual art displayed in galleries, and how that related to their sense of well-being. The following considers how the meanings that were created in response to the artworks allowed participants to construct a sense of identity that placed them within a life course narrative which they, to an extent, were more able to control.

This project recruited 38 older people in five groups (aged between 62 and 92), with numbers ranging from six to nine people in each group. Ethical approval was applied for and received from Newcastle University, UK. None of the participants suffered from dementia, and guidance on capacity was provided by Newcastle University's Institute for Ageing and Health. All participants gave informed consent, and it was emphasised that they could leave the project at any point without consequence. The five groups were recruited from categories that were identified by Keaney and Oskala (2007) as being liable to exclusion from the arts. These categories were limiting disability or illness, low income, living alone, low levels of educational achievement and low socio-economic status. In order to provide a point of comparison, those who did not fall into any of these categories were also recruited.

The groups were either pre-existing or came together for the research. They included a sheltered accommodation group (Gateshead), a writers' group (Sunderland), a group recruited from an advocacy organisation for older people (Gateshead), a group recruited from a daytime film club for the over-60s (Newcastle upon Tyne) and a group recruited from a 'Live at Home' scheme (Gateshead). In addition to these groups, a 92-year-old isolated female took part in the research. Each group visited three contemporary visual art venues over the lifetime of the project, with the final visit chosen by the group members. The venues were the Northern Gallery for Contemporary Art, Sunderland; the BALTIC Centre for Contemporary Art, Gateshead; the Shipley Art Gallery,

Photo 3.4: Discussing an art exhibition

Photo taken by Andrew Newman

Gateshead; the Belsay Hall, Castle and Gardens, Northumberland; the Great North Museum: Hancock, Newcastle upon Tyne; and the Hatton Gallery, Newcastle upon Tyne. The writers' group chose the Great North Museum: Hancock – displaying a mixed historical collection rather than contemporary visual art.

Focus groups or one-to-one interviews with the participants were used to collect some baseline data including demographic information and their understanding of, and responses to, contemporary visual art. The participants were taken to the gallery, given lunch and then given a guided tour around the show by a curator or education officer. Focus groups were then used to record their responses to the experiences of the visits.

A dominant social narrative was that of decline and social exclusion, which was internalised by some of the participants. The 92-year-old isolated female, who uses a wheelchair, stated:

> "Sometimes the way we are treated at a certain age makes you feel that, oh well, they're past it, it's not worth doing anything to help."

Her lack of mobility prevented her from doing things she wanted to do, and because of her age, many of her friends had died, so she had lost her purpose in life. She went on to say:

> "Sometimes I wish I was dead, I'm just waiting; I feel I have outlived my normal span. I don't really feel I'm justifying what existence I've got, I'm literally waiting to die."

However, other participants who had similar feelings responded politically by making a plea for older people to be seen as being active and part of mainstream society. A member of the writers' group made the following comment at the end of the project. This person is a 74-year-old female:

> "I mean we are not old but we have a young outlook and I think, you know, people sort of realise that you are not catering for the old, you are catering for the older people who are wanting to be stimulated, you know, want new ideas brought into their lives, something they can focus on and feel as though they are still part of society, you know."

For this person it was important for older people not to be written off as passive and somehow different from the rest of society. A member of the same group, a different 74-year-old female, made the same point:

> "I mean we all have the same ideas only in a different way we still have a mind that's sharp as a button."

Some of the participants felt that the negative social representation of ageing was changing, albeit slowly. An 81-year-old retired civil servant, who was a member of an advocacy organisation for older people, felt that society had accepted that older people could be more active than they had been in the past:

> "It's not just a question now of stick granny in a corner and give her knitting and tell her to shut up you know as it used to happen generations ago – they are now more acceptable that people of our age will come out and join in – to actually want to take part in things. You've got grannies that go abseiling now and do all sorts of weird and wonderful things you know. So I think society as a whole is more able

to accept that because we are old it doesn't mean to say
our life has come to an end; we are still able to take part."

He also felt that older people should stretch themselves and take
advantage of the opportunities that were now available, stating:

"We never got a chance to do what the young ones are
doing today; this is our chance now."

Despite this acceptance that there were changes in the ways that they
were viewed and that there were new opportunities for them, there
was still a sense that they needed to challenge the dominant view of
older people. The impact of real or anticipated age-associated deficits
could be combated through activity, both physical and intellectual.

The importance of learning was emphasised by a member of the 'Live
at Home' scheme who was an 84-year-old male. He stated:

"I've always thought of life as being one big school because
you are always learning and you are always seeing different
things. You watch people grow and this, that and the other.
It's forever one big school because people think they come
out of school that's it, it's not, you're forever learning."

An 87-year-old member of the writers' group commented on the
importance of keeping mentally active. She stated:

"I think I'm the oldest here being in my 80s; I feel that these
things have just kept me going, you know, I must admit
because I think I would just be sitting at home sleeping or
doing nothing if I hadn't this education, all these museums
and places we go to, I think they are wonderful. You know
when I think of my mother, she died at 59, when we all
grew up she hadn't much left to do, that's a terrible thing
to say about your mum, she hadn't much."

This might be seen as an example of Ekerdt's (1986, p 26) 'busy
ethic', with its 'emphasis on activity, exercise, travel, eating out, self-
maintenance and self care' for older people – preventing them being
classified as perhaps they see other older people being classified by
mainstream society.

These older people responded politically by emphasising the
importance of cultural engagement to their well-being. They suggested

changes to provision, such as the timing of activities and the need for transport that would facilitate their engagement. They are purposely developing an activist counter-narrative, not just in an abstract way to respond to issues around ageing, but in an attempt to achieve a definite political objective.

Particular artworks were more personally relevant to some of the participants and attracted more detailed recollections. For example, in response to 'Parrworld' by Martin Parr (a collection of photographs and assorted objects documenting historical and political moments), displayed at the BALTIC Centre for Contemporary Art, Gateshead, a 68-year-old member of the sheltered accommodation group commented:

> "With the miners' strike it was a situation that my husband was put in because he was a policeman, he was born in a mining village and there's dates and everything and all his family was miners, his brother was still in the pits so my husband was on the frontline in the miners' strikes and it caused a lot of animosity."

This artwork prompted her to express something that was of significance in her life and representative of her age and class. She felt comfortable in talking about something that was socially divisive. Although she had not played an active role in the miners' strike, she was emotionally drawn into it through her husband's role. Now the artwork provided her with an opportunity to talk about it.

The same exhibition allowed a 79-year-old wheelchair user to reach back into her past to holidays with her family when she was young:

> "I mean there was Lindisfarne and there was Bognor Regis because I was at Bognor Regis and Butlins[2] in the '70s with the kids and that was just the lounge thing, I just thought it was fantastic, I did, I really enjoyed it, really enjoyed it."

This mingling of difficult and happy moments in their lives enabled them to grasp that life was not always one or the other, but a series of changing events which they had come through.

The participants constructed a series of narratives in response to the artworks that they encountered which projected them into what Rowles (1983, p 306) has called 'incident places' that were closely related to their sense of self. These narratives were used to construct a sense of continuity and life course progression as well understanding their place in wider society. To quote Kroger (2002, p 7): 'through its processes and contents it provides meaning, form and continuity to one's life experiences.' Kroger emphasises the importance of the processes of identity revision and maintenance, which 'refer to those mechanisms that individuals use to maintain or revise a sense of who they are within their immediate and broader social networks and contexts' (2002, p 7), which are important for the well-being of older people.

Ages and stages

Performance and drama have been part of human society for millennia. They are a means not only of entertainment but also of conveying new ideas and encouraging debate and discussion about contemporary and historic issues. Both involve narrative as spectacle. They encourage us to reflect on our current social arrangements and introduce ideas about new ways of living, sometimes through a focus on the past, either through the canon of classical drama, or through drama that engages with a community's past. But there remains the question of whose past, and whose experience of ageing? If Samuel Beckett has brought powerful critical reflections on the meaning of ageing to the modern stage (for instance, *Krapp's last tape*), many still recall the classic rendering of the seven ages of man in Shakespeare's *As you like it*.

It is important to develop theatrical perspectives on ageing in ways that challenge ideas about ageing as deficit and inevitable decline. The 'Ages and stages' project (Bernard et al, 2013) explored not only the character of social representations of ageing but also how they were challenged in a particular theatrical context. The project focused on the New Victoria Theatre in the Potteries district of North Staffordshire. This theatre was established by Peter Cheeseman in the 1960s, and had a remit to represent and engage local residents. Over a period of 50 years it developed a substantial reputation for its 'documentary' theatrical productions, which took up local issues and encouraged local discussion.

The 'Ages and stages' project developed over three strands. The first explored the substantial archival material which Peter Cheeseman had developed over the years, and which provide a veritable treasure trove of textual and audio-visual material of about life in, and the history of, the Potteries. The second strand was a series of 79 individual/couple interviews (96 people in total) and 10 group interviews (51 people) with audience members, volunteers, theatre employees and actors, and those who were sources for the original documentaries. The third strand brought these two strands together in the development of a new documentary performance exploring ageing, inter-generational relations and the role the theatre has played – and continues to play – in the creative life of the people of Stoke-on-Trent and North Staffordshire.

Theatre archives are valuable resources for informing researchers about a community's identity, its past and the social attitudes on which it was founded, as reflected through its artistic repertoire. The Vic Theatre archive is no exception, while also offering researchers something representationally unique in the form of original materials on which the documentaries were based. When the theatre was established, Peter Cheeseman made it a matter of policy that the company's repertoire should reflect the community's history and identity back to its audience – hence 'documentaries' that were based on the pottery industry in the Victorian period (*The jolly potters*), the history of the local railway line that linked the urban communities of the Potteries together (*The Knotty*), local campaigns to save industrial resources from decline and closure during the 1970s and 1980s, such as *The fight for Shelton Bar* (steel), and *Nice girls* (mineworks and coal). In Cheeseman's method of documentary theatre, writers and actors became researchers, making the production from representations from the past. They did this initially through newspaper stories and ballads, published in the 19th century (*The jolly potters*).

Photo 3.5: Collecting stories for *The fight for Shelton Bar* (1974)

Copyright Guardian News & Media Ltd 1973.

Photo 3.6: Rehearsing The Knotty (1966)

Over time, they graduated to the use of tape recorders for capturing living people's experiences of and stories about working life on, for example, the railway in *The Knotty*. These interviewees were often older people, whose memories became crucial to this form of research, for representations of past experience captured on tape could include powerful inter-generational memories, handed down through a family. Of course, the archive includes both the original recording, and the transcription made of such moments that were shaped, artistically, into narratives, and arranged alongside other artistic material (such as songs), which could transform a representation into a narrated spectacle that would come to life in performance. Such performances had the potential to challenge received ideas about ageing and identity. For instance, in *The Knotty*, a performed story of 'granddad Preston's' induction into railway life as a young man in the 1840s, based on the memory of an interviewee in his 70s, passing on his grandfather's story in the 1960s, would be performed by a vigorous young actor on stage.

The archive valuably records the process by which original materials were gathered by writers and actor researchers, to be transformed into powerful narrative representations for the theatre. It enabled us, as researchers, to explore the creative interface between social attitudes, contexts and the production of new art forms. In addition, the archive valuably records those numerous extracts of interviews, often, indeed, whole interviews, which were not selected for inclusion in the final documentary theatre productions. Although ageing is very much the urgent focus of the research context of our own time, it was not always a consciously formulated focus in the theatre's history and its approach to its art. But still, the attitudes to ageing, and reflections on the experience of ageing as a community and its industries transformed, are valuably still recorded in the archival materials, even when they failed to be selected as a 'source' for dramatic representation and narrative. Over time, the project has come to formulate a sophisticated sense of narrative possibilities that have been preserved, although thus far 'un-articulated', in the archive's materials – for instance, narratives about ageing and its emotional impact that constitute alternative iterations of the story that the community could tell of itself as it fought the decline of its industrial heritage while challenging that loss.

Our interview methods and practice can consequently be seen as an extension of the methods already developed by the theatre as an organisation committed simultaneously to the production of art and social research; the extensive interview material that we captured can be seen as yet another source of critical challenge to narratives about ageing. In the following discussion, we make reference to some of the material from a selection of the interviews which highlight how involvement in the theatre provides an opportunity for older people to experience and represent ageing and later-life transitions in positive ways and combat some of the negative social representations of ageing. Reading through this wealth of material it was apparent that, while the theatre represented particular images of growing older, it also provided opportunities for challenge and resistance of various forms. We consider some examples of this process.

For some of the participants the theatre provided a sense of continuity. They could recall their early contact with the theatre with animation, and continued to experience that sense of wonder and also of community. As one audience member said:

> "I've always been involved in theatre right from a child. It's something which has always been my first hobby and still exists, and so it hasn't changed for me as I've got older."

Interviewees articulated a sense of belonging in relation to the theatre, and appreciated the social contact it offered. Importantly, the Vic was seen as a 'comfortable' place for people to visit on their own – something that was particularly valued by older women. The theatre could therefore provide an opportunity to combat feelings of social isolation. As one woman said:

> "It is a social occasion when you go to the Victoria Theatre. This is one of the things that matters, and it matters to older people because some people can spend a day without seeing anybody ... and usually if you are on your own, which I do do occasionally, you find that somebody will speak to you, you know it's a very relaxed atmosphere I think and that's important as you get older."

A dominant image of ageing is one of loss. As people grow old, their children often move away from the family home, and they lose connections with work colleagues. When one partner in a couple dies, the experience of loss of social contacts is accentuated. Our interviewees rarely produced narratives of ageing as loss or isolation. In contrast, many interviewees had become *more* involved with theatre following bereavement or retirement, and talked about the increased social networks and sense of community it provided. One volunteer said:

> "I've made some wonderful friends and I love the camaraderie that we have there. It's a very nice place to be and work and as I say people are there year in year out ... we don't lose a lot of people and I like that sort of steadfastness that it has.... People don't move on, and I like that sense of security that it gives me."

The many social roles which people have in terms of family and work can fade as they grow older. Theatre participation can provide a renewed sense of purpose and value, particularly for older people who volunteer following retirement. This was expressed clearly in a group discussion with women volunteers:

> "I think it gives you a role again."
> "It does."
> "Because when you've been working most of your life you've got a role and in lots of cases you were quite an important person. And then when you retire, after a while, you've been talking about."
> "Being invisible?"
> "Being invisible. You're nearly disappearing. So coming to somewhere like this you feel, yes, yes."

"Yes, because the people that come to the theatre, they treat you as if like this is a really important, well it is an important job ... they treat you as if you're important, you know, as if you have got a really good role in the theatre. Yes."

Being active in various roles attached to the theatre provided an ongoing opportunity to resist the public representation of ageing as a period of decline. One audience member and former theatre volunteer summed up this view in a group discussion:

"But I sense among us a slight resistance to categorisation of older people. We don't see ourselves, except in so far as physical incapacity is concerned, as being very different to what we were, and where we can look for expansion of these things we do."

Finally, interviewees appreciated the potential of theatre to broaden their horizons and provide ongoing challenges in later life, again challenging the idea of ageing as decline or loss. An older woman who had been trained by the theatre to be an audio-describer following her retirement said:

"I think that as you do get older, if you don't have a manageable challenge ... you're not developing yourself any more, and I think that's one of the things that the theatre does, not just for the young people but for us. It's still developing us, and that's what's so great."

From our body of interviews, it is apparent that older people's theatre participation challenges the negative social representation of ageing as a period of decline and social exclusion. This includes participation through attending as an audience member or in a more active manner through becoming a volunteer or starting or continuing to participate in creative theatre work.

The project team were keen to take this challenge to a higher level through the development of a verbatim documentary performance, drawing from the earlier interviews, and titled *Our age, our stage*. Participants and performers ($n=25$) were older people (aged 59–92) interviewed for Strand 2, and members (aged 16-19) of the New Vic Youth Theatre. Devised through weekly workshops using and discussing findings from the interviews and archival analyses and materials, the

Photo 3.7: *Our age, our stage* (2012)

Photo taken by Miriam Bernard

hour-long documentary was designed to ask questions of the audience and to challenge this 'narrative foreclosure'.

Visual representations and narrative potential

'Counter-stories' were the starting point for the 'Representing self – representing ageing' project, the specific focus of which was the representation of older women in the media. The 2002 Second World Assembly on Ageing had identified the need to involve older people in media representations of their activities and concerns (United Nations, 2002, p 39). The importance of creating new images of ageing was identified as a particular concern in relation to older women. While in general, older people are heavily under-represented within our image-saturated society (Woodward, 1999), cross-national studies evidence the particular paucity of images of women's ageing compared with those of men (Zhang et al, 2006). Contemporary visual representations of middle-aged and older women are increasingly diverse, but also more likely to misrepresent women through digital enhancement or airbrushing (Hurd Clark, 2010). When not hidden from view, the physical signs of ageing for women are framed by narratives of negative stereotyping, humour, or of an ever-expanding sexualised beauty industry (Greer, 1996; Hurd Clarke, 2010). Commentators have been concerned with the 'straight-jacketing' of older women (Twigg, 2004; Hurd Clarke, 2010) and the assigning of social value, resources and opportunities by such narratives (Arber and Ginn, 1991), which are perpetuated through popular media channels (Gill, 2006).

The originality of the 'Representing self – representing ageing' initiative lay in the direct involvement of 'ordinary' older women in creating visual counter-stories to those dominant narratives. Older women worked together to critique dominant images of women and, using creative arts, to make their own individual images of ageing. A total of 41 women were involved in the project from start to finish, and their ages ranged from 43 to 96. They participated in workshops using art therapy, phototherapy and community arts-based approaches. The images produced were displayed in an exhibition entitled 'Look at me!', held in a range of venues in Sheffield in the North of England.

Participants were interviewed before and after the workshops. In most cases they were also filmed during the workshops. Both interviews and filming led participants to reflect on the personal meanings of their artwork. This not only elicited detailed narratives about specific pieces of artwork and motives for creating that work, but also the process of involvement. Some of the women who took part were drawn to the project because they had prior experience of or an interest in the creative arts, but this was by no means true of all.

Existing 'Representing self – representing ageing' publications have documented the kinds of visual representations salient to women's understanding of ageing and women's responses to those representations when invited to challenge dominant media images (Hogan and Warren, 2012; Warren and Richards, 2012). Their auto- and co-produced images explored wrinkles, broken veins and greying hair, for example. They also captured various experiences from continued public involvement, friendships and fun to fears of increasing limitations and invisibility. Independent of the actual representations produced, the women's collaborative involvement in generating artwork which was displayed in exhibitions contributed to additional narratives of creativity, challenge and positive identity (Reynolds, 2008, p 137), and also of solidarity and ownership of the research process, having an impact on well-being and a feeling of public validation.

Previous analyses of the project have also shown some of the factors having an impact on and the difficulties of creating 'alternative' images of older women (Richards et al, 2012). For example, in the community arts workshops, where professional photographers were employed to give visual form to the women's narratives on ageing and their lives as older women, the types of images produced were affected by the artistic style and preferences of the photographers and their respective ages. While images produced avoided replicating the common 'heroes of ageing'/'bodily decline' binary (Featherstone and Hepworth, 2005), they did not escape other dualistic nostalgic/melancholic or humorously carnivalesque categorisations.

Studies of annual calendars have argued that the meanings of the photographs they contain may be 'bounded' by themes and use of text: textual additions to images bind the two and steer our interpretations of images (Zalot, 2001; Fairhurst, 2011). Nevertheless, Bytheway (2011, p 79) has noted that 'Visual, in contrast to verbal, images often have a power that overshadows the impact of any accompanying text.' The project collected verbal narratives from participants about their individual images and/or the production of those images, and these were made available alongside the artwork. This proved no guarantee that the images were read by others in a way that was consistent with participants' stories or the overall project goals. Understandings reflected a complex negotiation of the relationship between the image, accompanying text or video, different cultural narratives of ageing (Gullette, 2004) and the contexts within which individual viewers experienced their own ageing or interest in representations of ageing (Bytheway, 2011). Exhibition feedback provided illustrations of this.

A questionnaire, used at the Workstation and Jessop West exhibition sites, asked visitors to record tick-box responses to a short set of questions on what they thought of the exhibition, with space for written comments, as well as collecting basic demographic data.[3] There was a visitors book for unprompted feedback, and individuals were also invited to give their opinions to camera at the Workstation and shop window exhibition sites. At all sites, exhibition signage included panels explaining the project and the aims of each workshop. In the majority of cases, individual pieces of artwork were accompanied by labels, with quotes from the interviews with the participant which captured the essence of the image and/or its production. All labels were carefully checked with and approved by participants. In some cases, participants edited the quote, provided new words or chose not to have any accompanying words. An additional photo diary provided by the facilitator of the phototherapy workshop was available at the Workstation and Jessop West sites, where videos of the different workshops and of individual participants also ran in a loop.

Collectively, the questionnaires (*n*=242) demonstrated the success of the exhibition, with visitors judging it 'good' or 'very good' (87 per cent), describing it as 'thought-provoking' (83 per cent) and 'desirous of seeing more images of older women in public' (88 per cent). However, a more detailed analysis of feedback began to uncover more nuanced/ complex responses.

One female visitor (aged 46–55), who described her occupation as 'theatre', appeared disillusioned by the need for the exhibition:

> "I don't see individuals – just women once more forced to defend themselves in imagery."

It was not clear from her comment whether this was because she saw the continued misrepresentation of older women in the media as provoking collective action or because she believed the chosen way of challenging that misrepresentation to be rather hackneyed and staged. However, the result was the judgement of the exhibition as 'depressing' and a failure to see any kind of individual narrative.

Other visitors were concerned with resisting the reproduction of stereotyping. For example, a female lecturer (aged 36–45) observed:

> "I understand the work with wigs etc but think there are more interesting and challenging images to display. Don't make women look ridiculous – fashion does this all the time already."

For her, the Green Estate portraits, which had been displayed locally in a health centre prior to the exhibitions, were "positive and an antidote to advertising using 50+ women".

Photo 3.8: Green Estate exhibition at a local health centre

Photo taken by Fiona Oliver.

She articulated the distinction between the written, spoken and visual stories, admitting that she was:

> "… more interested in the photo diaries and women's narratives and new senses of community than in the images of the women."

The reason for this was the failure of dominant media images to offer older women any openings for narrating their stories:

> "That 'non-invisible' older women are forced to conform to a 'Good Housekeeping' style of acceptable glamour that says nothing about their personality – and in this project women were enabled to express what made them unique and what energised them."

Participants in the project were predominantly white, and a black adult education officer and white project officer (both aged 46–55) registered their disappointment at the absence of images of black and minority ethnic women: "Would have been interesting to see their view of ageing." Others were, in the words of a retired woman (aged 66-75): "Surprised at the young ages of some of the women involved." A male occupational therapist (36–45 years) observed:

> "This may be a reflection of the people I work with (the over-80s), but I didn't consider many of the people in the exhibition old."

The project had deliberately recruited 'self-defined' older women and was about 'ageing', but some visitors clearly expected representations of old age which, in this instance at least, were likely to be informed by the categorisations – 'the over-80s' – and context of care provision. In this respect, 'Someone who does not have any signs of age such as a lined face, clothing characteristic of older people, spectacles, a walking stick or a carer in attendance, is someone who will look "far too young" to represent old age' (Bytheway and Johnson, 2005, p 185).

If some visitors read the exhibition in terms of one dominating narrative, others were inspired by the "diversity of ways people expressed their thoughts on ageing", exposing ageing in a "new dynamic way" and "enjoying the subversion". Commenting on the image of Jude doing a handstand, a young man said to camera:

Photo 3.9: Jude in collaboration with Sue Hale

Photo taken by Sue Hale.

> "I think it's funny an old woman should try and recreate what she did in the playground as a youth. I didn't think an old woman could do a handstand – I can't."

> "I'm this mischievous little girl, looking off to the side and clearly planning the next exploit. As a child, I was often in trouble, not keeping myself clean, making mischief with my cousin. I wanted to try and recreate those feelings."

Others commented on the diversity of the form of images. The photograph entitled simply 'Barbie's bottom drawer, aged 50' – a collection of pills, creams, plasters and sprays, but including UHU glue, wood filler and a potato masher – was appreciated by many participants for its humorous representation of the many familiar tools of bodywork in later life: "I know about this" (female ex-teacher, aged 56–65).

A young female artist (aged 26–35) appreciated the materials and textures of Barbara Gibson's 'Balding pubic area'. Constructed from a pair of tights and straggling cotton threads, it was making public "an unspoken issue in a slightly shocking way. Shocking because [you] don't expect an older lady to produce this!"

Photo 3.10: Barbie's bottom drawer, aged 50

Photo taken by Amanda Wells.

Photo 3.11: 'Balding pubic area'

Photo taken by Deborah Gibson.

> "There are so many elements of ageing that don't make it into the media. These sorts of things, like the balding pubic area, for example, are missing from the whole story about ageing."

A woman engineer (aged 36–45) observed that the exhibition offered "Many ways of approaching the same subject so there's a good chance one will connect with you and your own life." For many women visitors, this was a positive connection:

> "Very enlightening, made me feel it was normal to be this 'owd woman'." (retired woman, aged 56–65)

It extended to "being represented as creative people" (woman, aged 56–65).

However, the connection was more mixed for others. A male artist in his 60s classed the exhibition as thought-provoking but "Not easy to view – I felt mildly intrusive". He was conscious of the women in the phototherapy session having "enjoyed the male gender-free environment in order to express themselves in a more uninhibited manner than generally meets society's expectations of people in their 50s". Locating his response in his own biography, he explained, "I bore some of the blame for what these women were doing or not doing – I felt a bit excluded – like I did when a group of women would dance together in a disco." Since he believed older people to be "abhorred and dismissed, some pitied and excused", he felt there to be an unsettling "air of regression and a somewhat forced [for the camera] liberty". Nevertheless, his final written exhortation was to "Keep this sort of stuff up!"

Conclusion

In her recent memoir, Jeanette Winterson (2012, pp 5-6) describes how in writing fiction she was challenging the dominant story of her life shaped by her adoptive mother:

> It's why I am a writer – I don't say 'decided' to be, or 'became'. It was not an act of will or even a conscious choice. To avoid the narrow mesh of Mrs Winterson's story I had to be able to tell my own. Part fact part fiction is what life is. And it is always a cover story. I wrote my way out.

This chapter was designed to explore how through participating in a range of artworks older people began to explore their own life narratives in relation to wider social narratives on which culture draws. In doing so they often surprised each other with their talents, and were keen to go further. Freeman (2011, p 15) has written about the existence of two competing narratives – one of a 'vital, self-sufficient individual, who resists the kind of fragility, vulnerability, and dependency that growing old sometimes brings in tow', and the other of 'inexorable decline'. While the older participants in our studies were aware of the latter narrative, through collectively participating in the different artworks they were beginning to explore the alternative narrative of creativity and possibility.

The novels read in the reading group provoked discussion and debate about broader social representations of ageing as a period of decline. In their discussions they emphasised that this may have been the case many years ago, but it was no longer the case for everyone today. In many ways they considered that some of the novelists they had read were living in the past in purveying such stereotypical views about older people. Nevertheless, in addressing these fictional narratives, many of the study participants empathised with many features of the older people portrayed, but their diaries allowed them to consider contrary examples and variations drawn from personal experience. The active study of fiction not only provided a catalyst for reflection, but also an insight into how social attitudes and processes were sustained, and might be radically challenged.

The community arts activities provided an opportunity for the older participants to reflect on their creative talents, which they felt had been largely ignored all their lives. Now they had the opportunity to show themselves and others what they could do. They were beginning to shape a counter-narrative of creativity and solidarity. Several of them recalled experiences of art making when they were at school or later. Unfortunately, due to lack of opportunity and, in some cases, negative comments from teachers, they had turned away from something they had enjoyed, and began to think of themselves as having little artistic talent. One man recalled: "they said my art was so good they couldn't believe that I hadn't traced it". Participation in the community arts projects with community residents with whom they felt comfortable allowed them the opportunity to reassess that representation of themselves and instead to develop a new narrative of imagination and possibility.

The art gallery project encouraged wider reflection on the older participants' lives. It allowed them to respond to wider narratives associated with older people, making a plea for them to be seen as productive members of mainstream society rather than as passive and excluded. Participation in the project widened their horizons and encouraged them to think that older people should take advantage of the many opportunities that were available to them. The narratives constructed in response to the artworks became an opportunity to share stories that their generation and class had in common. It allowed them to weave a personal and community narrative, providing a sense of solidarity and continuity. Within limits, it also empowered them to decide on the content of those narratives, determining the emphasis that might be placed on one event rather than another. This was achieved through the memories that were prompted and the themes identified that they associated with the artwork.

The theatre project explored the cultural and historical change in local narratives about ageing, and how the theatre itself could become an agent for greater reflection on dominant social representations. It also illustrated how participation in the theatre provided an opportunity to do more than was traditionally expected of older people. The development of the new performance extended this opportunity by enabling older and younger people to explore the character of dominant representations of ageing to a range of audiences in different settings.

Visual images produced by ordinary older women clearly have the power to challenge invisibility and the 'fabulous narrations' dominating popular media representations of gender and ageing, foregrounding creativity and engagement. However, we cannot assume a simple relationship between image and meaning, even when visual narratives are accompanied by verbal or textual narratives which 'add flow'. Pursuing the relationship between exhibition materials and visitor feedback gives insight into the complex ways in which meaning depends on how 'we' – the unknown audience (Bytheway, 2011, p 89) – 'see' the visual images and reflexively elaborate on them through text and video (Fairhurst, 2012).

Overall, involvement in the artwork provided an opportunity to reflect on and challenge the dominant narratives of ageing as inevitable decline. Participants instead began to consider their potential of developing counter-narratives of capability, creativity and camaraderie. Involvement in the various artworks encouraged them to reflect on their experiences and collectively begin to generate new narratives of community well-being, quality of life and cultural agendas for all – of life's worth rather than net worth (Groombridge, 2007, p 3).

Notes

[1] David Lodge's *Deaf sentence* (2008), Jim Crace's *Arcadia* (1992), Caryl Phillips' *A distant shore* (2003), Hanif Kureishi's *The body* (2002), Trezza Azzopardi's *Remember me* (2004), Angela Carter's *Wise children* (1991), Barbara Pym's *Quartet in autumn* (1977), Norah Hoult's *There were no windows* (1944) and Fay Weldon's *Chalcot Crescent* (2009).

[2] In the 1970s holiday camps were an affordable family holiday in the UK (see www.butlins.com).

[3] *What do you think of the exhibition?*

1 = very good; 2 = good; 3 = ok; 4 = variable; 5 = disappointing; Further comments....

How would you describe the exhibition?

Challenging; Thought-provoking; Offensive; Interesting; Uplifting; Depressing; Surprising; Stereotypical; Other....

Did the exhibition make you feel differently about representations of older women?

Yes; No; Don't know; *In what way?*...

Was there a particular image that you liked?...

Would you like to see more images like this in public?

Yes; No; Maybe; *Where?*...

Further comments...

Demographics

Sex; Age; Occupation; Ethnicity

FOUR

Maintaining health and well-being: overcoming barriers to healthy ageing

Sara Arber, Ann Bowling, Andrea Creech, Myanna Duncan,
Anna Goulding, Diane Gyi, Susan Hallam, Cheryl Haslam, Aadil Kazi,
Liz Lloyd, Janet Lord, MAP2030 team, Mike Murphy, Andrew Newman,
Anna C. Phillips, Ricardo Twumasi and Jane Upton

This chapter concentrates on health and well-being, drawing on 11 New Dynamics of Ageing (NDA) projects covering the whole range, from basic biology to the arts and humanities. Our main purpose is to employ the findings from our projects to examine the barriers to healthy ageing and how to overcome them. By way of introduction to this discussion of healthy ageing we first consider some key concepts in this field: ageing and ill health, older age, quality of life and subjective well-being. We begin with an overview of the main demographic changes that underline the importance of research on healthy ageing.

Key concepts for healthy ageing

Demographic changes

Major demographic shifts are currently under way in countries of the developed world such as the UK. In the 25-year period from 1985 to 2010 the number of adults aged over 65 in the UK increased by 1.7 million, and the number of those aged over 85 almost doubled to 1.4 million (ONS, 2011a). This is partly due to improvements in mortality leading to higher numbers in old age. Life expectancy is increasing at a rate of two years per decade in developed societies. However, there are sharply divergent views about how trends in life expectancy may develop during this century. For example, Christensen et al (2009, p 1196) pointed out, 'if the pace of increase in life expectancy in developed countries over the past two centuries continues through the 21st century, most babies born since 2000 ... [in] countries with long life expectancies will celebrate their 100th birthdays ... research suggests that ageing processes are modifiable and that people are living longer without severe disability.' On the other hand, Olshansky et al (2005, p 1142) stated, 'as a result of the substantial rise in the prevalence of obesity and its life-shortening complications such as diabetes, life expectancy at birth and at older ages could level off or even decline within the first half of this century'.

The magnitude and implications of population ageing depend heavily on the magnitude of mortality improvement in decades to come. At present, overall age-standardised mortality rates (both sexes combined) are improving at about 2.5 per cent per annum in the UK (based on ONS, 2012a), but current trends are heavily influenced by patterns at ages where deaths are concentrated. In 2010, half of UK deaths occurred to people born between 1925 and 1945. These birth cohorts, sometimes referred to as the 'golden generations', have exhibited faster-than-average rates of mortality improvement in recent decades (Dunnell, 2008, p 19). As these cohorts are replaced in the main mortality age groups by less favoured cohorts, rates of mortality improvement are expected to fall. Official projections assume that mortality improvement will decline to an underlying value of 1 per cent per annum from about 25 years after the 'golden generations' effect has worked itself out of the system (ONS, 2012b). The extent to which the current high annual rate of improvement is directly linked to these cohorts, or alternatively, whether it is a more generalised period phenomenon, is contested (Murphy, 2009). Future prospects are likely to depend on a number of factors, especially the current obesity epidemic. Olshansky et al (2005) identified this as a major threat, whereas the Government Office for Science (2007, p 38) concluded that increases in obesity will have surprisingly little impact (less than a year) on the life expectancy of the population in the first half of this century, a period when official projections assume that life expectancy will rise by around eight years for men and seven years for women. While obesity has a substantial impact on *morbidity* status, as a risk factor for cardiovascular disease, stroke, arthritis and dementia, it is unlikely to have much impact on numbers of older people in the next quarter century or so, and in any case, there will be offsetting factors such as lower levels of smoking among later cohorts (Murphy and di Cesare, 2012).

Assuming life expectancy grows in line with the principal Office for National Statistics (ONS) 2010-based population projection, the numbers of people in the UK aged 65 or over will rise by 64 per cent over the period 2010–35, from roughly 10 million to 17 million (ONS, 2012b). However, the increase in numbers of people over the period would be between 58 and 73 per cent, a difference of 1.3 million older people, based on the alternative rates of mortality improvement in these projections (see Table 4.1). The 'oldest old' age group, people over 85, is anticipated to grow the fastest, by 147 per cent under the principal projection. Uncertainty in the projections is greatest at the oldest ages, when the need for care is greatest, and the actual increase over the period could be anywhere between 122 and 172 per cent, a difference of around 700,000 people (Table 4.1).

Table 4.1: Population aged 65 and over and 85 and over, and growth in period 2010–35, UK

	Year and life expectancy projection type			
	2010	2035		
		Principal	High	Low
Size (000s)				
65 and over	10,304	16,948	17,572	16,307
85 and over	1,411	3,483	3,837	3,138
% increase over 2010 value				
65 and over	–	64.5	70.5	58.3
85 and over	–	146.9	172.0	122.5

Source: Derived from ONS (2012b)

Ageing and ill health

With increasing life expectancy, a key question is the extent to which the extra years will be healthy, active and productive. There is considerable uncertainty about future levels of health and disability (Jagger et al, 2007; Donald et al, 2010; FUTURAGE, 2011). Disability depends substantially on a range of major disabling diseases (arthritis, coronary heart disease, peripheral vascular disease, hypertension, stroke and dementia). Under the assumption of constant disease prevalence, thus representing ageing of the population alone, there would be an increase of 89 per cent in the numbers of older people aged 65 years and over with significant disability and an expansion of disability, since years with disability beyond age 65 would increase by 1.1 years for men and 1.2 years for women between 2010 and 2030. Even reductions of 10 per cent in the prevalence of these major disabling diseases would not result in an absolute decrease in the years with disability beyond age 65, although the proportion of remaining life spent with disability beyond age 85 would decrease (Jagger et al, 2009).

As the population ages there are increasing risks of ill health. Doing nothing to improve the health of older people is an expensive and unethical choice. Social care costs for older people in the UK amounted to £9.1 billion in 2008/09 and 10 million working days were lost through musculoskeletal conditions alone in 2006/07, with a cost to the NHS of poor musculoskeletal health close to £6 billion per annum. In addition, 370,000 older adults fall each year in the UK; 76,000 of these falls result in hip fracture and this is predicted to rise to 120,000 by 2015 (Johnell et al, 1992). A fall combined with hip fracture is a leading cause of older adults making a move into a care home, as a necessity because they are no longer able to be supported at home. Analysis of trends in risk factors for and incidence of dementia suggests that focusing on treatments that extend survival with dementia rather than on interventions that might reduce its disabling effects would significantly increase the population burden of disability over the next 20 years (Jagger et al, 2009). These are just a few examples of the consequences of unsuccessful ageing. If we are to ensure old age is enjoyed and not endured, we need to understand the barriers to healthy ageing in order to develop interventions to remove or minimise those barriers.

Conceptualising older age

In the context of these demographic changes, a re-examination of what being older actually means has become a critical issue. According to Laslett (1989), later life comprises a third and fourth phase. The 'third age' is a time when individuals, post-work and free from some of the responsibilities of earlier adulthood, may still pursue goals and lead creative, fulfilling lives, prior to the 'fourth age', which is characterised by physical and cognitive decline. Laslett acknowledged the difficulty of attaching a chronological age to these phases, and argued that the third age represented a quality of life, rather than a specific age band.

Others have argued that becoming 'post-work', associated with reaching the third age, is a transitional process, rather than a specific event (Hodkinson et al, 2008). For example, Schuller and Watson (2009) point out that within the UK social context there is a general move to enabling people to work longer and to consider 'retirement careers' for reasons related to both public finance and personal well-being. As a result, diverse processes of exit from employment are increasingly evident, raising important questions about the division of the life course into age bands (Gilleard and Higgs, 2009). Moreover, it is important to bear in mind the impact of socio-economic inequalities in people's life expectancy at retirement. Nevertheless, despite these shortcomings, 'the use of age bands has now become an accepted way to explore and to try to understand the experiences of different cohorts' (Withnall, 2010, p 118).

Quality of life

In recent years the notion of quality of life has been the focus of much research, for example, under the Economic and Social Research Council (ESRC) Growing Older Programme (Walker, 2006). A plethora of definitions of this concept has emerged, varying widely in scope and indicators (Smith, 2000; Bowling et al, 2013). Broadly, two major strands may be identified, one focusing on economic conditions and resources, the other on subjective experience of life. Veenhoven (2000) reconciles the two strands of research, interpreting these two perspectives on quality of life as 'life chances' and 'life results'. His model of quality of life proposes four dimensions: 'liveability' (the external environment), 'life-ability' (individual internal resources making it possible to exploit life's opportunities), 'utility of life' (a sense of utility to others, giving one's life meaning beyond personal pleasure) and finally, 'appreciation of life' (positive appraisals and positive emotional responses to life).

In research concerned with older populations, health and longevity have tended to be treated as proxies for well-being (Higgs et al, 2003). The result has sometimes been that quality of life has been interpreted as quantity of life. Hodge (1990), for instance, criticises the idea that quality of life may be captured in a concept of 'health years'. Higgs et al (2003) argue that treating health as a proxy for well-being reinforces a paradigm of ageing that is dominated by notions of decline and dependence, and largely ignores the capacity of older people to adapt and compensate for changes in health and mobility. They further argue that in a social context where older people are living longer and healthier lives, and where the 'younger old' have been said to have reached the 'crown of life' (Laslett, 1989), such a perspective on quality of life does not sufficiently account for the active and reflexive dimensions of later life.

Mainstream interpretations omit to consider older people's own definitions of, and priorities for, their quality of life, despite publications identifying these. Fry's (2000) research was based on a combination of survey data and in-depth interviews with older people in Vancouver. She concluded that older adults valued personal control, autonomy and self-sufficiency, their right to pursue a chosen lifestyle and a right to privacy. Farquhar's (1995) in-depth interviews with people aged

65 and over in East London and Essex reported that family, social activities and social contacts were the three commonly mentioned areas that gave quality to their lives. Browne et al (1994), on the basis of semi-structured interviews using the Schedule for Self-Evaluation of Quality of Life (SEIQoL) with people aged 65 and over in Ireland, reported that both family and health were nominated by people as most important to their QoL, with almost equal frequency, followed by social and leisure activities. Population surveys of all adults and people aged 65 and over have reported that people themselves have identified a wider range of life areas as important to them, and to their QoL (Bowling, 1996; Bowling et al, 2003; Gabriel and Bowling, 2004). The core components, and the central planks, of QoL, which were consistently emphasised by qualitative and quantitative methods, were self-constructs and cognitive mechanisms (psychological outlook, optimism-pessimism, independence and control over life), health and functional status, personal social networks, support and activities, neighbourhood social capital and financial circumstances (Bowling et al, 2003; Bowling, 2005; Gabriel and Bowling, 2004). There is also a dynamic interplay between people and their surrounding social structures, which influences QoL.

Since the turn of the 21st century broader QoL measures for older people have been developed and tested, with good results. The Older People's QoL (OPQoL) questionnaire (Bowling and Stenner, 2011) was derived from older people's views, in mixed-methods survey and qualitative interviews, about what gave their lives quality, what took quality away from their lives, and their relative importance, and compared with psycho-social theory (Bowling et al, 2003). These open-ended questions, which are of value when examining people's own views of their QoL, are shown below.

Open-ended questions to elicit views of QoL

'Thinking about your life as a whole, what is it that makes your life good – that is, the things that give your life quality? You may mention as many things as you like.'

'What is it that makes your life bad – that is, the things that reduce the quality in your life? You may mention as many things as you like.'

'Thinking about all these good and bad things you have just mentioned, which one is the most important to you?'

'Again, thinking about the good and bad things you have mentioned that make up your quality of life, which of the answers on this card best describes the quality of your life as a whole? 7-point QoL self-rating scale: QoL so good, could not be better – QoL so bad, could not be worse.'

'Thinking about all these good and bad things you have just mentioned, which one is the most important to you?'

'And what single thing would improve the quality of your life?'

'And what single thing, in your opinion, would improve the overall quality of life for people of your age?'

Source: (Bowling et al, 2003)

The full version of the OPQoL has 35 items covering: Social relationships and participation; Independence, control over life, freedom; Psychological and emotional well-being; Perceived financial circumstances; Area: home and neighbourhood; Life overall; Health; Religion and culture. A short version has been developed with good reliability and validity (Bowling et al, 2013). The OPQoL was shown to have better psychometric properties than two comparable measures of broader QoL for older people: the CASP-19 and WHOQoL-OLD (Bowling and Stenner, 2011). The CASP-19 has 19 items within four domains of control, autonomy, pleasure and self-realisation (Hyde et al, 2003), but this was developed 'top down', based on a theory of needs satisfaction and self-actualisation. The World Health Organization's (WHO) QoL measure for older people, the WHOQoL-OLD, contains 24 items within six subscales: sensory abilities, autonomy, past, present and future activities, social participation, death and dying, and intimacy (Power et al, 2005). This was based on WHO's multi-dimensional definition of QoL (see above). It was tested across countries with convenience samples. The WHOQoL-OLD consists of the pre-existing main WHOQoL questionnaire developed for all adults (Power et al, 2005), with physical functioning added, as suggested by focus groups. Apart from the OPQoL, most investigators have developed their outcome or QoL measures primarily based on pre-existing definitions, theory or on 'expert opinions' of relevant domains to include.

Subjective well-being

There are differing perspectives relating to an understanding of the essence of subjective well-being. It is generally accepted that this is a multi-dimensional concept that contributes to quality of life and may be measured through observation, self-report or multi-item scales that focus on cognitive, emotional and motivational attitudes towards life (Daatland, 2005). There is some debate over whether, in fact, basic needs may be conceptualised as being stable across time, space and cultures. The contrasting perspectives are encapsulated by Hodge (1990) who distinguishes between utilitarian and existential theories of well-being. While the utilitarian perspective presupposes a universal and inherent notion of quality of life, the existential approach is underpinned by the idea that quality of life is self-determined, pluralistic and diverse in nature. Some argue that a view of universal needs may be insensitive to differences between social groups and societies and indifferent to the dynamic nature of attitudes (Hornquist, 1990; Allison et al, 1997). Basic needs such as food, shelter and warmth, as set out in Maslow's (1954) widely known model representing a 'hierarchy of needs', are not contentious. However, other essential needs such as autonomy and self-realisation are more difficult to define and, not least, to measure. Nevertheless, others have put forth a convincing case for the idea that human needs 'are neither subjective preferences ... nor static essences. They are universal and knowable and the satisfiers necessary to meet them are dynamic and open ended' (Doyal and Gough, 1991, p 14). This view is supported by evidence that well-being is only weakly related to demographic variables such as age, sex, marital status and ethnicity, with these demographics explaining less than 10 per cent of variability in measures of well-being (Andrews and Robinson, 1991). On the other hand, positive affect, control beliefs and (in older age) accommodation have been associated with cognitive and emotional well-being (Lang and Heckhausen, 2001).

Higgs et al (2003) argue that the changing nature of ageing demands a special consideration of what the essential needs might be in older age. Within a context where significant numbers of older people remain active, relatively healthy and keen to develop a variety of leisure interests (Scase and Scales, 2000), the psychological needs for social participation, autonomy and choice are particularly salient. McKenna et al (1999) suggest that any model of basic needs in older adult life must move away from a focus on function per se and should instead emphasise the reasons why individuals want to accomplish things. From this perspective, leisure activities and social networking provide the means by which needs may be fulfilled. Thus, lifestyle, comprising goal-directed activities and social relationships, may be seen as the narrative of self (Higgs et al, 2003). This self-narrative, underpinned by agency and autonomy, in turn becomes the route to self-actualisation. Daatland (2005, pp 375-6) supports this view, suggesting that 'successful ageing, and indeed quality of life, has to do with the road (process) more than the destination (end state) – to have goals and a motivation to try and reach them.'

Barriers to healthy ageing

This section considers some of the many barriers to healthy ageing and poor quality of life in old age. These include economic barriers, physiological barriers (with reduced immunity as an exemplar), mobility issues, poor sleep, loss of paid work and barriers to paid employment and psychosocial barriers. It is also important to recognise that the aims of healthy ageing should apply throughout the life course, including to the end of life, rather than being seen merely as a way of saving long-term care resources. Taking a broad and inclusive view of health, which includes psychological and spiritual dimensions, it is possible and highly desirable to promote health even in circumstances of physiological or mental decline associated with the fourth age (Lloyd et al, 2014). Without such a commitment it cannot be said that there is equity in health for older people.

Economic barriers

As their populations age, countries across the developed world are recognising the need to reconsider and reform their policies for older people, driven in large part by concerns over their future affordability and sustainability in the face of rising demand and decreasing support ratios (the ratio of the population of working age to the post-working age population). In England (and the UK more generally), recent debate has focused on the reform of the pensions and long-term care systems. While several reforms for pensions have been announced and legislated for, few have so far been enacted for long-term care.

In the summer of 2010 the Coalition government established the Dilnot Commission on Funding of Care and Support, which reported in July 2011 (Commission on Funding of Care and Support, 2011). Members of the NDA-funded MAP2030 project team, including Ruth Hancock and Raphael Wittenberg, contributed to the development of this report continuing their earlier work in this area, which systematically examined a number of alternative proposals for funding long-term care in England that had been made over previous decades. Following the publication in July 2011 of the Dilnot report (Commission on Funding of Care and Support, 2011), in July 2012 the government's White Paper, *Caring for our future: progress report on funding reform* (HM Government, 2012), accepted the principle of a cap on the lines recommended by the Commission. At the time of writing, the UK Parliament is currently considering the Care Bill, which seeks to implement reforms announced in the White Paper, and subsequent government decisions on the funding of care and support. Despite the interconnectedness of the pensions and long-term care systems, the debates concerning reform have so far taken place independently, an area that MAP2030 research also addressed.

Over the period examined here, from 2007 to 2032, the effect of improvements in life expectancy on state expenditure on pensions and long-term care are as expected: expenditure on pensions and associated benefits is projected to rise in future years because of the increasing numbers of pensioners (Pensions Policy Institute, 2011). Expenditure on long-term care is projected to rise, at an even faster rate than pensions expenditure, partly as a consequence of the faster rate of growth of the 'oldest old', the group where need for care is the greatest, compared to the older population as a whole.

If life expectancy improves more than is assumed under the principal population projection (Table 4.1), the effect on state pension and long-term care expenditure could be quite substantial. If life expectancy rises in line with the high life expectancy variant with long-term mortality annual improvement of 2 per cent, then by 2032, the UK government would need to find an additional 0.2 per cent of GDP to finance the pensions system and an additional 0.1 per cent of GDP to finance the long-term care system. Should life expectancy increase at a long-term annual rate of 3 per cent, then by 2032, the government would need to find an additional 0.6 per cent of GDP, equivalent to roughly £11 billion per annum, to finance the pensions system, and an additional 0.2 per cent of GDP, or £3.4 billion, to finance the long-term care system. The effect of improvements in life expectancy on pensions and long-term care expenditure taken together represent a substantial amount of state expenditure, projected to rise from 5.6 per cent of GDP in 2007 to 7.8 per cent of GDP by 2032 under the principal life expectancy assumption, and 8.6 per cent under the very high life expectancy (Malley et al, 2011). Given the uncertainty surrounding life expectancy projections, it is important that the government allows for the possibility of faster than expected improvements in life expectancy on a range of programmes when considering the potential costs of policy reforms and life expectancy on the affordability and sustainability of state-funded programmes.

Older people's income from private pensions is also projected to increase over the period examined here, although the rise is significantly less than for state pensions (and could be further tempered if pension providers reduce annuity rates in response to increases in life expectancy). Income from private pensions is expected to increase initially, but will start to fall back as defined benefit (DB) pensions are replaced by defined contribution (DC) schemes. In contrast, spending on state pensions increases more strongly over the period as the numbers over state pension age increase and pensions become more generous.

Private expenditure on long-term care is projected to grow faster than public expenditure on long-term care over the period examined here, accounting for 40 per cent of total expenditure by 2032 compared to 36 per cent in 2007. This is due to an increase in the proportion of care recipients who fund 100 per cent of their care, which is largely explained by further increases in owner-occupation at the oldest ages. The reliance on private funding highlights the challenges there are around reforming the long-term care system, since most private expenditure is out of pocket, and a small proportion of people can face costs that are 'catastrophic': it has been estimated that 7 per cent of people aged 65 will face lifetime care costs of at least £100,000, and 5 per cent of at least £200,000 (Fernández and Forder, 2011). Policy makers will need to respond to these challenges in taking forward proposals for long-term care reform. Such reform will need to take into account not only economic factors but also factors related to the quality of care and support provided to the end of life. There is growing evidence concerning the importance of dignity in care and of the difficulties of achieving this in the context of an overriding economic imperative (Tadd and Calnan, 2009; Lloyd et al, 2014).

Compromised immunity

It is now well established that the efficiency of the immune system declines with age (Shaw et al, 2010). This 'immunesenescence' is associated with an increased risk of morbidity and mortality from infection (Fein, 1999; Bonomo, 2002; Gavazzi and Krause, 2002), particularly following a physical trauma (Papia et al, 1999). (For more detailed information, see Chapter Two, this volume.)

A common physical trauma in older adults is hip fracture, the prevalence of which in the UK is projected to rise to 120,000 by 2015 (Johnell et al, 1992). Hip fracture is associated with poor outcomes; approximately one-quarter of patients are dead one year post fracture (Haentjens et al, 2007), and one-quarter are discharged into rehabilitation centres or care homes rather than returning home (Birge et al, 1994). Few regain pre-fall levels of quality of life (Chaudhry, 2007), and a high proportion (studies vary between 9 and 47 per cent) report depressive symptoms (Holmes and House, 2000). In one study of older (>65 years) hip fracture patients, 37 per cent had succumbed to serious infections requiring readmission to hospital within 4-6 weeks of the fracture (Butcher et al, 2005). These figures for reduced immunity after hip fracture are supported by data from a large study of 531 hip fracture patients, which revealed that post-operative chest infections were the major six-month mortality risk factor, and that pneumonia was the cause of death in 43 per cent of patients (Wood et al, 1992). This has been confirmed more recently in a smaller-scale study where hip fracture patients had significantly diminished neutrophil antimicrobial function (generation of superoxide), which was greatest in those patients who succumbed to bacterial infection (Butcher et al, 2005). Interestingly, this effect of trauma on neutrophil function and infection rates was not observed in a group of younger (aged <35) fracture patients matched for the level of clinical trauma (Butcher et al, 2005). This suggests that the immune impact of physical stress is worsened by the presence of an already impaired immunity through immunesenescence.

It is now well accepted that prolonged exposure to stress, whether psychosocial or physical, has detrimental effects on immunity (see Chapter Two, this volume). The trauma of hip fracture is also associated with the release of stress hormones including cortisol (Butcher et al, 2003), which has potent immune-suppressive properties (Cupps and Fauci, 1982). This negative effect is counteracted in part by the simultaneous production of another adrenal hormone, dehydroepiandrosterone (DHEA) and its sulphated form, DHEAS, which is immune-enhancing (Radford et al, 2010). DHEAS production declines with age (termed adrenopause), but cortisol production is unchanged, resulting in a relative preponderance of immune suppressive with potentially detrimental consequences for immunity in older people (Duggal et al, 2013). Adrenocortical hormone balance may thus be a major determinant of immunity in older hip fracture patients.

The combined immune and endocrine effects of both hip fracture and depression in the context of immunesenescence has been examined in a study funded under the NDA Programme. This study tested the hypothesis that the addition of psychological distress to the physical stress of hip fracture might work synergistically to amplify effects of stress on immunity in older adults. The findings suggest that in fact, depression in hip fracture patients is the driving force behind reduced immunity and increased infections. Further, the cortisol:DHEAS ratio is higher in depressed hip fracture patients than non-depressed hip fracture patients or a healthy control group (Duggal et al, 2013).

This finding might be evidence for the treatment of depression in this patient cohort in order to improve immunity and overall outcome. Such patients may benefit from DHEAS supplementation. For example, it has been shown that DHEA replacement improves mood and well-being in patients receiving chronic glucocorticoid replacement for adrenal insufficiency (Coles et al, 2005) or in patients on chronic glucocorticoid treatment for systemic lupus erythematosus (Nordmark et al, 2005). Further, DHEA supplementation has been shown to improve minor and major depression in older individuals (Morsink et al, 2007).

Mobility and its consequences for health and well-being

Maintaining physical activity and mobility are often cited as key aspects leading to a healthy older age (Depp and Jeste, 2006), as it has been found that the more physically active a person is, the more they are viewed as having aged successfully (Baker et al, 2009). 'Out-of-home' mobility, that is, the ability to go out of the home and move around in the community, has been found to be vital to quality of life and well-being (see Oswald et al, 2010). Indeed, older people often state 'being able to stay mobile' as their prime concern as age advances – maintaining mobility helps maintain independence, a key aspect of successful ageing (Mollenkopf et al, 2004). However, ageing is generally associated with a decrease in mobility with people aged over 70 making fewer and shorter journeys than younger people (ONS, 2005). Government reports have also noted the stark fact that 36 per cent of people aged over 65 and 55 per cent of people aged over 75 self-report problems with their mobility (ONS, 2000), and that 43 per cent of people over the age of 50 report a deterioration in their walking speed (Science and Technology Committee, 2005). The importance of these statistics becomes apparent when one considers that a decline in mobility has been shown to be linked to a restriction in social life (Morris et al, 2004), increased feelings of social isolation and depression, limitations in access to leisure and cultural activities (see Shoval et al, 2011), and reduced access to a variety of shops leading to a restriction in choice of foods and ultimately healthy nutrition (Wylie et al, 1999). Additionally, changes in mobility have been associated with chronic illnesses and loss of bone density to the extent that a decline in mobility can act as an early predictor of physical disability among older people (Fried et al, 2000; Hirvensalo et al, 2000). At its most extreme, mobility has been found to be a predictor of mortality (Melzer et al, 2003; Newman et al, 2006). It is therefore apparent that a decline in mobility can be a barrier to healthy ageing.

Understanding levels of mobility, predictors of mobility and how to improve levels of mobility are therefore crucial to improving the health and well-being of older people. There is clearly scope and a need for interventions to improve mobility and to alleviate some of the risks associated with mobility impairment. Understanding levels of mobility among older people is a crucial first step in order to determine if interventions are successful or not. Until recently, methods to assess the extent to which older people are mobile in their home and in their community have typically relied on self-report studies in which participants maintain an activity diary noting periods of mobility. As with all self-report studies they can be influenced by compliance and memory and are, of course, subjective. New technologies, however, are offering more sophisticated methods to assess mobility through the means of general positioning satellite (GPS) systems and accelerometry. These tools enable more accurate indices of mobility to be gathered unobtrusively, and place little cognitive or time demands on those who are being assessed.

Location-based tracking using GPS is increasingly being made available as part of an assistive technology package to those for whom 'wandering' may be a problem, as is typically found in Alzheimer's disease and related dementias. Tracking technologies allow the carer(s) to identify the location of the person who has wandered, and to note routes taken (Miskelly, 2005; Rasquin et al, 2007; Shoval et al, 2008; McShane and Skelt, 2009; Robinson et al, 2009; Landau et al, 2010; Oswald et al, 2010). Use of such technology has been met with varying degrees of success and usability which can be influenced by the degree of cognitive impairment shown by the user. However, it is foreseeable that such technology could be useful to a much wider population, including those who are cognitively intact, as a means of assessing mobility. In particular, a mobility monitoring device could be used by a wide range of people of all ages to provide quantifiable measures of mobility based on measuring distance travelled and routes taken. In a similar way as a pedometer counts steps to give a proxy measure of movement and activity, a GPS device could give an indication of how far someone has travelled or how stationary they have been in their community (Shoval et al, 2010). When mobility levels are deemed to be low, then the device could act as a motivator to encourage the user that more mobility is required or indeed, such a device could act as an early warning that health and well-being may be at risk if a person's mobility levels have declined over a period of time. Limitations with GPS technology at the moment, however, mean that it is really only suitable for out-of-the home mobility where GPS signals can be received. While this out-of-the-home mobility is important for maintaining social contacts, access to leisure activities and shops, for example, levels of mobility only based on mobility out-of-the-home may give a false indication of low levels of mobility for someone who is very active indoors but who has not ventured out of the home. Information from both sources (in-home mobility and out-of-home mobility) is therefore needed to provide a more accurate account of mobility. Accelerometers, which register the stepping movements of the legs and changes in body position, are becoming popular as a means of quantifying activity in older adults (Pruitt et al, 2008). While accelerometry can measure activity by counting stepping movements and indicate amount of time spent standing, walking, sitting/lying and transitions from one state to another, accelerometry on its own gives no indication of the context of the activity, for example, whether the person is inside or outside of their home. Together, the two devices (GPS and accelerometers) can be used to provide a more comprehensive measure of mobility. Once mobility levels are established on either an individual or population basis, then identification of thresholds of low levels of mobility can be made and possible interventions made to improve levels of mobility.

Interventions to improve levels of mobility are closely tied to methods to improve physical activity and exercise per se. Levels of physical activity among the older population, and indeed, across the whole age range, are lower than UK government recommendations, despite physical activity being critically important for the prevention of disease and upholding quality of life (DH, 2004). Indeed, the Royal College of Physicians of Edinburgh (2005) have reported that physical activity is the major modifiable influence on health in old age. Improving physical activity may therefore be one means of avoiding a decline in mobility.

However, improving physical activity and exercise may only be one way to improve the mobility of older people. Mobility is more than just 'being able to move' as it also includes engaging with the world (Adey, 2010). To this extent there is a need to investigate the predictors of mobility. Gait speed has been identified as a predictor of adverse outcomes in older people (Abellan van Kan et al, 2009), and it would seem reasonable to expect that it is also a predictor of mobility.

Nilsson, Avlund and Lund (2011) found that low financial assets and poor social relations increased the odds ratios for onset of mobility limitations. More research is therefore needed on other social, physical and cognitive determinants of mobility so that interventions can be targeted for maximum impact.

Engagement with the world is also an important aspect of maintaining dignity in the sense of upholding an individual's sense of self-respect and their individual identity. Being isolated is likely to lead to a significant loss of dignity, particularly in the fourth age, when dignity is already compromised by declining health (Tadd and Calnan, 2009). In conclusion, maintaining physical activity and mobility are important for health and well-being at all ages, but especially for the older population. Monitoring levels of mobility is becoming easier with advances in technology. Intervention studies to increase mobility are needed to improve health and well-being for future older cohorts.

Poor sleep

Health promotion over the last two decades has emphasised the importance for health and well-being of the 'big four' – a good diet, physical exercise, not smoking and restricting alcohol consumption. A fifth health promotion message is also essential for good health and well-being, namely, sleep (Arber and Venn, in press). Sleep of a sufficient duration and quality is particularly important for healthy ageing. Lack of sleep is a significant cause of car and other accidents, and in later life is a major contributory factor for falls. Sleep is also important for cognitive functioning and memory consolidation. Prospective epidemiological studies demonstrate that short sleep duration (under six hours) is associated with elevated mortality, especially from cardiovascular disease (Ferrie et al, 2010). It is well-known that depression is associated with sleep problems, although recent research has shown that sleep problems often predate depression, and may therefore be a causal factor in the development of depression (Ferrie et al, 2011). Linked to the section above, there are few studies of the effect of poor sleep on immunity, although one study of shift workers with chronic sleep disruption did reveal an increased rate of infections in this population (Mohren et al, 2002).

Physiological research on sleep in later life has found that changes take place to sleep as we age, in particular, greater difficulty initiating sleep and an increased likelihood of awakening during the night (Dijk et al, 2010; Maglione and Ancoli-Israel, 2012). These studies show that with ageing the amount of time spent in deep, slow wave sleep diminishes, along with a decrease in REM (dreaming) sleep, whereas the time spent in lighter, stage 1 and stage 2, sleep increases. The result is that older people may find it takes longer to get to sleep, have more fragmented sleep and wake up earlier. Other physiological changes to the ageing body affect sleep including an increased propensity to daytime sleep and nocturia (Venn and Arber, 2011). However, while many sleep researchers view sleep purely as a physiological process, social scientists have increasingly shown how a range of societal factors associated with individuals' roles, relationships, family circumstances, daytime activities and environmental factors have an impact on sleep quality and duration (Williams et al, 2010; Arber et al, 2012). It is relevant to consider how social factors influence sleep, since poor sleep quality can adversely affect older people's well-being and autonomy. Given the importance of good quality sleep for health, well-being and having the energy to be active during the day, a later section of this chapter examines interventions to improve sleep and thus healthy ageing.

Loss of work and barriers to paid employment

Paid work is a major aspect of a person's identity. Unemployed individuals have to negotiate a variety of problems, especially the stigma of unemployment. This is particularly important for older people, as those over the age of 50 are more likely to suffer long-term unemployment than younger people (Tinsley, 2012). Being unemployed and seeking work can profoundly influence a person's self-image and self-esteem. When job applicants perceive they have been labelled as 'old' by others (for example, potential employers), they begin to define themselves as 'old' (Berger, 2006).

Following the introduction of the Employment Equality (Age) Regulations (2006) and the Equality Act (2010), recognition of age discrimination has dramatically increased. Riach and Rich (2007) empirically tested for age discrimination in recruitment by using matched pairs of job applications (matched in all respects except age). The method was similar to that of Jowell and Prescott-Clarke (1970) who developed the technique to investigate racial discrimination in employment. One of the most striking findings from the Riach and Rich (2007) study was that the rate of discrimination against older graduates and against older waiters in applications was higher than rates previously recorded for racial discrimination. Conversely, applications for retail manager positions showed significant bias in favour of older workers. Tinsley (2012) used a matched pairs method to explore age discrimination in hiring for bar work and personal assistant roles.

Results found statistically significant bias against older workers when applying for these positions. The clearest bias was observed with applications for bar work, with a response rate of 16.4 per cent for the 25-year-old applicant but only a 7.3 per cent response rate for the 51-year-old, implying that a younger applicant was more than twice as likely to get a response as an older applicant.

Taylor and Walker (1998) carried out a survey of personnel managers and directors in 500 large organisations to explore the relationship between attitudes towards older workers and employment practices. Attitudes that were found to be associated with recruitment, training and promotion practices were: perceived trainability, creativity, cautiousness, physical capabilities, the likelihood of having an accident, and ability to work with younger workers. Attitudes which showed no relationship with employment practices were: perceived productivity, reliability, ability to adapt to new technology, interest in technological change, and flexibility. The findings highlight the need to target stereotypical attitudes towards the older workforce if age barriers to employment are to be removed.

There has been considerable debate in the literature regarding the physical capacity of older workers to maintain their health and productivity (Ilmarinen, 1997; Kisner and Pratt, 1997; Wegman, 1999; Ng and Feldman, 2008). In a survey of 273 supervisors, Henkens (2000) found that most were not in favour of employees working beyond the age of 65, and that this was related to expectations regarding the loss of human capital and sickness absenteeism. However, research suggests that these concerns regarding the older workforce are largely unfounded. For example, Pransky et al (2005) conducted a survey of over 3,000 workers who had recently lost time due to a work injury, and found that older workers appeared to fare better than younger workers; their relative advantage was considered to be primarily due to longer workplace attachment and the healthy worker effect. A systematic review by Crawford et al (2010) on the health, safety and health promotion needs of older workers found that the physical and psychological changes occurring over the age of 50 are subject to large individual differences and can be moderated by maintaining physical activity, intellectual activity and other lifestyle factors.

Psychosocial barriers to participation in organised leisure and health promotion activities

Psychological barriers to arts engagement and learning are identified in the results of the NDA Programme-funded projects. These need to be addressed if interventions utilising these themes are to be successful. Older persons' engagement with art has been explored by Keaney and Oskala (2007) who analysed the results of 'Taking Part', a large-scale survey of arts participation and engagement undertaken for the UK's Department for Culture, Media and Sport (DCMS, 2007). They found that while those in the 55–64 age group were among the most active, the engagement of those over 64 decreased markedly. Keaney and Oskala (2007) identified lower rates of engagement among men; those with a limiting disability; those suffering from illness; people from minority ethnic backgrounds; those in lower socio-economic groups; and people living alone. A strong marker for arts engagement is access to education that tends to be lower among older people (Newman et al, 2013).

Withnall (2010) suggests that barriers to participation for older learners in a range of activities can be psychosocial factors such as fear of failure, reluctance to engage with unfamiliar tasks and perceptions of procedures as being very complex. Other barriers may be situational, relating to the social or physical environment, institutional, relating to the extent to which institutions exclude particular groups of learners, and informational, relating to the efficiency of communication about learning opportunities (Darkenwald and Merriam, 1982; Hallam et al, 2011). For example, the UK Audit Commission (2008) identified information barriers in local authorities, whereby older people were often found to lack access to good information systems about interesting and worthwhile activities.

Interventions to support well-being and healthy ageing

So what can be done to support well-being and healthy ageing? This section provides examples of interventions which promote well-being and healthy ageing, including financial interventions; exercise; interventions to improve sleep and thus healthy ageing; extending the working life; participation in making music; and visual art.

Financial interventions

The MAP2030 research team examined the impact of a range of potential reforms to the funding system for long-term care in England. They investigated the current and projected future public expenditure costs of long-term care for older people under various reform options, and the implications of those options for the costs of care borne by individuals in different income groups.

The existing funding system for adult social care in England requires recipients of publicly funded care to meet user charges based on their incomes and savings, and excludes entirely from public support those with savings (generally including the value of their home for those admitted to care homes) above an upper capital limit, at the time, of £23,500. The reform options considered included a version of free personal care, based on the recommendations of the Royal Commission on Long-term Care (1999); a version of free personal care, as proposed by the then Prime Minister at the 2009 Labour Party Conference; and several versions of a partnership model along lines suggested by the Labour government's 2009 Green Paper on care and support (HM Government, 2009). The proposals of the Commission on Funding of Care and Support (2011) have also subsequently been considered.

The analyses were conducted using two linked models – the CARESIM microsimulation model and the Personal Social Services Research Unit (PSSRU) cell-based long-term care finance model. The PSSRU model makes projections of demand for long-term care and associated expenditure, under clearly specified assumptions (Wittenberg et al, 2011). It makes projections of future numbers of older people with disabilities; future levels of long-term care services and disability benefits; future public and private expenditure on long-term care; and the future social care workforce. CARESIM simulates the incomes and assets of future cohorts of older people and their ability to contribute towards care home fees or the costs of home-based care, should such care be needed.

The partnership scheme examined as an alternative to the current system was designed to address some of the perceived failures of the current system, notably, that it produces significant unmet need (Wanless, 2006; Commission for Social Care Inspection, 2008) and creates disincentives to save and plan for long-term care needs (Mayhew et al, 2010). The proposal was that everyone who qualifies for care and support on the basis of their care needs would be entitled to have a set proportion of their basic care and support costs met by the state. The proposal has a progressive element such that older people with fewer means will have more of their costs met by the state, and those with the fewest means will have all their care costs met by the state (HM Government, 2009). The research team assumed that all those who qualify for care are eligible to have one-third of their personal care costs met by the state, and that all those who, under the current funding system are entitled to a state contribution of more than one-third of their care costs, continue to receive the same state contribution as under the current system. This particular version of the partnership scheme would require the state to find an additional 0.1 per cent of GDP by 2032 to finance it. The largest gains would accrue to the highest income group of older people.

A number of limitations to the analyses should be noted. A key question is how the revenues to meet reforms would be raised. The impact on different income groups will depend on how monies are raised as well as how they are spent under the reform options. Another important issue is the extent to which reforms would lead to increased demand for care. A more generous system may lead to increased demand for care, but there is little evidence on which to base assumptions about demand effects.

A further limitation is that the analysis accounts only partially for the links between spending on pensions and long-term care at the micro level, which are important for understanding the effects of potential reforms. Since long-term care is a means-tested system, any increases in pensioners' incomes and wealth shifts the balance of funding away from the state on to individuals.

Exercise

Increases in physical activity can prevent or reduce the risk of developing chronic illnesses such as cardiovascular disease (Lee et al, 2003), coronary heart disease (Morris and Heady, 1953), hypertension (Choquette and Ferguson, 1973), cancer (Thune et al, 1997), obesity (Brown et al, 2005), diabetes (Helmrich et al, 1991), osteoporosis and osteoarthritis (Warburton et al, 2006) and depression and anxiety (Ströhle, 2009; Porter et al, 2011). It is estimated that the direct cost of physical inactivity to the UK NHS is £1.06 billion a year (Allender et al, 2007).

In June 2011, the Chief Medical Officer (DH, 2011) published new physical activity guidelines. This was the first report to represent UK-wide guidelines and included recommendations for different age groups, including early years (under five-year-olds) and older adults (over 65-year-olds). Its recommendations state that adults should aim to be active daily, and accumulate at least 150 minutes of moderate intensity activity per week. Moderate intensity activity is defined as activity that raises the heart rate and increases oxygen intake, but at a level where you can still hold a conversation. An example of moderate intensity physical activity is brisk walking (Pate et al, 2012). Alternatively, similar benefits can be achieved through 75 minutes of vigorous intensity activity per week, or a combination of both moderate and vigorous. Vigorous intensity activity is defined as activity that causes rapid breathing and a substantial increase in heart rate, for example, jogging (Haskell et al, 2007).

The recommendations also state that adults should undertake physical activity to improve muscle strength on at least two days per week, and for the first time, the guidelines recommend that adults should minimise the amount of time spent being sedentary (including sitting). For older adults (over-65s), the guidelines include all of the recommendations that have been highlighted for adults, but are further extended to include physical activity to improve balance and coordination on at least two days a week. These new additions provide challenges for both health professionals and individuals to determine if these guidelines are being met, because there are no optimum thresholds to aim for. The guidelines have been criticised as they fail to provide information on the optimum levels of muscle strength activities and do not provide examples of the correct coordination activities older people should aim to complete.

Time spent engaging in physical activity has been shown to decline as age increases (Caspersen and Merritt, 1995). Research has reported incidental activity and movement levels in older adults, aged 71–81, to be 29 per cent less than adults aged 28–48. This difference has been attributed to older adults walking on average three miles less per day than younger adults (Harris et al, 2007). Furthermore, many older adults spend 10 hours or more sitting each day, making them the most sedentary population (DH, 2011). Therefore, meeting the Chief Medical Officer's activity recommendations may be unrealistic, especially since over 60 per cent of older adults do not participate in regular exercise (Crespo et al, 1996). However, the guidelines for physical activity recognise that they may not be feasible and suggest that even if older adults are not meeting all the recommendations, small increases in physical activity will still provide benefits to both their mental and physical function.

There is strong evidence to show that while physical ability to work declines with age, the effects of this decline can be delayed by exercise. Regular physical activity contributes to better balance, coordination, agility and cognitive function, which may help prevent falls in older people (Pate et al, 1995; Weuve et al, 2004). Physically active adults aged 65 or older have a lower incidence of chronic diseases, higher levels of cardio-respiratory fitness and improved physical function than those who are inactive (DH, 2011). The type of physical activity performed is not of primary importance; the key factor is total energy expenditure (Blair et al, 1992). Some physical activity is better than none, and higher levels of physical activity provide greater health benefits. Research has shown that older adults who participate in 20 to 30 minutes of moderate intensity exercise on most days have better physical function than older adults who do not exercise (Brach et al, 2004).

Mounting evidence shows that sedentary behaviour represents a significant health risk, which is independent of physical activity levels. In developed countries, adults report prolonged periods of sitting at work, during leisure time and for transport (Chau et al, 2010). Recent research has demonstrated that in physically active individuals, prolonged sitting was associated with an increased risk of premature mortality, and high levels of sitting cannot be compensated for by leisure time physical activity, even if activity levels exceed current guidelines (Katzmarzyk et al, 2009). Therefore, it appears that sedentary behaviour should not be viewed as simply the absence of physical activity or as the extreme lower end of the physical activity continuum (Owen et al, 2009). Moreover, increased sedentary behaviours contribute to obesity due to a lack of energy expenditure occurring throughout the day. For example, Hamilton et al (2007) reported that sedentary workers expend 700 kcal/day compared to the 1,400 kcal/day expended by standing workers.

One of the biggest changes affecting physical activity levels is occupational-based physical activity (Stamatakis et al, 2007). Probert et al (2008) demonstrated that occupational physical activity is associated with reduced risks of developing chronic illnesses independent of leisure-time physical activity levels. Therefore, work-related physical activity is an important contributor to daily levels of energy expenditure (Miller and Brown, 2004). The change from a manufacturing industry to service-type office work, automation and technological advances have not only contributed to a lack of physical activity, but they have also contributed to a sedentary lifestyle by increasing sitting requirements at work and at home (Sherwood and Jeffery, 2000). Research has demonstrated that over half of the total time spent sitting per day occurs at work (Miller and Brown, 2004). Given that many adults spend more than half of their waking hours at work, the workplace is clearly an ideal arena for implementing health promotion initiatives.

Loughborough University's 'Working Late – Ageing productively through design' project has explored organisational strategies aimed at maintaining the health and workability of employees. The research examined employee's self-reported activity levels, work ability, psychological and physical well-being. Findings from the initial cross-sectional survey were in line with those of Miller and Brown (2004), indicating that, on average, people spend a large proportion of the overall daily sitting time in the workplace. More time was reported sitting at work (5 hours and 7 minutes) than any other sitting activity, with work sitting time accounting for more than half of the average sitting time on a workday (55 per cent). On average, more time was spent sitting on a workday (9 hours and 18 minutes) than a non-workday (8 hours and 25 minutes). The mean sleeping time on a workday was 6 hours and 42 minutes whereas on a non-workday this was reported as 7 hours and 20 minutes. These results indicate that employees spend more time sitting than they do sleeping.

The 'Working Late' data also explored the relationship between sitting time at work, sitting time outside of work and total sitting time on a workday. Findings indicated that individuals who sat for longer at work were more likely to sit for longer outside of work. In terms of engagement with physical activity, two-thirds (66.7 per cent) of the respondents indicated they regularly engaged in physical activity and/or exercise during their leisure time. However, only around a quarter met the Chief Medical Officer's minimum recommended guidelines for physical activity.

It is increasingly acknowledged that in order to change employees' habitual sedentary activity levels and to promote the adoption of healthier, active lifestyles, interventions must take a life course perspective and include individuals of all ages. For populations to be healthier in later life, individuals must adopt positive health-related behaviours as early as possible. Occupational physical activity programmes are often poorly attended because they do not meet the individual needs of employees (Wong et al, 1998). It is important for health interventions to provide tailored health information which is relevant to an individual's needs. Health interventions that promote walking activities, provided in a tailored fashion, have been demonstrated to be more effective, especially in targeting individuals who are mostly sedentary or most motivated to change (Ogilvie et al, 2007).

The 'Working Late' research team have developed innovative workplace physical activity interventions involving multi-disciplinary collaborations and underpinned by extensive user engagement. The interventions have adopted a tailored approach based on the stage of change model (Prochaska and DiClemente, 1983; Prochaska et al, 1992). This model suggests that individuals attempting to change a health behaviour move through a series of distinct stages: precontemplation (not intending to change and/or not accepting the need for change); contemplation (recognition of the problem and considering making changes); preparation (intending to change soon and/or making plans to change); action (changed behaviour less than six months ago); maintenance (successfully changed behaviour for over six months); and relapse. Movement through these stages can occur in a cyclical, rather than linear pattern because individuals may make several attempts to change behaviour before they reach their goals (Marcus et al, 1996). According to the model, health education needs to be tailored to the individual's stage of change, for example, precontemplative individuals require consciousness-raising messages whereas those considering change require skills training and practical help to make changes. The model has been applied to a range of health behaviours such as smoking, and has also been very successful in workplace interventions aimed at reducing musculoskeletal disorders (Whysall et al, 2007).

Even though older adults may understand the benefits of physical activity, and the majority think they do enough to remain healthy, their average activity levels have been shown to be low. Lack of interest in exercise, joint pain, dislike of going out alone, accessibility issues and reduced energy levels are just some of the factors that have been identified to deter older adults from being more physically active (Crombie et al, 2004). Further to this, self-efficacy, past exercise habits, stigma and embarrassment have been shown to be influential factors when determining older adult's engagement in physical activity interventions (Bunn et al, 2008). It is therefore important to consider how the individual views 'exercise' before trying to intervene to increase activity levels.

Overall, walking is an ideal form of exercise (Morris and Hardman, 1997), and is one of the most popular forms of physical activity because it does not require any special equipment, training or any formal facility (Hillsdon et al, 1995). Walking and gardening are both among the most common forms of leisure-time activities practised by older adults (Weuve et al, 2004). Moreover, walking programmes have been shown to produce gains in fitness, reductions in blood pressure, improvements in blood lipid profiles, increases in bone density and enhanced mood state, with the greatest gains being observed in older adults, and in sedentary and obese individuals (Shephard, 1997). Consequently, there is wide scope to promote walking-based activities to both the working and retired population and, potentially, manifold benefits, both at the micro and macro level.

Interventions to improve sleep and thus healthy ageing

We turn now from walking activities to sleep. Among older people, untreated chronic sleep disturbance degrades quality of life, inhibits recovery and rehabilitation following illness, and is an independent risk factor for falls and depression. Older people, both at home and in care home settings, are the most likely and most vulnerable recipients of hypnotic drugs which, in this age group, are associated with risks of impaired daytime functioning, and compromise well-being. Among the very old, poor sleep quality *and* hypnotic drug use have been shown to exacerbate frailty and cognitive impairment. The need to reduce hypnotic drug prescribing, and provide effective non-pharmacological approaches to sleep management, are recognised policy and practice objectives.

The SomnIA ('Sleep in Ageing') collaborative research project (funded by the NDA Programme) was designed to address these issues. It focused on understanding the meanings and determinants of poor quality sleep among older people in the community and in care homes by assessing social, psychological and environmental factors, medication use and health status, and identifying potential solutions. SomnIA also investigated potential solutions, including self-management of insomnia (Cognitive Behavioural Therapy for Insomnia, CBT-I) among older people with chronic disease, evaluated the role of bright light and 'blue-enriched' light in improving the sleep of older people in the community and in care homes, and developed sensor-based products to optimise sleep for frail older people at home and in care homes.

The premise of 'active ageing' assumes that older people have the capacity to be active and productive in later life (Bowling, 2008). Yet there is also a need to acknowledge that some bodily changes which accompany ageing, such as poor night-time sleep, will have an impact on tiredness and energy levels during the day, and therefore constrain the number and duration of activities that older people may wish to undertake. Maintaining an active lifestyle was regarded as very important by all older participants in the SomnIA research (Venn and Arber, 2011). They placed great emphasis on the desirability of undertaking physical exercise, such as walking, swimming or cycling; leisure activities, such as socialising and attending clubs or church; and mental activities, such as learning how to use a computer and reading. Being active was universally regarded as desirable and even essential.

Many older participants reported that having a nap, or 'dozing off' during the daytime or early evening, were valuable in terms of being able to maintain their desired activity levels (Venn and Arber, 2011). Napping was sometimes planned before a proposed leisure activity, such as playing bowls, or going out for an evening, in order to be refreshed and have enough energy to enjoy the activity. Thus, planned or unplanned napping was seen as acceptable compensation for a poor night's sleep, or a series of poor nights, so that productivity could be re-established. By accepting napping as part of their everyday routines, older poor sleepers can be enabled to continue to be active and productive and maintain their 'busy' lives.

Hitherto, the main intervention to improve older people's sleep has been the use of sleeping medications, but these have adverse consequences, increasing the risk of falls, and confusion. In the SomnIA study, most older people gave a range of reasons why they did not seek medical help to improve their poor night-time sleep, in particular, not wanting to take prescribed sleeping medication (Venn and Arber, 2012). The SomnIA project assessed several non-pharmacological interventions to improve sleep, two of which are briefly discussed.

A major reason for poorer sleep quality with increasing age is due to chronic ill health which causes pain and discomfort at night (Maglione and Ancoli-Israel, 2012). Not only is the sleep of chronically ill or disabled people likely to be disturbed by their health condition, but also the sleep of family members and their caregivers (Arber and Venn, 2011). Therefore, it is important to reduce the sleep problems of older people with chronic illnesses.

Within the SomnIA project, a randomised clinical trial evaluated the effectiveness of cognitive behavioural management for insomnia (CBT-I) delivered through a programme of six self-help booklets, which were sent out weekly (Morgan et al, 2011, 2012). This structured psycho-educational programme addressed the key components of treatment and health education typically included in therapist-delivered CBT-I, such as the basic 'do's' and 'don'ts' for optimal sleep, the importance of establishing and keeping to routines, setting realistic expectations for sleep, and strategies for 'winding down'. The study found that self-help CBT-I could significantly improve global sleep quality, and improve sleep on a number of dimensions over a six-month follow-up period. These effects suggested that weekly self-help books can make a major difference in improving sleep, and that their use should be more widespread among older patients consulting their doctor with problematic sleep. They represent a cost-effective alternative to sleeping medication that has no longer-term adverse effects.

Sleep problems and decreased daytime alertness among older people may, in part, be caused by a dysfunction of the circadian body clock. Light is known to be a major factor influencing the body's biological clock and sleep/wake patterns, and changes in the eye with increasing age reduce the amount of light reaching the 'body clock' (Revell and Skene, 2010). Older people thus require more light than younger people.

A simple way to improve night-time sleep can be by increasing the amount of daytime light received, which can be achieved in a number of ways. Older people can be encouraged to spend more time outdoors to maximise their daylight exposure, whether engaging in physical activity or simply sitting in the garden or a park. Alternatively, brighter lights can be used or artificial 'blue-enriched' light can be obtained by having special lights in the home that have more short wavelength blue light (Skene, 2009). The SomnIA research evaluated the effectiveness of two light conditions in an 11-week at-home study involving older people with poor sleep. Compared to traditional white light, 'blue-enriched' light significantly delayed the time that older people went to sleep in the evening. In summary, good sleep is essential for well-being and quality of life. There are various personal strategies that older people can adopt to improve their sleep, as well as non-pharmacological means of optimising sleep, such as CBT-I, and ensuring greater daytime exposure to 'blue' light.

Extending the working life

Many work environments are challenging due to exposure to risks such as lifting and carrying, constrained and awkward postures, repetitive tasks and sometimes adverse conditions such as noise, or high/low temperatures. Positive perceptions are that older workers are experienced, dedicated and reliable, but there are also negative perceptions, such as, that they have reduced capacity, are slower, tire more quickly, are weaker and more vulnerable (Buckle et al, 2008). The ageing process combined with the effects of previous injury or disease will have an impact on the physical capabilities of older workers and therefore on performance at work. For example, reduced depth perception may make trips and falls more likely if preventive measures are not taken, such as sturdy footwear, or route planning to compensate. However, older people also show the greatest individual variability of any age cohort, and so reliance on chronological age as a predictor of physical and behavioural aspects is likely to be unreliable (Voorbij and Steenbekkers, 1998). It is therefore important that individuals of all ages take responsibility for looking after their body while undertaking paid work.

The 'Working Late' research project concerned the role of good design and ergonomics in healthy working. Active participation from industry collaborators was central to developing and guiding the research, and has directly informed the development of an online resource, Organiser for Working Late (OWL). The project's philosophy is that industry can learn from older experienced workers in terms of facilitating healthy behaviours by good design. OWL contains tools for encouraging active engagement and communication with workers of all ages about healthy working and workplace design, and therefore how best to support employees in 'Working Late'.

Workplace design is important to support the ageing workforce, and needs to adapt to accommodate changing physical and cognitive abilities throughout the occupational life course. In response to an ageing workforce, the automotive company BMW conducted field research and re-designed one of its factories in Germany for and with older workers (Loch et al, 2010). Their findings suggest that workers can successfully provide useful input to improve the design of their workplace and reduce physical stress on the body, for example, wooden flooring to reduce knee/ankle fatigue, larger typefaces to reduce eyestrain and minimise errors, and manual hoisting cranes to reduce strain on the back. Design changes to the workplace can reduce wear and tear on the body and thus the likelihood of ill health.

Participation from industry was important for this research and the aim was to secure collaboration from several large organisations. This benefited the research in two main ways: first, specific worker samples could be identified; and second, researchers could engage with different industrial sectors with different worker needs. The research involved four main phases, some of which have been reported elsewhere (Gosling et al, 2012; Williams et al, 2012a, 2012b) but are summarised here:

- Phase 1: Questionnaire survey of workers (n=719) across 21 industrial sectors. Triangulation interviews (n=21). Discussion document presented to collaborator organisations (n=4).
- Phase 2: In-depth data collection interviews, ergonomics observations and objective measurements, 'a half-day in the life of ...' with four collaborator organisations (n=32). Co-designing focus groups with each organisation.
- Phase 3: Development and synthesis of the OWL resource.
- Phase 4: Evaluation and refinement of OWL. Launch of the OWL online resource.

Following the questionnaire survey, four collaborator organisations agreed to work closely with the research team. Each identified workforce health needs for specific co-selected work tasks: hand tool design, temporary office environments, working in confined spaces and vehicle design. To enable in-depth data collection on design and healthy working, a 'toolbox' of methods was created which, as well as in-depth interviews, included questionnaires (for example, NMQ – Kuorinka et al, 1987), observation tools (for example, REBA – Hignett and McAtamney, 2000), pedometer step count and foot discomfort maps (Salles and Gyi, 2012). Six to nine people from each company took part (*n*=32), and more than 200 design ideas for healthy working were generated by these workers, half of which were deemed as low or no cost. Personal design stories were selected to populate the OWL resource; some were already in practice by workers, and some were co-developed by encouraging workers to think more about what would help them improve their own health and well-being at work through better design.

Data collected through the interviews and observations also identified key themes that were used to develop and synthesise the OWL resource. OWL is hosted online (www.workinglate-owl.org) and provides a suite of discussion tools and resources to facilitate and support healthy ageing at work. It also aims to encourage employers to engage with and respond positively to diversity (such as ageing) in the workforce. The resource hosts participatory design tools, personal stories, video and audio clips. It is based around two themes identified through the research: understanding the 'body at work' and 'healthy ageing through design'. One of the design tools is a suite of image and word cards, '@ work cards', which can be used to explore opinions in relation to the body at work and the tasks, actions, environments and/or tools and equipment used to perform different jobs. Specific @ work cards were designed relevant to each collaborator organisation to facilitate discussion: body @ work (for example, skin, lungs, muscles and joints), action @ work (for example, drilling, ingress/egress from vehicles), equipment @ work (for example, Personal Protection Equipment, ladders), weather @ work (for example, rain, wind), talking points @ work, and even blank @ work which can be made up by the company to suit their specific needs. Examples of the cards are shown below, in Figure 4.1. Although OWL evolved and has been refined with input from workers and managers in the collaborator organisations, the design ideas/solutions in the resource were selected to be as generic as possible. Positive comments have included the practical ideas/stories, good visual impact and flexibility in its use. Future work needs to define more clearly how OWL can be adopted by other organisations (including small and medium-sized enterprises) and any support/training needed for implementation.

Figure 4.1: Examples of @ work cards

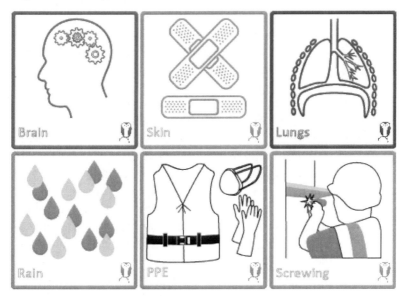

Source: www.workinglate-owl.org

Participation in making music

Participating in active music making offers the potential for enhancing health and well-being for older adults. Social networks that focus on participation in creative, active and social leisure activities such as music have been found to contribute to recovery from depression and maintenance of personal well-being (Fullagar, 2008). There are therapeutic interventions using music with older people suffering from, for example, dementia, where participation in singing has reportedly been associated with short-term increases in positive mood, sociability and self-confidence (Lesta and Petocz, 2006; Svansdottir and Snaedal, 2006). Research concerned with the role of music in the lives of 'well' older adults has demonstrated that listening to music forms part of many everyday activities, and represents a frequent source of positive emotions (Hays and Minichiello, 2005; Laukka, 2007; Saarikallio, 2010), and that there is social and emotional value to senior citizens of intergenerational music activities (Darrow, Johnson and Ollenberger, 1994; Bowers, 1998; Varvarigou et al, 2012a) and active engagement with making music (Kalthoft, 1990; Hillman, 2002; Gembris, 2008; Saarikallio, 2010). Playing a musical instrument has been shown to contribute to feelings of satisfaction, achievement and self-confidence (Taylor and Hallam, 2008), and group singing can promote social and personal well-being, encourage social participation and reduce anxiety and depression (Clift et al, 2010). Direct health benefits have also been suggested with lower mortality rates evident among those who make music or sing in a choir (Bygren et al, 1996). For instance, Cohen et al (2006, 2007) carried out non-randomised controlled studies with 166 participants with a mean age of 80 who participated in 30 singing workshops and 10 performances over one year. The participants, in comparison with control groups, reported fewer health issues, fewer falls, fewer doctor visits and less use of medication.

Building on this earlier research, the 'Music for Life' project investigated the social, emotional and cognitive benefits of community music making among older people, aiming to explore the ways in which participating in creative music making could enhance the lives of older people, while exploring the specific process through which any such impact would occur. Three case study sites acted as partners in the research: The Sage, Gateshead; Westminster Adult Education Service; and the Connect programme at the Guildhall School of Music. The Sage, Gateshead offered an extensive programme of choirs and instrumental groups facilitated by community musicians. Some groups took place in The Sage, Gateshead, an iconic arts centre/concert hall, while others took place in outreach locations around the wider area. The Music Department of the Westminster Adult Education Service was a more formal adult learning context, offering choirs, music appreciation classes and keyboard classes. Finally, the Guildhall Connect programme offered creative inter-generational music workshops within sheltered housing centres, delivered by facilitators who had been trained as community outreach music leaders. Overall, the musical activities engaged with included singing in small and large groups, rock groups, and classes for guitar, ukulele, steel pans, percussion, recorder, music appreciation and keyboard. A control group was made up of individuals attending language classes (four groups), art/craft classes (five groups), yoga, social support (two groups), a book group and a social club.

The research methods included questionnaires for participants, music (n=398) and non-music (n=102), at the beginning of the research, including the CASP-12 measure of quality of life and the Basic Psychological Needs Scale (Deci and Ryan, 2010); questionnaires for music participants at the end of the nine-month period (n=143); individual interviews with music participants (n=30); focus group interviews with music participants (15 focus group interviews); videos and observations of music sessions (45 videos, notes made of 25 sessions); videos and observations of musical performances (3); data relating to drop-outs from musical activities (records of the participating providers); questionnaires for music facilitators including two scales (assessment of views of successful leadership, Basic Needs Satisfaction at Work Scale; see Deci and Ryan, 2010); interviews with music facilitators (12); and interviews with area coordinators of Age UK (responses representing the views of over 40 people concerned with the welfare of older people in all three partner areas).

The majority of the sample was female (80 per cent) and white, despite attempts of the research team to recruit members of a range of minority ethnic groups. The age range was 50–93. The majority of those participating in the music groups had been involved in professional occupations. There was no statistically significant difference in this respect between the music participants and those in the other groups.

Consistently more positive responses were found among the musical groups in response to the well-being measures in the questionnaires. In order to ascertain whether the two quantitative measures shared underlying conceptual constructs, a factor analysis was undertaken using the items from the CASP-12 and the Basic Psychological Needs Scale. This produced three factors. The first related to having a positive outlook on life (purpose), the second to lack of autonomy and control (autonomy/control), and the third to positive social relationships, competence and a sense of recognised accomplishment (social affirmation). Comparisons of those engaged in music making with those participating in other activities revealed statistically significant differences on all three factors, with the music groups having more positive responses. Comparisons of those in the third and fourth age in the music groups revealed no differences in relation to factors relating to autonomy/control or social affirmation, although there was a deterioration in relation to sense of purpose (Hallam et al, 2011).

High ratings were given by those participating in music and non-music groups to a series of statements relating to the benefits of group participation, including sustaining well-being, quality of life and reducing stress; acquiring new skills; providing opportunities for mental activity and intellectual stimulation; promoting social activity and involvement in the community; providing opportunities for demonstrating skills and helping others; and maintaining physical health. There were no statistically significant differences in response to the elements outlined above between music and non-music groups with the exception of enjoyment, where those participating in the music groups reported higher levels. A multiple regression analysis revealed that for those involved in musical activities (but not for those involved in other activities) high scores for the third well-being factor – social affirmation – were predicted by strong agreement that participation in their groups provided opportunities to remain involved with the community, were intellectually stimulating, helped to manage stress and provided opportunities for performance (Hallam et al, 2011).

The individual and focus group interviews with participants and facilitators revealed a range of perceived benefits of active musical engagement including those related to social activity, cognition, emotional and mental health and physical health. Social benefits included a sense of belonging, a sense of playing a valued and vital role within a community, having fun and having contact with younger people in inter-generational groups. Participants also noted that being a member of a musical group helped to provide a routine and structure to their daily lives, providing motivation for leaving the house and for engaging in daily individual practice. Those who participated in inter-generational activities reported that it was fun and enjoyable, challenged stereotypes, and facilitated peer learning and the sharing of expertise. Cognitive benefits included rising to new challenges, acquiring new skills, improved concentration and memory and a general sense of achievement related to their accomplishments in music making. Progression played a key role in underpinning these benefits. Participants spoke of how they valued remaining mentally agile, and how they derived great pride in their musical competencies and achievements. Participants and facilitators also noted many examples of improved mental and physical health. Physical health benefits included a renewed sense of vitality and rejuvenation and improved mobility. Many mental health benefits were also reported, including protection against stress and depression, a sense of purpose in life, enhanced confidence, positive feelings about life in general and support following bereavement. Overall, when questioned about what was special about music as opposed to other activities, many participants attributed positive benefits to the creative and expressive qualities of music (Hallam et al, 2012; Varvarigou et al, 2012b).

Visual art

There is a long history of research into the social and individual benefits of engagement with the arts (Bygren et al, 1996; McCarthy et al, 2004; Greaves and Farbus, 2006; Belfiore and Bennett, 2007). However, there is little that attempts to explain the mechanisms through which that benefit develops and is sustained over time. For example, Johansson et al (2001) concluded that any benefits were lost if attendance at cultural events declined, but could not explain why. There is also very little research that explores the consumption of art by the older population, as Scherger (2009, p 23) states, 'most social science studies of cultural activity focus on class, gender and ethnicity and at best treat age as a background variable that is rarely questioned further.'

In response to this, the 'Contemporary visual art and identity construction' project used a qualitative approach in an attempt to understand the complex and multiple processes which older people go through as they engage with contemporary visual art in art galleries. It aimed to identify how engagement with art facilitated identity processes that contributed to participants' well-being. The focus on contemporary art was a consequence of the fact that its aesthetic, conceptual and even moral value is frequently questioned and contested by publics and in the media. This gives it particular power to prompt people to engage in identity construction processes through their imaginative and/or critical responses to it.

The project sought to understand the benefits for those who engage frequently with the arts, those, who, through circumstance had ceased to do so, and those who had not engaged prior to the intervention. While those in the 55–64 age group are among the most active, the engagement of those over 64 decreases markedly (Keaney and Oskala, 2007) as barriers take more effect. Those who were considered 'non-engaged' were drawn from categories identified by Keaney and Oskala, including men; those with a limiting disability; those suffering from illness; people from minority ethnic backgrounds; those in lower socio-economic groups; and people living alone.

Over 28 months, 38 participants, in five groups, were given guided tours around three galleries in North East England. The groups consisted of:

- sheltered accommodation unit, Gateshead, Tyne and Wear
- writers' group, Sunderland, Tyne and Wear
- advocacy organisation for older people, Gateshead, Tyne and Wear
- daytime film club for the over-60s in Newcastle upon Tyne, Tyne and Wear
- 'Live at Home' scheme for men in Rowland's Gill, Tyne and Wear.

The venues were:

- BALTIC Centre for Contemporary Art, Gateshead, Tyne and Wear
- Belsay Hall, Castle and Gardens, Northumberland
- Great North Museum: Hancock, Newcastle upon Tyne
- Hatton Gallery, Newcastle upon Tyne

- Northern Gallery for Contemporary Art, Sunderland, Tyne and Wear
- Shipley Art Gallery, Gateshead, Tyne and Wear.

Participants visited the galleries in their existing groups, and were interviewed before and after about their experiences. Baseline interviews were held to get a sense of the participants as individuals and in an attempt to understand the visits within the wider context of their lives.

The theoretical framework that guided the analysis is that of identity maintenance and revision processes as described by Marcia (1980, 2002), Kroger (2002) and Kroger and Adair (2008). Building on the work of Erikson (1968) and Kroger (2002), the research emphasised the importance of the processes of identity revision and maintenance, which 'refer to those mechanisms that individuals use to maintain or revise a sense of who they are within their immediate and broader social networks and contexts' (Kroger, 2002, p 7). Consumption of art in a gallery context provided resources for identity processes, aiding participants with maintaining continuity with earlier life and to deal with change, important for well-being among older people.

When asked to give their opinions about what they had seen, the respondents who had little knowledge of art history or visiting art galleries naturally interpreted what they saw in terms of aspects of their identity. The meanings representing links to families, friends, past events and personal histories could be interpreted in terms of maintaining a sense of continuity with the past. The art pieces in the exhibitions were being harnessed for a particular purpose, becoming a way through which an identity could be performed. What was distinctive about these meanings was that they were associated with families and communities. While they did not recognise many of the meanings encoded by the artists, they did recognise themes which became a conduit for memories. For example, an art piece displayed at Shipley Art Gallery prompted an 82-year-old female respondent, who lived in the sheltered accommodation unit, to recall memories of bombing in the Second World War. In a similar way, in response to an exhibition featuring knitted objects ('Knitted Lives', Shipley Art Gallery), an older female respondent who was a 79-year-old wheelchair user stated she would make her children's clothes because she could not afford to buy them. She had given away her knitting needles when she had moved into a sheltered housing unit, and noted that since having had a stroke, she had less feeling in her hands. As part of the exhibition there was the opportunity to knit, and despite her reservations regarding her ability, she successfully completed a few lines. This person's declining health, associated with her age, had interfered with her sense of self that engaging with the exhibition had helped to re-establish. Members of this group discussed setting up a knitting group in the future.

Those who already had a pre-existing identity-defining commitment to art used the experience of visiting the exhibitions to explore that commitment in depth (Luyckx et al, 2006). Participants in this position viewed the visits as an educational experience and wanted to do research on the artists before the visits. They did not construct meanings in terms of their own life histories, but in terms of what they imagined the artist wished to communicate. This group also saw keeping mentally active as important for well-being, possibly keeping illness, such as dementia, at bay. They viewed engaging with art galleries as an important way of doing this.

It can be concluded that engaging with contemporary visual art facilitated identity processes that contributed to participants' well-being. Whether participants liked or disliked the contemporary art was unimportant, but in asserting preferences, they were able to make an identity commitment. In this way, participants' rejection of the art, or assimilation into existing schema about the self, seemed to contribute to identity optimisation. It could also be seen as a way of helping participants respond to change, such as moving into sheltered accommodation, or coping with ill health by adjusting their self-construct or identity.

Conclusion

The NDA findings set out in this chapter suggest that there is much that can be done to promote well-being in older people. However, especially in a time of 'financial austerity', there remain a great many challenges. A key issue for policy makers is whether it would be more economical in the longer term to provide a range of activities which would promote health and well-being in currently 'well' older people in preference to meeting the costs of the more intensive care which may be required without this provision. There is also considerable work to be undertaken in changing public perceptions of older people, their capabilities and their capacity to make a valuable contribution to society. The way that older people are perceived in the UK is not universal. It is a cultural phenomenon, and as such, can be changed.

Challenging deficit models of ageing

There are a great many myths about older people which have served to influence prejudices at the individual and societal level (Withnall et al, 2004). For instance, there is a perception that older people are all the same, whereas, as a result of accumulated life experiences interacting with biological and psychological factors, individual differences within the population become greater with age. Similarly, there is a belief that older people are not interested in engaging in any new activity or learning new skills. The University of the Third Age has clearly demonstrated that this is not the case, as have a number of the NDA projects discussed above, both showing that even well into the fourth age older people form goals and feel motivated to attain, achieve or re-experience something. Just as for younger people, feeling competent and purposeful is a crucial part of positive well-being in later life.

While there may be deterioration in some cognitive capacities with age, this is not inevitable. For instance, it is estimated that in the UK approximately 1 per cent of people aged 60–64 suffer from some form of dementia, rising to approximately 12 per cent for those aged 80–84 and 25 per cent for those aged over 85. This indicates that the majority of older people do not develop dementia. Among the 'well' population of older people, while there is some evidence of cognitive change with ageing, there is striking variation in the extent to which this is experienced. Fluid intelligence, associated with processing speed and short-term memory, may decline as humans age, but crystallised intelligence, acquired through experience and reflection and associated with knowledge and wisdom, has been found to remain stable or even increase (Glendenning, 2000). Maintaining an active life and engaging in a range of social and cognitive activities offers some protection against decline (Hanna-Pladdy and MacKay, 2011). Later life can be a period of profound creativity, where older people use creative outlets for reflection on their own unique stories and for personal healing and problem solving (Hickson and Housley, 1997; Boulton Lewis, 2010).

While old age is frequently perceived as being defined by physical decrepitude, in fact, most older people have sufficient mobility to lead active and independent lives, although they may experience some loss of visual acuity (at age 85 it is approximately 80 per cent less than at age 45), and hearing problems can have an impact on self-confidence and lead to feelings of isolation. However, there are many ways in which these difficulties can be ameliorated.

Considerable work is required to challenge the myths associated with ageing, particularly with those providing services for older people and working closely with them. Staff working with this group need to be trained to treat each older person as an individual and be flexible in their practices to meet individual needs. The interpersonal qualities of staff are of crucial importance (Hickson and Housley, 1997; Duay and Bryan, 2008; Villar et al, 2010; Hallam et al, 2011). Qualities that have been identified as contributing to positive outcomes when staff are facilitating activities include enthusiasm, respect for participants, clarity and organisation, interest in participants' prior knowledge, subject knowledge and the ability to respond to diverse needs within a group. Effective facilitators employ a range of strategies to spark interest and sustain motivation including adopting an open style of questioning, time for discussion and managing interactions so that they are not dominated by particularly vocal individuals, and time for social interactions and practising new skills. The use of humour, clear visual and aural stimuli and stress-free activities that avoid timed tasks are also important (Duay and Bryan, 2008).

Identity, possible selves and resilience

How people face the ageing process is important in terms of the extent to which they are able to meet the challenges that it presents. One way of conceptualising this is in terms of the 'possible selves' that older people may hold (Markus and Nurius, 1986). Possible selves are ideal and hoped-for selves or alternatively, selves that are feared and dreaded which comprise the 'motivational component of the self system' (Frazier et al, 2002, p 308). They are domain-specific, guiding action and influencing decisions with regard to what to expend effort on and what to abandon (Smith and Freund, 2002), and are dynamic, in the sense that individuals are thought to reframe their possible selves in response to life transitions, motivated by the desire to preserve well-being (Cross and Markus, 1991). Smith and Freund (2002) focused on whether the motivational orientations of possible selves among older people would indicate desires for self-improvement or, alternatively, would be concerned with efforts to prevent losses. Positive and negative possible selves were collected via face-to-face interviews from a sample of 206 people aged 70–103, drawn from the Berlin Ageing Study. Four years later, the possible selves interviews, whereby participants were asked to generate two hoped-for and two feared possible selves, were repeated. Across all ages of participants, the dominant motivational orientation for hoped-for selves was the desire to attain, achieve or re-experience something, while for feared possible selves the dominant orientation was avoidance. The emerging possible selves were found to be highly personalised, dynamic and varied, covering a range of domains, even among the oldest old, suggesting that 'the future-oriented motivational system associated with possible selves functions relatively well into very old age' (Smith and Freund, 2002, p 498), and late adulthood need not be interpreted as a period of disengagement from planning for new possibilities and experimenting with new possible selves.

Future-oriented images of self among older people seem to be underpinned by identity-relevant goals (Frazier et al, 2002). Hoped-for and feared possible selves reported by 151 residents, aged 60 to 96, of senior residential communities in Florida revealed that overall, leisure, health and enhanced abilities/education were the most important hoped-for possible selves. Abilities/education were the most important domain for possible selves among those in their 60s and 70s, while health was the most important domain for those aged 80+. Frazier et al concluded that through pursuing goals associated with possible selves, individuals continued to construct their own development through the latter stages of life. Adults who experience major life transitions may have to adjust their goals, leading to 'lost possible selves' and the need to re-evaluate their place in the world (King and Hicks, 2007, p 626). For well-being to be maintained, lost possible selves must cease to be salient to individuals.

In developing new possible selves in response to transitions, individuals need to be resilient, that is, have the capacity to cope with stress and adversity through adapting their behaviour (Rutter, 2008). The major challenge may be to find ways to support people as they age to become resilient so that they are able to reframe their thinking, seeing problems as challenges and opportunities, and developing a range of coping strategies to deal with practical and psychological issues.

Evidence from the study of 'Maintaining dignity in later life' (Lloyd et al, 2014) identifies a range of ways in which older people attempt to retain a sense of continuing identity in the face of wholesale changes in life brought about by the onset of illness. In this study, older participants were able to pinpoint a time when their circumstances changed irreversibly. For most, it was the onset of illness that made them feel old, and this was linked to a sense of being 'a fish out of water', as their normal way of life was altered irreversibly. These changes were also reflected in major changes in relationships as family members. Such changes pose significant challenges to personal identity and highlight the extent of change and the emotional effort required of older people. Lloyd et al (2014) discuss the exercise of 'mind over matter' that research participants often described, which was an attempt to maintain personal identity and, thus, dignity. However, it was also clear that participants also recognised that in time they would no longer be able to exercise 'mind over matter' because their illnesses were long term and would be with them until their deaths. They therefore needed to make an adjustment between their aspirations and their physical and mental capabilities.

Promoting health in the context of long-term care

The promotion of health in the context of long-term conditions remains a major challenge for health and social care services, particularly within the contemporary policy context. The tertiary model of prevention holds that health can be promoted in the context of chronic illness, and the analysis of demographic trends in this chapter highlights the increasing importance of this sphere of practice. Older people remain active in promoting their own health, as demonstrated by the participants in the 'Maintaining dignity' study, who spent a considerable amount of time and energy researching ways to make the most of the health they still had. Strategies they employed included getting out of the house as regularly as possible, watching their diets, taking supplements and promoting their mental agility through puzzles and word games. They also took responsibility for monitoring their health through regular tests, for example, on sight, hearing, heart rate and blood pressure. They monitored the dosages of their medications, looked out for side effects and frequently attended surgeries with a GP and consultants. In short, they had engaged with health policies on self-care to maintain their self-respect. For this group, barriers to maintaining health included physiological barriers, such as the inevitable progress of illnesses such as Parkinson's disease and cancer, but also psychological and social barriers. As pointed out above, there is a difficult psychological task to be undertaken in maintaining a sense of self in the context of long-term illness, but this is aided significantly by supportive family relationships, friendships and relationships with practitioners. Services were, of themselves, a barrier to health when they were over-bureaucratic and treated participants as numbers in the system. Being treated badly or being neglected in care services was a major barrier to psychological health and well-being as well as a disincentive to older people seeking the help they needed. Conversely, where services were courteous and efficient and treated participants as individuals with specific needs and preferences, the impact on health extended beyond the immediate treatment to encompass a broader sense of well-being.

Acknowledgement

We would like to greatly acknowledge the help and support of Sarah Howson in the preparation of this chapter.

FIVE

Food environments: from home to hospital

Janice L. Thompson, Sheila Peace, Arlene Astell, Paula Moynihan and Alastair Macdonald

Introduction

As explained in Chapter One, a major focus of the New Dynamics of Ageing (NDA) Programme was nutrition, and the two connected critical issues concerning older people: malnutrition and obesity. Malnutrition is defined as a state in which there is a deficiency, excess or imbalance of energy and nutrients which leads to adverse effects on body tissues, function and/or clinical outcomes (MAG, 2011). In the UK, it is estimated that at any one time under-nutrition affects over three million older people (The Advisory Group on Malnutrition, 2009). Approximately 10–14 per cent of people living in sheltered housing have been found to be at risk of under-nutrition, as well as 30–42 per cent of residents recently admitted to care homes (BAPEN Quality Group, 2010, p 4). Even older adults living at home are at risk – data from the 2012 Health Survey for England (HSCIC, 2013) indicate that 0.5 per cent of those aged 65–74 and 1.3 per cent of those aged 75 or older are underweight (defined as a body mass index <18.5kg/m^2). Concurrently, overweight and obesity are a growing concern in older adults as they increase the risks for, and complications of, chronic diseases such as cardiovascular disease, type 2 diabetes, hypertension and some cancers. The prevalence of obesity in the UK is 34.1 per cent in men and 35.9 per cent in women aged 65–74, and 29.8 per cent in men and 28.7 per cent of women 75 years or older, respectively (HSCIC, 2013).

Various important contributors to under-nutrition, overweight and obesity in older adults have been identified. These include medication use, age-related physiological and psychological changes such as reduced mobility or problems with chewing and swallowing, depression or social isolation, cognitive factors such as dementia or other neurological illnesses, financial limitations, low levels of physical activity and function, limited access to affordable and appetising healthier foods, and difficulties in acquiring, preparing and consuming healthier meals (Brownie, 2006). These factors can result in an inadequate nutritional intake or an imbalance between energy intake and expenditure, both of which increase the risks for malnutrition and related acute and chronic illnesses.

Maintaining independence and autonomy are critical features of healthy and successful ageing. This includes being able to look after oneself, including shopping and preparing meals (McKie, 1999; Rioux, 2005). Changing environments and life course events are such that maintaining control over one's food intake and subsequent nutritional and health status is not always possible. Consequently, needing assistance with any aspect of eating, such as provision of meals, is seen as an indicator of change in a person's independence, and may herald the start of a more serious decline. Early intervention could potentially be very beneficial in reducing the risks for malnutrition, but it is currently difficult to detect in people at risk, for example, isolated older people in the community. In part this is due to a limited number and range of sensitive measures with predictive value that can detect early signs of change. However, there is also a lack of joined-up systems, in that no one in particular has responsibility for keeping track of an individual's overall health and well-being, including their nutritional status, other than the individual him or herself.

The consequences of under-nutrition once an older adult is admitted to hospital are of particular concern. The unacceptable scale, significance and economic dimensions of malnutrition in older hospital patients within the UK's NHS are well documented elsewhere (The European Nutrition for Health Alliance, 2005; MAG, 2011). Each individual patient, but particularly those in vulnerable groups, such as those suffering from stroke, dementia and hip fracture, requires specific nutrient and fluid targets to be met daily dependent on their nutritional status, medical condition, body weight and mobility level. To date, a solution to the problem of hospital malnutrition in older patients in the UK has not been found through previous approaches using isolated interventions. Although tools and processes are in place for the screening of malnutrition, the current food system for food provision is unable to adequately manage, deliver and monitor food, nutrient and fluid intake on an individual basis; neither is there an audit trail of management and accountability to ensure patients' individual nutritional requirements are being met.

It is clear that whether an older person lives independently at home, in a care home or in hospital, the acquisition, preparation and consumption of food are significantly influenced by that person's environment. To date, limited research has been conducted examining the diverse food environments of older adults and how differences inherent in these environments may have an impact on older adults' relationships with food and the potential to optimise or compromise health in advancing age.

To address some of the existing gaps in the research literature, this chapter draws from the data and experiences of four nutrition-focused projects funded under the NDA Programme to provide an overview of the role of food in the lives of older people, with a particular focus on food environments and how these may change across the life course. A description is provided of the multidisciplinary and mixed-methods approaches that were used to examine historical, cultural, social, lifestyle and contextual factors that influence and shape the diverse food environments of older adults. The environments explored in these project include the home, the wider community, supportive housing (extra-care and sheltered), and in hospital. The chapter seeks to augment the discussion of specific questions of nutrition with insights into the social aspects of eating – what we regard as a novel contribution of the NDA Programme.

Project descriptions

'Transitions in kitchen living' (TiKL)

The 'Transitions in kitchen living' (TiKL) study (see www.newdynamics.group.shef.ac.uk/kitchen-living.html) brought together social gerontologists with ergonomists and designers. This two-year project aimed to investigate historically and contemporarily the experience of the kitchen for people currently in their 60s, 70s, 80s and 90s living in a variety of mainstream and supportive housing in England. Secondary analysis of previous research concerning spatial dimensions of the housing circumstances of older people (Hanson et al, 2002), and the relationship between environment and identity (Peace et al, 2006), provided background material to the study.

The research aimed to contribute a historical understanding to the use of the contemporary kitchen, an essential 'food environment', as well as a rich data bank of stories concerning kitchen living which also identified the introduction of certain household services such as running water, electricity and kitchen equipment. In terms of the contemporary kitchen, diversity among participants, an examination of age, gender, health and well-being enabled further understanding of person–environment congruence, which is a central focus of environmental gerontology (Rubenstein and de Medeiros, 2004; Peace et al, 2007). Therefore the project planned to re-examine theoretical perspectives through multi-disciplinary research alongside providing a contemporary understanding of the current material, social and psychological environment of the kitchen that would contribute to user requirements for inclusive kitchen design or adaptation.

To capture this diversity of interest, a mixed-methods approach was adopted including oral history and semi-structured interviews, records of routine activities and visual representations of the physical environment. Methods were developed through detailed pilot testing with five older people living in Loughborough and the London Borough of Haringey. These included a couple interviewed together and three people on their own; people living in bungalows, semi-detached housing and extra-care housing; and people from minority ethnic groups (that is, Black African and Black Caribbean). The main study was undertaken in Loughborough and Bristol, with a purposive sample of 48 older people chosen to meet the following criteria: (i) housing type to cover at a ratio of 2:1 – (a) detached, semi-detached, terraced, bungalow, high rise and low rise flats, and (b) sheltered housing, retirement housing, extra-care housing; (ii) age groups: 60–69, 70–79, 80–89, 90+; and (iii) gender – women and men with a ratio of 2:1 to reflect life expectancy differences. In Loughborough the team had access to a panel of people who were screened by these criteria. In Bristol this was not the case, and in both locations participants were found through discussions with housing managers, talks to community groups and other forms of advertising. In the outcome relatively few people met the 90+ years age category; these participants were combined with those aged over 80. However, the views of participants from four generations enables an understanding of contextual changes over time.

'Migration, nutrition and ageing across the life course in Bangladeshi families. A transnational perspective' (MINA)

The Bangladeshi population is one of the fastest growing ethnic groups within the UK, and among the most socially disadvantaged. They have poorer self-reported and measured health status indicated by higher rates of disability, centralised obesity and chronic diseases such as type 2 diabetes and cardiovascular disease (HSCIC, 2006). Older Bangladeshi women are particularly affected as they play a lead role in caretaking for multiple generations within relatively large extended families, and many struggle to cope with the complex challenges of ageing, poverty, racism and social exclusion. MINA (see www.newdynamics.group. shef.ac.uk/mina.html) was a three-year project that examined ageing, migration and nutrition across two generations of Bangladeshi women. This research builds on the existing literature focusing on migration and ageing among the UK Bangladeshi population (Gardner, 2002; Phillipson et al, 2003), providing new insights into, specifically, food, nutrition and their interactions with ageing and migration among UK Bangladeshi families living in communities outside of Tower Hamlets, London.

MINA brought together experts in public health nutrition and exercise, public health nursing, biological anthropology, health psychology, ethnobotany, and environment and multimedia design. MINA used an intergenerational and transnational approach incorporating multi-disciplinary methodologies. The inter-generational component included a sample of older women (aged 45+; $n=40$) who migrated from Sylhet, Bangladesh to Cardiff, UK and their younger adult daughters (aged 18–35; $n=37$) born to migrants in the UK or who immigrated to the UK as children. The transnational component included women (mothers, $n=22$, and daughters, $n=22$) of the same two age groups, who were interviewed and assessed in Sylhet, Bangladesh, giving us a continuum to understand the influences of migration, nutrition and eating patterns on ageing. Participants in both countries were recruited across the range of socio-economic deprivation.

MINA used a participatory, mixed-methods approach to gather and analyse data. Nutritional status, physical function and bone health (UK participants only) were measured using anthropometry, a standardised battery of tests for lower body physical function (Guralnik et al, 1994), and via estimates of heel bone density using quantitative ultrasound. Food ethnobotanical knowledge and uses of traditional food plants, analysis of home gardens/allotment gardens managed by Bangladeshi migrants in the UK and in Bangladesh, including frequency of botanical species, analysis of the management and organisation of food plants in the home gardens, assessment of the social meaning of these for the community, and analysis of the 'emic' perception of food plants and plant-based culinary preparations as traditional medicines were assessed using focus groups, interviews, participant observation, collection of botanical species and seeds and visual anthropological methods.

Differences between life course experiences and the typical 'food environments' of the Bangladeshi community in the UK and in Bangladesh were assessed using a semi-structured questionnaire, in-depth interviews, participant observation and photoethnography. Detailed accounts of migration and biographical experiences were gathered to assess their impact on nutritional status, health behaviours and transmission of nutritional knowledge cross-generationally and transnationally. Additionally, the influence of cultural beliefs on nutrition, health and health-seeking behaviours and how this has changed across the lifespan and between generations were examined. The impact of social inequalities on nutrition and health status, changes in the roles, position and responsibilities of women in the household and the impact on their nutrition, the family unit and wider community were also assessed.

'Novel assessment of nutrition and ageing' (NANA)

The aim of the NANA project (www.newdynamics.group.shef.ac.uk/nana.html) was to improve the collection of information about free-living older adults' diets through technology designed to make the process quicker and easier. By using a touchscreen computer, NANA aimed to support an older adult to collect information about his or her food and drink intake, which was then used to provide an estimate of their energy consumption. In addition, the NANA system collected information on a person's physical activity, mood and cognitive function, to help inform understanding of their current context and nutritional status, with a view to potentially detecting early signs of change. As frailty is closely linked to malnutrition, an additional feature of NANA was the capacity to measure grip strength, one of the five indicators of frailty (Fried et al, 2001). As part of the NANA validation process we also collected data on the other four indicators: unintentional weight loss (>10lbs in the past year), self-reported exhaustion, slow walking speed and low physical activity.

NANA's holistic approach was intended to reflect the way individuals see the interactions between the various aspects of their lives and their food environment, and to promote understanding of the relationships between nutrition, cognition, mood and physical activity. Over the three years of the NANA development and validation project, 100 older adults aged between 65 and 95 trialled the different versions of the NANA system in their homes, for between 10 days and three weeks. An additional 270 older adults took part in various experiments, focus groups and user-testing studies, both in their own homes and laboratory settings, to inform the development of the NANA system.

As NANA was aimed at supporting people to live and age well at home, a critical feature of the project has been spending time with older adults to understand their daily lives in context. In addition to the data required for the development and evaluation of the NANA system, this approach produced insights into the role of food, from preparation to consumption, in the lives of the older adults who participated in the NANA validation. This is important for improving detection of people at risk of malnutrition and targeting interventions aimed at prevention.

'Multidisciplinary approaches to develop a prototype for the prevention of malnutrition in older people' (mappmal)

The mappmal project (www.newdynamics.group.shef.ac.uk/mappmal. html) was a three-year multi-disciplinary research project that exploited new technologies to re-think and test new ways that the food provision to, and nutritional intake of, older patients can be managed and monitored in hospital using a 'joined-up' approach that considers all stages of the food journey, from production to consumption (that is, products, people, places and procedures). The amenability of this new systems prototype to become embedded in current UK practice in hospitals and other care settings was also investigated by engaging end users and key stakeholders throughout the development. An iterative and participative process was used throughout all phases of the project, and methods were employed that engaged users and key stakeholders in the co-design of the prototype system (Macdonald et al, 2012).

The methods used to inform the design and development of the prototype included: (i) an ethnographic study of current food provision in the elderly care setting in hospitals to highlight opportunities for intervention; (ii) a survey and evaluation of product available on the market; (iii) a literature review highlighting design studies which informed the approach to categorising patient needs and providing best practice exemplars; (iv) the analysis of findings and concepts arising from a series of five user workshops; and (v) semi-structured interviews with users and stakeholders throughout the duration of the project.

This research resulted in the 'hospitalfoodie' concept and demonstration prototype (see www.hospitalfoodie.com). Hospitalfoodie comprises a number of separate but integrated elements. A nutrition management system is accessed on touchscreens at the patient bedside and on staff interfaces. The system facilitates the provision of tailored menus enabling personalised food choice and allowing ordering closer to time of consumption. The hospitalfoodie system enables the provision of six smaller energy- and nutrient-dense 'mini-meals' per day by supplementing existing catering systems with ward-based food provision, using a new 'mini-meal' trolley. At each meal, nutrition intake is monitored through an innovative 'wipe away' food monitoring application linked to a nutrition composition database. Patients' nutrient intake can be compared with their individual requirements in real time. In the event of a shortfall in intake of nutrients, alerts prompt time-limited actions that are allocated to an appropriate staff member, building accountability, providing performance data for auditing requirements, and facilitating increased management of food and nutrition. The system is also designed to engage all types and grades of staff in the process of providing adequate nutrition to patients, and thereby raises the profile of food provision and nutrition management as part of total patient care. In addition to nutrition management and monitoring and the provision of appropriate foods, the hospitalfoodie concept intends to promote an environment that is conducive to eating.

Food environment

The following section provides a synthesis of findings from these four distinct projects brought together to address a number of related themes. The factors discussed include: historical; lifestyle, including physical, social and familial contexts; health and well-being; and when independence goes.

Historical – past lives

Everyone has something to say about food – from basic likes and dislikes, to religious meaning, to the way food fits with the routines of life and the variety of places they may eat. Globally, the food environment can encompass both public and private spaces and places. In this chapter attention is focused on experiences within the UK, and embraces its cultural diversity. At one extreme the food environment may be the domestic home where the kitchen will be seen by the vast majority of people as the place for food preparation, and often or sometimes as a place to eat. At the other extreme there are a variety of public and institutional environments that range from the most exclusive restaurant, to the dining room in retirement housing, to the hospital ward (Cieraad, 1999; Freeman, 2004; Llewellyn, 2004). These communal settings are more or less familiar to different groups of people depending on their social circumstances, health and well-being. They are also places where other people may have greater control over food preparation and management, and the individual more or less control over choice and preference.

In considering the food environment for people in later life – from their 60s onwards – looking backwards sometimes helps us to look forwards. The oral history interviews carried out with the predominantly white British participants in the TiKL project, whose ages ranged from 61 to 91, meant that for some, childhood years were in the 1920s, while for others, this was the late 1940s. Their reflections indicate a range of housing types, forms of accommodation and the development of modernity and material culture. This gives an insight into how a life course perspective enables greater understanding of the current food environment. Talking about their lives, these participants have commented on more than 300 kitchens, a majority of which were in the UK (but some were overseas). People are concerned about space, the development of domestic equipment, routines for different tasks, storage, social etiquette, changes over time and personal meaning.

The following two quotes have been chosen because they illustrate aspects of the food environment from the past for people of quite different socio-economic status. The kitchen, which has long been discussed as gendered space (Ardener, 1997; Silva, 2000), is seen here as a place where mothers passed on skills to their children, as well as a place where men may cook (but here were seen as relieving the wife of particular duties). Also, through looking at the past, in days before refrigeration, different types of food were more commonly enjoyed by different generations.

The first woman remembered a kitchen from a semi-detached house in the 1930s:

"... there was a long kitchen table at which my mother cooked and we used to take it in turns to help her make the pastry and that sort of thing ... the larder had open shelves just behind mother, so she just needed to turn around and reach the flour and so on ... at the end, away from the yard, there was a big what was called 'A meat safe'.... To keep the flies out. And things were, in a sense, more organised in those days because for instance if you were roasting you saved the fat but there was a separate jar for beef, mutton or pork.... It always had to go into the correct jar.... No fridge of course.... I mean we used to eat quite a lot of fat, one of the favourite dishes was larded toast, where the actual lard was spread onto the toast, it was delicious [laughs]." (Woman, aged 88)

The kitchen was also a place to eat meals, and having enough space for the kitchen table was essential. Social etiquette is also important and there are generational, social and cultural issues as to what and who eats in the kitchen or in the dining and living rooms on different days and at different times. This oral history data tells us about variation in the domestic food environment and the importance of spatial layout. Post-Second World War the dining room and living room became more accessible through material and social change. Architecturally there was the development of the hatch between the kitchen and the dining room, and the gradual opening up of through-rooms and designs that were more open plan. Media expansion and cultural diversity had an impact on eating environments, and routines were also influenced by social interaction between family members and generations.

> The kitchen in a 1950s council house in a northern town lived in since the age of 2:
>
> "That's where we all sat to eat ... and where we always had to sit and eat at the table together. Especially sort of at the tea time.... My mother insisted ... on that ... it was a real treat if you were allowed to take a sandwich and perhaps sit down in the front room.... It was a treat for you to be able to do that ... that was your Saturday night treat [laughs].... Oh yes, yes. No, we always had to sit at the table to eat breakfast and what have you, so.... Yes, because there was a table and five chairs.... I mean my dad did use ... he did cook the Sunday lunch. Nearly always ... it was my mother's day off from cooking." (Woman, aged 62)

Within the NANA project, a subsample of 20 participants who lived in the St Andrews and Fife area reported having a traditional Scottish background which continued to influence their eating habits in older age. These 20 participants all lead busy and active lives, with some still in paid employment, most engaged in community and charitable pursuits, and all endeavouring to follow guidance on a healthy lifestyle. As a group they provide some interesting examples of what an active and fulfilling older age can look like, and how their life histories and current lifestyles influenced their eating behaviour.

Based on experiences from childhood they are used to eating breakfast and lunch, with 'tea' between 5–6 pm and then a small 'supper' later in the evening, which they had carried on into adult life. Those who worked or were not Scottish ate later in the evening. The majority of the participants snacked regularly throughout the day. It was particularly noticeable in the 'leftover' items recorded into the NANA system that this generation did not really have 'leftovers'. They indicated many times that they had been brought up always to clear their plates. This may have influenced their habit of over-eating and many expressed regret at the amount of food which they became aware that they ate, either by using the NANA system or writing the food diary.

The MINA project results highlight how food, including its procurement, preparation and consumption, is central to the lives of Bangladeshi women and their families. The food environments identified by UK-based participants not only included the home kitchen, but also home gardens and allotments, various food-related shops and businesses supplying ingredients, and restaurants (both sit-down and 'takeaway' types) that are frequented. Arguably, however, the home kitchen and serving areas are most central to participants' lives. Women historically and currently play major roles in food choice, shopping and cooking of meals and snacks. However, men can play influential roles as well, particularly regarding food shopping and influencing what is cooked due to personal preferences.

Migration history, cultural influences and role expectations are key themes identified within MINA as having an impact on how women perceive and function within their food environments. Here their historical biography was very different to the TiKL and NANA participants. All of the UK-based older women participating in MINA were born and lived a considerable portion of their lives in Bangladesh. Seventeen (46 per cent) of the UK-based adult daughters were born in Bangladesh and migrated to the UK during childhood or adolescence, with the average age of migration approximately eight years (Bogin et al, 2014); the remainder were born in the UK. These varied histories exert differential effects on nutritional status (both in childhood and adulthood), personal food preferences, levels of daily physical activity and the role that traditional food and cooking practices play in one's daily life.

Lifestyle – physical, social and familial contexts of food environments in present-day housing ('mainstream' and 'supportive')

Where and with whom people live has a direct impact on food preparation and consumption, which has an impact on their health and well-being. The TiKL study included 21 participants who lived with a spouse or partner at the time of interview, and 27 who lived on their own. Those who were 80 (n=16) and older were the most vulnerable. They are predominantly older women more likely to be living alone with the lowest income spread, to be experiencing mobility problems and most likely to be living in supportive housing. In contrast, 10 of the 16 participants (62.5 per cent) in their 60s were living with their spouse.

The impact of the past on the present is seen in the way activities are habit-forming and part of personal continuity. These participants are able to record a specific routine for their current kitchen activities that is often centred round food and drink preparation, and they have developed certain preferences. Analysis of participants' daily activities records show that people move in and out of the kitchen throughout the day preparing food, making drinks and doing other domestic tasks. However, there is evidence of changing eating and drinking habits as people get older. Those in their 80s and 90s were more likely to have their main meal at mid-day with a light supper or snack, and a small number of the eldest reported that they either ate communally in retirement housing, went to a day centre for meals, or were just less interested in their food. In contrast, participants in their 60s and 70s were more inclined to have a light lunch and their main meal in the evening. The youngest participants commented that planning for mealtimes and food preparation was more likely to depend on their other daily activities.

As noted, for many in the TiKL study the kitchen had been a hub and a place of social interaction. It was still the place of food preparation, but in later life, those whose family had moved away and who may have lost their partner, could find that living alone had changed or reinforced their routines. Interestingly, the location where people ate their meals did not vary by age; rather, the size of the kitchen, the type of meal, whether this was a meal taken alone or with company, and eating comfort were important. The size and shape of the contemporary kitchen did not always allow space for a kitchen table, and even if there was a table, eating in the kitchen was not as common as the oral history accounts had shown for the childhood days of the oldest participants. It was still common for people to eat a hot meal at a table that may be in a dining room/area, while a lighter meal could be taken on a tray watching television in a lounge.

The town of St Andrews, and its surrounding area, is considered to be an affluent one, comprising many farmers, professionals, academics and retired individuals from all over the UK. The lifestyle of the NANA participants living in Scotland reflected a high-end socio-economic group. All were of retirement age and were well educated including a retired doctor, teacher, academic, NHS manager, engineers and a BBC researcher among them. Their cognitive assessment was within normal limits for their age and education, and no one showed signs of cognitive decline during the research period. All participants in this subsample owned their homes and had cars. Some had chosen to remain in either part-time, or, in one case, full-time employment, not from necessity but from the desire either to serve the community or to alleviate boredom. The majority had time-consuming hobbies, which involved them in a supervisory or leadership role. Consequently, their daily routines were punctuated by meetings, planned activities or leisure pursuits. Most of their immediate family lived some distance from North East Fife; therefore they were often receiving visitors or travelling to meet family. This had an impact on their type, pattern and amount of food intake. For example, it could disrupt a routine or cause them to eat out more often.

Most NANA participants living in Scotland were part of a couple, and a few were widowed or divorced. If in a couple, the eating habits of their partner would sometimes affect the size and type of food eaten by the participant. If they lived alone, they might sometimes report over-eating (on snacks) or missing meals. However, the majority were conscientious about eating regularly. All of the participants were able to do their own shopping and, even when part of a couple, it was obvious that both men and women made decisions about what was bought and cooked. Cooking, however, was left to the female partner, although the male participants did show an interest in food and diet quality in particular. Most of the participants ate their main meal at a table, with some in a separate dining room. There was not much evidence of food being eaten on a tray, even when living alone.

Many meals that were recorded in the NANA study are described in a family context with several members round the dining table.

This group did not show any signs of serious low mood or depression. Instead, they often remarked how lucky they were, and could not understand how anyone in their position could have 'low mood'. It was clear that these participants were living comfortably with few health or financial worries. One was bereaved during the project, when his mother died, but this did not seem to affect his mood or food intake, although he seemed distracted by executor duties for many weeks. Participants ate out a great deal, particularly at lunchtime, but, as the project took place during the summer, when they had visitors, many of them had celebratory dinners in a restaurant.

All of the NANA participants had very well-established food routines, especially for breakfast. On weekdays many would eat exactly the same thing such as porridge or toast every day. At weekends, they tended to eat a 'full fry' or brunch. None of these participants missed breakfast regularly. If anything, lunch was the most moveable meal of the day. One participant did not eat lunch at all, nor did she snack throughout the day, preferring to drink milky coffee as a substitute meal or snack. This was a retired doctor and one of the few participants whose BMI was within normal limits.

The more solitary existence of some TiKL participants was very different from the NANA and younger MINA members, although similarity is seen among some of the older MINA participants. In MINA, 62.5 per cent of older women were married with the remainder widowed; 92.5 per cent lived in households with at least two generations, with 50 per cent living in nuclear-structured households. Despite just one participant living alone, many older participants reported feelings of isolation and loneliness. Many did not get out and about into the community very often due to limitations in language skills, lack of social activities and environments that were culturally appropriate, and concerns about safety. Many compared their current household and social environments to that in Bangladesh, where regular visits with family, friends and neighbours were part of daily life. Among younger MINA participants, 32.5 per cent were single, 55 per cent were married and two women (5 per cent) were divorced. Almost all (97.3 per cent) lived in households with at least two generations, with 61 per cent of married daughters living in nuclear-structured households. Thus, not all participants lived in large households with multiple generations.

Across the range of family structures and relationship status, the majority of MINA participants commonly prepare two home-cooked meals per day, spending on average over two hours a day preparing food. Although this activity is time-consuming, participants see this activity as a highly important role and a way to exert control within the family and their environment (Jennings et al, in press). Cultural influences, personal food preferences and preferences of husbands (or other male members of the household) and children are key factors affecting the purchase, preparation and serving of food in the home.

Although participants reported eating a range of food types, virtually all described cooking and consuming at least one or more 'traditional meal' per day, which included rice and a curry dish. Older participants more commonly reported eating only one or two 'meals' per day, stating challenges with eating (loss of appetite, digestion problems, attempts to change eating behaviours to promote health). In contrast, younger participants typically consumed only one traditional 'meal' per day (usually at dinner), and ate 'Western' or 'English' food for the remaining meals. Not all younger participants cooked – many who were not married reported that their mothers, older sisters or sisters-in-law may do the majority of the cooking, as their work or school responsibilities limited their time to prepare foods in the home.

The MINA participants expressed competing pressures of trying to prepare, serve and consume more healthy foods, with the expectation that women provide delicious, ample meals for both family and guests, who may visit at any time, and thus women within the home must be ready to provide meals and snacks at a moment's notice. There is considerable pressure felt by women to prepare foods that illustrate their skills and promote their status as a good hostess. Typically this includes foods high in energy, fats and sugar, such as curries cooked with relatively high amounts of oil, fried snacks and traditional sweets that contain high levels of both sugar and fat. However, this could also include 'Western' snacks such as crisps, biscuits, sweetened beverages and chocolates.

Although MINA participants recognised that food is critical to health and well-being, and understood the importance of good nutrition, they were less inclined to alter food choices and cooking preparation methods unless they had been diagnosed with something. This was because of the commonly shared view that healthy modifications resulted in food being less palatable. Frequent consumption of fried foods is of particular concern among younger MINA participants, with 60 per cent reporting eating fried foods at least one or two times per day. Adding salt to food during cooking was reported by 100 per cent of participants, and less than 10 per cent reported consuming the recommended five portions of fruit and vegetables each day. Seven older participants no longer added salt to their food after cooking, and had altered their dietary intake subsequent to disease diagnosis, and many complained of stomach and intestinal irritation when eating foods they used to enjoy; they subsequently limited the use of spices and consumption of many of their favourite foods. However, these dietary changes as one ages, and differences in food preferences and health status in multi-generational households, have an impact on the food environment of all family members, and can lead to challenges with trying to accommodate all family members within environments of communal cooking and food consumption.

The term 'meal' has a specific connotation with MINA participants; when used by researchers during data collection, it elicited responses that virtually always referred to a meal composed of rice and curry. This finding has important implications for assessing dietary intake in this population, as many individuals report only eating one 'meal' per day, but when queried further, describe a number of other foods and snacks consumed throughout the day (which would not be reported or considered by participants if the interviewer only uses the word 'meal'). Other challenges to dietary intake assessment in this population include the tradition of eating communally out of large dishes, as portion sizes are extremely difficult, if not impossible, to estimate. Additionally, meals are prepared and served across the day at various time to accommodate the range of work and school schedules of husbands and children, which promotes over-eating among adult women and limits time for health-promoting physical activities.

   NANA participants also reported preferences towards consumption of 'traditional' foods. This group showed distinct food preferences in their diets recorded using a four-day diary and the NANA recording system. They frequently ate local specialities such as haggis, scotch eggs, 'bridies' and potted haugh; however, their diets also included items such as mangos and quiche containing smoked salmon and asparagus. These participants had clear preferences for how they cooked food, which did not vary across meals. For example, some always steamed their vegetables whereas others always boiled them. It was noticeable that, at the end of the project, the most common comment about using the NANA system was the regret that they had not used the 'favourites' option more often. This is a function of the system that allows people to record a sample of a favourite meal that they always prepare and serve in the same way; this function helps participants save time when entering their meals. By the end of the data collection period, many of the participants had realised just how much of the same foods and meals they were eating, and recognised how using the 'favourite' option more often would have saved them a great deal of time. This finding has implications for how to guide participants in using the NANA system in future studies.

   Both extremes of the physical activity continuum were captured within these projects. Of course, very inactive lifestyles were noted among many participants in all studies, and this is associated with lower physical function. Many older women in the MINA study report being socially isolated and lonely, and some reported feeling depressed; their role in food environments may be limited either due to health issues or as a reflection of their role as a respected elder female which results in their doing very little physical movement or work (and thus has an impact on health and well-being). This situation can limit independence and interactions with family and friends. They described how they missed eating and visiting in communal settings, and compare life in Bangladesh as being more favourable and supportive of regular social interactions and feelings of belonging and higher self-worth, with food considered 'fresh' and thus more healthy than in the UK. A comparison of the physical function levels of UK-based and Bangladesh-based older participants confirm clear differences in levels of physical function – the mean physical function score of older women living in Cardiff was significantly lower than that of older women living in Sylhet (6.3±3.0 versus 9.4±1.9 points on a scale of 12), and indicative of high risk for frailty. Additionally, many older adults no longer have children living in the UK who are in a position to care for them, or their children live globally and cannot provide the care needed as one ages. This means that most older participants expressed a concern about provision of housing, healthcare and social care as they age, and some are fearful for the future.

The majority of NANA participants living in Scotland reported being physically active. They either played sport (mainly golf, but also cycling, swimming and walking) or performed regular gardening, with some housework also part of their regular routine. Two participants were relatively physically inactive due to illness and they scored lower on the grip strength test and had a slower walking pace. Two participants were particularly active and, on closer inspection, were both 'young' older adults (aged 65) living on their own. One of these very active people lived in a remote cottage with a great deal of land on which he grew vegetables and kept animals; the other was a keen birdwatcher who walked for many hours most days of the week. One female (aged 78), who worked full-time, five days a week, cycled two miles to a bus stop to and from work before coming back to her 'estate' on which she grew fruit and vegetables and managed rented farm cottages. Other participants used their retirement years to attend various activity classes, meet with friends and family and champion good causes or local campaigns. Only one female was relatively housebound as she was waiting for a replacement hip operation. As a group, their levels of physical fitness were most apparent when they performed a 10m walk under clinical conditions and a 3m walk in their own home. All of the participants walked over 1m per second, which is considered the minimum speed for healthy older adults (Studenski, 2011). None of these participants showed risk of frailty using the five indicators proposed by Fried et al (2001) over the four-month period of the NANA validation study.

Health and well-being – contribution of food and the food environment

In the TiKL study, activity within the domestic food environment is fundamental to how some participants defined personal identities. However, changes in personal health and well-being were both lifelong and ongoing, and through detailed discussion of everyday living, many indicated a degree of difficulty in the kitchen that was due to sensory impairment and issues of agility. Seventeen participants had problems due to changes with their sight, 13 with their hearing, 26 with reaching, and 19 with carrying out tasks that demanded dexterity. The most common problems reported were reading small instructions on packaged food or other kitchen products, and seeing the cooker controls. Lighting levels for different areas of each kitchen both with and without artificial light were measured. It was found that the food preparation areas were the most poorly lit, both naturally and artificially, and fell well below recommended minimum light levels. Despite the use of hearing aids by some, several people experienced problems, such as hearing the phone ring with the kettle on.

As people experienced these difficulties, the kitchen as a food environment could become problematic in terms of the material environment, but everyone developed different coping strategies. For example, to address problems of reaching or stretching down to the floor or to use appliances or cupboards, participants coped by crouching rather than bending down to the oven, using steps to get to higher shelves, and pulling themselves up using the worktop.

Many people owned special gadgets for opening jars, cans and milk cartons to overcome limitations of dexterity, mobility and strength. Although several people received help from others with shopping, many did it themselves, sometimes using mobility aids such as a stick or scooter. No one stated that they shopped online. Physical disability was the main barrier to preparing food, for example, pain and lack of strength when peeling and chopping, backache when standing for baking, and so on. Sitting for food preparation (requiring a lower work surface) and taking rest breaks were useful strategies adopted to overcome challenges.

Some solutions appeared to involve more risk-taking. For making a hot drink, one woman found her kettle heavy and unsafe to lift, and so slid it to the tap, filled it, and then slid it back to turn it on. Others used a small lightweight kettle or a microwave instead of a kettle. It was also commented that adequate light and colour contrast for crockery, surfaces and surface edges was needed for those with impaired vision.

Of course, domestic equipment constantly develops, and it is true that for some people staying put in their own home is possible because of a microwave, as they are no longer able to prepare food for themselves. However, the research also showed that for the people who owned a microwave, there could be problems with the appliance being at the wrong height, the door being on the wrong side, cooking the food for too long, and transporting food from the microwave (when hot) to the table or work surface. Simple operation of a microwave was seen as important (and not always delivered), and an oven/microwave combination was also found useful and convenient.

While these views from the TiKL study indicate the ways in which domestic space is embodied, leading people to cope and adapt in different ways, other research set out to clinically assess health circumstances in greater detail alongside food intake patterns and food environments. The low levels of physical activity and relatively high and frequent consumption of energy-dense foods among UK-based MINA participants is reflected in their high levels of risk for being overweight (30 and 22.5 per cent of older and younger women, respectively) and obesity (65 and 42.5 per cent of older and younger women, respectively) (Bogin et al, 2014; overweight and obese categories based on BMI cut-points for Asian populations; see WHO Expert Consultation, 2004). Additionally, over 75 per cent of older women living in Cardiff reported having a long-standing illness, with approximately one-third reporting their health as being poor or very poor.

Despite the high levels of activity reported among the NANA participants, the majority were overweight, with some in the obese category, according to their BMI. This finding of high levels of overweight and obesity among UK older adults is consistent with regional and national data (Thompson et al, 2011; HSCIC, 2013). A review of their food intake revealed that some ate a great deal of food that some would describe as 'unhealthy.' In conversations about food, many indicated that they knew what constituted healthy food, and they tried to include some of this in their diet, but they supplemented this with a lot of unhealthy food. It was obvious that food was important to the majority, and perhaps this was motivating factor for them volunteering to participate in the project. One participant enjoyed the experience most of all because it gave her a change to monitor her intake and to reduce her current food intake (from embarrassment at the amount she was entering into the NANA system). All of them prepared at least one meal a week from scratch, using fresh ingredients (and some only ate this type of food); one participant (who lived on his own) had a diet of mainly inexpensive convenience foods. Most ate meat nearly every day, with only the rare vegetarian and one vegan.

When independence goes – eating out, being in retirement housing, care homes, hospital

As mentioned in the introduction, the public and private nature of the food environment can be central to the ways in which a diversity of complex issues concerning choice, preference, preparation, nutritional content, dignity, comfort and contentment are experienced. The research featured in the NDA Programme captures this complexity, and indicates how, within the domestic home and supportive settings of housing with care, people may begin to change their ways of eating as they age. Our last theme concerns 'when independence goes', and while this has been touched on already, we turn to the 'mappmal' project and the food environment of the hospital.

Current systems for food provision in hospitals in the UK offer the patient little individual choice. Food is often ordered over a day in advance, meaning that food for the incoming patient may be that ordered by the previous patient occupying the bed! Although menus offer some level of choice, they are not tailored to patient preferences and do little to stimulate patient appetite and enjoyment of food. It was therefore important that the new prototype for food provisions for hospitals enabled more tailored food choice and reduced the time between food ordering and consumption. The hospitalfoodie system enables the patient to enter their likes and dislikes into the bedside food ordering system so that the food choices presented to them are always ones that they like. This enables the patient to maintain a level of autonomy while in the hospital environment.

The Care Quality Commission report on the Dignity and Nutrition Inspection Programme (CQC, 2012) highlighted that a limited range of foods to consume outside set mealtimes were available at ward level, meaning that patient food choice is often limited, contributing to a low overall nutrient intake. The mappmal project aimed to address this issue by developing a range of energy and nutrient-dense food items designed for provision at ward level, including nutrient-enriched biscuits, cakes, savoury scones, soups and ice creams, thus increasing the range of both sweet and savoury options available to patients.

The hospital eating environment for older patients is currently far from ideal. Patients are faced with eating in bed or, if able, while seated at a bedside chair. The mappmal project found that eating often takes place in a cramped, cluttered, sometimes unpleasant environment, and that patients do not always have the necessary equipment to eat properly.

To address this, and to maximise patient comfort and enjoyment at mealtimes, the hospitalfoodie system includes a pre-meal checklist for staff that includes guidance on helping the patient into a safe and comfortable position for eating. The pre-meal checklist that appears on the bedside touchscreen interface also prompts staff to offer the patient hand wipes and provide any personal equipment, for example, dentures, spectacles or assistive cutlery. This serves as an *aide-mémoire* for staff; however, ethnographic data from the mappmal study emphasised that patients need to be 'emphatically assisted' at mealtimes, and this requires skilful good practice that is sometimes taken for granted as a non-technical task (Heaven et al, 2012).

The bed and bedside environment is a multi-functional space which has to accommodate many different activities in addition to eating and drinking, for example, temporary storage of urine bottles and a place to keep personal possessions. In view of this, the hospitalfoodie prototype includes a specification for both an appropriately designed chair and dedicated dining surface which together: (i) maximise patient comfort; (ii) adjust to accommodate the anthropometric range of sizes and postures of older people; (iii) provide a dedicated dining surface separate from clinical and other functions of the bedside environment; and (iv) are able to be routinely cleaned to required health and safety standards, and therefore enable an environment more conducive to safe and enjoyable eating. The mappmal team evaluated a number of products on the market to identify those which embody the desirable features and meet design specifications.

When an older person is admitted to acute or long-term care it is often difficult for families and relatives to communicate with staff about their family member's food needs and to obtain feedback on their food intake. Sometimes relatives of patients with dementia or stroke are prevented from assisting at mealtimes due to dangers of the patient choking, and this can be emotionally difficult for relatives who wish to help. Data from the mappmal study found that managing family expectations of mealtimes and food provision was a common issue raised by ward staff. The hospitalfoodie prototype helps facilitate communication around food between staff and relatives, and enables the relatives to become 'involved' with their relative's food provision by enabling them to enter into the system the food preferences of their family member and to see information on what foods have been consumed. Information on patients' food preferences is valuable to those providing food to the older person, especially when the patient is unable to communicate their food preferences themselves (for example, patients with dementia or following stroke). The hospitalfoodie system also enables staff to share information on the food intake of their relative, thus enabling them to be reassured about the nutritional care received.

The rationale for the mappmal project came from the recognition that adequate intake of food and nutrient intake while in hospital is fundamental to the healing process, yet approximately 40 per cent of those aged 65 and over become malnourished or their situation worsens while in hospital (MAG, 2003). Malnutrition delays recovery from illness, increases mortality and risk of complications, and has a negative impact on patient morale and quality of life. Inadequate nutritional status impairs immune function, which subsequently increases susceptibility to infections. Wound healing is impaired in malnutrition and this, coupled with muscle weakness, impairs mobility and increases the risk of pressure sores and delays return to full mobility.

Furthermore, malnutrition causes apathy and depression which impairs morale and will to recover. Becoming malnourished in hospital also increases the likelihood of discharge into long-term care, thereby reducing quality of later life and increasing healthcare costs.

The hospital eating environment for the older patient may threaten the patient's dignity, especially if a patient is unable to eat independently or if their condition means that they dribble or eat messily (Heaven et al, 2012). Therefore, in addition to optimising the physical environment as discussed above, ward staff also have an important role to play in preserving dignity at mealtimes – a factor that is easily overlooked on busy wards where technical duties take precedence.

Conclusion: future research and policy

When introducing this chapter it was noted that over the past decade we have seen a wealth of policy documents concerned with both the malnutrition of older people, particularly those living within institutional settings, but also issues for those who are overweight and obese living throughout the community. Organisations such as BAPEN, NICE, Age UK (Age UK, 2010) and CQC (CQC, 2012) have developed numerous initiatives including standards and indicators to help bring the issue to wider attention and prompt the development of action on the ground. At the national level proposals are being made, for example in Wales, as the Welsh Assembly has developed a nutritional strategy for older people (WAG and Food Standards Agency Wales, 2003), and there has been acknowledgement of the specific needs to recognise malnutrition in both community and care home settings (WAG, 2007, 2008). Yet throughout this period of policy development, change has been variable and BAPEN, in their document *Malnutrition matters*, says: 'The nutritional care that results must be focused on each individual and must be comprehensive and seamless across all care settings' (BAPEN Quality Group, 2010, p 6). This statement identifies the importance of people and place, and relates clearly to the results of NDA research.

The four research projects discussed here have identified a myriad of ways in which to address the food environment, working across a continuum from the individual themselves to the complexity of meeting needs within an institutional setting. In reflecting on the NANA study, the definition begins by seeing the food environment as the embodied self, which, by focusing on diet, brings together issues of nutrition, cognition, mood and physical activity for the individual, setting that individual in context. As we have seen, the purpose here is to develop nutritional assessment through providing a usable technology that captures this complexity. The way forward for the results of NANA has to be through incorporating additional or more appropriate assessments and further validation among culturally diverse older adults living in the UK.

Aspects of the complexity are looked at in greater detail within the MINA and TiKL projects which focus on cultural, material and social environments that influence food environments for people living domestic lives with family, friends or as a part of communal housing for older people. The older person is seen as someone of diversity, a person of ethnicity, generation, gender, socio-economic status and ability whose biography brings a unique approach to the ways in which they engage with the food environment, and through which they need to be considered should they find themselves in a care environment.

The concept of transitions is also central to an understanding of food environments. For the women in the MINA study, some will have migrated to the UK from Bangladesh, while other family members may have been born Asian British. The experience of West European and Asian cultures sit in parallel and affects the ways in which food is procured, prepared and eaten. The study highlights the importance of traditional foods which families may grow themselves and see as having therapeutic benefits. The results from the MINA project will be used to develop resources for health and social care practitioners to enhance cultural awareness and improve the quality of care delivered to Bangladeshi older adults, to develop culturally tailored nutrition resources for communities, to provide guidance on the availability and delivery of culturally tailored social care and healthcare services, to recognise the need to design living environments that are acceptable and appropriate for older adult migrants, and to inform policies that can be implemented to reduce exiting health inequalities and promote health and active ageing among Bangladeshi families. This example from the Bangladeshi community in Cardiff addresses the needs of the most socially deprived group for whom both malnutrition and obesity are part of their everyday lives. It is a model for testing with other minority ethnic groups and for learning from. Changes in family structures and living arrangements noted in the research should lead to new food environments such as day centres that target specific cultural needs.

While the social environment has been central to MINA, the TiKL study has captured the physical/material food environment of the kitchen using personal biography to show how interaction can change over time, demonstrated not only in routines, mealtimes and meal types, but also through material environments that can be more disabling than enabling. The value of this research lies in understanding the variation of person–environment interaction for people across the last 30 years of their lives. During this time accommodation and care needs may change, and yet the kitchen can remain central to both mainstream and supportive housing. The TiKL results demonstrate that ageism in design needs to be challenged, for at present, where the environment no longer meets the person's needs, then continuity relies on coping skills alongside material adaptation. In 2008, the then Labour government published *Lifetime homes, lifetime neighbourhoods*, a national strategy for housing an ageing society, which stated:

> Inclusive design must become part of mainstream thought in designing every aspect of our environment. We need to ask fundamental questions about the design faults of our most familiar and important home products. Our brightest designers should be challenging the everyday: stairs, chairs, baths, beds, everything including the kitchen sink. (Department of Health, Department for Work and Pensions, 2008, p 93)

At present there is need to revisit these wishes. For the TiKL study, the importance of knowledge transfer and further verification across the diversity of stakeholders is central to recognising the complexity of the food environment in later life.

Finally, while each of these studies has developed particular expertise across an aspect of the food environment, the mappmal study seeks to encompass the food journey for those older people who are hospital patients. We have noted the outcry concerning malnutrition among older patients, and reiterate once more the findings of the CQC's report *Meeting nutritional needs*:

> Where we did find problems, key themes were that:
>
> • Patients were not given the help they needed to eat, meaning they struggled to eat or were physically unable to eat meals.
> • Patients were interrupted during meals and had to leave their food unfinished.
> • The needs of patients were not always assessed properly, which meant they didn't always get the care they needed – for example, specialist diets.

- Records of food and drink were not kept accurately, so progress was not monitored.
- Many patients were not able to clean their hands before meals. (CQC, 2012, p 7)

Yet malnutrition and help with eating and drinking are a continuing challenge to the delivery of person-centred care. At present, nobody is solely responsible for the provision of adequate nutrition intake for older people in hospitals, food intake is inadequately monitored, shortfalls go undetected and nobody is held accountable. What are needed are clear policy standards for the prevention of malnutrition in the UK while embedding clear pathways to detect and treat malnutrition in all social and health care settings. Ethnographic evidence from the mappmal study shows that the hospitalfoodie system offers potential practical solutions to delivering this essential level of care by introducing and auditing a chain of accountability, and by increased patient involvement in their food and nutritional care across all health and social care settings.

These pieces of research stand alone and yet are interrelated, each with the potential to learn from the other. The way forward has to be through the investment of resources to put such valuable research into policy and practice.

SIX

Participation and social connectivity

Penny Vera-Sanso, Armando Barrientos, Leela Damodaran, Kenneth Gilhooly, Anna Goulding, Catherine Hennessy, Robin Means, Michael Murray, Andrew Newman, Wendy Olphert, Jatinder Sandhu, Philip Tew, Janice L. Thompson, Christina Victor and Nigel Walford

Introduction

Extending participation and social connectivity is now widely accepted as central to adding life to years as well as healthy years to life, while participation in the life of the community is seen as critical to well-being (Sen, 1992, p 39), and capable of addressing older people's rights, extending inclusion, reducing exclusion, easing demand on national budgets and building social cohesion. The central conundrums of increasing participation and social connectivity are, first, the intermeshing of personal, local, meso and macro level factors in shaping participation and social connectivity, and second, how the drive towards increased participation can be included in framing policy in such a way that participation is individually meaningful, social connectivity is enhanced and benefits flow to participants and to society in general. Underlying the application of the concepts of participation and social connectivity to older people is the idea that old age places people outside the mainstream: that older people's participation and social connectivity is wanting in scale or scope, that they do want or should want to participate more and that it is chiefly the impediment of old age that constrains their participation. Categorised as outside the mainstream, older people become defined by their age rather than those other salient aspects of their social identity, class, sexuality, ethnicity, education, histories and personal outlook that policy makers and implementers find difficult to respond to in relation to older people. This chapter examines older people's experiences of participation and social connectivity across a range of geographical and social locations within the UK and within low and middle-income countries, in order to test conceptualisations of older people's participation and social connectivity against experience, and to begin to trace the individual, local, meso and macro factors and linkages that need to be addressed to extend meaningful participation and engagement for *people* who happen to be older.

The World Health Organization's (2002) concept of active ageing as a process of optimising opportunities for health, participation and security in order to enhance people's quality of life as they age is now widely accepted (EuroHealthNet, 2012), in part because it provides an umbrella for a wide number of perspectives and objectives, ranging from neoliberal and austerity perspectives, demanding contraction of state services and expansion of individual responsibility, to grass-roots organisations focusing on older people's rights (Walker, 2009). Research on the positive impact of participation on mortality (Bennett, 2002; Menec, 2002), cognition (Fratiglioni et al, 2004), mental health (Greaves and Farbus, 2006) and well-being (Morrow-Howell et al, 2003) has provided common source material for both promoting older people's participation in order to reduce demands on the state and increasing well-being, extending inclusion and reducing exclusion within and between generations.

Historically, the demand for increased participation came from those outside the circle of economic and political power; in the second half of the 20th century it also became a tool of governance, a means of controlling participation and containing dissent. In the field of international development, where participation and social connectivity ('social capital') came to be seen as a key means of alleviating poverty and powerlessness for the majority poor, participation became a standardised demand of power holders as well as those fighting for social and economic justice. Research has shown that participation can become a tyranny in itself (Cooke and Kothari, 2001): that there is a wide difference between increased time spent participating and effective access, that there can be significant opportunity costs to community participation and, of more concern, that increased participation may not only structurally reproduce exclusion but also deepen inequalities (Cleaver, 2005). In high-income countries participation is often presented as local democracy and choice; and while it can give greater local control to resources generated at or supplied to the local level, it can also reinforce local-level inequalities and fail to challenge regional disparities. Participation can no longer be seen as an unequivocal good, and calls for participation need to be unpacked. Participate on what terms, and with what effect? Which forms of participation and social connectivity are promoted, which are ignored or underplayed, and by whom? These questions are as critical to extending older people's well-being through participation and social connectivity as they are for younger generations.

Access and participation

Access is the most fundamental requirement of participation and social connectivity, yet access alone is not sufficient to ensure either greater inclusion or reduced exclusion. To increase inclusion participation must be experienced in the short and long term as meaningful, spurring further and deeper participation. The measure of meaningful participation is persistent participation. Insufficient or incomplete access and superficial participation will deepen inequality by allowing the better-off in health, wealth and social connectivity terms to find avenues for bridging the access and participation gap in ways that others are not able to do.

Spatial access

Active ageing includes participation in social, economic, cultural, spiritual and civic affairs as well as physical activity and participation in the labour force (WHO, 2002), and central to all these is the capacity to access both well-known and unfamiliar places. Changes in people's use of different spaces as they grow older come from alterations in their personal circumstances and physical or mental well-being, and from adjustments to the environments that they encounter. The interplay of these factors can mean that people who were formerly 'spatially gregarious' may be deterred from visiting unfamiliar places, and previously familiar places can take on an unfamiliar nuance. The 'Older People's Use of Unfamiliar Space' (OPUS) project examined people's use of different spaces as they grow older, finding that it was not just alterations in personal circumstances and physical and mental well-being that determined older people's experience of way-finding in familiar and newly unfamiliar spaces. Rather, adjustments to the environments that older people encountered also constrained their spatial access by making previously familiar places take on an unfamiliar nuance and by deterring people from visiting unfamiliar places.

The OPUS study focused on older people's navigation and way-finding in unfamiliar places: it combined a quantitative assessment of the physical, built environment by adapting existing street audit tools (Cunningham et al, 2005; Ewing et al, 2006) with participants' qualitative appraisal of places never previously visited. Fifty older people from Swansea in South Wales were given the opportunity to 'visit' an unfamiliar place by viewing a predetermined filmed walking route in Colchester, in the north-east of Essex. The route included residential and shopping streets, and led the 'virtual visitor' on a visual and auditory experience, incorporating panoramas at selected locations (Walford, et al, 2011). A group of older people were also escorted on a visit to Colchester, providing them with the opportunity to walk the filmed route, to meet local older residents and to discuss their feelings about the town with planners and urban designers (Phillips et al, 2012).

The findings offer some important insights into the strategies adopted by older people when faced with unfamiliar environments. Over-reliance on transferring experience and norms from a familiar environment to an unfamiliar one proved to be an unhelpful guide to navigating new places. Familiar 'high street' brands such as shops with a national profile may provide reassurance in unfamiliar places, but can also be too commonplace, detracting from their usefulness as navigational landmarks. Distinctive, unusual structures, such as churches, castles and historic buildings, can help older people to find their way around an unfamiliar place, but disorientation can arise if changing sightlines mean these disappear from view. Study participants who experienced difficulty in following directions were more inclined to walk or use public transport as opposed to venturing into unfamiliar areas by means of private transport.

Undoubtedly, while visiting adjusted environments and unfamiliar places contributes to active ageing by being both a rewarding and stimulating experience and a basic requirement for participating in social, civic and economic life, a focus on inclusive design that creates accessible and navigable environments for everyone will be as beneficial to older people as to people of all ages and abilities – as was amply demonstrated during the London Olympics in 2012. Critical to using public space is understanding the cultural context in which shared spaces are used, and the exclusionary effect of lack of familiarity with custom and practice in unfamiliar places, including places that have become unfamiliar, may be as important in deterring access as not having previously visited the location. Signage can aid navigation and make the experience less disconcerting. Yet, while an indication of distance or time to the featured destinations can ease uncertainty, too much information may contribute to sensory overload and confusion. As built environments undergo regeneration and renewal, it is essential to make the outdoor, public environment convenient and usable by older people (and others) in ways that go beyond the current limited requirement to address the issue of physical ingress and egress to buildings. Spatial access is central to increasing participation and social connectivity, but measures that are task-and-effort focused, rather than experience-and-expectation focused, will not fully grasp why older people (and others) choose or feel forced to restrict mobility. People-unfriendly environments reinforce inequalities based on age, cognition, ability and class.[1]

Digital access

As social, civic, cultural and economic transactions and information and knowledge exchange become increasingly located in digital space, older people's digital access becomes critical to their participation and social connectivity. While older people (aged 50+) are still among the minority in terms of computer usage, the number of new 'silver surfers' is increasing at a steady rate – and the growth rate is indeed fastest among the over-75s (ONS, 2010). To date there has been little research to understand the nature of older people's computer usage and the challenges that they may face in remaining digitally connected as they age. The 'Sustaining IT use by older people to promote autonomy and independence' (SUS-IT) research project aimed to fill this gap, collecting data through a questionnaire-based survey of more than 750 older people across the UK, supported by a number of in-depth interviews and case studies. The project explodes the popular myth that older people typically shy away from use of new technologies. The survey explored the extent of older people's digital engagement, and found that the majority of older people were using a wide range of digital technologies on a regular basis. Almost 80 per cent used a mobile phone daily or several times a week, and almost 70 per cent used a computer daily or several times a week. Digital technologies are integral to the daily lives of many older people, the centrality of which was epitomised by one respondent's statement that "The computer is one of the 5 'C's in my life – the others being children, church, car and cat." Respondents graphically summarised the significance of 'digital connection' to participation and social connectivity when answering the open question, 'How would you feel if you had to stop using the computer?': "devastated", "alone", "isolated", "powerless" and as having "lost independence".

The study also challenges the myth that older adults are reluctant to learn new things. Findings show that while some only learn the basics associated with using digital technologies for a narrow range of tasks relevant to their everyday lives, others will go on to master the use of digital technology and to find new and creative ways of applying it. While the 'oldest old' in this sample (80- to 89-year-olds) tended to use their computers for fewer tasks, around 50 per cent of the 60- to 80-year-olds used their computers for a wide diversity of tasks. Some have developed in-depth expertise using particular software relevant to their pursuit of hobbies and interests, such as photography. Further, a third of respondents were keen to extend their current use of digital technologies. The desire for personal development, to keep up with the times or to acquire a new skill were by far the most frequent reasons cited for using digital technology. As one respondent put it, "I feel that if I cannot use modern communication technology it would be similar to being unable to read." Keeping in touch with friends and family via email/Skype is also a popular activity – especially when faced with reduced mobility or geographical separation – and was often cited as a reason to get online.

Social connectivity is not only a positive outcome of digital connectivity; it is a key factor in both becoming and staying connected. Social inclusion and digital inclusion are widely recognised to be closely related (Selwyn, 2002). Older people's awareness of this inter-relationship, from the perspective of personal experience, explains their exceptional tenacity to remain digitally connected – often persisting in the face of obstacles posed by changes in physical ability, memory, support and/or technology problems/changes. For more than a quarter of respondents, human help and encouragement was the most important factor that enabled them to use technology successfully and to sustain their usage. Participants emphasised the importance of accessing face-to-face support for digital connectivity – expressed as "being around people who you can talk to and who can help you". There appears to be a strong consensus among many older users that they prefer their learning and use of ICT to be a social process in which knowledge and experience are shared, relationships nurtured, communication enjoyed – often inter-generationally – hobbies and interests pursued, and problems of many different kinds can be resolved. Yet current provision of both learning and support opportunities for older people in the UK is patchy, and only partially meets these expressed needs.

In addition to busting myths regarding older people's wish or capacity to keep up with the changing social and technical environment, this study demonstrates the centrality of social connectivity to secure digital connectivity – social connectivity is not just the outcome but the means. The interconnection between spatial and digital access, the ability to go somewhere for face-to-face support and the costs in doing so means that under current arrangements spatial and digital access are likely to deepen inequalities among older people while easing inter-generational inequalities for some.

Institutional access

The capacity of people to move institutions with a duty of care to protect them and the capacity of institutions to identify when they should act reflects gaps in connectivity at a range of social and institutional levels. This is particularly apparent with the general rise in financial abuse, and the financial abuse of older people is a growing concern due to the substantial and increasing numbers of frail and cognitively impaired older people living in the community (Kemp and Mosqueda, 2005). Financial abuse can take many forms, from that perpetrated by family, carers, 'befrienders' and rogue tradesmen to that of postal, telephonic and digital scammers. It is through the vulnerable older person's connection with health, social care and banking professionals or through connections with family, friends and neighbours that financial abuse is often detected and acted on. Applying a 'bystander intervention model' (Gilhooly et al, 2013) to the study of decision making by professionals in detecting and preventing elder financial abuse is complex. Complexity arising from the presence or involvement of other people in the care of the older person and from organisational constraints, including policy and procedural rules, plays a part in determining what interventions may be possible or likely to occur. The 'Decision making in detecting and preventing financial abuse of older adults' study identified five decision-making stages:

1. The professional must notice or be told by another party that something unusual is happening.
2. The situation has to be interpreted as suspicious.
3. The decision maker must decide what kind of intervention can be provided.
4. The decision maker has to decide what they can or should do.
5. The decision maker has to consider the rewards and costs of intervening.

Interviews with professionals in health, social work and banking as well as an experimental study of decision making found that all three professional groups showed a high level of consistency in their decision making. This indicates that the individual professionals had stable strategies for dealing with cases which would yield similar decisions for similar cases. Of the many cues that could be used in deciding whether financial abuse is taking place, only a few seemed to influence the decisions and the actions taken (Davies et al, 2011). The cues that exerted the greatest influence were the mental capacity of the older person, the nature of the financial problem and, in the case of those in banking, who was in charge of the money.

The study addressed the connectivity of vulnerable older people to the agencies entrusted with protecting them from financial abuse. The agencies are often dependent on other parties such as relatives, friends and neighbours, as sources of information about possible abuse. However, for an abuse case becoming known to an agency, 'bystander intervention' issues arise. Should a neighbour report tradesmen harassing the older person? Or decide it's not their business? If the neighbour decides he or she should report the matter, to whom should they report? If the neighbour reports to a GP, then the GP has to decide whether to report to the police or to social services. If a neighbour contacts social services directly, should the professional receiving the report decide that a single report is enough to take action, or should further reports be awaited? Thus, victims are dependent on the decisions of individuals in a complex network that connects them to those who can take effective action. A sequential form of 'bystander intervention' is occurring throughout the network in which potential informers may or may not contact appropriate agencies, that may or may not then take action. The cumulative effect of such a sequential process, that can lead to 'no action' at each choice point, is the 'iceberg' phenomenon, where for every case investigated and substantiated, there are many more cases not investigated (NCEA, 1998).

This study not only highlights the lack of connectivity between institutions with a duty of care and older people, but also points to the need for wide social connectivity and a range of access (spatial, digital, institutional) for older people in order that they or others can identify financial abuse. As services move from neighbourhoods to the high street and on to the digital high street, the importance of widening social connectivity and participation increases, and inequalities in being able to do so widens.

Access to social and political organisations

Older people's access to social and political organisations is critical to their ability to participate in the 'life of the community'. It both shapes and reflects their capacity to maintain, diversify or expand their participation and social connectivity in line with their circumstances. While the common assumption is that participation in social and political organisations or associations will decline with age, cross-national research provides a more nuanced picture which does not uphold a presumption of an inevitable decline.

The 'Ageing, Well-being and Development' project studied a sample of older people and their households in poor areas in Brazil and South Africa with the aim of assessing the impact of individual ageing on well-being. The research studied older people within their households, taking care to include intra-household relations and decision making. To this end, the study asked questions of the most knowledgeable person in the household and of every person in the household aged 60 and over, in 2002 and 2008. Social and political participation and connectivity were included as significant dimensions of well-being, and the cross-country comparative approach was helpful in isolating the influence of institutions and culture.

The older person survey asked whether respondents participated in a range of social and community organisations. Some were common to the two countries, such as social clubs, community organisations, church groups, school and sports organisations, trade unions and political organisations. In South Africa, two additional organisations were included due to their importance in the life of poor households: stockvels (saving clubs for the purpose of covering burial costs) and burial societies. Older South Africans in poor households, particularly black households, feel a strong need to make provision for their burial.

The study found that there was a significant difference in participation in social and political organisations by older people in the two countries. Taking all forms of participation and connectivity as a whole, levels of participation were much higher in South Africa, by an order of magnitude. In Brazil (n=1,193), by far the largest form of participation was membership of a church group. Around one in three people aged 60 and over reported membership of a church group, but participation in other organisations was marginal. Around 2 per cent of older people reported participating in a social club (women's or men's clubs), and this was the next highest participation level reported. In South Africa (n=514), just over one-third reported participating in a church group, but 27 per cent reported participating in a community organisation, and 10 per cent in a social club. Strikingly, two-thirds of older people in the South Africa sample reported participation in a burial society or stokvel, and one in four reported participation in a political organisation. It is, in fact, the latter form of participation that accounts for the difference in participation and connectivity between poorer South African and Brazilian older people. The study found that higher levels of participation and connectivity are an important factor, explaining higher levels of satisfaction with their family and community relationships among older people in South Africa compared to Brazilian older people (Lloyd-Sherlock et al, 2012). The share of older people reporting no participation in political and social organisations is of particular concern – around three in five in Brazil and around one in five in South Africa. While there are many factors explaining the absence of participation and connectivity, health and economic barriers are significant. The concern is that to the extent that older people are disconnected from their communities and their polities, their voice is unlikely to be heard, and social and political exclusion might have adverse implications for their well-being. The longitudinal nature of the study posed the question as to whether participation and connectivity declines with individual ageing. Despite a six-year gap between visits to panel respondents (2002 and 2008), only marginal changes in participation over time were found. In Brazil, the proportion of the sample reporting no form of participation declined by around 5 percentage points in 2008, while in South Africa there was no change over time. This would suggest that, for the group of older people taken as a whole, social participation and connectivity might not necessarily decline with age, and it is necessary to look elsewhere for explanations of low participation and connectivity.

As with the discussions of spatial, digital and institutional access, it is clear that some are better positioned than others to belong to social and political organisations, and those that are can sustain participation into old age. However, the Brazil/South Africa comparison, both of which are classified as upper middle-income countries by the World Bank, demonstrates that it is not necessarily comparative wealth at a national level or absolute poverty at an individual level that determines social and political access, although it may determine differentials *within* countries. The fact that, despite greater levels of persistent poverty (Barrientos and Mase, 2012), the South African panel's participation was greater than the Brazilian panel, and remained greater over a six-year period, is reflected in the fact that their levels of satisfaction with family and community relationships were comparatively greater. This suggests that South Africa is organised to be more socially and politically inclusive of older people than is Brazil.

Having seen that older people are not intrinsically less able or less willing to participate in a range of activities, this chapter turns to uncovering the arenas in which older people actively participate, and in doing so, challenges negative stereotypes.

Challenging negative stereotypes of older people

The stereotype of declining participation in old age derives from the assumption that the arena of work and work-associated participation in unions and associations are the main or most important forms of participation and social connectivity. This reflects a productionist, male-breadwinner bias that promotes a discourse of old age and retirement as a physiologically rooted, individual experience rather than a socially structured condition and a socially constructed experience. The idea of retirement is a construction of the late 19th and early 20th centuries, arising from the needs and impacts of industrialisation (Walker, 1980). It arose in the context of industrial competition, worker mobilisation, a declining need for labour due to automation and, in the United States, in-migration and the combination of the ascendency of 'scientific management' of the labour process and the 'wear-and-tear' theory of biological ageing that posits that people have a fixed capacity to work (Atchley, 1982, pp 269-70). People in mid and later life were being forced out of their workplace to face a labour market marked by age discrimination and rigid working conditions (hours, tasks, processes and so on). Yet throughout history, across the globe most people have undertaken paid and unpaid work as well as unmonetarised socially necessary activities into deep old age. This remains the case today.

Rural community capital

While rural older people are known to experience a variety of barriers to social inclusion such as isolation, poor public transport and problems with access to needed services, far less is understood about the positive aspects of rural ageing and the role of older people in rural community life. In particular, although older people's contributions to rural civic society are recognised as a significant source of community cohesion in many rural areas (Le Mesurier, 2003), the nature, context and extent of their civic engagement has been under-researched. Guided by a perspective on older people as rural community capital, the 'Grey and Pleasant Land' project ('An interdisciplinary exploration of the connectivity of older people in rural civic society') investigated older people's connections in rural communities and the ways in which these links affect their participation in civic life. A community survey of 900 people aged 60 and over in six differentiated rural locations in South West England and Wales examined the circumstances and experiences of older people's connectivity to community life. Participants were asked about their involvement in activities such as volunteering, and membership in community or other groups, as well as factors underlying the type and levels of their participation. Qualitative research was also used to explore experiences of community connectivity among diverse groups of older rural residents.

Community participation was highest for informal activities to assist others and for formal voluntary work. Those who were more likely to be involved in civic activities included married people, the 'young old' and those with better self-rated health, higher former occupational status or educational qualifications. Individuals' financial status, their length of residence in their rural community and levels of friendship, did not, however, affect their civic engagement. What was defined as older people's leisure functioned as a significant means of creating social capital (networks of social ties, reciprocity and trust), or social glue, within communities through activities such as volunteering for charities or other groups, serving on parish councils or other organisational boards, and helping with fundraising. For some, while involvement in civic groups was on a smaller scale, they experienced satisfaction in being able to make some contribution such as collecting items for jumble sales to benefit local senior citizens' clubs.

The principal barriers to community participation reported by rural elders included limitations in health, lack of time, lack of access to transport and, significantly, lack of interest. In relation to mobility within their communities, few respondents reported feeling excluded due to this reason, and more reported difficulties in accessing specific necessary and discretionary activities, including specialist hospitals and cinemas (Shergold and Parkhurst, 2012). Car availability was not a strong predictor of overall inclusion, although non-availability could limit access to particular types of location. The relatively short travel distances required to access community activities was a key factor in the high levels of community inclusion; however, because of dependence on car travel there is a rising risk of mobility-related exclusion among older people in rural areas, particularly among the 'old old'.

Specific subgroups of older rural residents reported a varied experience of connection to community. In qualitative interviews with respondents in low-income households, a strong sense of community inclusion with reference to neighbourliness and informal social support systems was expressed in parallel with reports of conditions of financial hardship (Milbourne and Doheny, 2012). Members of minority groups, however, including gay and lesbian older people and gypsy travellers, could and did experience forms of disconnectivity and exclusion from mainstream community activities.

This work challenges dominant problem-based views of rural ageing populations through highlighting the contributions and experience of older people in rural areas as a source of community capital. It emphasises the need to step away from perceptions of what older people are capable of, and instead to identify, support and extend what they wish to do. At the same time, it emphasises the need to raise awareness of the continuing barriers to older people's connections to community for maximising participation and well-being in later life.

Economic contributors

Older people's economic contribution draws negligible attention, although what evidence there is suggests that older people's engagement in work may be increasing in countries with large informal sectors and negligible pension provision (Alam and Barrientos, 2010). In India, the dominant discourse on old age posits a norm of old age withdrawal from social connectivity and participation and dependence on the family (Lamb, 2000). However, the 'Ageing, poverty and neoliberalism in urban South India' project found that in the context of insecure incomes, significant material and social deprivation and limited state support, families living on low incomes cannot afford for their elderly to withdraw from economic and family life (Vera-Sanso, 2012). A survey of 800 households living in five low-income settlements of Chennai, India's fourth largest city, in-depth qualitative research with 179 households and 30 months' observation of one street market between 2007and 2010 demonstrate that older people remain active in economic and family life. The mismatch of the norm of family support and low-income families' capacity to provide such generates deeply ambiguous feelings. Feeling at times rejected, isolated or let down, older people also understand the difficulties their adult children face and, not wanting to become a burden themselves, strive to mitigate these difficulties in the interests of the family as a whole. They do so by earning an income, 'helping out' in a family business or by taking on the caring and domestic work of younger female relatives in order that they can enter the workforce. To continue working as long as they can, older people tailor their paid work to their capacities and needs by moderating working hours and intensity.

While policy makers and others consider older people's participation in paid work as a marker of filial indifference and neglect, and unpaid family domestic work as not such, the older urban poor do not necessarily see it this way. In a context where people live in congested conditions, without piped water and drains for sewage or storm water (and are hence regularly flooded with contaminated water and have difficulty accessing basic domestic inputs), domestic work is both onerous and arduous. As one elderly woman who walks from office to office in temperatures of up to 40 degrees centigrade to clean office telephones and computers succinctly put it, "Whether I'm at home or not I have to work, and I prefer this to working at home." In a context of low-quality housing, negligible comforts and high levels of school participation, homes are lonely and uncomfortable sites of strenuous work, alternating with periods of boredom and hunger that older people escape by sleeping until children return from school and adults from work. In this context social connectivity is extended by economic participation. Vending in street markets, working alongside a daughter or daughter-in-law in a family business, or waiting with known cycle rickshaw pullers or construction workers for piece-rate work is as much about social connectivity and meaningful activity as it is about economic participation.

While economic participation is experienced as providing more opportunity for social connectivity than unpaid domestic work or no work, the pay-off in terms of social recognition is constrained by ageism. Older people's labour is considered by others, and sometimes by themselves, as having little or no economic value. Working in a family business is described by family members as merely "helping out" or "passing time", even if the older person, usually a woman, is the only one working in the business. Men also experience age discrimination which locks them out of work or prevents them earning equal incomes (Harriss-White et al, 2013). Skilled construction workers, who are the most skilled in low-income settlements, rile against perceptions of age, skill and strength that misrepresents their capacities and reduces their incomes, forcing them into small, piece-rate repair work rather than being hired for their skill and experience to do design work, train and oversee younger workers.

This study has revealed that dominant ideas of what is best for older people, a withdrawal from economic life and dependence on family support, is neither feasible nor desirable in a context of significant poverty and poorly resourced homes without basic services. Instead, social connectivity, participation in meaningful activity and a sense of self-worth is often facilitated by working outside the home. Yet the lack of recognition for older people's economic contribution and the lack of a pension sufficient to enable them to say no to the most onerous and demeaning work available to them constrains the benefits they draw from working.

Both these studies on older people as rural community capital and economic contributors demonstrate the erroneousness of the view that older people cannot and do not make important contributions to society and the economy through their paid, unpaid and voluntary activities. In addition to highlighting the value of older people's participation to their own well-being and that of others, they also demonstrate that the benefits that older people can potentially draw from participation are undercut by ageism and by a series of barriers, which, although they may be experienced as individual barriers, are instead socially structured.

Structural factors

The chapter has demonstrated that older people *do* participate and are tenacious in their participation, but that a range of accesses are closed to many older people, creating inequalities in the scope, extent and benefits of participation. Taking an experiential focus on structural inequalities uncovers nuances in older people's positioning that research and policy needs to take on board in order to increase their participation and social connectivity.

Cross-generational ramifications of economic participation

The MINA project (described in detail in Chapter Five, this volume), examined the impact of migration, nutrition and ageing among two generations of Bangladeshi women (older women, aged 40–70) and their adult daughters (aged 17–36) in Cardiff, UK, and Sylhet, Bangladesh. Approximately 63 per cent of older women living in the UK were married, with the remainder widowed, with 50 per cent living in a 'nuclear' structured household including themselves, their husband and children. Among the UK daughters, 35 per cent were single, 60 per cent were married, and two women (5 per cent) were divorced, with 61 per cent of married daughters living in 'nuclear' structured households, illustrating that not all participants live in large, multi-generational households.

There were distinct differences in levels of social participation and connectivity between the generations and transnationally. Despite just one older participant reporting living alone, many of the older Cardiff participants reported feelings of isolation and loneliness, which is consistent with previously published research examining the lives of older Bangladeshis living in Tower Hamlets (Gardner, 2002). Lack of fluency in English, limited social activities and community spaces that are viewed as culturally acceptable, and concerns regarding physical safety, vulnerability and racism, severely limit older women's social connectivity and engagement with wider society. Older women expressed not only discomfort related to the cold weather, but that actually fearing the cold is a barrier to leaving their homes to socially engage. These issues were highlighted as major concerns by the women themselves, and were shared and reinforced by family members.

The cultural norm to honour one's elders by encouraging very little physical movement was described by older women and adult daughters. The older women in Cardiff compared the differences between living in the UK and Bangladesh. In Bangladesh there is a great deal of social interaction in homes between family, neighbours and friends; older adults described daily visits with people coming in and out of their home throughout the day. This degree of social interaction does not occur in the UK. Interestingly, a significantly higher proportion (33 per cent) of UK mothers reported their perceived health as poor or very poor, compared to 23 per cent of older mothers living in Bangladesh. Older women in Cardiff expressed the view that their lives would be of higher quality in relation to social participation and feeling connected if they were living in Bangladesh as an older person, but most stated they would stay in the UK throughout the remainder of their lives because of existing family connections.

Daughters, by contrast, provide a strikingly different picture. For the daughters living in the UK, particularly those who are bi-lingual, most have benefited from gaining their education in the UK and engage fully in paid or voluntary work, further education, doing much of the shopping, and taking their children to school and other activities. During qualitative interviews, the adult daughters living in the UK expressed a higher satisfaction with their quality of life than their counterparts living in Bangladesh, and both groups described the benefits of education toward enhancing social mobility, connectivity and life opportunities. Smith, Kelly and Nazroo (2009) confirm a significant increase in educational attainment between first- and second-generation Bangladeshis in the UK, and this is associated with increased socio-economic status and improved self-reported general health. Although these findings are positive for the adult daughters living in the UK, their enhanced social connectivity and participation may result in increased isolation for older women, as men are also fully engaged in work, social, and religious activities outside of the home.

This project amply demonstrates the need to study older people's lives in the context of wider social changes. In this example the social change is initiated by migration, but what is most enlightening is that the greater participation of some, here younger women, can lead to the greater isolation of others. This study has also busted the myth that older Bangladeshi women self-exclude from participation outside the home; instead, they enthusiastically engaged in the project's data collection events including the associated social and physical activities provided, suggesting that rather than an unwillingness to participate, these women lacked sufficiently meaningful opportunities to encourage them to do so.[2]

Social class and cultural capital

The benefits of engagement with culture have been shown by a number of studies. For example, Bygren et al (2009) demonstrated, through a large-scale quantitative study in Sweden, that people attending cultural events live longer than those who rarely attend, and Greaves and Farbus (2006) and Cohen et al (2006) were able to show the positive effects of creativity and social engagement on the health and well-being of older people. However, while this can be demonstrated, barriers to engagement are significant for those without the cultural capital and subsequent habitus (Bourdieu, 1984), making decoding contemporary visual art problematic. For others, their cultural tastes shaped their personal networks (Lizardo, 2006). How social participation and connectivity influence engagement with art, both in terms of overcoming barriers and decoding the art on display, is discussed below using the results from the 'Contemporary visual art and identity construction – well-being among older people' project.

As described in more detail in Chapter Four, the project recruited six groups of older people from a variety of backgrounds, including people who had a history of visiting art galleries and people who did not. They were taken to galleries, based in North East England, UK, three times, over 28 months (May 2009–October 2011). Differences in responses could be identified between broad groupings of working-class participants aged 68–91 and middle-class participants aged 61–65. The variable of class is defined by Silva (2008, p 268) as 'the positions in a hierarchical social order occupied by individuals in social space, according to which aesthetic engagements will vary'. Many of the working-class participants would not have attended the venues without the opportunity presented by the research project, and those who had attended before did not have meaningful experiences. For example, a 68-year-old whose occupation was classified as semi-routine (National Statistics Socio-economic Classification[3]) stated during her visit to the BALTIC Centre for Contemporary Art as part of the research project:

> "I've been before. I came down when it was first opened but I'll be very honest with you, I didn't really get much further than the first floor. I was a little bit lost then but I found it a lot easier now."

By contrast, the middle-class participants generally had greater educational attainment and responded very differently compared to those who were working class. For them, discussing the work was important, enabling them to challenge each other's perceptions, and to use their collective resources to decode the artwork. For example, a 63-year-old male participant's response to the group's discussion was:

> "If we'd been to see Rembrandts today or Constables or Turners we wouldn't be banging on about what material they were made out of. We would be talking about how good the paintings were, which is the main difference between what I would call classical good art and modern artists. [Modern art's] ideas either work for you or they don't – it's not [about] a skill in great painting."

Within the visiting groups, of whatever class and age, habitus became coordinated through social dynamics, which resulted in differences in opinion becoming fewer as the visits progressed. For the younger/middle-class participants, cultural tastes both influenced and generated social networks as they recognised and attempted to improve their position within the field of contemporary visual art. This was not observed in the responses of the older/working-class participants, although there was evidence that when accompanied by friends, older/working-class people attending the BALTIC Centre as part of the research were more enabled to engage with modern art in a way that would otherwise have been very difficult.

While engagement with expressive arts is recognised as important to health and social engagement, and is reflected in preferential pricing for senior citizens, it is clear that a large proportion of older people are excluded from this arena of social and creative engagement – in part, for want of the out-reach strategies, that are well-established in relation to children in recognition of the centrality of social interaction in developing and sustaining engagement with art.

Ethnicity and social connectivity

Within the broad demographic trend of population ageing, the communities who moved to Britain in the decades from the 1950s–1980s from the Caribbean and South Asia (notably India, Pakistan and Bangladesh) are also beginning to age. In 2007 it was estimated that 17.5 per cent of the 'white' population were aged 65+ compared with 4 per cent for the Chinese, Pakistani and Bangladeshi populations, 7 per cent for the Indian population and 13 per cent for the Caribbean group (Livesley, 2011). Future decades will see substantial absolute and relative increases in the size of these groups.

The ageing of the UK's minority communities is an important but relatively neglected issue in terms of research, policy and practice. Despite pioneering efforts (Blakemore, 1982; Boneham, 1989), the ageing experience of older black and ethnic minority adults is a relatively new field of research within the UK (Koehn et al, 2013). This research has focused on specific issues among individual minority populations, often within particular locations and often with a 'problem-focused orientation', for example, social support systems of older South Asians in the West Midlands (Burholt, 2004), social exclusion of older Bangladeshis in East London (Phillipson et al, 2003) and family care among elderly Chinese in London (Chiu and Yu, 2001). The 'Families and caring in South Asian communities' project sought to take a broader perspective on the daily lives and experiences of people growing older from Pakistani and Bangladeshi communities. Using a mixed-methods approach, the project was able to compare participants' perceptions of relations and places with its substantive findings relating to daily life (see Victor et al, 2012). This gave the project a strong methodological component focusing on some of the specific challenges in working with minority populations (see Zubair et al, 2012a, 2012b).

In an attempt to understand networks from the participant's viewpoint, the project invited them to draw social network maps to support the details gathered on their social relationships. The initial intention was to invite participants to complete the formalised concentric circle map employed by Pahl and Spencer (2004), with the individual at the centre and relationships decreasing in strength from them. This was abandoned at the pilot stage as participants found this difficult to conceptualise, and an 'open-ended' approach was used. Participants were invited to map out, on a blank sheet of paper, those relationships, both to people and places, that were most important to them. This exercise generated 109 'maps' from the study participants, of which 42 were in the 'classic' spidergram form and 67 were textual (with and without hierarchies of attachment). Examples of these differing formats are illustrated by Figures 6.1 and 6.2. Undertaking this exercise generated a number of challenges. First, for many participants, the interviewer had to act as the scribe for individuals who were not literate. Second, where individuals were literate, many maps had to be translated into English for analysis by the team. Third, when participants did rank relationships in order, it was not always clear that there was an intended hierarchy of relationships. Given the challenges, what did we learn from this exercise? It very clearly demonstrated the primacy of the family in our

Figure 6.1: A 'traditional' style network map with the participant at the centre

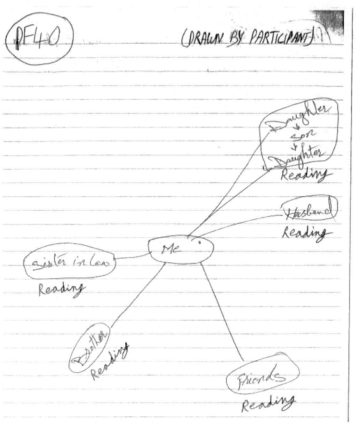

Figure 6.2: A textual network list

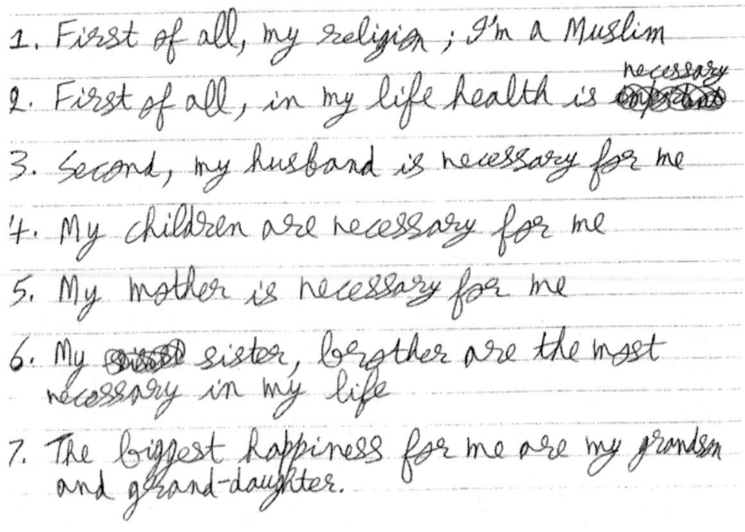

1. First of all, my religion ; I'm a Muslim
2. First of all, in my life health is ~~important~~ necessary
3. Second, my husband is necessary for me
4. My children are necessary for me
5. My mother is necessary for me
6. My ~~sister~~ sister, brother are the most necessary in my life
7. The biggest happiness for me are my grandson and grand-daughter.

participant's social networks, with virtually no references to friends in these relationship networks. And the importance of deceased family members to individuals was evident but had never been articulated within the project interviews. Finally, participants' 'maps' emphasised the fundamental importance of religion to daily lives.

By allowing older people from Pakistani and Bangladeshi communities to express their perspectives on their most important relationships to people and places, this project was able to identify categories of relationships that held the greatest meaning for these older people – that of family and religion. In diasporic communities, the categories of family and religion carry local and national and international dimensions, and those spatial connections also link past, present and future across generations, including the deceased who continue to have an active presence in older people's perception of their relations to people and place.

These three projects, along with the study of older people's participation in rural Britain and the study of older people working in urban India, challenge negative stereotypes of older people by demonstrating how socio-economic and spatial positioning shape older people's participation and social connectivity. There are two common threads to these projects. First, that it is not age that determines participation and social connectivity, but social and economic structures that position people differently in relation to the economy, culture and society at local and wider levels. These structures have an impact on individuals, both older and younger, within the family, community and economy. Those without jobs, cars, the local language, particular cultural habitus(es) or experiences will find themselves excluded from, or less able to participate in, certain social, economic and cultural arenas and less able to derive the various benefits such participation can provide. What is specific to older people, however, is the way age becomes the reason for undervaluing older people's participation or for justifying reduced participation and social connectivity. The second thread is that older people are not interested in participation and connectivity *per se*; they are interested in *meaningful* participation, and the point to be noted here is that it is participation that *they* find meaningful. This brings us to the final section of this chapter – older people's response to attempts at increasing their participation.

Generating meaningful participation and social connectivity

Research, programmes and projects assessing or designed to expand older people's participation and social connectivity often take a top-down approach that is based on an 'othering' of older people – an othering derived from the distillation and application of expertise that positions older people as the objects of study and action. A bottom-up approach, by contrast, transfers direction into the hands of older people, repositioning older people as the authors, not objects, of knowledge. While top-down approaches now regularly include a consultation strategy, a participation approach requires that older people play an active part, having a significant degree of power and influence (Burns et al, 2004). Very few studies have asked older people what makes participation in organised activities meaningful for them. A study undertaken in the US found that a lack of 'meaty' or meaningful personal roles in group activities provided little more than escape from boredom and isolation (Ward, 1979). Eakman et al (2010) produced a tool for assessing the meaningfulness of daily activities by asking participants to identify the activities to be studied, and to self-rate their frequency and its meaningfulness. This study found that participation in activities deemed meaningful have more influence on psychosocial well-being and health-related quality of life than participation in a greater number of lesser-valued activities. Two New Dynamics of Ageing (NDA) projects took the bottom-up approach, one taking a locale-specific facilitator approach, and the other an activity-specific trigger approach.

Promoting social engagement among older residents of disadvantaged urban neighbourhoods

In response to the frequently reported decreased levels of older people's social engagement and higher levels of loneliness, particularly among older residents of disadvantaged neighbourhoods where there are fewer resources and facilities, the 'CALL-ME' study undertook the participatory development and evaluation of a series of community projects in disadvantaged areas of the large urban centre, Manchester, UK. A range of different community activities – including arts, gardening and physical activities – were developed together with groups of older residents in four different neighbourhoods. The groups raised funds from local authorities and in some cases developed inter-generational projects. Public events (for example, exhibitions, demonstrations) were organised as part of the projects to draw in other community residents and to promote broader awareness of the activities (Murray and Crummett, 2010; Middling et al, 2011).

As part of the project of developing community activities a survey of older participants was undertaken that revealed participants' low levels of social engagement outside of the project (Beech and Murray, 2013). Individual and group interviews confirmed that older people identified very closely with their immediate neighbourhoods. Many had lived in the same house for 30 or more years. They often stressed the positive features of their neighbourhood, and resented it being labelled as deprived. They emphasised the importance of neighbourliness: "They're all very good on our close ... if anybody's ill or they need anything they're there and I'm one of those people – I'll be there first." However, those who lived in apartment blocks felt cut-off from social interaction. As one older man said: "It's a different way of life. It can be isolating. It can be so that you don't have contact with other people."

Work outside the district had been an important source of social interaction, particularly for men. However, once they retired, their social circle became very reduced. In a discussion group, one man said: "Well, I used to work and obviously most of my activities were connected with that, and my leisure." There were limited social facilities in these neighbourhoods, and much of what there had been is now closed. The men often complained about the loss of the local pub: "The older you are the less opportunities you have to make friends, and in this neighbourhood, particularly, there are no pubs. [Pubs] were the hub of communities."

Even though the neighbourhoods had limited local facilities, participants were reluctant to take part in activities outside their immediate communities without the support of others. A common view was that such facilities and activities were not designed for them but for members of another community. As one woman said: "I know they have things going on in other centres further down but we don't belong to them – really, those things are for them that live there."

While older residents had extensive experience of participating in social activities with family and neighbours, they had, until then, little experience of taking responsibility for organising group activities. So, despite expressing enthusiasm about the opportunity provided by organised group activities, they were anxious about taking on any leadership responsibilities. One woman said: "I don't know if people would like to do it themselves, it depends. Some of the people wouldn't do it themselves. They like somebody there to show us." Further, taking on community responsibility could sometimes lead to conflict with neighbours, as one woman explained: "I've had a lot of grief about it all really, you know, tongues wagging. There was some that thought that I was getting paid. They couldn't get it into their heads, see, that people would do work voluntarily." So, while they were delighted that someone could take the lead in organising group activities, they were also emphatic that the group membership should be local. As one man said: "We want to stay our own group, we don't want it so that we get taken over", demonstrating a wish to remain in control.

Older residents of disadvantaged neighbourhoods are enthusiastic about the opportunity of participating in local group activities. However, although they are keen to be involved in the planning, they can be anxious about taking responsibility without support. While group projects can be established, there is a need to plan carefully how they can be sustained and resourced and, critically, older residents need to be centrally involved in the development and ongoing planning of community activities.

While the 'CALL-ME' survey suggested hesitance and apprehension about taking on leadership roles, this is likely to be temporary if there is a widespread policy acceptance of older people's capacity to direct projects designed by them to meet their self-identified needs. Top-down projects position older people as passive beneficiaries. Bottom-up projects can provide spaces for meaningful participation. They can create "a sense of individual and community achievement and bring back a bit of the old community spirit", as participants in the 'CALL-ME' projects described the experience and outcome of the projects.

Triggering cultural engagement and authorship

The 'Fiction and cultural mediation of ageing' (FCMAP) project undertook qualitative research exploring what response older people have when they engage with formal representations and narratives of ageing, as well as those encountered in their everyday lives. Analysis assessed whether and how participants regarded such representations in terms of their capacity to shape either their own self-image or other social attitudes towards ageing. One element of the project comprised 90 volunteers organised in eight volunteer reading groups in and around London in collaboration with the University of the Third Age (U3A). Participants were recruited to read and react to the selected British novels published after 1943 that focused variously on ageing.

Volunteer reading group participants submitted periodically for analysis mass observation-style diary entries (recorded anonymously in either electronic or written form) in response to fictional *and* social narratives. FCMAP created an open space for participants to offer often extended views related to: fictional content; their opinions of volunteer reading group discussions; and views of existing social and policy issues. While not directed towards any particular view or any particular format, participants added commentary as they wished on relevant events, aspects of culture and the ways older people are treated, as well as any images or concepts concerning ageing they found relevant. The structure of combining reading, diary entry and volunteer reading group participation solicited such responses. The participants were not only given voice, but their diaries allowed the FCMAP team to chart both patterns and noteworthy personal narratives, which, when taken together, offered clusters of experiential knowledge. A plethora of insights included the following: most feared residential care; older women felt marginalised in terms of visibility, especially sexual; none actively feared crime; and Alzheimer's troubled nearly all of them. Their responses were often radically different from stereotypical views held by others about ageing subjects and their conceptual parameters of life. The diaries were replete with insights into normal and everyday life, relevant to not only social policy issues, but also ways of challenging attitudinal norms. This included a potential inter-generational impasse, recorded as: 'it is difficult for the old to really understand what is going on in the culture of the young – and vice versa.' Furthermore, the diaries also offered powerful insights into social attitudes, which many felt as equally important in framing the condition of their lives as are governmental manoeuvres, amply represented by one journal entry:

> Does age render one anonymous or invisible? I don't find that to be the case. I find the problem to be more often a patronising attitude that might be called the "poor old dears" syndrome. This leads to an unwillingness to listen seriously to what I say, and an attempt to carry out tasks for me, whether I wish it or no.

Younger people and policy makers might consider age as the dominant social factor in later life. This misrepresents older people's experience – they consider ageing to be both varied and contextual. Underlying the volunteer reading group, however, as with all examples of participative social groupings, were certain ideological realities, as one respondent signified:

> I do not yet feel free to speak openly in the group. I begin to realise that we separate into 2-3 groupings for beliefs and

values; class position; issues of politics [guessed at]; social issues, etc. Interesting that it's hard to think about age and the process of ageing without being forced to encounter in some form or another our philosophy of life.

Her commentary questions the efficaciousness of other modes of research, such as focus groups, in offering valid interconnectivity while sustaining the individual perspective. As in life generally, ideology permeates, having an impact on shared conceptual understanding. In contrast, the FCMAP diaries allowed a far less inhibited, less structured or researcher-influenced space than is found in most other gerontological approaches. Participants were freer to synthesise opinions, reflections and experiential knowledge of the life-world that might otherwise be considered less credible or acceptable than the option of either reflecting existing norms or responding to innate or self-evident clues from researchers. In so doing, genuine and valid social connectivity is potentiated, whereas other modes of inquiry often pre-determine the kinds of inter-subjective exchange researchers prefer. FCMAP facilitated radical critical reflection on otherness and selfhood. As one respondent pondered, 'I used to think that, fundamentally, in essence I had not changed; I was still "me". The more I engage in this project the more I am unsure whether I am, in any way, who I was.' FCMAP respondent diaries demonstrated that ageing is contextual, differentiated and shaped and understood in terms of intersecting personal and social narratives, and that older subjects should be involved in these narratives, not as failing individuals concerned only with health and mental health issues, but subjects with agency, many of whom develop and change throughout their third and fourth ages.

Like the 'CALL-ME' project, FCMAP initially met with some resistance as older people are accustomed to being directed through top-down programmes and projects that reflect others' perceptions of older people, their needs and capacities. The success of this project for meaningful and creative participation and social connectivity and personal development, which stands in marked contrast to the assumption of old age decline, is demonstrated by one of the volunteer reading groups choosing to carry on with readings, discussions and journal entries for one year after the life of the project, incorporating members from other groups.[3]

Conclusion

While supporting the importance of participation and social connectivity for health, well-being and rights, the projects on which this chapter is based have challenged many of the underlying assumptions and stylised facts that inform knowledge about and policies aimed at older people. By placing older people's experience at the centre of research, it is clear that they *are* participating in a great many arenas of life, but that their participation is hampered, unacknowledged or undervalued. The studies on spatial and digital access clearly indicate that older people are keen to deepen their engagement with new and changing places and new technologies, but for many, their access is hampered. When linked to the project on connectivity of older people to institutions entrusted with protecting them from financial abuse, as well as the increasing trend of moving institutions out of neighbourhoods and on to the digital high street, issues of spatial and digital access take on further significance. Failure to deal with these access issues will deepen inequalities between older people themselves and between generations as well as increase old age vulnerability.

Projects on participation in social and political organisations in Brazil and South Africa, voluntary work in rural Britain and paid and unpaid work in urban India demonstrate that it is not age that determines participation. Rather, the opportunities provided for older people's participation not only determine how much and how they participate, but also the recognition they receive for doing so – to the point that they may be contributing in ways that are essential to family, community, society and economy, but these are unrecognised or undervalued. Structural constraints on access, lack of recognition and undervaluation inevitably impinge on older people's rights and well-being.

Digging deeper into structural issues, examining how older people are situated differently within families, communities and within the population of older people themselves, it is clear that they need to be understood within the wider networks and contexts of which they are a part. Increasing participation of younger female Bangladeshi migrants in London's economy can leave older women isolated, which can easily be misread as an age or cultural issue rather than what it is, the uneven and unequal integration of different age groups in society and the economy. Differing cultural backgrounds, generated by class, education, religion and ethnic differences as well as personal histories position people differently, creating diverging impediments to participation. However, the projects emphasising structurally generated differences between older people as well as the projects designed to generate meaningful participation and social connectivity amply demonstrate that older people do enthusiastically take up opportunities to participate in activities *they* consider meaningful, and are keen to participate in projects that do not assume that older people are failing physically and socially and for whom low-value, generic services are sufficient to meet assumed needs. Taken together, all the projects demonstrate that older people do participate and want to participate more, that older people want to take part in new activities, new ways of doing and new ways of thinking, but they want to do so in ways that *they* determine.

Old age is not the problem; the problem is the widespread negative stereotypes and prejudicial discourses found in the media, research, policy and taken up by stakeholders. While the objective may be to improve older people's well-being and rights, portraying older people as needy and declining because of their age, rather than systematically disadvantaged by the way society is organised, will not enable the development of policies and practices that fully acknowledge the diversity of what older people do, need and want. Until older people are positioned as authors of knowledge about themselves, rather than the objects of knowledge by experts, the goal of addressing older people's rights and well-being, of extending inclusion and reducing exclusion, will remain elusive.

Notes

[1] See Tilt et al, 2007; Cattell et al, 2008; Crawford, 2010, on the link between health, capacity, mobility and class.

[2] Eighteen months after completion, project researchers were still being asked to run another MINA event, and subsequent doctoral research in Cardiff on older women's health, including a physical activity assessment study, has had an enthusiastic response from the Bangladeshi community. Unexpectedly, Pakistani women approached the doctoral student to also include them in the study, demonstrating that the concept of 'hard-to-reach' communities is not applicable if the mode of engagement and activities on offer are deemed interesting, appropriate and inclusive.

[3] See www.ons.gov.uk/ons/guide-method/classifications/current-standard-classifications/soc2010/soc2010-volume-3-ns-sec--rebased-on-soc2010--user-manual/index.html

[4] Extracts of the data produced by the FCMAP can be found in the Demos policy report, 'Coming of age' (Bazalgette et al, 2011).

SEVEN

Design for living in later life

Mike Timmins (Chapter Coordinator), Alastair Macdonald, Constantinos Maganaris, Cheryl Haslam, Diane Gyi, Eleanor van den Heuvel, Irene di Giulio, Jane McCann, Martin Maguire, Sheila Peace and John Percival

> The need has never been greater for products, services and environments to be developed in such a way that they do not exclude, but instead reflect more accurately the diverse demands of today's users – particularly older and disabled people. (Professor Sir Christopher Frayling, Foreword, in Clarkson et al, 2003)

Introduction

Knowledge transfer is the starting point for this chapter, which has been crafted by members of six collaborative research teams who have been involved in unique projects concerning aspects of everyday living for older people, addressing issues of technology and design from a human perspective. A real dichotomy underpins this work, because while the focus has been on working with and learning from people in later life, all address issues that may affect people of all ages. So there is a real sense that while we may continue to highlight the underpinning ageism of designers, retailers and the youth-obsessed market, what we are really demonstrating is the importance of inclusive or universal design (Coleman, 1994) throughout the life course, or what has been called 'transgenerational design' (Pirkl, 1994). In recognising this we can see that this body of work from the New Dynamics of Ageing (NDA) Programme builds on the seminal research carried out for the i-design consortium funded by the Engineering and Physical Sciences Research Council (EPSRC) (2002–07) that brought together researchers in engineering and design (see Clarkson et al, 2003; Royal College of Art, 2012). It also recognises the dynamism of design outlined here by Fuad-Luke (2009, p xix):

> The real JOY of design is to deliver fresh perspectives, improved well-being and an intuitive sense of balance

with the wider world. The real SPIRIT of design elicits some higher meaning. The real POWER of design is that professionals and laypeople can co-design in amazingly creative ways. The real BEAUTY of design is its potential for secular, pluralistic expression. The real STRENGTH of design is this healthy variance of expression. The real RELEVANCE of design is its ability to be proactive. The real PASSION of design is in its philosophical, ethical and practical debate.

The NDA researchers also include a wide range of disciplines, bringing together social and medical scientists and the humanities alongside engineering and design colleagues. The researchers are textile designers, electrical, mechanical and biomedical engineers, specialists in muscle mechanics, design experts for health and social care, ergonomists and social gerontologists, and draw on both the wider skills of others who are clinical consultants, design anthropologists, psychologists and urologists, alongside the vital component, the knowledge of older lay experts. One strategy has been an inclusive co-design approach, embracing all stakeholders, in the iterative research and development process. Collaborative design engagement informed 'shared (lay) language', in raising awareness of older user needs and aspirations, between users, cross-disciplinary researchers, and industry collaborators, in user engagement throughout near-market prototype development.

While people are living longer and have more healthy lives into advanced age (Westendrop and Kirkwood, 2007), their social roles and activities have also become more complex (see Chapter One, this volume). They may continue in active paid employment for longer than the traditional retirement age and combine this role with active unpaid employment, caring for both younger and older family members, and also friends. They may wish to go on living in their home of many years or continue to take exercise for as long as possible or to wear comfortable clothing that continues their interest in style and fashion. But as people get older, these aspects of lifestyle may seem to slowly move out of reach as discrimination through age rears its head. Discussion continues over the diversity of the older population and the distinction that can be made between the third and fourth agers (Rees-Jones et al, 2008), the 'haves' and 'have nots', and the ways in which people can be targeted in different ways within our consumer culture in relation to different goods and services (Jones et al, 2009). It is certainly true that although many people may live with long-term health conditions, the ageing body is a centre of continuity and change where different needs have an impact on that congruence between the person and their environment.

Appropriate design is recognised as key to the acceptance and uptake of products, services and environments. There has been a lack of understanding of the actual and potential role of technological advances in the everyday lives of older people, and developments have often failed to address their aspirations. Here, discussion of the biology of human ageing enables us to recognise that you can design to enhance the well-being of people as they age. Huppert (2003, pp 30-57) has provided an important overview of implications of changes in physical, sensory and mental capabilities and their implications for inclusive design. We consider a few key points with particular relevance to the research outlined here. In terms of physical capabilities, muscle strength and power, flexibility, balance and cardio-respiratory endurance are highlighted as key to maintaining an independent lifestyle through continued physical engagement.

Understanding the size and shape of the changing older human body is of relevance to many areas of design. Due to difference in body size, women are not as strong as men and have weaker muscles; consequently, certain activities become more arduous, such as lifting, carrying and climbing stairs. Indeed, Huppert (2003, p 33) suggests that the older women should be 'a priority target group for inclusive design'. Height difference between older and younger people, due to both generational and age-related issues, means that the design of many household items (such as the height of kitchen cupboards in the 'Transitions in Kitchen Living' study) are too high for comfort. The last sizing survey, relevant to garment design, was carried out in the 1950s when the average female size was imperial size 12, which has now risen to approximately size 15. NDA research has involved the first study in capturing the size and shape of active agers, within the 60–75 year age range, to inform, for example, the design of a functional clothing 'layering system' as an assistive 'wearable technology platform'.

Such technological advances may be utilised to promote health and well-being but may not be readily accepted by some older users due to badly designed user interfaces that have small controls or displays that may prevent someone with minor impairment from using them effectively. Turning to sensory capabilities, the five senses – vision, hearing, taste, smell and touch – can all experience change through ageing. Throughout our lives people experience such change but cure, improvement, assistance and support by various means are available. Here we consider vision and hearing. Changes in our ability to see in detail are age-related, and contrast in terms of brightness when moving from dark to light can be an issue. This has particular importance for lighting levels which enable older people to see a level of detail and objects more clearly. Alongside vision, hearing problems can lead to communication difficulties that are increased when there is background noise, making listening more difficult.

This discussion highlights important implications for design, and this is also seen in relation to cognitive capabilities when developing new products and services to ensure that they are appropriate to the real-world needs of older users. Increasing development of cognitive impairment through degenerative brain disorders in advanced age has led to particular environmental design developments (Dementia Services Development Centre, 2012). More commonly, difficulties will also be experienced with multi-tasking, maintaining concentration and attention, memory change and numerical and spatial ability. Here the implications for design often relates to how information is presented and the complexity required.

This brief summary of issues relating to the embodiment of ageing begins to demonstrate some of the concerns that must be taken on board when considering different ways of developing the field of design. There are implications for undertaking research that enable us to learn more about the ways in which people both present themselves and interact with their environment, and how design may assist their well-being.

The ageing community may be seen as the 'new consumer majority' (Wolfe and Snyder, 2003, p xii). To date, a product is generally developed in relation to last year's sales and trend forecasting. As there is virtually no positive design trend for ageing, there needs to be major intervention in 'business as usual' to inform new routes to this new potential market. Here are just some of the questions being considered that have potential for changing lives:

- How can we bring a positive image to ageing/create up-beat trend information – not just boring statistics?
- How can industry learn from older workers to facilitate healthy behaviour in good design?
- Can we develop wearable technology that assists active ageing by monitoring heart rates yet is comfortable and something people would be pleased to wear?
- How can we help to prevent falls which occur more often for people when going down stairs?
- What about the embarrassment for older people of knowing that they are no longer as continent as they used to be? Can we design

washable fabric for underwear that is wetness-sensing, and odour-free?

- Daily routines in the kitchen will have developed over lives and relate to gender, culture and generation, and the physical environment may no longer be enabling, so how do older people cope and adapt?
- Can we develop a way of looking at changes in mobility as people age that would help in designing a better fit between the person and their environment?
- How do we effectively communicate what we have learned through user engagement (over time) to designers and product developers new to ageing design?

To address these research questions the teams developed, with growing innovation, user research methods that strengthen understanding of the experience of living into old age and the impact of the past on the present. Through collective consideration of the findings from the range of research projects presented here, a number of central themes that cut across and underpin this work have been addressed.

Projects selected from the New Dynamics of Ageing Programme

Drawn from the full complement of 35 NDA projects, the six projects considered in this chapter are as shown in Table 7.1. They were chosen as having high design content across a range of fields, and as being highly relevant to the subjects outlined in the introduction to this chapter. More detailed descriptions of these projects, and of the other projects forming the whole NDA Programme, are available from the NDA website (see www.newdynamics.group.shef.ac.uk).

Table 7.1: NDA projects contributing to this chapter

Project short name	Project full name	Topic
DFAW	Design for Ageing Well	Improving quality of life for the ageing population using a technology enabled garment system
Envision	–	Innovation in envisioning dynamic biomechanical data to inform healthcare and design practice
TiKL	Transitions in Kitchen Living	The role, function and design of the kitchen within the lives of older people
SOS	Safety on Stairs	Biomechanical and sensory constraints of step and stair negotiation in old age
TACT3	Tackling Ageing Continence through Theory, Tools and Technology	Reducing the impact of continence difficulties for older people
Working Late	–	Strategies to enhance productive and healthy environments for the older workers

Aspects analysis

This section considers the relationships, differences and similarities that arise from the six NDA projects. It is based around a list of 'aspects' developed by the project team leaders as being important in affecting the design process. Each aspect is taken in turn, and considered in light of the material contained in the third section in this chapter, on page 223. The list in its final form consisted of 11 items, shown in Table 7.2 as follows:

Table 7.2: Aspects of the design process

Aspects
Staying active
Answering need
Answering desires/wants
Inclusive for all
Improving confidence/competence
Feeling connected
Improving image
Empowering
Usability
Clarity
Independence

This list is not prioritised, and there is inevitably some overlap between the aspects listed.

A superficial assessment might conclude that there is little apparent commonality between the different projects outlined above. But all of them, setting aside the obvious link that they are concerned with older people, have a strong design emphasis. As well as this consideration, each project has developed its own approach to ensuring that the user is part of that process. Each project, too, although it may concentrate on the end user in providing advice, or in some cases, actual products to use, contains much to guide and advise other stakeholders. This is particularly the case in the Envision programme, where the movement and posture of older people is considered, and in the DFAW project, where the different body shapes of older people are recognised, perhaps for the first time. In both these cases, as well as in those of other projects, product designers and manufacturers will find valuable information.

The question then naturally arises, 'Who, then, are the stakeholders in this set of projects?' The first on the list has to be the end user, because it is their life that the outcomes of the project are designed to improve. Second, as mentioned, designers and providers of products and services will find both the outcomes and design processes resulting from the various projects commercially valuable. Carers, formal and informal, the latter often family members, make yet another stakeholder group. They will be reassured that someone with continence problems can carry out a more normal life (TACT3), or that assistance can be called if an accident happens when a relative is out walking (DFAW). Finally, medical and paramedical specialists should find their job eased by recommending the adoption of some of the solutions outlined.

Although the projects discussed necessarily take the point of view of meeting the needs of an older clientele, in many instances, the outcomes can apply directly or with some modification to all ages. Similarly, some outcomes for older people have their roots in well-researched existing design outcomes and processes, for example, ergonomics (both in the home and at work) and clothing. This consideration is expanded on later.

Staying active

One of the principal platforms of the group of projects is that older people are helped to stay active. In some cases this may be deliberate, such as longer walks or exercise recommended by a medical professional, or incidental, such as ordinary daily activities around the home or in the immediate locality. Staying active may be approached directly, as in the example of DFAW, where the emphasis is on functional clothing as a 'platform' for wearable technologies to enable the user to feel more confident in taking exercise by walking, or in the TACT3 programme, where outdoor activities may be considered to be limited by those affected by continence issues. In these situations, the TACT3 solutions can help to keep those affected stay active. Less direct influences occur in, for example, the TiKL and SOS outcomes, where well-designed and easy-to use kitchens and stairs can encourage greater use, and hence greater activity. Badly designed facilities can restrict active use, based on the idea that too much effort is required to use such facilities. Indirect effects on staying active are exemplified in the Envision programme, whereby using that project's outputs, medical professionals can work out appropriate programmes of rehabilitation therapy designed to keep the patient mobile and active.

Answering need

All of the projects described in this chapter have as their basis identification of a possible need, establishing that the need does actually exist, and collecting data about the need, proposing and verifying solutions and shepherding these solutions into practical application. The needs identified cover a particularly wide spectrum, from situations in daily life at home (TiKL, SOS) to workplace-based needs for older workers (Working Late). Some needs are answerable by simple, traditional online methods, such as the TACT3 Great British Public Toilet Map, whereas others can only be met by more complex electronic systems, such as vital signs monitoring in the DFAW project and odour detection in TACT3. Outputs from some of the projects can be used directly by the older person her/him self, whereas in other cases, the identified need can only be solved by taking the project findings and using them as part of a future design brief. Examples of this latter point would include informing kitchen and stairway designers of the recommendations as they apply to older people (TiKL, SOS). Even here, however, some needs can be provided for by relatively straightforward changes of lighting, floor covering and wall colour that can be undertaken directly by the older user (with help, if needed) – so guidance needs to come in different forms. Similarly, changes in the workplace (Working Late) to accommodate older workers' needs should be readily achievable, both by employing organisations and their older employees – particularly where legislation is in place concerning workplace risk assessments. In DFAW the adoption of a co–design approach, that has involved direct engagement between older research participants, researchers and industry stakeholders, has given clear feedback, on real-world user needs and limitations, to industry for ongoing product development. Stakeholder engagement, in product prototyping, helps to ensure the realistic selection of commercially available materials and the application of novel processes that can bring research outputs nearer to market. The Envision programme approach could be seen as the prime example of indirect ways of meeting needs, but it would be quite within the bounds of possibility for an older person to use the Envision approach to understand and perhaps take action on their various aches, pains and stiffness.

Answering desires/wants

A designer's first priority may be to meet the older (or any) client's need, but to assume this is all that is required would be a mistake. For solutions to be effective, individual client tastes need to be taken into account. Clothing specifically cut to fit older body shapes, whether electronically enabled or not (DFAW), may fulfil the need of the wearer, but be rejected because the colour is wrong, or even where a manufacturer's embroidered logo is seen to be given undue prominence. Continence products may be made to be very efficient, but if too bulky or obvious, will be rejected by the potential user (TACT3). A work area – whether in an employer's premises or a home kitchen – may meet all the user's needs, but a desk in a draughty corner or floor covering not to the client's taste will not meet the user's wants and desires (Working Late, TiKL, SOS). A rigorous approach, such as the co-design method used in the DFAW programme, recognises that clothing has to both function and be aesthetically pleasing, in respect of the culture of the identified end user. Meeting both needs and desires, however, through stakeholder engagement, is a process that can be time-consuming and resource-hungry.

Inclusive for all

Although the projects in this section, being under the umbrella of the overall NDA Programme, are firmly based in designing solutions to problems encountered by older people, the solutions proposed will have wider applicability. Not only this, but solutions already in existence, with younger age ranges in mind, can inform the outcomes for the NDA Programme. In this way, the solutions become more inclusive across the entire age range – noted in the introduction as 'transgenerational design'. The DFAW project used body scanning to capture the size and shape of the changing older figure to inform the cutting of the smart clothing 'layering system'. Of particular note is the DFAW project's methods of specifying and incorporating electronic systems into garments, designed with older body shapes in mind. These methods can readily be applied to garments for every age range, and in its turn will inform the merging of electronics and textiles in the design of this type of garment. Similarly, good staircase and kitchen design (TiKL, SOS) will be applicable to all age groups, and the solutions proposed by the TACT3 programme will also have wider application, since continence problems are not restricted to older members of the population. The visualisation approach taken in the Envision programme, although developed with older adult data, is adaptable for using a variety of movement and biomechanical analyses in a number of rehabilitation therapies across the age range. Working in the other direction, the extensive body of knowledge of workplace ergonomics, as well as health and safety legislation, informs the development of special considerations for older workers (Working Late). These synergies represent an important outcome of the NDA Programme, and so this important aspect topic is revisited in some detail in the fourth section of this chapter (see page 234).

Improving confidence/competence

At least one of the NDA design projects has 'increasing confidence' as a major stated outcome (DFAW), but improving confidence/competence is at least implicit in all the projects represented. The DFAW project is designed to enable older people to feel more confident in planning where they travel, monitoring aspects of their walking performance, in having methods of emergency contact and enhanced confidence through overall clothing comfort and protection. Similarly, the TACT3 project builds confidence in going out and about, rather than being restricted to the home. For older people still in work, Working Late provides the confidence that their special needs, especially but not exclusively in health and safety matters, are being met. Well-designed kitchens and stairs (TiKL, SOS) mean that these facilities are likely to be used with more confidence and competence. For example, a kitchen that is more comfortable to use can promote confidence in food preparation, leading perhaps to better and healthier eating habits.

As is the case in some of the other aspects under consideration in this chapter, it is not just the users' confidence that project outcomes can improve. Although a largely incidental effect, family members not resident with the older person may have their confidence improved by knowing that their relative is safer in the kitchen and on the stairs, and that the older person is more confident and competent when they are out and about in the open air (TiKL, SOS, DFAW).

One additional facet of this aspect is that where a particular NDA project has promoted collaborative research, informed through meaningful user engagement, inclusive design practice has in turn built up the confidence of the academic teams in cross-disciplinary dialogue and the sharing of best practice in addressing the design requirements of the ageing population.

Feeling connected

It is by no means unusual for older people to feel disconnected from society. Age-related illnesses, particularly when such afflictions restrict mobility, can result in feelings of isolation. Outcomes from the projects in this chapter can alleviate some of the effects of these feelings. As a first example, having a kitchen that an older person is confident in using can encourage cooking and socialising, and thus a feeling of being more connected (TiKL). A further example would be project outcomes that encourage older people to be active outside the home, and to mix confidently with other people. Both the DFAW and TACT3 programmes encourage older people to be out and about, thus allowing for a greater chance of interacting with others. It is axiomatic that those older people who are still active in the workplace will have contact with others – very few occupations, if any, are carried out in complete isolation (Working Late). It even remains possible that the reason for remaining at work is to alleviate the feeling of being disconnected, and so arrangements for older people to remain working can encourage the feeling of remaining linked with society. In respect of electronic communications, a limitation to feeling connected is the problem of usability of poorly designed technology user interfaces, and often, a lack of standards that allow different devices to interact with each other (DFAW, Working Late).

Improving image

Technology has immense potential for making life easier for everyone. It is almost impossible for a 21st-century Western individual to live without the technologies on which we have all, to some extent, become dependent. Cars, phones, washing machines, fridges and televisions are simply part of the fabric of our lives. For some older people no longer able to cook for themselves, the microwave has enabled them to 'stay put' in their own home. Technological solutions designed to make life easier for older people and people with disabilities have not always benefited from the same user-focused design input as products aimed at the mass market. Classic examples of these ugly, stigmatising products are hearing aids and raised toilet seats. An important objective of the NDA Programme has been the involvement of older people at every stage of the research, including the design and development of products and services. Involving older people has been the key to developing aesthetically pleasing technology that complements older people's self-image as competent adult members of society. The DFAW project has worked to raise the profile of clothing for older people, designing for comfort, practicality and fit as well as for sustainability and attractiveness. TACT3 provides underwear that alerts the wearer to continence pad leakage, allowing them to change before wetness spread to outer clothing, helping to preserve their privacy and dignity. In the home, a kitchen designed with older people to be practical and attractive helps to maintain the self-image of the user and the image and value of the home (TiKL). Similar considerations apply to staircase design – safer stairs that don't look 'adapted' are also valuable (SOS).

Empowering

All the design-focused NDA projects have aimed to empower older people not only in the eventual technological design solutions, but also by close cooperation with stakeholders, particularly older people themselves, in every stage of the research programme. The Envision project empowers older people to discuss the issues affecting their mobility with healthcare professionals and designers. Both the TiKL and SOS projects are empowering people to live more comfortably and safely in their own homes. DFAW provides comfortable clothing solutions with a feel-good factor for getting out and about. TACT3 also empowers people to keep active by providing technologies to promote confidence and self-esteem, and by providing accurate information on publically accessible toilets with a web resource that mines 'OPEN DATA' provided by local councils, updating the vital information on a daily basis.

Usability

Usability can be regarded as the intuitiveness and ease of use of equipment, products, information or interactive systems. If designed and tested to ensure that they are as usable as possible, this makes them much easier to employ for everyone, not just older age groups. Usability can even be said to contribute to an enjoyable user experience. The design of wearable technology (DFAW) is a good example. Such clothing and the wearable devices should be appropriate in terms of size and fit for changing older bodies, comfortable, attractive to the culture of the end user, functional and easily understood. Similarly, the technology user interface to the clothing should be appropriate for ageing eyesight, hearing and dexterity, simple and intuitive in use. Another example is TACT3 where the Great British Public Toilet Map, odour detector and Smart underwear were all designed for usability. For instance, the Smart underwear has no on/off switch so there is no possibility of accidentally not switching it on, or accidentally switching it off. The TiKL project has developed guidelines for consumers to help make their kitchens more usable. This includes aspects such as reducing reaching and bending, improving layout and co-location of work areas, facilitating sitting down to work, and improving lighting. In the Envision project, the development of a visualisation tool based on biometric analysis illustrates points of stress and strain on the human body during movement, which makes data interpretation easier, more intuitive and reduces dependence on interpretation and subjective judgement. Professionals also felt that data specific to an individual's needs could be interpreted with more objectivity, allowing a more detailed and accurate diagnosis.

Clarity

It has been said that the most important thing a web page can do is be crystal clear about exactly what you can do on that website. The same can be said for products in general, so that if the purpose of an item and the method of using it is clear, this will make it attractive to use. Relating this concept to current technical clothing and technology interfaces, they typically have a profusion of confusing icons, buttons, connections, and so on. Technology providers and their teams need to engage, with older users, preferably with a co-design approach, with designers and other stakeholders, in order to understand the needs, wants and aspirations of those who are ageing, but active, and do not perceive themselves as 'ill'. The output will be clearer technology, as demonstrated in the DFAW project. In the Envision project, visualisations enable lay people to contribute to discussions about biomechanics. From both the written responses and subsequent discussions it was clear that the 'traffic light system' was effective as an indicator of the degree of 'pain' or 'stress' being experienced during certain activities, with green indicating 'okay' and red illustrating the peak point. This clarity in understanding of the dynamic visualisations enabled the participants to effectively contribute to the discussion and interpret chronic conditions such as the flexibility of joints and which joints were more or less painful. Many older kitchen users find appliance labels with poor contrast or small instructions on packaging difficult to read. TiKL project guidance on better task lighting, suggestions for use of magnifiers, or text scanning and read out devices can all help to overcome the problems by making labels and instructions clearer.

Independence

Maintaining independence is an important aim for people in later life. The TiKL researchers recorded problems experienced by older people in carrying out kitchen tasks. Adaptations they had made to overcome these problems were also identified. These were then used as examples within a kitchen guide to promote independent living at home, for example, extra shelving at a convenient height, installing a carousel rack to make reaching into cupboards easier, or extra lighting to assist with kitchen tasks. Wearable technology developed in the DFAW project has the potential to enable older people in their everyday lives to connect with friends and family, call for help (in case of falling or getting lost), route finding and locating their friends (while outdoors), checking on wellness (vital signs), and to keep them warm. Within TACT3, the Smart underwear and odour detector have the capacity to improve the independence of the older users as they will cut down on washing and basic care requirements. The Great British Public Toilet Map will allow greater freedom to travel for people with continence problems. Similarly, the SOS guidelines for stair dimension based on an elderly population will allow anyone, in particular older people, to negotiate a staircase because the new dimensions are designed for safe foot placement. The recommendation of successful strategies to negotiate difficult staircases and the training programme that can be adopted to improve the individual's difficulty in stair negotiation will improve the confidence and consequent independence of the individual. Within Envision, the visualisation of movement and stresses and strains on the human body facilitate an understanding of differences between individuals. The visualisation tool demonstrates the variance in capacity of different individuals conducting the same task, for example, in rising from a chair, bending or climbing stairs, or the same individual conducting a task in different ways, thereby allowing more customised rehabilitation therapy programmes.

Consideration of these themes across six rigorous pieces of research demonstrates the potential for real practical application, both as individual recommendations and, as addressed in the final section of this chapter, as added value synergies.

Designer competencies and interactions with client/user groups

Competency

As described earlier in this chapter, designers become involved in a wide range of topics. They design physical entities, systems and processes, frequently under a series of constraints. These include externally dictated regulations such as the need to use fire-retardant fabrics for furniture, restrictions on the use of certain substances in electronic equipment and various building regulations. Additional constraints from within the designer's organisation may also exist, such as quality and environmental standards and, crucially, finance. Designers work across such wide topic areas that it is easy to assume that the different design specialisms have little in common. It turns out, however, that a series of designer attributes ('competencies') can be identified, not all of them necessarily based on the design specialism, but all necessary for success.

This section also identifies the various methods available to the designer in involving, to a greater or lesser extent, the client/user in the design process, again referring to competency issues. It also touches briefly on the need, in the context of the NDA Programme – and doubtless others – for a cross-discipline common language.

As is often the case, the word 'competency' has a common usage and a specialist one. Both are linked, and associated with a person's ability to perform a set of tasks, but the common use has a flavour of an individual's performance being just about adequate, whereas the specialist meaning carries with it the concept of a person being fully trained and having the skills, knowledge and attitudes to be excellent at their job. It is perhaps unfortunate for the clear understanding of this important topic, that:

> In the past, HR professionals have tended to draw a clear distinction between 'competences' and 'competencies'. The term 'competence' (competences) was used to describe what people need to do to perform a job and was concerned with effect and output rather than effort and input. 'Competency' (competencies) described the behaviour that lies behind

> competent performance, such as critical thinking or analytical skills, and described what people bring to the job. (Chartered Institute of Personnel and Development, www. cipd.co.uk, accessed 31 May 2014)

More recent usage does not make this distinction, however, and Lucia and Lepsinger (1999, p iii) offer the following definition of competency: '... a cluster of related knowledge, skills and attitudes that affect a major part of one's job ...'. Within this definition, of course, the use of the terms knowledge, skills and attitudes need, in their turn, to be defined:

- *Knowledge:* that which is known and usually remembered, acquired by deliberate learning or observation and experience.
- *Skill:* the ability to interact at a practical level with equipment and tools, or in more abstract senses, to be able to communicate, instruct and guide.
- *Attitude:* personal philosophy in relation to tasks and situations experienced, and motivation to carry them out.

This approach can be used to describe the knowledge, skills and attitudes required in designing for older people. As a simplified example, a garment designer might have regard to the following competency aspects:

Knowledge of:

- How a garment is constructed
- The use to which the garment may be put
- The most appropriate fabric for the particular garment
- Any limitations imposed by the garment manufacturing process

Skills in:

- Accurately interpreting expressed buyer/client needs into a working garment design
- Laying out, cutting and assembling a trial garment in inexpensive fabric
- Economically cutting out and assembling the prototype version of the garment

Attitudes to:

- Meeting deadlines
- Delighting the client/buyer with the finished product
- Finishing garments neatly and professionally

The advantage of using this competency approach is twofold. First, the approach provides a framework for analysing and understanding the nature of a complex topic such as design, and second, it can provide a logical yardstick against which a designer can be selected and assessed. (There is a third use, not pursued further here, in which the analysis can help with training, as knowledge, skills and attitudes often need different training approaches.) It is worth noting that as with all classifications of this type, boundaries are not always rigid between the three aspects – cross-boundary movements can easily occur.

Competency for designers

In the field of design the competency approach is by no means unknown but tends to be located in particular subject specialisms. One example of this is graphic design, where the AIGA (previously American Institute for Graphic Arts) has identified 13 so-called 'designer competencies for 2015' (AIGA, 2012). Although AIGA uses the word 'competency' as synonymous with knowledge or skill or attitude, these will nonetheless provide a useful framework for that profession. Similar analyses exist in the medical field, the construction industry and even in the design of training and learning materials. An example of an attempt to work on a more general level was made by Bakarman in a somewhat obscure but useful survey of approaches to competency. In his report, *Attitude Skill and Knowledge (ASK): a new model for design education* (Bakarman, 2005), he prefers to reorder the three topics, and arrives at the following analysis:

Attitude

- Expert behaviour in handling a design problem
- Dedication and motivation to be a good designer
- Knowledge acquisition and managing that acquisition
- Excellent teamwork
- Ability to run the task smoothly

- Good time management
- Responsibility for the outcomes

Skills

- Task clarification
- Concept generation
- Evaluation and refinement
- Detailing design
- Communication of results
- Overall skill displayed in carrying out the necessary processes
    Skill in handling appropriate hardware and software

Knowledge

Descriptive knowledge
    Use of appropriate tools, including software and computer and other hardware
    Identification and exploration of emergent tools and techniques
Normative knowledge
    Recognition and understanding constraint
        Of the materials to be used
        Of organisational requirements – quality, procedures, communications
        Of financial requirements and constraints
Operational knowledge
    The commercial climate within which the design is being created

It should be noted that although the above is what Bakarman found (and those who provided the sources from which he drew), it will always be possible in a particular design process to identify other skills, knowledge and attitudes that relate to that design, and that the above represents a core that can be added to if needed. The importance of keeping abreast of new competencies and their required attitudes, skills and knowledge is particularly important where rapid developments and changes occur, not infrequently associated with very rapid changes in technology. (The italicised material has been added to Bakarman's analysis for the purposes of incorporation into this chapter, and one or two minor grammatical changes made to the original to improve clarity.)

In this section so far, competencies have been dealt with on a general basis. Sometimes, however, it is useful to establish the knowledge, skills and attitude required in a single topic area. This may be the case when a fuller understanding of that topic area is needed where the topic is new, or represents a substantial part of a design project. So, a particular project might rely heavily on 'communicating with older people'. While it is true that the human communication process is broadly the same over a wide age range, there is additional competence required for communicating with older people, and thus further knowledge, skills and attitudes needed. Among others:

- *Knowledge:* that older people not infrequently lip read, even though they are not clinically deaf, and may not consider themselves hard of hearing.
- *Skill:* speaking at the correct pace from the right position.
- *Attitude:* preparedness to spend time ensuring the message is properly understood.

Analysis in this way shows that successful communication with older people may need more effort than might at first be apparent.

Communication across disciplines

Communication channels in NDA projects

Any project uses a range of communication channels to try to ensure that all stakeholders are kept appropriately informed. These channels are varied, depending on need, but commonly used in the six projects are meetings, interviews, newsletters and websites. As well as these well-known communication routes, there are two points of particular interest: one concerned with communication within the professional project staff, and another concerning communication with the older people who make up the wide range of users/clients forming the subjects of questionnaires and surveys, members of focus groups and co-design teams, as well as potential clients. For this second group, mention has already been made of the competencies needed by those communicating with older people. Since older people comprise a substantial proportion of the people who, for example, are interviewed by project researchers, it is important that their needs are taken into account.

Arising from the first point above, further considerations emerge about communications within each project. To start with, in this series of projects it is quite usual to draw project team members from different types of organisation, such as universities, private companies and professional bodies. Members of this rich mixture will each have their own systems and procedures, and attempting to reconcile them requires a considerable amount of project management communication effort. Again, members of the project team may come from organisations that are widely separated geographically, and there is a considerable risk that stretched and far-flung communication links can lead to misunderstanding.

In addition to these considerations, there are many examples in the six projects of the need for a particular subject specialist to work with someone of an entirely different specialism. Each subject will have its own language and set of competencies, and some of these will overlap and some will not. In the cases of the TACT3 and DFAW programmes, for instance, electronic systems specialists need to collaborate with clothing designers to make sure that the needs of both specialisms, and especially the needs of the user, are met. Communicating across these design boundaries may mean that in addition to the designer's topic-related competencies, new methods of achieving common understanding may need to be developed. As Taylor (2011, p 1) puts it:

> The communication challenge within the development process is brought into focus when considering the broad range of inputs from these (widely differing) areas of expertise and the overlap between the disciplines.

For different specialisms the same word may have different meanings – and those meanings may be different from the everyday use of the word, as in the competency example above. In different ways each project faces the problem. Some use glossaries, word lists and 'frequently asked questions'. Others, following Taylor, adopt an information graphics approach, and it could be argued that the whole of the output of the Envision project is a very special variety of information graphic. An example of a different approach to building a common language across a wide range of specialists in their own field is the use in the DFAW project of concept maps. Used in selected cases these concept maps explore terminology and may offer advice – an example, relating back to the ideas on communicating with older people referred to at the beginning of this section, is given in Figure 7.1 (on pp 230-1 below).

Involving the end user in the design process

Good designs are based on imagination and flair. Excellent designs are based on imagination, flair and end user involvement in the design at as deep a level as possible. In any design activity this involvement will be needed at an early stage, in order to give direction to the activity.

In this part of the chapter, differing end user involvement strategies are outlined, and examples of the use of such strategies are provided, drawn from practical experience within the different NDA projects. Reference is made too to the 'competences' (as outlined earlier in the chapter) that the designer may need to draw on when adopting the different involvement strategy groupings.

Table 7.3 (on p 233) summarises some of the principal methods the designer can use to interact with the client/user group. There is no 'best way', because the choice depends on the situation. For example, although an online survey may be quick, cheap and allow a large client/user group to be surveyed, that group's views are interpreted, and possibly misinterpreted, through at least one person. On the other hand, a fully-fledged co-design approach is expensive and time-consuming, but ensures the client/user has every opportunity and encouragement to express any views they hold.

In the next section of the chapter, the above user/client involvement processes are examined in the context of such processes in the NDA Programme. Some processes of involvement are relatively common and used in many cases, but others used in very few instances. Two examples, drawn from the six projects considered in this chapter, have been chosen to illustrate possible approaches to user involvement.

Examples of user involvement in the Design for Ageing Well project

In this project several approaches to user involvement have been used, of which three have been selected as having particular importance. These are questionnaire-based survey, body scanning and co-design.

At the start of the project, an initial survey of some 50 individuals in the age range of 60–75 was made. The aim was to establish the extent to which this end user group used differing items of technology (mobile phone, pedometer, GPS system and the like) that individuals in this user group took with them when they were out walking. This information from them was used to make an initial assessment of the technology that might be included in the proposed electronically enabled layered garment system. There was little, if any, direct involvement of the group surveyed with the process, other than to provide information. The competencies required by the person carrying out this work – in this case, not a designer – would be knowledge of how to produce a survey and analyse the results, skills in writing survey questions and a rigorous attitude to timescales and interpreting off-scale results.

Figure 7.1: Communicating with older people

COMMUNICATING WITH OLDER PEOPLE

* THE COMMUNICATION PROCESS
* COMMUNICATION CHANNELS
  - ONE & TWO WAY
* SOME BARRIERS TO COMMUNICATING
  WITH OLDER PEOPLE
* TWELVE TIPS FOR GOOD COMMUNICATION

TWELVE TIPS FOR COMMUNICATING WITH OLDER PEOPLE
- Use simple language and don't use jargon and/or initials - but don't patronise
- Speak clearly but naturally, not too fast and not too slow
- Check for hearing difficulties, face the listener and don't cover your mouth when speaking - older people often unconsciously lip read
- Where a carer is involved, communicate directly with the receiver, not the carer (unless this is a requirement for the particular message)
- Test understanding early in (and regularly during) the communication, as well as the end
- Find out the extent of the receiver's knowledge early on in the communication process - the receiver may know more (or less) than you think
- Establish early on how the individual prefers to be addressed (Mr/ Mrs/Ms/Miss, full first name, shortened first name), & record for future use
- Avoid over-familiarity - avoid using words like 'dear', 'love' and similar terms
- For written communication, don't use very small typefaces (14 point minimum font size recommended)
- Avoid fancy, difficult-to-read typefaces   14 pt. Helv .
  - consider using Helvetica or Times   14 pt. T.N.R.
  New Roman for example
- Speak directly into a telephone and keep the handset still
- Check sound systems (such as microphone and induction loops) are actually working before attempting their use

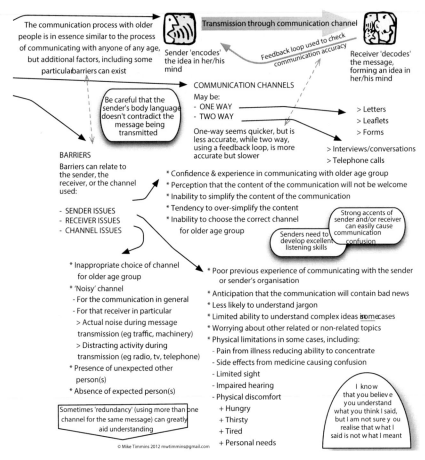

The communication process with older people is in essence similar to the process of communicating with anyone of any age, but additional factors, including some particular barriers can exist

Transmission through communication channel

Sender 'encodes' the idea in her/his mind

Feedback loop used to check communication accuracy

Receiver 'decodes' the message, forming an idea in her/his mind

Be careful that the sender's body language doesn't contradict the message being transmitted

COMMUNICATION CHANNELS
May be:
- ONE WAY
- TWO WAY

One-way seems quicker, but is less accurate, while two way, using a feedback loop, is more accurate but slower

> Letters
> Leaflets
> Forms
> Interviews/conversations
> Telephone calls

BARRIERS
Barriers can relate to the sender, the receiver, or the channel used:

- SENDER ISSUES
- RECEIVER ISSUES
- CHANNEL ISSUES

* Confidence & experience in communicating with older age group
* Perception that the content of the communication will not be welcome
* Inability to simplify the content of the communication
* Tendency to over-simplify the content
* Inability to choose the correct channel for older age group

Senders need to develop excellent listening skills

Strong accents of sender and/or receiver can easily cause communication confusion

* Inappropriate choice of channel for older age group
* 'Noisy' channel
  - For the communication in general
  - For that receiver in particular
    > Actual noise during message transmission (eg traffic, machinery)
    > Distracting activity during transmission (eg radio, tv, telephone)
* Presence of unexpected other person(s)
* Absence of expected person(s)

* Poor previous experience of communicating with the sender or sender's organisation
* Anticipation that the communication will contain bad news
* Less likely to understand jargon
* Limited ability to understand complex ideas in some cases
* Worrying about other related or non-related topics
* Physical limitations in some cases, including:
  - Pain from illness reducing ability to concentrate
  - Side effects from medicine causing confusion
  - Limited sight
  - Impaired hearing
  - Physical discomfort
    + Hungry
    + Thirsty
    + Tired
    + Personal needs

Sometimes 'redundancy' (using more than one channel for the same message) can greatly aid understanding

I know that you believe you understand what you think I said, but I am not sure you realise that what I said is not what I meant

© Mike Timmins 2012 mwtimmins@gmail.com

At a later stage in the project, when a formal user group of some 12 individuals had been recruited, further and more complex involvement was made with them. Most sport-related garments are designed to fit younger body shapes, but older people are shaped differently. For active pursuits such as walking, good garment fit is essential, and so full body scans were made of each member of the user group so that a correct fit of the garment could be made. The process involved the use of a specialised body scanning booth, and its experienced operator. The user group were thus deeply involved with this process. Designer competencies for this required knowledge of this equipment's existence, use and limitations, organising skills in arranging the availability of the equipment and the user group members, and a flexible attitude when parts of the scan programme had to be altered.

For the DFAW project, the co-design process was particularly important. The user group met at regular intervals with the clothing and electronic system designers in a series of about 12 full-day seminars, each seminar focusing on a detailed examination of one aspect of the layered garment system being designed (outer layer, electronic equipment choice, colour, and so on). In the co-design process, the end user's views are regarded as equally valid as the specialist designers' present, and so this process represents perhaps the highest possible level of end user involvement. Competencies of the designer here are knowledge of the 'technical' side of the topic under discussion, skills in communicating and organising, and an attitude that allows her/him to realise that all inputs need to be carefully considered, and that none is rejected without due consideration.

User involvement in the Transitions in Kitchen Living project

This study was based on interviews with 48 participants (aged between 60 and 91) alongside other data collection. The first interview gathered from each participant an oral history of kitchens they had experienced across the life course, informed by a housing history record and a life event guide, for example, first remembered home, parental home when a teenager, leaving home and setting up first house as an independent person. The second semi-structured interview focused on the present kitchen, how well it met the person's abilities and needs, and any coping strategies they adopted. It contained both multiple choice and open-ended questions. The interview also considered the person's health and well-being as well as their activities. It covered aspects such as physical abilities (mobility and dexterity), sight, hearing, whether the person cooked, what they liked to eat and then discussion about difficulties completing various tasks such as cooking, washing, ironing, recycling and feeding pets. Prior to this meeting, self-completion records of routine kitchen activities and basic demographic information were kept. Both user opinions and discussion of ergonomic problems in their current kitchen informed by their kitchen history led to a better understanding of user needs for inclusive kitchen design. Further research into user needs in relation to future technological support in the kitchen was also carried out based on a survey of 45 older participants. In all these examples the designer/researcher would need knowledge of the various methods of interaction, skills in designing and administering questionnaires and managing interactions, and a patient and rigorous attitude to discovering the required information.

Table 7.3: Processes for involvement of users with the designer

Type of involvement	Designer knowledge for this strategy grouping	Designer skills for this strategy grouping	Designer attitudes for this strategy grouping	Level of client involvement in the design process	General comments
Scanning - Exhibitions - Trade journals - Catalogues - Trade fairs	The rapidly changing field of exhibitions and trade fairs	Choosing the most appropriate route without wasting time	Willingness to network effectively	Minimal, largely zero	Can be a useful first stage in establishing a starting point
Surveys - Questionnaires - Online surveys	The design of the overall scope of the survey and of the questions within it	Planning and execution of the survey process	Time management and motivation of self and others	Minimal, rare for the group to have further involvement	Often subject to rigorous statistical analysis, can look neat and tidy, but fails to pick up often important detail
Interviews - Structured - Less formal conversations - Focus groups	Know when this cluster of involvement techniques is appropriate	Skills in arranging the event including designing the question framework Interpreting results	Willingness to allot the necessary time and resources to the process	Largely one-off events with users having little further involvement	Allows some dialogue between the user group and designer, but may be time-hungry. Can allow ideas not considered by the designer to be detected
Other and emergent involvement routes - Co-design - Body scanning - Animation - Wearer/user trials	Used in specialised situations, the knowledge set will depend on the consultation process chosen	Similar considerations	Similar considerations	The involvement process tends to be pre-eminent in these specialist situations	In some particular situations the involvement process may have to be developed from scratch

Synergy

The fact that synergy exists between the outputs of the six projects was noted earlier in the chapter, and in this section the nature of the links introduced earlier are enlarged. Each project had identifiable outputs that stand alone in the context of that particular project – this is, after all, usually the reason for the project in the first place. In these cases recommendations from individual projects can lead to interesting future project work around the same topic, but more interesting are those cases where outcomes from similar projects can be combined to open up new fields of investigation. Even more interesting and potentially more rewarding are situations where projects have apparently very different outputs, but can, in fact, be related. This synergy can be related to tangible outputs (prototypes, specifications), or to processes (novel user engagement methods, data visualisation techniques), or a mixture of the two. Synergy can also mean reaching out to entirely different projects in other institutions, thus enriching the outputs of both activities.

As a first example, although the outputs of the TACT3 and DFAW programmes may be very different, both are concerned with clothing that contains electronic systems. Both projects have faced issues concerning the degree of integration of the electrical/electronic system in the garment, the need to clean the garments designed in the project, provision of signal and data-processing systems and power supplies. To deal with these issues, the TACT3 and DFAW projects have independently taken the route of using mobile phone technology. This would give future projects faced with similar issues the confidence that mobile phone technology, representing a medium level of garment/system integration, would be the appropriate starting point. Remaining with these two programmes, the TACT3 output of the Great British Public Toilet Map (now independent of the NDA Programme) could be accessed through the mobile phone technology used in DFAW, but additionally expanded to meet the DFAW user group request for travel and refreshment stop information.

The guidance and advice outputs from the TiKL and SOS programmes could be the foundation for, say, bathroom design for older people, or even the design of gardens for this age group. The idea of designing in flexibility to the original design of the kitchen, put forward in the TiKL programme, of taking account of the changing needs of people as they get older, may seem a small point, but could readily be used as the starting point for design of a house that could meet the owner's needs throughout her/his life, and that of any family. That programme also illustrates examples of synergy links in discussions with entirely different projects – Ambient Kitchen (Newcastle University), Future Bathroom (Sheffield University) and TSB COBALT (Foundation for Assistive Technology).

Also contributing to understanding older user needs in such projects based in the home are the outputs from the Envision programme. It would for, say, a bathroom project, be entirely appropriate for the designer to employ Envision approaches as one tool in his/her design methodology in order better to understand the space needs and movement patterns of older clients.

Synergy can exist between unlikely-sounding projects. One of the outcomes of the Working Late project is concerned with advice about travel to work, including walking. The DFAW programme does not exclude walking to work from its analysis of walking types, thus building a link between the two projects. Another synergy between these two projects is the WalkingWorksWonders initiative of the Working Late programme, where participants record pedometer readings on the website for analysis and feedback, and the record kept of individual walk data (including distance walked) by users in the DFAW project.

Envision does hold a special place in this grouping of projects. One outcome of this programme is that older people themselves can usefully gain information about how their body reacts as they perform daily tasks, with a view to adopting less stressful methods of task performance. At least as important – and perhaps even more important – is the added value to other programmes that could be achieved by using the Envision approach to underpin and inform the final design. Envision has great value in programmes where analysis of bodily movement patterns forms part of the requirement. This analysis occurs in such programmes as TiKL, SOS and Working Late, where in the latter case, patterns of movement in and around the workplace may be different for older workers. The nature of one of the Working Late programme outputs is largely based around the idea of the older worker going out from home to a place of work, but it is by no means unusual for older workers to work from home. In these cases, the recommendations of TiKL and SOS will be highly relevant. The value is not all one way, however. While designers should be able to cope with Envision stick figures, they may be less appropriate for some audiences. It is interesting, therefore, to speculate about whether the data obtained about older people's body shapes in the DFAW project by a body scanning process could be used to 'clothe' the Envision figures.

Some synergies are related to processes used in the various projects rather than the outcomes formally described in a project's aims and objectives. Often these processes are hidden within the project management systems of the programme, but when located and recorded, form valuable foundations for future projects. An example here would be the use of a co-design approach in the DFAW project that is a similar to, but somewhat more complex than, the end user involvement process in the TiKL programme. The formal use of storytelling and reminiscing as a method of older user engagement and data provision in the same TiKL project has no parallel in other projects. The phenomenon is, however, easily observed when occasions such as focus groups of older people are drawn together. This approach could thus be developed to provide a valuable tool. A further example of this would be the work station risk assessments with older workers in mind, a necessary part of the Working Late programme, which could, with minor alterations, be usefully employed by kitchen, staircase and bathroom designers.

Project outcomes are based on providing direct advice and assistance to the end user, in various forms, but in addition to this, many have the function of providing advice and guidance to various forms of decision makers working with or on behalf of older people. Outputs from Envision, SOS and TiKL will be of interest to architects and designers, Working Late to employers, and the caring professions will be interested in TACT3 and possibly DFAW. Currently the required information is in varying formats and accessed on an individual basis, and for these professional stakeholders, considerable synergy would result from accessing the information via an online portal.

Two final points remain. First, synergistic relationships are not confined to the six projects considered in this chapter, and many more added value instances can be found in relationships with the wider set of NDA projects. Just one example will suffice to illustrate the point, that of synergy between DFAW, designed to increase confidence in walking by the use of an electronically enabled garment system, and the OPUS project, designed to give confidence to older walkers in urban settings – both using smart phone technology. Outcomes of these programmes, if combined, would cover the full range of walking likely to be undertaken by the older walker.

Finally, in addition to these considerations, the second section of this chapter introduced the idea that the outcomes of the projects can have implications for clients/end users who are younger than the NDA target age group. Again, such considerations can result in added synergy, not just of this chapter's projects, but a range of others as well. Perhaps the most obvious point is that limitations in capability are not confined to older age groups, and that many younger people can have similar limiting conditions to those existing in older people. In these cases, the outcomes could well be directly relevant. For programmes such as TiKL and SOS, the parameters for designs for safety and convenience of users have relevance for any age, and, since their outcomes may need to remain in place over an extended period of time, taking into account future possible limitations can obviate future structural alterations in the home. Similar considerations apply in the case of Envision and Working Late. Here, the Envision outputs can be used with little regard to age, and although the literature on workplace ergonomics is substantial, Working Late good practice can apply in other situations than for older workers in the workplace.

It must also be remembered that the outcomes of the projects are not necessarily confined to older age groups or to those with some kind of limiting health condition. Younger people with perfectly normal health, and those advising them, will find much of value in the outcomes, direct and less obvious, of these projects.

Conclusion

Each of the six projects referred to in this chapter had its own aims, objectives and outcomes. Very briefly described in Table 7.1 and described more fully in the NDA website (see www.newdynamics. group.shef.ac.uk), these individual attributes are the main focus of the work carried out in the individual project. The outcomes of each project are self-contained, and stand on their own, as is required for effective project management. These individual outcomes are very varied. In some cases they affect older people directly by providing tangible items to help improve their lives (DFAW, TACT3). In other cases, they provide advice for older people directly (TIKL, SOS, Working Late), while in others, they will be used by professionals advising their older client group (TIKL, SOS, TACT3, Working Late). Some outcomes (Envision, DFAW) provide tools that can be used in further research, and this research need not necessarily be restricted to older people.

These latter considerations underpin the view that many of the projects have an additional set of clients/end users to the older client group. Project outcomes in TiKL and SOS will be highly relevant to architects, house construction companies and planning regulators, while the medical, nursing and other caring professionals will find outcomes from TACT3, Envision and possibly DFAW relevant to their work. Even family members of the older person could in some cases be regarded as a client. They may be less concerned about their relative's safety if they are aware that outcomes of, for example, TiKL, SOS and DFAW, have been implemented (and possibly paid for by them). Employers of older people will naturally be interested in the Working Late outcomes.

This chapter, however, is concerned with linkages and similarities associated with the six projects, rather than the differences between them. Three main approaches have been adopted. The third section dealt with 11 'aspects' – matters agreed by the principal investigators of the projects as having particular importance across the projects. Here, a cross-project analysis based on these 11 aspects shows a remarkable set of linkages as they apply to the various projects, notwithstanding the different outputs of each the particular programme. This leads to the interesting speculation that if a similar analysis were to be made across more of the 35 NDA projects than the six in this chapter, the 11 identified aspects could form some kind of universal linkage binding the projects together into a strong cohesive whole. Even if this were not to prove to be the case, the activity of identifying a possibly different set of common aspects could produce interesting and valuable guidance for planning future projects.

The second approach was to examine, in the fourth section, the concept of competency, linking this topic with the essential matter of client/user involvement in the design process. Competency frameworks are not common in the design field, but are well established in industry, particularly in manufacturing. In the industrial context, competencies are the central core of the UK National Vocational Qualifications programme, but in this chapter, competency is coupled with client/user involvement in the particular project concerned, in order to help to provide a framework to assist in clarifying this complex topic. Reference here is also made to the need for cross-disciplinary understanding and clear communication channels free from jargon and other interferences.

The third approach was to identify synergy linkages between the different projects, discussed in the fifth section. This aspect is particularly important, representing an added-value component to the outputs to two or more projects. Already alluded to in Chapter Five is the synergy between TIKL (kitchen) and SOS (staircase), leading to these essential central features of a home being designed around the needs of older people. But the concepts enshrined in these two projects could be taken even further. With appropriate input from architectural design specialists, the 'Lifetime Home' where within the same four-walled structure the changing needs of a starter home, family house, and older people's living space could be accommodated. In addition to this example, it would again be interesting to speculate about synergy links with other projects than the six represented in this chapter.

Finally, as shown in even this small sample of six projects, designers are involved in many activities producing a range of outputs. Sometimes the outputs are physical items used by the client, and sometimes they are processes. Design solutions may address an immediate problem, or may have a long-lasting effect. They may affect just one individual, or large populations – and span narrow or wide age ranges. Designed solutions may be provided for the use of the general public, or solely for fully competent specialists, not necessarily in the design field. As Fuad-Luke (2009, p 27) neatly puts it:

> Design crosses a diverse range of subject fields and disciplinary borders (and) is manifest in all facets of contemporary life…. It is design's ability to operate through 'things' and 'systems' that makes it particularly suitable for dealing with contemporary societal, economic and environmental issues.

EIGHT

A new policy perspective on ageing

Alan Walker

This is the first excursion into what is boldly claimed to be a new science of ageing. Assertions of this nature are asking to be contested. But before the open season begins, let's be clear what is being suggested. Rather than a puffed-up claim of novelty, it is a simple recognition of a transition that is indisputably already under way. The main lines of change in the ageing research agenda have been plotted in Chapter One: more multi-disciplinary collaboration, a much broader than hitherto multi-disciplinarity, and an increasing explicit life course focus. This is not to suggest that all ageing research must follow this path. While it is essential to support single disciplinary inquiry, arguably, such research would benefit from a multi-disciplinary context. Nor is it claimed that this volume is the last word on the subject – first word, more like it, because a transition is under way, and what my New Dynamics of Ageing (NDA) colleagues have accomplished here is not yet sufficiently integrated in its analysis. We can go further in this direction. It is incredibly difficult to achieve even a basic degree of fusion across disciplines, beyond, that is, the obviously cognate ones. This was not due to lack of commitment or effort.

Nor can this account of ageing be described as definitive. (Perhaps only an encyclopaedia could be so described.) Its contents were determined by the NDA Programme and, despite its wide brief, it was not able to cover every base in a highly complex field. There are many pieces of the ageing jigsaw missing that others will have to investigate. Mental capacity is a huge one and unequal ageing another (FUTURAGE, 2011). But what the NDA researchers have demonstrated collectively is a great willingness to undertake multi-disciplinary research, when the research questions demand it, and considerable talent in doing so. They have cleared away a lot of the debris from the path towards a new science of ageing and, hopefully, will encourage others to go further along it.

As well as new scientific approaches, a new policy perspective is also called for to enable the UK and other countries to adjust successfully to the ageing process. The main contender for this position is 'active ageing', which has been taken up in many different contexts – local, national, regional and global. The team responsible for the Road Map for the Future of Ageing Research in Europe (FUTURAGE, 2011) placed active ageing at the centre of its research priorities. In other words, the main *purpose* of ageing research, they argue, is to promote active ageing across the life course, to ensure that, as people age, they are able to maximise their opportunities for participation and well-being. Given the global significance of active ageing as a policy prescription, the bulk of this concluding chapter is devoted to its discussion. The emphasis here is on the policy level in contrast to the discussion of active ageing in Chapter Three, which focuses on its meaning to older people and how to measure it.

As well as the Road Map for European Ageing Research (FUTURAGE, 2011), the research foundations for an active ageing policy focus are also located firmly in the NDA Programme. In addition to a specific project focused on this topic (see Chapters One and Three), many of the other projects espouse an active ageing approach. In fact, active ageing is a, largely invisible, thread linking all of the chapters in this book and most of the NDA projects. This includes the obvious associations with health and well-being, in Chapter Four, where activity is pinpointed as a positive influence on both physical and mental status; with social participation in Chapter Six, which starts from the assumption that active engagement is essential for later-life well-being and examines the barriers to it; and with design, in Chapter Seven, where a key goal of inclusive approaches is to ensure that, as people age, they are enabled to remain actively engaged. Similarly with the issues at the heart of Chapter Five, under- and over-nutrition, it is obvious that these have direct links to both physical and mental capacity and activity levels. Less obvious, perhaps, in the discussion of representations of later life in Chapter Three, it is 'activity' in the form of a positive interaction with social and artistic environments that provides a unifying focus of the projects involved. Thus a clear message from the NDA Programme is that activity, in a wide variety of forms, is a key to well-being in later life, hence the focus of this chapter. This is where the trouble starts, however, because active ageing, like ageing itself, is a contested concept.

To understand the potential of active ageing as a policy paradigm, as well as the risks of misrepresentation it entails, it is necessary briefly to locate the discourse surrounding it within a broader social and political framework. Three parallel developments associated with population ageing may be distinguished: *in society* changes in the politics of ageing and, in particular, the emergence of more active citizenship among older people; *in the scientific and practitioner communities*, the development of various activity paradigms which have culminated in the concept of active ageing; and *in the world of policy*, a new political economy of ageing which has taken the idea of active ageing from science and moulded it to its own purposes. However, the policy response to societal ageing does not yet measure up to the potential created by the other two developments because, essentially, it is dominated by a narrow, top-down productivist orientation. Missing are the critical social and political dimensions. Without them the possibilities for later-life citizenship remain severely constrained. Thus, after examining the origins of active ageing, the chapter concludes by arguing that a new, more comprehensive approach to it would promote both citizenship and social inclusion.

From passive to active citizenship

The current close relationship between ageing and public policy was forged in the UK, as in some other developed countries, in the so-called 'golden age' of welfare state construction following the Second World War. This association between older people and the welfare state produced both positive and negative outcomes for this age group. Summarising drastically, on the one hand, it raised their living standards substantially in most Western European countries. Thus the welfare state formed the essential basis for social citizenship in old age (Marshall, 1950). On the other hand, however, it contributed to their social construction as dependent in economic terms, and encouraged popular ageist stereotypes of old age as a period of both poverty and frailty (Walker, 1980; Townsend, 1981, 1986; Binstock, 1991). Although many stereotypes have some tangential relationship to reality, in this case the high levels of poverty in old age in most European countries in the 1950s and 1960s (one in three in the UK and one in five in Germany), they tend to exert a disproportionate influence on public perceptions and discourses even long after the grain of truth has disappeared. Thus age discrimination is a universal feature of European countries even though the standard of living experienced by older people differs widely and, in some, poverty has been virtually eradicated (Naegele and Walker, 2009).

The close relationship between older people and the welfare state is also a powerful factor in determining the current nature of ageing discourses. All welfare states originated, to a large extent, in provision for old age and public pension systems. Now they constitute not only the biggest items of national social expenditure, which pose sharp policy questions about future sustainability, but they also comprise the heart of the particular welfare regime found in each country. This means that the character of a country's retirement pension system tends to have a major role in determining the rest of the welfare regime (Esping-Andersen, 1990, 1999; Walker, 2003). Notwithstanding variations in regime types between European countries, however, there was a common stereotype of older people as, essentially, passive recipients of pensions and, in the case of those reliant on social assistance, welfare dependants, albeit deserving ones. In other words, even under contrasting Beveridge (UK) and Bismarck (Germany) pension systems, similar discourses of dependency were found although they were, and are, contingent on the broad social legitimacy of a national pension scheme.

This generally negative social construction of old age and older people was reinforced by their social exclusion from the political and policy-making systems. The key development here was superannuation: the expectation that older people would leave the labour force at fixed (arbitrary) ages, exchange wages for pensions and disengage themselves from formal economic activity (Phillipson, 1982; Walker, 1980). Retirement also operated as a process of social and political exclusion: older people were simultaneously detached from paid work together with the main sources of political consciousness and channels of representation. This exclusion contributed to the popular perception of older people as being politically, as well as economically, inactive. This then fed into age discriminatory stereotypes that portrayed older people as passive, acquiescent, family-orientated and disinterested in social and political participation.

Other factors also operated to reinforce these stereotypes of passivity. For example, age was less significant than it is today: there were fewer older people; they were less healthy; and retirement acted as an efficient regulator of labour force exit. Also, in political terms, old age was less salient because it was not yet perceived as an economic threat and, in any case, attention was directed at rebuilding the physical infrastructures of the UK and other European countries following the Second World War and constructing the major institutions of modern society, including the welfare state.

Emergence of a new politics of ageing

Summary accounts such as the preceding and following ones are prone to sweeping generalisations. They are, nonetheless, necessary here to convey the important broad transformations that have taken place in the public policy discourses accompanying population ageing (for fuller accounts, see Walker and Naegele, 1999; Walker, 2006). The tide in public discourses on ageing began to turn in the 1970s. At the macro level policy makers began to reject the welfare state consensus and to question, more openly than hitherto, the cost of population ageing. Underlying this tidal shift in policy discourses were macro-economic developments: first, the fiscal crisis of the 1970s following the Yom Kippur War and then, in the 1980s, the rising influence of neoliberalism with its inherent critique of public welfare. Because pension systems are the keystones of welfare states, they came under close scrutiny from this new doctrinal perspective. Moreover, this change in economic and political ideology coincided with the maturation of some national pension schemes and the beginning of the present concern with projections of the future costs of long-term care.

It was in this period, too, that the UK and other European countries witnessed the huge growth of early exit from the labour force (Kohli et al, 1991), which exacerbated the financial consequences of population ageing for national exchequers. All European countries began to focus on the ageing issue at the highest levels of policy making. Few took significant action, however, which emphasises the essential role of political/economic ideology in shaping policy responses to demographic change as well as the urgency of their introduction. Thus there were big variations between European countries at this stage, ranging from substantial reductions in public pensions in the UK (under the Thatcher governments) to the maintenance or improvement of existing pension systems in many other countries (Pierson, 2000; Scharpf and Schmidt, 2000). Despite the negative consequences of the public policy measures encouraging early exit, all of them remained in operation apart from the UK's. It was not until the latter part of the following decade that a different policy perspective emerged in the majority of European countries, one which, as outlined below, portrayed an active role for older people.

Globalisation was yet to have its later decisive impact on the spread of neoliberal ideas including those concerning ageing and its economic consequences (Estes and Phillipson, 2002; Walker and Deacon, 2003). The early signs of what would become common ground among the international governmental organisations (IGOs) appeared in the late

1980s in the form of two Organisation for Economic Co-operation and Development (OECD) (1988a, 1988b) reports. These set out, and were followed by others in the same mould, a 'burden of ageing' discourse, and advocated policy prescriptions that involved a reduction in public pay-as-you-go and private/occupational defined benefit pension schemes and an increase in private, defined contribution ones (The World Bank, 1994; OECD, 1998). The IGOs made much, some would argue too much, of the 'ageing crisis' and, in doing so, reinforced negative perceptions of ageing and older people (Quadagno, 1989; Walker, 1990; Vincent, 1996). Not all policy makers accepted the idea of the public burden of ageing, nor the neoliberal prescriptions that accompanied it. There remained substantial variations across the European continent: in the West only the UK went along this policy route wholeheartedly, while, in the East, the key roles played by the IGOs in advising the ex-communist bloc countries meant that the neoliberal prescriptions were followed more closely (Ferge, 2002).

There is a 'structural lag' between social and cultural changes and institutional ones (Riley, 1992). So, while the public policy discourses were dominated by either the deserving model of ageing or the public burden one, or sometimes a mixture of both, within some European countries new grass-roots discourses were emerging. For example, in the late 1980s and early 1990s, there was a growth in direct political participation among older people (Goerres, 2009). Such action is invariably a minority pursuit but, nonetheless, new or reconstituted movements of older people were seen in Denmark, Germany and the UK, while, in 1992, the Italian pensioner party, the oldest of its kind in Europe, had its first representative elected to the regional government in Rome. A year later seven pensioner representatives were elected to the Dutch Parliament (Walker and Naegele, 1999). The character of the political and policy discourses emanating from these social movements were, of course, fundamentally different from the public policy ones. In contrast to the latter the grass-roots movements emphasised human (including welfare) rights, participation, social inclusion, and fiercely opposed age discrimination regardless of whether it was blatant or benign.

These new social movements of civil society often reflected the close relationship between ageing and the welfare state in two separate ways. On the one hand, the success of Western European welfare provision meant that increasing numbers of older people were not only surviving longer than previously but also, were doing so in better health. On the other hand, the negative impact of the changes in economic and political ideology discussed earlier had a mobilising effect, and led to direct action in the form of protests against cuts in pensions, health and social services. Policy makers in several countries have responded to this new politics by, for example, establishing advisory boards of older people at the local level. Non-governmental organisations (NGOs) have also often supported the activities of older people engaged in this new, more direct, politics of ageing (Walker and Naegele, 1999; Durandal, 2002).

Intertwined with this growth in social movements concerned with ageing issues has been the cultural shift in society usually labelled as the transition from modernity to late modernity/post-modernity (Harvey, 1989). The key dimension of this transition, for this account, is the rise of individualistic consumerism. Its effects are apparent in both the state and the market sectors (and, of course, its spread is closely related to neoliberal economic globalisation). As far as the state is concerned, the pressures for more individually tailored services and for a participating voice by service users has led to new, more flexible forms of service provision, such as individual payments in Germany and the UK in lieu of services, and the establishment of user groups to represent the interests of older users, as in Denmark. On the market front, the emergence of the 'older consumer' and the 'silver economy' over the last decade can be seen across Europe. Indeed, one comparison between Germany and the UK concludes that differences are greater between age cohorts *within* the two countries that between them (Potratz et al, 2009). In other words, new generations of younger-older people who, as a result of continuous employment and pension scheme maturation, are more affluent then their forebears, also display higher levels of hedonism concerning consumption and lifestyle. This finds its expression in a wide variety of forms, from anti-ageing medicines to 'silver travellers' (Potratz et al, 2009).

In sum, the last four decades in the UK and other parts of Western Europe have seen the emergence of two interrelated discourses on citizenship in old age. First, a new macro-political economy of ageing which has transformed the deservingness stereotype of older people, which accompanied welfare state formation, into a threat to economic sustainability. This neoliberal policy orientation is more visible in some countries than others, and is especially so in the Anglo-Saxon ones. Second, partly in response to the macro-political economic changes, a new micro and meso politics of old age has emerged. Although this affects only a minority of older people, there is no doubt about the sea change in the desire for political participation on the part of older people (Durandal, 2002). No longer content to be the passive recipients of pensions, many are demanding an active voice in decisions which affect their lives.

Genesis of active ageing

The second critical development in the construction of later-life citizenship are the discourses concerning the nature of ageing which have culminated in the concept of active ageing. In order to comprehend the scope and potential of this concept, and to distinguish it from related notions such as healthy ageing, it is necessary to trace its origins, albeit briefly. It began life in the US in the early 1960s with the introduction of the 'successful ageing' paradigm (Pfeiffer, 1974; Rowe and Kahn, 1987). This goal could be achieved by the maintenance in old age of the activity patterns and values typical of middle age (Havighurst, 1954, 1963; Havighurst and Albrecht, 1953). In other words, successful ageing was a matter of denying the onset of old age and replacing those relationships, activities and roles of middle age that are lost with new ones, in order to maintain activities and life satisfaction. This theory of ageing was seen partly as a response to the then influential theory of 'disengagement', which viewed old age as an inevitable period of withdrawal from roles and relationships (Cumming and Henry, 1961).

Activity theorists recognised that this was a depressing picture of old age (and empirically wrong). But, and this is important for the contemporary present debate, their approach was regarded as too idealistic and grounded in American norms. It placed an unrealistic expectation on ageing individuals themselves to maintain the levels of activity associated with middle age through to advanced old age. It was pointed out that, in trying to do so, many older people faced biological limitations and, perhaps more importantly, that the economic, political and social structures of society sometimes inhibit and prevent people from remaining active – the obvious example being retirement (Walker, 1980). Activity theory was also criticised for making generalisations about the ageing process and homogenising older people. Nonetheless the empirical link between activity and well-being in old age, that was established by this school of thought, remains true today.

From productive to active ageing

In the 1980s the concept re-surfaced in the US in the guise of 'productive ageing'. Its emergence reflected various socio-political developments including the desire for more active citizenship outlined earlier. Researchers had begun to shift the focus of ageing research from older people to the process of human development over the life course. Underlying this attention to the life course was the realisation that chronological age is not a good predictor of performance. A significant group of older US citizens were making it clear that they wanted something else besides leisure and family obligations after traditional retirement, and 'productive ageing' became a rallying cry for elder advocates and others looking for a more positive approach to ageing (Bass et al, 1993). These changes chimed very closely with policy makers' growing concerns about the pension and healthcare costs of an ageing population, and they, too, were keen to extend productivity. Thus active ageing was raised at the G8 Summit in Denver in June 1997, and delegates discussed ways of removing disincentives to labour force participation and lowering barriers to part-time employment. Since then it has become a key feature of social policy proposals from the European Union (EU) and OECD.

Most of the variants of productive ageing are focused narrowly on the production of goods and services and, therefore, tend to be instrumental and economistic. For example, 'productivity' means 'activities that produce goods and services that otherwise would have to be paid for' (Morgan, 1986, p 74), or, more broadly, 'Productive ageing is any activity by an older individual that produces goods or services, or develops the capacity to produce them, whether they are paid for or not' (Bass et al, 1993, p 6).

A modern concept of active ageing

A new concept of active ageing began to emerge in the 1990s, under the influence of the World Health Organization (WHO), which, not surprisingly, emphasised the vital connection between activity and health (Butler et al, 1990, p 201), and the importance of healthy ageing (WHO, 1994; see also WHO, 2001a). Given the link with health and the influence of the EU on its development, this approach to active ageing has focused on a broader range of activities than those normally associated with production and the labour market, and has emphasised health and the participation and inclusion of older people as full citizens (see, for example, Walker, 1993, 1994). The thinking behind this new approach is expressed perfectly in the WHO dictum, 'years have been added to life, now we must add life to years'. This suggests a general lifestyle strategy for the preservation of physical and mental health as people age rather than just trying to make them work longer. Thus the essence of the emerging modern concept of active ageing is a combination of the core element of productive ageing, but with a strong emphasis on quality of life and mental and physical well-being (EC, 1999; Cabinet Office, 2000). The WHO (2001a, 2001b), for example, sees active ageing in terms of the health, independence and productivity of older people.

The new political economy of ageing

As already noted, the emergence of neoliberalism, first in the 1980s and then, more comprehensively, in the 2000s, led to a transformation in the attitudes of policy makers towards older people. No longer seen as the deserving recipients of welfare state 'largesse' they were, to a varying degree across different countries, increasingly viewed as a threat to economic performance. Of course this new political economy runs counter to the changing political aspirations of older people and, therefore, it acted as a spur to participation. For example, particularly at grass-roots level, older people have been mobilised as political actors (often for the first time) by campaigns against government cuts in benefits and services. It also has a close association with the second critical development in the construction of current later-life discourses, the emergence of active ageing. There is always a risk involved in the cross-over of ideas from science to policy that the evidence base and finer points of concepts will be lost in the process that translates into a political slogan. This is exactly what has happened in the case of active ageing.

This may be illustrated briefly with regard to the EU (for fuller versions, see Walker, 2009; Walker and Maltby, 2012). European policy makers enthusiastically took up the idea of active ageing in the late 1990s. Unfortunately, however, the origins of the concept and its potential to respond to the call for greater political participation in old age were completely overlooked. In practice, active ageing was reduced to the level of the lowest common denominator: a policy prescription to work longer. This was translated into EU policy by the Lisbon European Council (the Heads of State summit meeting), which established a 10-year strategy to make Europe 'the most competitive and dynamic knowledge-based economy in the world'. Central to this strategy was the achievement of 'full employment' by 2010. At the next summit in Stockholm in 2001, flesh was put on these bare strategic bones, and this included a specific target employment rate for older workers of 50 per cent. This target was translated into the EU's Employment Guidelines under which the member states report annually on progress (a system known as the Open Method of Coordination). Thus the idea of active ageing was turned, by EU policy makers, into a productivist reduction concerned with keeping older workers in the labour market:

> Member States should develop active ageing policies by adopting measures to maintain working capacity and skills of older workers, to introduce flexible working arrangements and to raise employers' awareness of older workers' potential. They should ensure that older workers have sufficient access to further education and training and review tax and social protection systems with the aim of removing disincentives and creating incentives for them to remain active in the labour market. (EC, 2001, p 50)

Inevitably, in a region as big as Europe and an organisation as complex as the European Commission, there is a range of different discourses, some of which are competing. So it is with active ageing, and there are examples of where a more expansive position has been taken (EC, 2006). Nonetheless the dominant policy concern was employment. This was emphasised by the aims of the 2012 European Year of Active Ageing and Solidarity between Generations:

> The European Year 2012 aims to help create better job opportunities and working conditions for the growing number of older people in Europe, help them take an active role in society and encourage healthy ageing. (EC, 2010)

As far as the UK is concerned, the zenith of its commitments to active ageing was the 2005 White Paper, *Opportunity age* (DWP, 2005), which established a broad programme of actions to promote social inclusion, albeit one that led with an employment rate target.

In sum, if we imagine active ageing as a continuum, in practical policy terms, at EU level it is stuck firmly at one end – the lowest common denominator. This productivist stance denies the potential of the concept, as demonstrated by its origins in activity theory and in subsequent research (see Chapter Four), to both enhance participation and well-being in later life, and to respond to the needs expressed by older people across Europe for a greater voice in decision making. It is the macro-political economy that is the main driver of this reduction but, in implementing it, policy makers are overlooking two important dimensions of active ageing. First is *social participation*. There is a clear relationship between participation and well-being, as illustrated here in Figure 8.1.

Figure 8.1: The cycle of well-being

Source: ODPM (2006)

In other words, social inclusion is good for people, including older people; it enhances their well-being and quality of life. Second is *political participation*. The beneficial impact of participation also applies to political engagement. Furthermore, in terms of human rights and social empowerment, it is essential that older people themselves play active roles in combating exclusion and in shaping the sort of citizenship they themselves want to experience. It is only when older people's voices are uppermost in this process that later-life citizenship will reflect their aspirations.

Making active ageing inclusive

The challenge, then, is to realise the true potential of the active ageing idea to promote social inclusion and active citizenship. To respond to this challenge requires a massive leap of the imagination to envisage a completely different model of active ageing and, indeed, of ageing, from the one currently favoured by policy makers in all developed countries, and not only those in the EU.

A good starting point is the WHO's multi-dimensional approach to active ageing. Not surprisingly this perspective is strongly health-orientated, but the WHO does take an extremely broad view of 'health'. Thus, according to the WHO (2002, p 12), active ageing is:

> ... the process of optimising opportunities for health, participation and security in order to enhance quality of life as people age. Active ageing applies to both individuals and groups. It allows people to realise their potential for physical, social, and mental well-being throughout their lives and to participate in society according to their needs, desires and capacities, while providing them with adequate protection, security and care when they require assistance.

This WHO policy represented the culmination of a long process of deliberation and discussion, with inputs from a variety of scientific and policy perspectives. It made two important contributions to European and global discourses on active ageing. First, it added further weight to the case for a re-focusing of active ageing away from employment and towards a consideration of all of the different factors that contribute to well-being. Specifically it argued for the linkage, in policy terms, between employment, health and participation, and echoed the similar case made by some within the EU. Second, and again along similar lines to the contributions of the European Commission and European scientists, it emphasised the critical importance of a life course perspective. In other words, to prevent some of the negative consequences associated with later life it is essential to influence individual behaviour and its policy context at earlier stages of the life course.

The WHO approach also contributed to the growth of the discourse on older people as active participants in society that had been present at the European level since the 1993 Year of Older People, encouraged by the European Commission's support of organisations such as AGE (the EU platform representing older people), and boosted by the European activities in the UN Year of Older People in 1999. The theme of older people's right to participate, as well as the key policy of active ageing, were further reinforced by the 2002 UN Madrid International Plan of Action on Ageing (MIPAA). The MIPAA gives prominence to active ageing as a strategic global response to population ageing, and this is reflected in the UN Economic Council of Europe's Regional Implementation Strategy (UN, 2002).

Despite the major contribution made by the WHO's active ageing strategy, there are several deficiencies inherent in its model. These are not fundamental, but suggest that a modified version is necessary. First, the inevitable emphasis on health implies a focus on physical health alone when it is also essential to preserve mental capacity. Second, the WHO model pays insufficient attention to inequality and heterogeneity in later life. These present barriers to the implementation of active ageing policies as well as indicating priorities for intervention. Third, along similar lines, variations in culture and institutions between countries and regions suggest the need for flexibility in application of the active ageing concept. For example, within one small EU country, Belgium, there is a need for different approaches to active ageing within the two communities of Flanders and Wallonia because of their contrasting age profiles. Fourth, the WHO model tends towards top-down prescriptions and does not, therefore, emphasise the critical role of empowerment in the active ageing agenda. Finally, a very broad understanding of 'activity' is required and of the policy levels that might be used to promote it.

Building on the foundations of the WHO model it is possible to outline what a comprehensive strategy would look like and the principles on which it should be based (EC, 1999; Walker, 1999a; WHO, 2001a, 2001b, 2002). By emphasising the health and well-being aspects of active ageing, this body of work represented a paradigm shift away from the 'productive ageing' one that had previously been prominent in the global discourse on ageing. There were certainly very positive discourses embedded within the US concept of productive ageing because it was born as a rallying cry for older people and their advocates who were campaigning against discrimination and calling for a positive approach to ageing (Bass et al, 1993). Moreover, it replaced the then prevailing concept of 'successful ageing', which was highly idealistic and strongly US culture-bound (Walker, 2002). Unfortunately, as we have seen, the idea of productive ageing usually focused narrowly on the production of goods and services and, therefore, lacked the emphases on the life course and well-being found in the active ageing paradigm. When the OECD (1998, p 14) tried to combine these two paradigms, the result begged more questions than it answered: active ageing is 'the capability of people as they grow older to lead productive lives in the society and economy'.

So, while the WHO conception prioritises health, the modified one advanced here places more emphasis on participation and well-being. Also, rather than assuming that the process of active ageing exists in practice, perhaps we should be more cautious. Thus, active ageing *should* be:

> … a comprehensive strategy to maximise participation and
> well-being as people age. It should operate simultaneously
> at the individual (lifestyle), organisational (management)
> and societal (policy) levels and at all stages of the life course.
> (Walker, 2009, p 86)

As mentioned and illustrated earlier, the twin emphases on participation
and well-being are derived from the scientific evidence of the
close interrelationship between them and the beneficial effects of
participation on positive well-being (ODPM, 2006).

A strategy for active ageing

Seven key principles have been proposed previously as the basis for a
strategy on active ageing to ensure that it is both comprehensive and
consistent (Walker, 2002).

First, 'activity' should consist of all meaningful pursuits which
contribute to the well-being of the individual concerned, his or
her family, local community or society at large, and should not just
be concerned with paid employment or production. Thus, in terms
of active ageing, volunteering should be as highly valued as paid
employment, and mental activities as relevant as physical ones.

Second, it should be primarily a preventative concept. This means
involving all age groups in the process of ageing actively across the
whole of the life course.

Third, active ageing should encompass *all* older people, even those
who are, to some extent, frail and dependent. This is because of the
danger that a focus only on the 'young old' will exclude the 'old old',
and the fact that the link between activity and health (including mental
stimulation) holds good into advanced old age (WHO, 2001a). There
is also an important gender aspect to this principle in that most of the
'very old' are women. Thus this strategy is framed to be gender-sensitive,
not gender-neutral (Foster and Walker, 2013).

Fourth, the maintenance of intergenerational solidarity should be
an important feature of active ageing. This means fairness between
generations as well as the opportunity to develop activities that span
the generations. In practice, active ageing should be as important for
younger as older generations.

Fifth, the concept should embody both rights and obligations.
Thus, the rights to social protection, lifelong education and training
and so on should be accompanied by obligations to take advantage
of education and training opportunities, and to remain physically and

mentally active in other ways. Again, from a gender perspective, this may require support to enable women to participate because of their caring responsibilities.

Sixth, a strategy for active ageing should be participative and empowering. In other words, there must be a combination of top-down policy action to enable and motivate activity, but also, extensive opportunities for citizens to take action, from the bottom up, for example, in developing their own forms of activity. Clearly, on its own, an active ageing strategy cannot overcome all forms of powerlessness that older people experience, but it should aim to contribute to empowerment. To achieve a broader change would require a wider cultural transformation in political democracy towards more participative forms.

Seventh, active ageing has to take account of inequality and heterogeneity, or unequal ageing (Cann and Dean, 2009), and also respect national and cultural diversity. For example, the significance of gender has been highlighted already but, unless the very different life courses of men and women are recognised, including different career opportunities and domestic responsibilities, women will not gain equal access to the potential benefits of active ageing (Foster and Walker, 2013), similarly with social class/socio-economic status inequalities. In all EU countries there are clear differences in life expectancy and healthy life expectancy based on occupational class (FUTURAGE, 2011). Active ageing has to take these into account and try to prevent them, otherwise the already most disadvantaged groups will be excluded from active ageing. Similar points may be made about racial and ethnic differences and the need to tailor policies accordingly.

With regard to national variations there are differences in the forms of participation undertaken between the North and the South of Europe, therefore value judgements about what sort of activity is 'best' are likely to be problematic (EC, 2006). As noted previously *within* some EU countries, there are major cultural variations that require a flexible approach to the implementation of an active ageing strategy.

These principles suggest that an effective strategy on active ageing should be based on a *partnership* between the citizen and society. In this partnership the role of the state is to enable, facilitate and motivate citizens and, where necessary, to provide high-quality social protection for as long as possible. This will require interrelated individual and societal strategies. As far as individuals are concerned, they have a duty to take advantage of lifelong learning and continuous training opportunities and to promote their own health and well-being throughout the life course. As far as society is concerned, the policy challenge is to recognise the thread that links together all of the relevant policy areas: employment, health, social protection, social inclusion, transport, education, and so on. A comprehensive active ageing strategy demands that all of them are 'joined up' and become mutually supportive. The primary discourse behind this strategic vision of active ageing is the UN's one of a society for all ages (see www. un.org/en/globalissues/ageing).

Thus what is envisaged here is a comprehensive model of active ageing which embodies both social inclusion and citizenship. It derives from a perspective on ageing which insists that it is every person's human right to age actively. While some may choose to neglect or ignore this right, it should be the duty of society and the state to facilitate it. Thus, ideally, active ageing would be a right of citizenship. Of course, as noted above, citizenship entails responsibilities as well as rights, but people cannot be forced to age actively. Instead, the critical test of the robustness of this right is the extent to which policies, practices and institutional regimes support and empower citizens to age actively. This means, for example, education in schools about ageing and its consequences, lifelong education and training, age management in employment, opportunities for physical activities and mental stimulation in all communities, preventative public health measures and inter-generational pursuits.

With regard to the scope of the actions necessary to achieve such a comprehensive strategy, the WHO has highlighted eight main determinants of active ageing: culture and gender (both of which are cross-cutting), health and social services, behavioural, the physical environment, the social environment, economic determinants and those related to the person concerned (such as biology, genetics, and psychology) (WHO, 2002). In both UK and EU policy terms this would mean linkage between policy domains that have hitherto been separated: employment, health, social protection, pensions, social inclusion, technology, economic policy and research.

Of course the key stakeholders are not dormant while they wait for the perfect strategic framework to be assembled. Thus there are countless examples of local community and grass-roots level initiatives by older people, NGOs and municipalities aimed at raising the participation and well-being of this group (Walker and Naegele, 1999; Durandal, 2002). In some countries there are national programmes to encourage healthy ageing such as 'FinnWell' in Finland. There is plenty of evidence, too, that some employers, albeit a minority, have developed a variety of age management measures designed to retain, recruit and maximise the potential of an ageing workforce (Walker, 1999b; Naegele and Walker,

2006). What is lacking at present, however, in the UK and other EU countries, is a comprehensive strategy on active ageing which includes the sharing of the many examples of good practice in different spheres.

Research and development have a critical role to play in advancing the active ageing agenda, and especially in providing the evidence base for policy. UK research such as the NDA Programme, and European research under Framework Programmes 5, 6 and 7, has already added considerably to this knowledge base. Also the future research priorities have been mapped by, for example, the ETAN initiative, coordinated actions such as FORUM and ERA-AGE (see http://era-age.group.shef.ac.uk) and, as noted at the start of this chapter, the Road Map for European Ageing Research (FUTURAGE, 2011) places active ageing as the central objective of research in this field.

Conclusion

Because of the need for a new policy approach to accompany the new science of ageing, this concluding chapter has focused on the relationship between active ageing, citizenship and social inclusion. Three parallel developments related to population ageing have been identified which have shaped discourses on both ageing and active ageing. It has been demonstrated that the concept of active ageing was rooted in the new politics of old age that began to take a recognisable shape during the 1980s. The transition from a largely passive to a more active political orientation among older people was echoed (and encouraged) by policy makers at both local and national levels. In Europe, the EU also played a leading role in the articulation of this new approach by and to older people. It facilitated the development of a new approach to active ageing with the potential to, on the one hand, reflect the discourses arising, bottom up, from older people and being reinforced by those with scientific expertise in health and well-being and ageing while, on the other, those coming, top down, from policy makers concerning the economic sustainability of the EU's social protection systems. In other words, active ageing is that rare policy concept that could unify the interests of all key stakeholders: citizens, NGOs, business interests and policy makers. Unfortunately, however, the radical potential of active ageing has not been realised in Europe because the productivist reduction has been dominant.

In contrast, the policy paradigm of active ageing proposed here consists of a comprehensive approach to the maximisation of participation and well-being as people age and one that, ideally, operates simultaneously at the micro, meso and macro levels. Comprehensiveness and consistency would be ensured by policies that reflect the seven key principles outlined earlier. Essentially these principles reflect the need for a partnership between the citizen and society if the comprehensive, inclusive and lifelong paradigm of active ageing is to be realised in a non-coercive fashion. Thus individual responsibility should be matched by policy action to connect all of the potential supports for active ageing that are usually separated into different administrative departments. Joining up separate policy areas, such as employment, health, pensions and education, is a pre-requisite for realising this comprehensive approach as well as for the creation of a society for all ages. At the core of the strategy must be a preventative, life course perspective. Citizenship should include the right and responsibility to age actively and, thereby, to maximise well-being. Only this comprehensive approach can do justice to three interrelated challenges: utilising the research riches produced by the new science of ageing, as represented by the NDA Programme, the need for transformational change in later life inequalities, and older people's demand for social inclusion.

Of course it is not the task of one policy strategy – active ageing – to create a new, deeper citizenship in later life but, as argued here, it could play a significant role in doing so. The essential ingredients are an inclusive approach, responding to unequal ageing, rejecting the ageist stereotypes that diminish old age and exclude many older people, and attempting to empower those engaged in the active ageing process. Thus, while the new science of ageing produces a holistic understanding of this lifelong process and its culmination in old age, a new policy paradigm, focused on active ageing for all, is essential to maximise participation and physical and mental well-being. A partnership between science and policy could transform the experience of ageing and later life. To do so, what is required is political commitment to undertake the far-reaching transformation in policy and practice needed to implement a comprehensive active ageing strategy.

References

Abele, D., Strahl, J., Brey, T. and Philipp, E.E. (2008) 'Imperceptible senescence: ageing in the ocean quahog *Arctica islandica*', *Free Radic Res*, vol 42, pp 474-80.

Abellan van Kan, G., Rolland, Y., Andrieu, S., Bauer, J., Beauchet, O., Bonnefoy, M., Cesari, M., Donini, L.M., Gillette-Guyonnet, S., Inzitari, M., Nourhashemi, F., Onder, G., Ritz, P., Salva, A., Visser, M. and Vellas, B. (2009) 'Gait speed at usual pace as a predictor of adverse outcomes in community-dwelling older people. An International Academy on Nutrition and Ageing (IANA) Task Force', *J Nutr Health Aging*, vol 13, no 10, pp 881-9.

Abrams, D.I., Shade, S.B., Couey, P., Mccune, J.M., Lo, J., Baccheti, P., Chang, B., Epling, L., Liegler, T. and Grant, R.M. (2007) 'Dehydroepiandrosterone (DHEA) effects on HIV replication and host immunity: a randomized placebo-controlled study', *AIDS Res Hum Retroviruses*, vol 23, pp 77-85.

Achenbaum, W.A. (1997) 'Critical gerontology', in A. Jamieson, S. Harper and C. Victor (eds) *Critical approaches to ageing and later life*, Buckingham: Open University Press, pp 16-26.

Adey, P. (2010) *Mobility*, Oxford: Routledge.

Advisory Group on Malnutrition, The (2009) *Combating malnutrition: recommendations for action*, Edited by M. Elia and C.A. Russell, Redditch: BAPEN (www.bapen.org.uk/pdfs/reports/advisory_group_report. pdf).

Aebi, U., Cohn, J., Buhle, L. and Gerace, L. (1986) 'The nuclear lamina is a meshwork of intermediate-type filaments', *Nature*, vol 323, pp 560-4.

Age UK (2010) *Still hungry to be heard: the scandal of people in later life becoming malnourished in hospital*, London: Age UK (www.ageuk. org.uk/Documents/EN-GB/ID9489%20HTBH%20Report%20 28ppA4.pdf?dtrk=true).

AIGA (American Institute of Graphic Arts) (2012) 'Designer of 2015 competencies', New York: AIGA (www.aiga.org/designer-of-2015-competencies).

Akbar, A.N. and Fletcher, J.M. (2005) 'Memory T cell homeostasis and senescence during aging', *Curr Opin Immunol*, vol 17, pp 480-5.

Alam, M. and Barrientos, A. (eds) (2010) *Demographics, Employment and Old Age Security: Emerging Trends and Challenges in South Asia*, New Delhi: Macmillan Publishers India.

Alkema, G.E. and Alley, D.E. (2006) 'Gerontology's future: an integrative model for disciplinary advancement', *The Gerontologist*, vol 46, pp 574-82.

Allender, S., Foster, C., Scarborough, P. and Rayner, M. (2007) 'The burden of physical activity-related ill health in the UK', *J Epidemiol Community Health*, vol 61, no 4, pp 344-8.

Allison, P.J., Locker, D. and Feine, J.S. (1997) 'Quality of life: a dynamic construct', *Social Sci Med*, vol 45, no 2, p 221.

Allolio, B. and Arlt, W. (2002) 'DHEA treatment: myth or reality?', *Trends Endocrinol Metab*, vol 13, pp 288-94.

Andrews, F.M. and Robinson, J.P. (1991) 'Measures of subjective well-being', in J.P. Robinson, P.R. Shaver and L.S. Wrightsman (eds) *Measures of personality and social psychological attitudes*, San Diego, CA: Academic Press, pp 61-114.

Arber, S. and Ginn, J. (1991) *Gender and later life: a sociological analysis of resources and constraints*, London: Sage.

Arber, S. and Venn, S. (2011) 'Caregiving at night: understanding the impact on carers', *J Aging Studies*, vol 25, pp 155-65.

Arber, S. and Venn, S. (in press) 'Sleep and healthy ageing', in C. Browning and S. Thomas (eds), *Interdisciplinary Perspectives of Healthy Ageing: Improving the Quality of Life for Older People*, New York: Springer.

Arber, S., Meadows, R. and Venn, S. (2012) 'Sleep and society', in C.M. Morin and C.A. Espie (eds) *The Oxford handbook of sleep disorders*, Oxford: Oxford University Press, pp 223-47.

Ardener, S. (ed) (1997) *Women and space. Ground rules and social maps*, Oxford and New York: Berg.

Aries, P.Y. (1962) *Centuries of childhood: a social history of family life*, New York: Vintage Books/Random House.

Arking, R. (2006) *The biology of ageing: observations and principles*, Oxford: Oxford University Press.

Aspinall, R. and Andrew, D. (2000) 'Thymic involution in aging', *J Clin Immunol*, vol 20, pp 250-6.

Atchley, R.C. (1982) 'Retirement as a social institution', *Annual Review of Sociology*, vol 8, pp 263-87.

Audit Commission (2008) *Don't stop me now: Preparing for an ageing population*, Local government national report, London: Audit Commission, (www.cpa.org.uk/cpa/Dont_Stop_Me_Now.pdf (accessed 17 August 2013).

Avenell, A., Gillespie, W.J., Gillespie, L.D. and O'Connell, D. (2009) 'Vitamin D and vitamin D analogues for preventing fractures associated with involutional and post-menopausal osteoporosis', *Cochrane Database Syst Rev*, CD000227.

Aviv, H., Khan, M.Y., Skurnick, J., Okuda, K., Kimura, M., Gardner, J., Priolo, L. and Aviv, A. (2001) 'Age dependent aneuploidy and telomere length of the human vascular endothelium', *Atherosclerosis*, vol 159, pp 281-7.

Bagley, M.C., Davis, T., Latimer, J. and Kipling, D. (2011) 'The contribution of biogerontology to quality ageing', *Quality in Ageing and Older Adults*, vol 12, pp 26-32.

Bagley, M.C., Davis, T., Murziani, P.G.S., Widdowson, C.S. and Kipling, D. (2010) 'Use of p38 MAPK inhibitors for the treatment of Werner syndrome', *Pharmaceuticals*, vol 3, pp 1842-72.

Bakarman, A.A. (2005) *Attitude, Skill and Knowledge (ASK): a new model for design education*, Riyadh, Saudi Arabia: King Saud University.

Baker, D.J., Wijshake, T., Tchkonia, T., Lebrasseur, N.K., Childs, B.G., van de Sluis, B., Kirkland, J.L. and van Deursen, J.M. (2011) 'Clearance of p16Ink4a-positive senescent cells delays ageing-associated disorders', *Nature*, vol 479, pp 232-6.

Baker, J., Meisner, B.A., Logan, A.J., Kungl, A. and Weir, P. (2009) 'Physical activity and successful aging in Canadian older adults', *J Aging Physical Activity*, vol 17, pp 223-35.

BAPEN Quality Group (2010) *Malnutrition matters – meeting quality standards in nutritional care: a toolkit for commissioners and providers in England*, Redditch: BAPEN (www.bapen.org.uk/pdfs/toolkit-for-commissioners.pdf).

Bargh, J.A., Chen, M. and Burrows, L. (1996) 'Automaticity of social behaviour: direct effects of trait construct and stereotype activation on action', *J Personality Soc Psychol*, vol 71, pp 230-44.

Barnes, S.K. and Ozanne, S.E. (2011) 'Pathways linking the early environment to long-term health and lifespan', *Prog Biophys Mol Biol*, vol 106, pp 323-36.

Barnes, M. and Walker, A. (1996) 'Consumerism versus empowerment – a principled approach to the involvement of elder service users', *Policy & Politics*, vol 24, no 4, pp 375-93.

Barrientos, A. and Mase, J. (2012) 'Poverty transitions among older households in Brazil and South Africa', *European Journal of Development Research*, vol 24, no 4, pp 570-88.

Barthes, R. (1972) *Mythologies*, New York: Farrar, Straus & Giroux.

Bass, S., Caro, F. and Chen, Y.-P. (eds) (1993) *Achieving a productive aging society*, Westport, CT: Auburn House.

Bauer, M.E. (2005) 'Stress, glucocorticoids and ageing of the immune system', *Stress*, vol 8, pp 69-83.

Bazalgette, L., Holden, J., Tew, P., Hubble, N. and Morrison, J. (2011) *'Ageing is not a policy problem to be solved...': Coming of age*, London: Demos (www.demos.co.uk/files/Coming_of_Age_-_web.pdf?1302099024).

Beech, R. and Murray, M. (2013) 'Social engagement and healthy ageing in disadvantaged communities', *Quality in Ageing and Older Adults*, vol 14, no 1, pp 12-24.

Bekesi, G., Kakucs, R., Varbiro, S., Racz, K., Sprintz, D., Feher, J. and Szekacs, B. (2000) 'In vitro effects of different steroid hormones on superoxide anion production of human neutrophil granulocytes', *Steroids*, vol 65, pp 889-94.

Belfiore, E. and Bennett, O. (2007) 'Determinants of impact: towards a better understanding of encounters with the arts', *Cultural Trends*, vol 16, no 3, pp 225-75.

Bengtson, V.L., Gans, D., Putney, N.M. and Silverstein, M. (2009) *Handbook of theories of aging*, New York: Springer Verlag.

Bennett, K. (2002) 'Low level social engagement as a precursor of mortality among people in later life', *Age and Ageing*, vol 31, no 3, pp 165-8.

Bennett, M.R., Macdonald, K., Chan, S.W., Boyle, J.J. and Weissberg, P.L. (1998) 'Cooperative interactions between RB and p53 regulate cell proliferation, cell senescence, and apoptosis in human vascular smooth muscle cells from atherosclerotic plaques', *Circ Res*, vol 82, pp 704-12.

Berger, E.D. (2006) '"Aging" identities: degradation and negotiation in the search for employment', *J Aging Studies*, vol 20, no 4, pp 303-16.

Berger, R., Florent, G. and Just, M. (1981) 'Decrease of the lymphoproliferative response to varicella-zoster virus antigen in the aged', *Infect Immun*, vol 32, pp 24-7.

Bernard, M., Rickett, M., Amigoni, D., Munro, L., Murray, M. and Rezzano, J. (2014) 'Ages and Stages: the place of theatre in the lives of older people', *Ageing and Society*, available on CJO2014. doi: 10.1017/S0144686X14000038.

Biggs, S. (2001) 'Toward critical narrativity: stories of aging in contemporary social policy', *Journal of Aging Studies*, vol 15, pp 303-16.

Binstock, R.H. (1991) 'From the great society to the aging society – 25 years of the older Americans Act', *Generations*, vol 15, no 3, pp 11-18.

Birge, S.J., Morrow-Howell, N. and Proctor, E.K. (1994) 'Hip fracture', *Clin Geriatr Med*, vol 10, pp 589-609.

Blair, S., Kohl, H., Gordon, N. and Paffenbarger, R. (1992) 'How much physical activity is good for health?', *Ann Rev Public Health*, vol 13, no 1, pp 99-126.

Blakemore, K. (1982) 'Health and illness among the elderly of minority ethnic groups', *Health Trends*, vol 14, no 3, pp 68-72.

Blasco, M.A. (2005) 'Telomeres and human disease: ageing, cancer and beyond', *Nat Rev Genet*, vol 6, pp 611-22.

Bogin, B.A., Harper, D., Merrell, J., Chowdhury, J., Heinrich, M., Garaj, V,, Molik, B., and Thompson J.L. (2014) 'Influence of adult knee height, age at first birth, migration, and current age on adult physical function of Bangladeshi mothers and daughters in the United Kingdom and Bangladesh', *Journal of Anthropology*, vol 2014, Article ID 808634, (http://dx.doi.org/10.1155/2014/808634).

Boneham, M. (1989) 'Ageing and ethnicity in Britain: the case of elderly Sikh women in a Midlands town', *New Community*, vol 15, no 3, pp 447-59.

Bonomo, R.A. (2002) 'Resistant pathogens in respiratory tract infections in older people', *J Am Geriatr Soc*, vol 50, S236-41.

Bostrom, N. (2005) 'The fable of the dragon tyrant', *J Med Ethics*, vol 31, pp 273-7.

Boubriak, I., Mason, P.A., Clancy, D.J., Dockray, J., Saunders, R.D. and Cox, L.S. (2009) 'DmWRNexo is a 3'-5' exonuclease: phenotypic and biochemical characterization of mutants of the Drosophila orthologue of human WRN exonuclease', *Biogerontology*, vol 10, pp 267-77.

Boulton-Lewis, G.M. (2010) 'Education and learning for the elderly: why, how, what', *Educational Gerontol*, vol 36, no 3, pp 213-28.

Bourdieu, P. (1984) *Distinction: a social critique of the judgement of taste* (translated by R. Nice), Cambridge, MA: Harvard University Press.

Bowers, J. (1998) 'Effects of an intergenerational choir for community-based seniors and college students on age-related attitudes', *J Music Therapy*, vol 35, pp 2-18.

Bowling, A. (1996) 'The effects of illness on quality of life: findings from a survey of households in Great Britain', *Journal of Epidemiology and Community Health*, vol 50, pp 149–55.

Bowling, A. (2005) *Ageing well. Quality of life in older age*, Maidenhead: Open University Press.

Bowling, A. (2008) 'Enhancing later life: how older people perceive active ageing?', *Aging Mental Health*, vol 12, pp 293-301.

Bowling, A., Gabriel, Z., Dykes, J., Dowding, L.M., Evans, O., Fleissig, A., Banister, D. and Sutton, S. (2003) 'Let's ask them: a national survey of definitions of quality of life and its enhancement among people aged 65 and over', *International Journal of Aging and Human Development*, vol 56, pp 269-306.

Bowling, A. and Stenner, P. (2011) 'Which measure of quality of life performs best in older age? A comparison of the OPQOL, CASP-19 and WHOQOL-OLD', *Journal of Epidemiology and Community Health*, vol 65, no 3, pp 273-80. (doi:10.1136/jech.2009.087668).

Bowling, A., Hankins, M., Windle, G., Bilotta, C. and Grant, R. (2013) 'A short measure of quality of life in older age: the performance of the brief Older People's Quality of Life questionnaire (OPQOL-brief)', *Archives of Gerontology and Geriatrics*, 56, no 1, pp 181-87. (doi:10.1016/j.archger.2012.08.012). (PMID:22999305).

Boyton, R.J. and Openshaw, P.J. (2002) 'Pulmonary defences to acute respiratory infection', *Br Med Bull*, vol 61, pp 1-12.

Brach, J., Simonsick, E., Kritchevsky, S., Yaffe, K. and Newman, A. (2004) 'The association between physical function and lifestyle activity and exercise in the health, aging and body composition study', *J Amer Ger Soc*, vol 52, no 4, pp 502-9.

Bridger, J.M. and Kill, I.R. (2004) 'Aging of Hutchinson-Gilford progeria syndrome fibroblasts is characterised by hyperproliferation and increased apoptosis', *Exp Gerontol*, vol 39, pp 717-24.

Bronfenbrenner, U. (1979) *The ecology of human development*, Cambridge, MA: Harvard University Press.

Brooke, A.M., Kalingag, L.A., Miraki-Moud, F., Camacho-Hubner, C., Maher, K.T., Walker, D.M., Hinson, J.P. and Monson, J.P. (2006) 'Dehydroepiandrosterone improves psychological well-being in male and female hypopituitary patients on maintenance growth hormone replacement', *J Clin Endocrinol Metab*, vol 91, pp 3773-9.

Brown, W.T. (1992) 'Progeria: a human-disease model of accelerated aging', *Am J Clin Nutr*, vol 55, pp 1222S-1224S.

Brown, W.T., Williams, L., Ford, J., Ball, K. and Dobson, A. (2005) 'Identifying the energy gap: magnitude and determinants of 5-year weight gain in midage women', *Obesity Res*, vol 13, no 8, pp 1431-41.

Brown, W.T., Kieras, F.J., Houck, G.E., Jr, Dutkowski, R. and Jenkins, E.C. (1985) 'A comparison of adult and childhood progerias: Werner syndrome and Hutchinson-Gilford progeria syndrome', *Adv Exp Med Biol*, vol 190, pp 229-44.

Browne, J.P., O'Boyle, C.A., McGee, H.M., Joyce, C.R.B., McDonald, N.J., O'Malley, K. and Hiltbrunner, B. (1994) 'Individual quality of life in the healthy elderly', *Quality of Life Research*, vol 3, no 4, pp 235-44.

Brownie, S. (2006) 'Why are elderly individuals at risk of nutritional deficiency?', *International Journal of Nursing Practice*, vol 12, no 2, pp 110-18.

Bruun, H., Hukkinen, J. and Klein, J.T. (2005) *Promoting interdisciplinary research: the case of the Academy of Finland*, Series #8/05, Helsinki: Academy of Finland.

Buckle, P., Woods, V., Oztug, O. and Stubbs, D. (2008) *Workplace design for the older worker*, Reading: SPARC (Strategic Promotion of Ageing Research Capacity) (http://www.sparc.ac.uk/media/downloads/executivesummaries/exec_summary_buckle.pdf).

Bunn, F., Dickinson, A., Barnett-Page, E., Mcinnes, E. and Horton, K. (2008) 'A systematic review of older people's perceptions of facilitators and barriers to participation in falls-prevention interventions', *Ageing Soc*, vol 28, no 4, pp 449-72.

Burholt, V. (2004) 'Transnationalism, economic transfers and families' ties: intercontinental contacts of older Gujaratis, Punjabis and Sylhetis in Birmingham with families abroad', *Ethnic and Racial Studies*, vol 27, issue 5, pp 800-29.

Burns, D., Heywood, F., Taylor, M., Wilde, P. and Wilson, M. (2004) *Making community participation meaningful: a handbook for development and assessment*, Bristol: Policy Press.

Burrig, K.F. (1991) 'The endothelium of advanced arteriosclerotic plaques in humans', *Arterioscler Thromb*, vol 11, pp 1678-89.

Butcher, S.K. and Lord, J.M. (2004) 'Stress responses and innate immunity: aging as a contributory factor', *Aging Cell*, vol 3, pp 151-60.

Butcher, S.K., Killampalli, V., Chahal, H., Alpar, E.K. and Lord, J.M. (2003) 'The effect of age on susceptibility to post traumatic infection in the elderly', *Biochem Soc Trans*, vol 31, pp 449-51.

Butcher, S.K., Killampalli, V., Lascelles, D., Wang, K., Alpar, E.K. and Lord, J.M. (2005) 'Raised cortisol:DHEAS ratios in the elderly after injury: potential impact upon neutrophil function and immunity', *Aging Cell*, vol 4, pp 319-24.

Butler, R., Oberlink, M. and Schecter, M. (eds) (1990) *The promise of productive aging*, New York: Springer.

Buvat, J. (2003) 'Androgen therapy with dehydroepiandrosterone', *World J Urol*, vol 21, pp 346-55.

Bygren, L.O., Konlaan, B.B. and Johansson, S. (1996) 'Attendance at cultural events, reading books or periodicals, and making music or singing in a choir as determinants for survival: Swedish interview survey of living conditions', *British Medical Journal*, vol 313, p 1577.

Bygren, L.O., Weissglas, G., Grjibovski, A.M., Karlsson, A.-B., Andersson, S.-O. and Sjöström, M. (2009) 'Cultural participation and health: a randomized controlled trial among medical care staff', *Psychosomatic Medicine*, vol 71, no 4, pp 469-73.

Bytheway, B. (2011) *Unmasking age: the significance of age for social research*, Bristol: Policy Press.

Bytheway, B. and Johnson, J. (2005) 'Cataloguing old age', in G. Andrews and D. Phillips (eds) *Ageing and place: perspectives, policy and practice*, London: Routledge, pp 176-87.

Cabinet Office (2000) *Winning the generation game*, London: The Stationery Office.

Campisi, J. (2000) 'Cancer, aging and cellular senescence', *In Vivo*, vol 14, pp 183-8.

Campisi, J., Andersen, J.K., Kapahi, P. and Melov, S. (2011) 'Cellular senescence: a link between cancer and age-related degenerative disease?', *Semin Cancer Biol*, vol 21, pp 354-9.

Cann, P. and Dean, M. (eds) (2009) *Unequal ageing*, Bristol: Policy Press.

Cannon, W.B. (1932) *The wisdom of the body*, New York: Norton.

Cao, K., Capell, B.C., Erdos, M.R., Djabali, K. and Collins, F.S. (2007) 'A lamin A protein isoform overexpressed in Hutchinson-Gilford progeria syndrome interferes with mitosis in progeria and normal cells', *Proc Natl Acad Sci USA*, vol 104, no 12, pp 4949-54.

Cao, K., Graziotto, J.J., Blair, C.D., Mazzulli, J.R., Erdos, M.R., Krainc, D. and Collins, F.S. (2011) 'Rapamycin reverses cellular phenotypes and enhances mutant protein clearance in Hutchinson-Gilford progeria syndrome cells', *Sci Transl Med*, vol 3, 89ra58.

Carnes, B.A. and Olshansky, S.J. (2007) 'A realist view of aging, mortality, and future longevity', *Pop Dev Rev*, vol 33, pp 367-81.

Caspersen, C. and Merritt, R. (1995) 'Physical activity trends among 26 states, 1986-1990', *Med Sci Sports Exercise*, vol 27, no 5, pp 713-20.

Cattell, V., Dines, N., Gesler, W. and Curtis, S. (2008) 'Mingling, observing, and lingering: everyday public spaces and their implications for well-being and social relations', *Health & Place*, vol 14, no 4, pp 544-61.

Champion, T. and Shepherd, J. (2006) 'Demographic change in rural England', in L. Speakman and P. Lowe (eds) *The ageing countryside: the growing older population in rural England*, London: Age Concern, pp 29-50.

Chang, E. and Harley, C.B. (1995) 'Telomere length and replicative aging in human vascular tissues', *Proc Natl Acad Sci USA*, vol 92, pp 11190-4.

Chau, J., van der Ploeg, H., van Uffelen, J., Wong, J., Riphagen, I., Healy, G., Gilson, N., Dunstan, D., Bauman, A., Owen, N. and Brown, W. (2010) 'Are workplace interventions to reduce sitting effective? A systematic review', *Preventive Med*, vol 51, no 5, pp 352-6.

Chaudhry, S. (2007) 'The management of subcapital fractures in the elderly – with an emphasis on economic aspects', *Trauma*, vol 9, pp 119-26.

Chiu, S. and Yu, S. (2001) 'An excess of culture: the myth of shared care in the Chinese community in Britain', *Ageing & Society*, vol 21, no 6, pp 681-99.

Chodosh, J., Kado, D.M., Seeman, T.E. and Karlamangla, A.S. (2007) 'Depressive symptoms as a predictor of cognitive decline: MacArthur studies of successful aging', *Am J Geriatr Psychiatry*, vol 15, pp 406-15.

Chodzko-Zajko, W.J., Proctor, D.N., Fiatarone Singh, M.A., Minson, C.T., Nigg, C.R., Salem, G.J. and Skinner, J.S. (2009) 'American College of Sports Medicine position stand. Exercise and physical activity for older adults', *Med Sci Sports Exerc*, vol 41, pp 1510-30.

Choquette, G. and Ferguson, R. (1973) 'Blood pressure reduction in "borderline" hypertensives following physical training', *Can Med Assoc J*, vol 108, no 6, pp 699-703.

Christensen, K., Doblhammer, G., Rau, R. and Vaupel, J.W. (2009) 'Ageing populations: The challenges ahead', *The Lancet*, vol 374, pp 1196-1208.

Chu, C.Y., Chien, H.K. and Lee, R.D. (2008) 'Explaining the optimality of U-shaped age-specific mortality', *Theor Popul Biol*, vol 73, pp 171-80.

Cieraad, I. (ed) (1999) *At home: an anthropology of domestic space*, Syracuse, NY: Syracuse University Press.

Clair, J.M. and Allman, R.M. (2000) *The gerontological prism: developing interdisciplinary bridges*, New York: Baywood Publishing.

Clarkson, J., Coleman, R., Keates, S. and Lebbon, C. (eds) (2003) *Inclusive design: design for the whole population*, London: Springer-Verlag Publications.

Cleaver, F. (2005) 'The inequality of social capital and the reproduction of chronic poverty', *World Development*, vol 33, no 6, pp 893-906.

Clift, S., Nicol, J., Raisbeck, M., Whitmore, C. and Morrison, I. (2010) *Group singing, wellbeing and health: a systematic mapping of research evidence*, Folkestone: Sidney de Haan Research Centre for Arts and Health, Canterbury Christ Church University, UK.

Cohen, G.D., Perlstein, S., Chapline, J., Kelly, J., Firth, K.M. and Simmens, S. (2006) 'The impact of professionally conducted cultural programs on the physical health, mental health, and social functioning of older adults', *The Gerontologist*, vol 46, no 6, pp 726-34.

Cohen, G.D., Perlstein, S., Chapline, J., Kelly, J., Firth, K.M. and Simmens, S. (2007) 'The impact of professionally conducted cultural programs on the physical health, mental health and social functioning of older adults – 2-year results', *J Aging, Humanities Arts*, vol 1, pp 5-22.

Coleman, R. (1994) 'The case for inclusive design – an overview', Proceedings of the 12 Triennial Congress, International Ergonomics Association and Human Factors Association of Canada, Toronto, vol 3, pp 250-2.

Coles, A.J., Thompson, S., Cox, A.L., Curran, S., Gurnell, E.M. and Chatterjee, V.K. (2005) 'Dehydroepiandrosterone replacement in patients with Addison's disease has a bimodal effect on regulatory (CD4+CD25hi and CD4+FoxP3+) T cells', *Eur J Immunol*, vol 35, pp 3694-703.

Colman, R.J., Anderson, R.M., Johnson, S.C., Kastman, E.K., Kosmatka, K.J., Beasley, T.M., Allison, D.B., Cruzen, C., Simmons, H.A., Kemnitz, J.W. and Weindruch, R. (2009) 'Caloric restriction delays disease onset and mortality in rhesus monkeys', *Science*, vol 325, pp 201-4.

Commission for Social Care Inspection (2008) *Cutting the cake fairly: CSCI review of eligibility criteria for social care*, London: Commission for Social Care Inspection, (www.cpa.org.uk/cpa/cutting_the_cake_fairly.pdf)

Commission on Funding of Care and Support (2011) *Fairer Care Funding: The Report of the Commission on Funding of Care and Support* ('Dilnot Commission'), (http://webarchive.nationalarchives.gov.uk/20130221130239/http://dilnotcommission.dh.gov.uk/our-report/)

Cooke, B. and Kothari, U. (eds) (2001) *Participation: the new tyranny?*, London and New York: Zed Books.

Corrigan, D.P., Kuszczak, D., Rusinol, A.E., Thewke, D.P., Hrycyna, C.A., Michaelis, S. and Sinensky, M.S. (2005) 'Prelamin A endoproteolytic processing in vitro by recombinant Zmpste24', *Biochem J*, vol 387, pp 129-38.

Cox, L.S. (2009) 'Live fast, die young: new lessons in mammalian longevity', *Rejuvenation Res*, vol 12, pp 283-8.

Cox, L.S. and Faragher, R.G. (2007) 'From old organisms to new molecules: integrative biology and therapeutic targets in accelerated human ageing', *Cell Mol Life Sci*, vol 64, pp 2620-41.

Cox, L.S. and Mason, P.A. (2010) 'Prospects for rejuvenation of aged tissue by telomerase reactivation', *Rejuvenation Res*, vol 13, pp 749-54.

Cox, L.S. and Mattison, J.A. (2009) 'Increasing longevity through caloric restriction or rapamycin feeding in mammals: common mechanisms for common outcomes?', *Aging Cell*, vol 8, pp 607-13.

Cox, L.S., Clancy, D.J., Boubriak, I. and Saunders, R.D. (2007) 'Modeling Werner syndrome in Drosophila melanogaster: hyper-recombination in flies lacking WRN-like exonuclease', *Ann NY Acad Sci*, vol 1119, pp 274-88.

CQC (Care Quality Commission) (2012) *Dignity and Nutrition Inspection Programme: national overview*, Newcastle upon Tyne: CQC (www.cqc.org.uk/sites/default/files/media/documents/20111020_dignity_nutrition_report_easy_to_read.pdf).

Crawford, J.O. (2010) 'Health at the heart of spatial planning', *Planning Theory & Practice*, vol 11, no 1, pp 91-113.

Crawford, J.O., Graveling, R.A., Cowie, H.A. and Dixon, K. (2010) 'The health safety and health promotion needs of older workers', *Occupational Medicine (Oxford, England)*, vol 60, no 3, pp 184-92.

Crespo, C., Keteyian, S., Heath, G. and Sempos, C. (1996) 'Leisure-time physical activity among US adults. Results from the Third National Health and Nutrition Examination Survey', *Arch Intern Med*, vol 156, no 1, pp 93-8.

Crombie, I., Irvine, L., Williams, B., McGinnis, A., Slane, P., Alder, E. and McMurdo, M. (2004) 'Why older people do not participate in leisure time physical activity: a survey of activity levels, beliefs and deterrents', *Age Ageing*, vol 33, no 3, pp 287-92.

Cross, S. and Markus, H. (1991) 'Possible selves across the life span', *Human Development*, vol 34, pp 230-55.

Cruess, D.G., Douglas, S.D., Petitto, J.M., Have, T.T., Gettes, D., Dube, B., Cary, M. and Evans, D.L. (2005) 'Association of resolution of major depression with increased natural killer cell activity among HIV-seropositive women', *Am J Psychiatry*, vol 162, pp 2125-30.

Cumming, E. and Henry, W. (1961) *Growing old: the process of disengagement*, New York: Basic Books.

Cunningham, G.O., Michael, Y.L., Farquhar, S.A. and Lapidus, J. (2005) 'Developing a reliable senior walking environmental assessment tool', *American Journal of Preventive Medicine*, vol 29, no 3, pp 215-17.

Cupps, T.R. and Fauci, A.S. (1982) 'Corticosteroid-mediated immunoregulation in man', *Immunol Rev*, vol 65, pp 133-55.

Daatland, S.O. (2005) 'Quality of life and ageing', in M.L. Johnson (ed) *The Cambridge handbook of age and ageing*, New York: Cambridge University Press, pp 371-7.

Dahl, K.N., Scaffidi, P., Islam, M.F., Yodh, A.G., Wilson, K.L. and Misteli, T. (2006) 'Distinct structural and mechanical properties of the nuclear lamina in Hutchinson–Gilford progeria syndrome', *Proc Natl Acad Sci USA*, vol 103, pp 10271-6.

Damjanovic, A.K., Yang, Y., Glaser, R., Kiecolt-Glaser, J.K., Nguyen, H., Laskowski, B., Zou, Y., Beversdorf, D.Q. and Weng, N.P. (2007) 'Accelerated telomere erosion is associated with a declining immune function of caregivers of Alzheimer's disease patients', *J Immunol*, vol 179, pp 4249-54.

Darkenwald, G.G. and Merriam, S.B. (1982) *Adult education: foundations of practice*, New York: Harper Row Publishers.

Darrow, A.A., Johnson, C.M. and Ollenberger, T. (1994) 'The effect of participation in an intergenerational choir on teens' and older persons' cross age attitudes', *Journal of Music Therapy*, vol 31, pp 119-34.

Davey, J. and Glasgow, K. (2006) 'Positive ageing: a critical analysis', *Policy Quarterly*, vol 2, no 2, pp 21-7.

Davies, M., Harries, P., Cairns, D., Stanley, D., Gilhooly, M., Gilhooly, K., Notley, E., Gilbert, A., Penhale, B. and Hennessy, C. (2011) 'Factors used in the detection of elder financial abuse: a judgment and decision making study of social workers and their managers', *International Social Work*, vol 54, no 3, pp 404-20.

Davis, T. and Kipling, D. (2006) 'Werner syndrome as an example of inflamm-aging: possible therapeutic opportunities for a progeroid syndrome?', *Rejuvenation Res*, vol 9, pp 402-7.

Davis, T., Tivey, H.S.E. and Kipling, D. (2009) 'Telomere dynamics and biology in human progeroid syndromes', in L. Mancini (ed) *Telomeres: function, shortening and lengthening*, New York: Novascience, pp 1-75.

Davis, T., Baird, D.M., Haughton, M.F., Jones, C.J. and Kipling, D. (2005) 'Prevention of accelerated cell aging in Werner syndrome using a p38 mitogen-activated protein kinase inhibitor', *J Gerontol A Biol Sci Med Sci*, vol 60, pp 1386-93.

DCMS (Department for Culture, Media and Sport) (2007) *Taking Part: The National Survey of Culture, Leisure and Sport*, Annual report 2005/2006, London: DCMS.

DCMS (2012) *Taking part 2011/12 quarter 4 statistical release*, London: DCMS.

Debusk, F.L. (1972) 'The Hutchinson-Gilford progeria syndrome. Report of 4 cases and review of the literature', *J Pediatr*, vol 80, pp 697-724.

Deci, E.L. and Ryan, R.M. (2010) *Self-determination theory: An approach to human motivation & personality* (www.psych.rochester.edu/SDT/).

de Fina, A. and Georgakopoulou, A. (2012) *Analyzing narrative. Discourse and sociolinguistic perspective*, Cambridge: Cambridge University Press.

de Grey, A. (2005) 'Aubrey de Grey: a roadmap to end ageing' (www. ted.com/talks/aubrey_de_grey_says_we_can_avoid_aging.html).

de Jager, C.A., Oulhaj, A., Jacoby, R., Refsum, H. and Smith, A.D. (2012) 'Cognitive and clinical outcomes of homocysteine-lowering B-vitamin treatment in mild cognitive impairment: a randomized controlled trial', *Int J Geriatr Psychiatry*, vol 27, pp 592-600.

Dementia Services Development Centre (2012) 'Design for dementia care', University of Stirling (www.dementia.stir.ac.uk and www.atdementia.org.uk/editorial.asp?page_id=163 – accessed 8 September 2012).

Deng, Q., Liao, R., Wu, B.L. and Sun, P. (2004) 'High intensity ras signaling induces premature senescence by activating p38 pathway in primary human fibroblasts', *J Biol Chem*, vol 279, pp 1050-9.

Department for Work and Pensions (DWP) (2005) *Opportunity age*, London: DWP.

Department of Health, Department for Work and Pensions (2008) *Lifetime Homes, Lifetime Neighbourhoods. A National Strategy for Housing in an Ageing Society*, London: Crown Publishing.

Depp, C.A. and Jeste, D.V. (2006) 'Definitions and predictors of successful aging: a comprehensive review of larger quantitative studies', *Am J Geriatric Psychiatry*, vol 14, pp 6-20.

DH (Department of Health) (2004) *At least five a week: evidence on the impact of physical activity and its relationship to health*, London: DH.

DH (2011) *Start active, stay active: a report on physical activity from the four home countries' Chief Medical Officer*, London: DH.

Dijk, D.J., Groeger, J.A., Stanley, N. and Deacon, S. (2010) 'Age-related reduction in daytime sleep propensity and nocturnal slow wave sleep', *Sleep*, vol 33, no 2, pp 211-23.

Dimri, G.P., Lee, X., Basile, G., Acosta, M., Scott, G., Roskelley, C., Medrano, E.E., Linskens, M., Rubelj, I. and Pereira-Smith, O. (1995) 'A biomarker that identifies senescent human cells in culture and in aging skin in vivo', *Proc Natl Acad Sci USA*, vol 92, pp 9363-7.

Ding, Z., Wu, C.J., Jaskelioff, M., Ivanova, E., Kost-Alimova, M., Protopopov, A., Chu, G.C., Wang, G., Lu, X., Labrot, E.S., Hu, J., Wang, W., Xiao, Y., Zhang, H., Zhang, J., Gan, B., Perry, S.R., Jiang, S., Li, L., Horner, J.W., Wang, Y.A., Chin, L. and Depinho, R.A. (2012) 'Telomerase reactivation following telomere dysfunction yields murine prostate tumors with bone metastases', *Cell*, vol 148, pp 896-907.

Donald, I., Foy, C. and Jagger, C. (2010) 'Trends in disability prevalence over 10 years in older people living in Gloucestershire', *Age and Ageing*, vol 39, no 3, pp. 337-42.

Douglas, M. (1996) *Natural symbols: explorations in cosmology*, London: Routledge.

Doyal, L. and Gough, I. (1991) *A theory of human need*, Hong Kong: Macmillan.

Doyen, S., Klein, O., Pichon, C.L. and Cleeremans, A. (2012) 'Behavioral priming: it's all in the mind, but whose mind?', *PLoS One*, vol 7, e29081.

Duay, D. and Bryan, V. (2008) 'Learning in later life: what seniors want in a learning experience', *Educational Gerontology*, vol 34, no 12, pp 1070-86.

Duggal, N.A., Upton, J.A., Phillips, A.C., Hampson, P. and Lord, J.M. (2013) 'Depressive symptoms are associated with reduced neutrophil superoxide generation in hip fracture patients', *Brain Behavior Immunity*, vol 33, pp 173-82.

Dunnell, K. (2008) 'Ageing and Mortality in the UK – National Statistician's Annual Article on the Population', *Population Trends 134*, Winter 2008, pp 6-23 (www.ons.gov.uk/ons/rel/population-trends-rd/population-trends/no--134--winter-2008/ageing-and-mortality-in-the-uk---national-statistician-s-annual-article-on-the-population.pdf)

Durandal, J.-P. (ed) (2002) *Grey power?*, 2 volumes, Paris: Fédération internationale des associations de personnes âgées.

Eakman, A., Carlson, M. and Clark, F. (2010) 'The meaningful activity participation assessment: a measure of engagement in personally valued activities', *Journal of Aging Human Development*, vol 70, no 4, pp 299-317.

EC (European Commission) (1999) *Towards a Europe for all ages*, COM (1999) 221, Brussels: EC.

EC (2001) *Guidelines for member states' employment policies for the year 2002*, Brussels: EC.

EC (2006) *The demographic future of Europe – from challenge to opportunity*, Brussels: EC.

EC (2010) *2012 to be the European Year for Active Ageing*, DG Employment, Social Affairs and Inclusion (http://ec.europa.eu/social/main.jsp?langId=en&catId=89&newsId=860).

Effros, R.B. and Pawelec, G. (1997) 'Replicative senescence of T cells: does the Hayflick limit lead to immune exhaustion?', *Immunol Today*, vol 18, pp 450-4.

Ekerdt, D. (1986) 'The busy ethic: moral continuity between work and retirement', *The Gerontologist*, vol 26, pp 239-44.

Emmerson, E. and Hardman, M.J. (2012) 'The role of estrogen deficiency in skin ageing and wound healing', *Biogerontology*, vol 13, pp 3-20.

Epel, E.S., Blackburn, E.H., Lin, J., Dhabhar, F.S., Adler, N.E., Morow, J.D. and Cawthon, R.M. (2004) 'Accelerated telomere shortening in response to life stress', *Proc Natl Acad Sci USA*, vol 101, no 49, pp 17312-5.

Erikson, E.H. (1968) *Identity: youth and crisis*, New York: Norton.

Eriksson, M., Brown, W.T., Gordon, L.B., Glynn, M.W., Singer, J., Scott, L., Erdos, M.R., Robbins, C.M., Moses, T.Y., Berglund, P., Dutra, A., Pak, E., Durkin, S., Csoka, A.B., Boehnke, M., Glover, T.W. and Collins, F.S. (2003) 'Recurrent de novo point mutations in lamin A cause Hutchinson-Gilford progeria syndrome', *Nature*, vol 423, pp 293-8.

Esping-Andersen, G. (1990) *The three worlds of welfare capitalism*, Cambridge: Policy Press.

Esping-Andersen, G. (1999) *Social foundations of postindustrial economies*, Oxford: Oxford University Press.

Estes, C. and Phillipson, C. (2002) 'The globalisation of capital, the welfare state and old age policy', *International Journal of Health Services*, vol 32, no 2, pp 279-97.

EuroHealthNet (2012) *Healthy and active ageing*, Brussels: Brundeszentrale fur gesundheitliche Aufklarung.

European Nutrition for Health Alliance, The (2005) *Malnutrition within an ageing population: a call for action. Report on the Inaugural Conference of The European Nutrition for Health Alliance*, London: The European Nutrition for Health Alliance (www.european-nutrition.org/index.php/events/malnutrition_within_an_ageing_population_a_call_for_action).

Evans, W.J. and Campbell, W.W. (1993) 'Sarcopenia and age-related changes in body composition and functional capacity', *J Nutr*, vol 123, pp 465-8.

Ewing, R., Handy, S., Brownson, R.C., Clemente, O. and Winston, E. (2006) 'Identifying and measuring urban design qualities related to walkability', *Journal of Physical Activity Health*, vol 3, suppl 1, S223-S240.

Fairhurst, E. (2011) '"Positive images" and calendars', in V. Ylänne (ed) *Representing ageing: images and identities*, Basingstoke: Palgrave, pp 189-206.

Farquhar, M. (1995) 'Definitions of quality of life: a taxonomy', *Journal of Advanced Nursing*, vol 22, no 3, pp 502-8.

Featherstone, M. and Hepworth, M. (2005) 'Images of ageing: cultural representations of later life', in M. Johnson (ed) *The Cambridge handbook of age and ageing*, Cambridge: Cambridge University Press, pp 354-62.

Fein, A.M. (1999) 'Pneumonia in the elderly: overview of diagnostic and therapeutic approaches', *Clin Infect Dis*, vol 28, pp 726-9.

Feinberg, C. (2010) 'The mindfulness chronicles', *Harvard Mag* (http:// harvardmagazine.com/2010/09/the-mindfulness-chronicles).

Ferge, Z. (2002) 'European Integration and the reform of social security in the accession countries', *European Journal of Social Quality*, vol 3, no 1/2, pp 9-25.

Fernández, J.-L., and Forder, J. (2011) *Impact of changes in length of stay on the demand for residential care services in England, report commissioned by Bupa care services*, PSSRU discussion paper 2771, Canterbury: PSSRU. (www.pssru.ac.uk/pdf/dp2771.pdf)

Ferrie, J.E., Kivimaki, M. and Shipley, C. (2010) 'Sleep and death', in F.P. Cappuccio, M.A. Miller and S.W. Lockley (eds) *Sleep, health and society: from aetiology to public health*, Oxford: Oxford University Press, pp 50-82.

Ferrie, J.E., Kumari, M., Salo, P., Singh-Manoux, A. and Kivimaki, M. (2011) 'Sleep epidemiology – a rapidly growing field', *Int J Epidemiol*, vol 40, pp 1431-7.

Fontana, L., Meyer, T.E., Klein, S. and Holloszy, J.O. (2004) 'Long-term calorie restriction is highly effective in reducing the risk for atherosclerosis in humans', *Proc Natl Acad Sci USA*, vol 101, pp 6659-63.

Foster, L. and Walker, A. (2013) 'Gender and active ageing in Europe', *European Journal of Ageing*, vol 10, pp 3-10.

Fratiglioni, L., Paillard-Borg, S. and Winblad, B. (2004) 'An active and socially integrated lifestyle in late life might protect against dementia', *The Lancet*, vol 3, no 6, pp 343-53.

Frazier, L., Johnson, P., Gonzalez, G. and Kafka, C. (2002) 'Psychosocial influences on possible selves: a comparison of three cohorts of older adults', *Int J Behav Dev*, vol 26, no 4, pp 308-17.

Freeman, J. (2004) *The making of the modern kitchen: a cultural history*, Oxford and New York: Berg.

Freeman, M. (2011) 'Narrative foreclosure in later life: possibilities and limits', in G. Kenyon, E. Bohlmeijer and W.L. Randall (eds) *Storying later life: issues, investigations and interventions in narrative gerontology*, New York: Oxford University Press USA, pp 3-19.

Fried, L.P., Bandeen-Roche, K., Chaves, P.H. and Johnson, B.A. (2000) 'Preclinical mobility disability predicts incident mobility disability in older women', *J Gerontol Series A: Biol Sci Med Sci*, vol 55, no 1, M43-M52.

Fried, L.P., Tangen, C.M., Walston, J., Newman, A.B., Hirsch, C., Gottdiener, J., Seeman, T., Tracy, R., Kop, W.J., Burke, G. and McBurnie, M.A. (2001) 'Frailty in older adults: evidence for a phenotype', *Journal of Gerontology: MEDICAL SCIENCES,* vol 56A, no 3, M146-M156.

Fry, P.S. (2000) 'Religious involvement, spirituality and personal meaning for life: Existential predictors of psychological wellbeing in community-residing and institutional care elders', *Ageing and mental health*, vol 4, no 4, pp 375-87.

Fuad-Luke, A. (2009) *Design activism: beautiful strangeness for a sustainable world*, London and Sterling, VA: Earthscan.

Fullagar, S. (2008) 'Leisure practices as counter-depressants: emotion-work and emotion-play within women's recovery from depression', *Leisure Sci*, vol 30, pp 35-52.

FUTURAGE (2011) *A road map for European ageing research*, Sheffield: Department of Sociological Studies, University of Sheffield (http://futurage.group.shef.ac.uk).

Gabriel, Z. and Bowling, A. (2004) 'Quality of life from the perspectives of older people', *Ageing and Society*, vol 24, no 5, pp 675-91. (doi:10.1017/S0144686X03001582).

Gardner, E.M. (2005) 'Caloric restriction decreases survival of aged mice in response to primary influenza infection', *J Gerontol A Biol Sci Med Sci*, vol 60, pp 688-94.

Gardner, K. (2002) *Age, narrative and migration: the lifecourse and life histories of Bengali elders in Britain*, Oxford and New York: Berg.

Gates, P.E., Strain, W.D. and Shore, A.C. (2009) 'Human endothelial function and microvascular ageing', *Exp Physiol*, vol 94, pp 311-16.

GavazziI, G. and Krause, K.H. (2002) 'Ageing and infection', *Lancet Infect Dis*, vol 2, pp 659-66.

Gembris, H. (2008) 'Musical activities in the third age: an empirical study with amateur musicians', Paper presented at the Second European Conference on Developmental Psychology of Music, Roehampton University, England, 10-12 September.

Geyer, G. (2005) 'Establishing the European research area in ageing: a network of national research programmes', *Experimental Gerontology*, vol 40, no 10, pp 759-62.

Gilford, H. (1904) 'Ateleiosis and progeria: continuous youth and premature old age', *Br Med J*, vol 2, pp 914-18.

Gilhooly, M.L., Cairns, D., Davies, M., Harries, P.H., Gilhooly, K.J. and Notley, E. (2013) 'Framing the detection of financial elder abuse as bystander intervention: decision cues, pathways to detection and barriers to action', *The Journal of Adult Protection*, vol 15, no 2, pp 54-68.

Gill, R. (2006) *Gender and the media*, Cambridge: Polity Press.

Gilleard, C.J. and Higgs, P. (2000) *Cultures of ageing: self, citizen and the body*, Harlow: Prentice Hall.

Giltay, E.J., van Schaardenburg, D., Gooren, L.J., von Blomberg, B.M., Fonk, J.C., Touw, D.J. and Dijkmans, B.A. (1998) 'Effects of dehydroepiandrosterone administration on disease activity in patients with rheumatoid arthritis', *Br J Rheumatol*, vol 37, pp 705-6.

Glendenning, F. (ed) (2000) *Teaching and learning in later life*, Aldershot: Ashgate.

Goerres, A. (2009) *The political participation of older people in Europe*, Houndmills: Palgrave.

Good, C.D., Johnsrude, I.S., Ashburner, J., Henson, R.N., Friston, K.J. and Frackowiak, R.S. (2001) 'A voxel-based morphometric study of ageing in 465 normal adult human brains', *Neuroimage*, vol 14, pp 21-36.

Gordon, L.B., Kleinman, M.E., Miller, D.T., Neuberg, D.S., Giobbie-Hurder, A., Gerhard-Herman, M., Smoot, L.B., Gordon, C.M., Cleveland, R., Snyder, B.D., Fligot, B., Bishop, W.R., Statkevich, P., Regen, A., Sonis, A., Riley, S., Ploski, C., Correia, A., Quinn, N., Ullrich, N.J., Nazarian, A., Liang, M.G., Huh, S.Y., Schwartzman, A. and Kieran, M.W. (2012) 'Clinical trial of a farnesyltransferase inhibitor in children with Hutchinson-Gilford progeria syndrome', *Proc Natl Acad Sci USA*, vol 109, pp 16666-71.

Gosling, E.Y., Gyi, D.E., Gibb, A.G. and Haslam, R.A. (2012) 'Ageing productively through design? A survey of cement workers', *Aging & Society*, vol 1, no 4, pp 1-18.

Goto, M. (1997) 'Hierarchical deterioration of body systems in Werner's syndrome: implications for normal ageing', *Mech Ageing Dev*, vol 98, pp 239-54.

Government Office for Science (2007) *Tackling obesities: Future choices. Foresight project report* (www.bis.gov.uk/assets/foresight/docs/obesity/17.pdf)

Graham, J.E., Christian, L.M. and Kiecolt-Glaser, J.K. (2006) 'Stress, age, and immune function: toward a lifespan approach', *J Behav Med*, vol 29, pp 389-400.

Greaves, C. and Farbus, L. (2006) 'Effects of creative and social activity on the health and well-being of socially isolated older people: outcomes from a multi-method observational study', *The Journal of the Royal Society for the Promotion of Health*, vol 126, no 3, pp 134-42.

Greer, G. (1996) *The change: women, aging and the menopause*, London: Hamish Hamilton.

Groombridge, B. (2007) *Extra time: arts, health and learning in later life*, Frank Glendenning Memorial Lecture, Leicester: National Institute of Adult Continuing Education.

Gullette, M.M. (2004) *Aged by culture*, London: University of Chicago Press.

Guralnik, J.M., Simonsick, E.M., Ferrucci, L., Glynn, R.J., Berkman, L.F., Blazer, D.G., Scherr, P.A. and Wallace, R.B. (1994) 'A short physical performance battery assessing lower extremity function: association with self-reported disability and prediction of mortality and nursing home admission', *Journal of Gerontology*, vol 49, M85-M94.

Haentjens, P., Autier, P., Barette, M., Venken, K., Vandersheuren, D. and Boonen, S. (2007) 'Survival and functional outcome according to hip fracture type: a one-year prospective cohort study in elderly women with an intertrochanteric or femoral neck fracture', *Bone*, vol 41, pp 958-64.

Hales, S. (1733) *Statical essays, volume 2, containing haemastaticks,* London and New York: Hafner, Publishing Co.

Hallam, S., Creech, A., Varvarigou, M., McQueen, H. and Gaunt, H. (2012) 'Perceived benefits of active engagement with making music in community settings', *International Journal of Community Music*, vol 5, no 2, pp 155-75.

Hallam, S., Creech, A., Gaunt, H., Pincas, A., McQueen, H. and Varvarigou, M. (2011) *Music for life project: promoting social engagement and well-being through community supported participation in musical activities: final report*, London: Institute of Education, University of London and Guildhall School of Music & Drama.

Hamilton, M., Hamilton, D. and Zderic, T. (2007) 'Role of low energy expenditure and sitting in obesity, metabolic syndrome, type 2 diabetes, and cardiovascular disease', *Diabetes*, vol 56, no 11, pp 2655-67.

Hammack, P.L. (2012) 'Narrative and the politics of meaning', *Narrative Inquiry*, vol 21, pp 311-18.

Hankiewicz, J. and Swierczek, E. (1974) 'Lysozyme in human body fluids', *Clin Chim Acta*, vol 57, pp 205-9.

Hanna-Pladdy, B. and MacKay, A. (2011) 'The relation between instrumental musical activity and cognitive aging', *Neuropsychol*, vol 25, no 3, pp 378-86.

Hanson, J., Kellaher, L., Rowlands, M., Zako, R., Marcoux, J.-S. and Percival, J. (2002) *Profiling the housing stock of older people: from domesticity to caring* (www.bartlett.ucl.ac.uk/graduate/research/space/research/equal-domesticity).

Harris, A., Lanningham-Foster, L., McCrady, S. and Levine, J. (2007) 'Nonexercise movement in elderly compared with young people', *Am J Physiol Endocrinol Met*, vol 292, no 4, E1207-E1212.

Harrison, D.E., Strong, R., Sharp, Z.D., Nelson, J.F., Astle, C.M., Flurkey, K., Nadon, N.L., Wilkinson, J.E., Frenkel, K., Carter, C.S., Pahor, M., Javors, M.A., Fernandez, E. and Miller, R.A. (2009) 'Rapamycin fed late in life extends lifespan in genetically heterogeneous mice', *Nature*, vol 460, pp 392-5.

Harriss-White, B., Olsen, W., Vera-Sanso, P. and Suresh, V. (2013) 'Multiple shocks and slum households in South India', *Economy and Society*, vol 42, no 3, pp 398-429.

Harvey, D. (1989) *The condition of postmodernity*, Oxford: Blackwell.

Haskell, W., Lee, I., Pate, R., Powell, K., Blair, S., Franklin, B., Macera, C., Heath, G., Thompson, P. and Bauman, A. (2007) 'Physical activity and public health: updated recommendation for adults from the American College of Sports Medicine and the American Heart Association', *Med Sci Sports Exerc*, vol 39, no 8, pp 1423-34.

Havighurst, R. (1954) 'Flexibility and the social roles of the retired', *American Journal of Sociology*, vol 59, pp 309-11.

Havighurst, R. (1963) 'Successful ageing', in R. Williams, C. Tibbitts and W. Donahue (eds) *Process of ageing*, vol 1, New York, Atherton, pp 299-320.

Havighurst, R. and Albrecht, R. (1953) *Older people*, London: Longmans.

Hawkes, K. (2004) 'Human longevity: the grandmother effect', *Nature*, vol 428, pp 128-9.

Hayflick, L. and Moorhead, P.S. (1961) 'The serial cultivation of human diploid cell strains', *Exp Cell Res*, vol 25, pp 585-621.

Hays, T. and Minichiello, V. (2005) 'The contribution of music to quality of life in older people: an Australian qualitative study', *Ageing Soc*, vol 25, no 2, pp 261-78.

Heaven, B., Bamford, C., May, C.R. and Moynihan P. (2012) 'Food work and feeding assistance on hospital wards', *Sociology of Health and Illness*, vol 41, no 2, pp 263-9.

Helmrich, S., Ragland, D., Leung, R. and Paffenbarger, R. (1991) 'Physical activity and reduced occurrence of non-insulin-dependent diabetes mellitus', *New Eng J Med*, vol 325, no 3, pp 147-52.

Henkens, K. (2000) 'Supervisors' attitudes about the early retirement of subordinates', *J Appl Soc Psychol*, vol 30, no 4, pp 833-52.

Hennessy, C. and Walker, A. (2011) 'Promoting multi-disciplinary and inter-disciplinary ageing research in the UK', *Ageing and Society*, vol 31, part 1, pp 52-69.

Hepworth, M. (2000) *Stories of ageing (rethinking agency)*, Buckingham: Open University Press.

Herbig, U., Ferreira, M., Condel, L., Carey, D. and Sedivy, J.M. (2006) 'Cellular senescence in aging primates', *Science*, vol 311, p 1257.

Heuser, I. (2002) 'Depression, endocrinologically a syndrome of premature aging?', *Maturitas*, vol 41, S19-S23.

Hickson, J. and Housley, W. (1997) 'Creativity in later life', *Educational Gerontology*, vol 23, no 6, pp 539-47.

Higgs, P., Hyde, M., Wiggins, R. and Blane, D. (2003) 'Researching quality of life in early old age: the importance of the sociological dimension', *Social Policy & Administration*, vol 37, no 3, pp 239-52.

Highmore, B. (2002) *Everyday life and cultural theory: an introduction*, London and New York: Routledge.

Highmore, B. (2010) *Ordinary lives: studies in the everyday*, London: Routledge.

Hignett, S. and McAtamney, L. (2000) 'Technical note: Rapid Entire Body Assessment (REBA)', *Applied Ergonomics*, vol 31, no 2, pp 201-5.

Hill, K. and Hurtada, A.M. (1996) *Ache life history: the ecology and demography of a foraging people*, New Brunswick, NJ: Transaction Publishers.

Hillman, S. (2002) 'Participatory singing for older people: a perception of benefit', *Health Education*, vol 102, no 4, pp 163-71.

Hillsdon, M., Thorogood, M., Anstiss, T. and Morris, J. (1995) 'Randomised controlled trials of physical activity promotion in free living populations: a review', *J Epidemiol Comm Health*, vol 49, no 1, pp 448-53.

Hirvensalo, M., Rantanen, T. and Heikkinen, E. (2000) 'Mobility difficulties and physical activity as predictors of mortality and loss of independence in the community-living older population', *J Amer Ger Soc*, vol 48, no 5, pp 493-8.

HM Government (2009) *Shaping the future of care together*, Cmnd 7673, London: The Stationery Office (www.gov.uk/government/uploads/system/uploads/attachment_data/file/238551/7673.pdf).

HM Government (2012) *Caring for our future: progress report on funding reform*, Cmnd 8381, London: The Stationery Office (www.gov.uk/government/uploads/system/uploads/attachment_data/file/216889/progress-report-on-social-care-funding-reform-Accessible-version1.pdf).

Hodes, R. (2003) 'NIA Symposium: research initiatives, funding and training opportunities at the National Institute on Aging', Presented at the 56th Annual Scientific Meeting of the Gerontological Society of America, San Diego, California.

Hodge, J. (1990) 'The quality of life: a contrast between utilitarian and existentialist approaches', in S. Baldwin, C. Godfrey and G. Propper (eds) *Quality of life: perspectives and policies*, London: Routledge, pp 42-57.

Hodkinson, P., Ford, G., Hodkinson, H. and Hawthorn, R. (2008) 'Retirement as a learning process', *Educational Gerontology*, vol 34, no 3, pp 167-84.

Hoen, P.W., de Jonge, P., Na, B.Y., Farzaneh-Far, R., Epel, E., Lin, J., Blackburn, E. and Whooley, M.A. (2011) 'Depression and leukocyte telomere length in patients with coronary heart disease: data from the heart and soul study', *Psychosom Med*, vol 73, pp 541-7.

Hogan, S. and Warren, L. (2012) 'Dealing with complexity in research processes and findings: how do older women negotiate and challenge images of aging?', *Journal of Women and Aging*, vol 24, no 4, pp 329-50.

Holmes, J.D. and House, A.O. (2000) 'Psychiatric illness in hip fracture', *Age Ageing*, vol 29, pp 537-46.

Holstein, J.A. and Gubrium, J.F. (2011) *Varieties of narrative analysis*, London: Sage.

Hornquist, J.O. (1990) 'Quality of life', *Scand J Public Health*, vol 18, no 1, pp 69-79.

Horrobin, S. (2006) 'The value of life and the value of life extension', *Ann NY Acad Sci*, vol 1067, pp 94-105.

HSCIC (Health & Social Care Information Centre) (2006) *Health Survey for England 2004: health of ethnic minorities – full report*, Leeds: HSCIC (www.hscic.gov.uk/pubs/hse04ethnic).

HSCIC (2013) *Health Survey for England 2012, Trend tables*, Leeds: HSCIC (www.hscic.gov.uk/catalogue/PUB13219).

Huhse, H. (1987) *The sanctity-of-life doctrine in medicine: a critique*, Oxford: Clarendon Press.

Hulstaert, F., Hannet, I., Deneys, V., Munhyeshuli, V., Reichert, T., de Bruyere, M. and Strauss, K. (1994) 'Age-related changes in human blood lymphocyte subpopulations. II. Varying kinetics of percentage and absolute count measurements', *Clin Immunol Immunopathol*, vol 70, pp 152-8.

Human Mortality Database (nd) 'England and Wales 5x10 life tables males' (www.mortality.org/hmd/GBRTENW/STATS/mltper_5x10.txt).

Human Mortality Database (nd) 'England and Wales 5x10 life tables females' (www.mortality.org/hmd/GBRTENW/STATS/fltper_5x10.txt).

Huppert, F.A. (2003) 'Designing for older users', in J. Clarkson, R. Coleman, S. Keates and C. Lebbon (eds) *Inclusive design: design for the whole population*, London: Springer-Verlag Publications, pp 30-57.

Huppert, F.A., van Niekerk, J.K. and Herbert, J. (2000a) 'Dehydroepiandrosterone (DHEA) supplementation for cognition and well-being', *Cochrane Database Syst Rev*, CD000304.

Huppert, F.A., Brayne, C., Jagger, C. and Metz, D. (2000b) 'Longitudinal studies in ageing: a key role in the evidence base for improving health and quality of life in older adults', *Age and Ageing*, vol 29, pp 485-6.

Hurd Clarke, L. (2010) *Facing age*, Lanham, MD: Rowman & Littlefield.

Hutchinson, J. (1886) 'Case of congenital absence of hair, with atrophic condition of the skin and its appendages, in a boy whose mother had been almost wholly bald from alopecia areata from the age of six', *The Lancet*, vol I, p 923.

Huyck, M.H. (2003) 'Is gerontology the Cheshire cat?', *The Gerontologist*, vol 43, no 1, pp 132-6.

Hyde, M., Wiggins, R., Higgs, P. and Blane, D. (2003) 'A measure of quality of life in early old age: the theory, development and properties of a needs satisfaction mode', *Aging and Mental Health*, vol 7, pp 186-94.

Iatsenko, D., Bernjak, A., Stankovski, T., Shiogai, Y., Owen-Lynch, P.J., Clarkson, P.B.M., McClintock, P.V.E. and Stefanovska, A. (2013) 'Evolution of cardio-respiratory interactions with age', *Phil Trans R Soc (Lond) A*, vol 371, 20110622.

Ilmarinen, J. (1997) 'Aging and work – coping with strengths and weaknesses', *Scand J Work Environ Health*, vol 23, suppl 1, pp 3-5.

Iwasa, H., Han, J. and Ishikawa, F. (2003) 'Mitogen-activated protein kinase p38 defines the common senescence-signalling pathway', *Genes Cells*, vol 8, pp 131-44.

Jagger, C., Matthews R., Matthews, F., Robinson, T., Robine, J.-M. and Brayne, C. (2007) 'The burden of diseases on disability-free life expectancy in later life', *Journals of Gerontology. Series A (Biological Sciences and Medical Sciences)*, vol 62, pp 408-14.

Jagger, C., Matthews, R., Lindesay, J., Robinson, T., Croft, P. and Brayne, C. (2009) 'The effect of dementia trends and treatments on longevity and disability: a simulation model based on the MRC Cognitive Function and Ageing Study (MRC CFAS)', Age and Ageing, vol 38(3), pp 19-25; discussion 251.

Jaskelioff, M., Muller, F.L., Paik, J.H., Thomas, E., Jiang, S., Adams, A.C., Sahin, E., Kost-Alimova, M., Protopopov, A., Cadinos, J., Horner, J.W., Maratos-Flier, E. and Dephino, R.A. (2011) 'Telomerase reactivation reverses tissue degeneration in aged telomerase-deficient mice', *Nature*, vol 469, pp 102-6.

Jennings, H.M., Heinrich, M. and Thompson J.L. (in press) 'Bengali-British food journeys: exploring the movement of food and plants across transnational landscapes', in C. Rey and P. Howland (eds) *Food, globalization and human diversity*, Oxford: Berg.

Johansson, S., Konlaan, B.B. and Bygren, L.O. (2001) 'Sustaining habits of attending cultural events and maintenance of health: a longitudinal study', *Health Promotion International*, vol 16, no 3, pp 229-34.

Johnell, O., Gullberg, B., Allander, J.A., Kanis, J.A. and the MEDOS Study Group (1992) 'The apparent incidence of hip fracture in Europe: a study of national register sources', *Osteoporosis Int*, vol 2, pp 298-302.

Jones, M. (2009) 'An overview of maggot therapy used on chronic wounds in the community', *Br J Community Nurs*, vol 14, S16, S18, S20.

Jowell, R. and Prescott-Clarke, P. (1970) 'Racial discrimination and white-collar workers in Britain', *Race & Class*, vol 11, no 4, pp 397-417.

Kajstura, J., Leri, A., Finato, N., di Loreto, C., Beltrami, C.A. and Aversa, P. (1998) 'Myocyte proliferation in end-stage cardiac failure in humans', *Proc Natl Acad Sci USA*, vol 95, pp 8801-5.

Kajstura, J., Pertoldi, B., Leri, A., Beltrami, C.A., Deptala, A., Darzynkiwicz, Z. and Aversa, P. (2000) 'Telomere shortening is an in vivo marker of myocyte replication and aging', *Am J Pathol*, vol 156, pp 813-19.

Kalthoft, G. (1990) 'Music and emancipatory learning in three community education programs', *Dissertation Abstracts Int*, vol 51, no 7, p 2239A, University Microfilms No AAT90-33861.

Kananen, L., Surakka, I., Pirkola, S., Suvisaari, J., Lonnqvist, J., Peltonen, L., Ripatti, S. and Hovatta, I. (2010) 'Childhood adversities are associated with shorter telomere length at adult age both in individuals with an anxiety disorder and controls', *PLoS One*, vol 5, e10826.

Katzmarzyk, P., Church, T., Craig, C. and Bouchard, C. (2009) 'Sitting time and mortality from all causes, cardiovascular disease, and cancer', *Med Sci Sports Exercise*, vol 41, no 5, pp 998-1005.

Keaney, E. and Oskala, A. (2007) 'The golden age of the arts? Taking part survey findings on older people and the arts', *Cultural Trends*, vol 16, no 4, pp 323-55.

Kemp, B.J. and Mosqueda, L.A. (2005) 'Elder financial abuse: an evaluation framework and supporting evidence', *Journal of the American Geriatrics Society*, vol 53, no 7, pp 1123-7.

Kendig, H. (2003) 'Directions in environmental gerontology: A multidisciplinary field', *The Gerontologist*, vol 43, no 5, pp 611-4.

Kiecolt-Glaser, J.K. and Glaser, R. (1995) 'Psychoneuroimmunology and health consequences: data and shared mechanisms', *Psychosom Med*, vol 57, pp 269-74.

Kiecolt-Glaser, J.K. and Glaser, R. (2002) 'Depression and immune function: central pathways to morbidity and mortality', *J Psychosom Res*, vol 53, pp 873-6.

Kiecolt-Glaser, J.K., Glaser, R., Gravenstein, S., Malarkey, W.B. and Sheridan, J. (1996) 'Chronic stress alters the immune response to influenza virus vaccine in older adults', *Proc Natl Acad Sci USA*, vol 93, pp 3043-7.

King, L. and Hicks, J. (2007) 'Lost and found possible selves: goals, development and well-being', *New Directions for Adult and Continuing Education*, vol 114, summer, pp 27-37.

Kipling, D., Davis, T., Ostler, E.L. and Faragher, R.G. (2004) 'What can progeroid syndromes tell us about human aging?', *Science*, vol 305, pp 1426-31.

Kirkwood, T. (2001) *Time of our lives: the science of human ageing*, Oxford: Oxford University Press.

Kirkwood, T. (2011) *Funders Round Table Discussion*, 14th Congress of the International Association of Biomedical Gerontology – 'The Science of Ageing: Global Progress', Brighton, 11-14 July.

Kirkwood, T.B. (1977) 'Evolution of ageing', *Nature*, vol 170, pp 201-4.

Kisner, S.M. and Pratt, S.G. (1997) 'Occupational fatalities among older workers in the United States: 1980-1991', *J Occup Environ Med*, vol 39, pp 715-21.

Klein, J.T. (1990) *Interdisciplinarity: history, theory and practice*, Detroit, MI: Wayne State University Press.

Klein, J.P. and Moeschberger, M.L. (2003) *Survival analysis: techniques for censored and truncated data*, New York: Springer Verlag.

Koehn, S., Smith, S., Kobayashi, K. and Khamisa, K. (2013) 'Revealing the shape of knowledge using an intersectionality lens: results of a scoping review on the health and health care of ethnocultural minority older adults', *Ageing & Society*, vol 33, no 3, pp 437-64.

Kohli, M., Rein, M., Guillemard, A.-M. and Gunsteren, H. (eds) (1991) *Time for retirement*, Cambridge: Cambridge University Press.

Kroger, J. (2002) 'Identity processes and contents through the years of late adulthood', *Identity*, vol 2, no 1, pp 81-99.

Kroger, J. and Adair, V. (2008) 'Symbolic meanings of valued personal objects in identity transitions of late adulthood', *Identity*, vol 8, no 1, pp 5-24.

Kuhn, T. (1962) *The structure of scientific revolutions*, Chicago, IL: University of Chicago Press.

Kumazaki, T., Kobayashi, M. and Mitsui, Y. (1993) 'Enhanced expression of fibronectin during in vivo cellular aging of human vascular endothelial cells and skin fibroblasts', *Exp Cell Res*, vol 205, pp 396-402.

Kuorinka, I., Jonsson, B., Kilbom, A., Vinterberg, H., Biering-Sørensen, F., Andersson, G. and Jørgensen, K. (1987) 'Standardised Nordic questionnaires for the analysis of musculoskeletal symptoms', *Applied Ergonomics*, vol 18, no 3, pp 233-7.

Kyng, K.J., May, A., Kolvraa, S. and Bohr, V.A. (2003) 'Gene expression profiling in Werner syndrome closely resembles that of normal aging', *Proc Natl Acad Sci USA*, vol 100, pp 12259-64.

Lacour, J.R., Kostka, T. and Bonnefoy, M. (2002) 'Physical activity to delay the effects of aging on mobility', *Presse Med*, vol 31, pp 1185-92.

Lakowski, B. and Hekimi, S. (1998) 'The genetics of caloric restriction in Caenorhabditis elegans', *Proc Natl Acad Sci USA*, vol 95, pp 13091-6.

Lamb, S. (2000) *White saris and sweet mangoes: aging, gender, and body in North India*, Berkeley, CA: University of California Press.

Lamond, A.J., Depp, C.A., Allison, M., Langer, R., Reichstadt, J., Moore, D.J., Golshan, S., Ganiats, T.G. and Jeste, D.V. (2008) 'Measurement and predictors of resilience among community-dwelling older women', *J Psychiatr Res*, vol 43, pp 148-54.

Landau, R., Werner, S., Auslander, G.K., Shoval, N. and Heinik, J. (2010) 'What do cognitively intact older people think about the use of electronic tracking devices for people with dementia? A preliminary analysis', *Int Psychogeriatrics*, vol 22, no 8, pp 1301-9.

Lang, F.R. and Heckhausen, J. (2001) 'Perceived control over development and subjective well-being: differential benefits across adulthood', *J Personality Social Psychol*, vol 81, no 3, p 509.

Langer, E.J. (2009) *Counter clockwise: mindful health and the power of possibility*, New York: Random House Inc.

Lansley, P. (2013) 'Multi-disciplinarity, user engagement and the design of special programmes of ageing research in the United Kingdom', *Ageing and Society*, vol 33, no 5, pp 727-60.

Laslett, P. (1989) *A fresh map of life: the emergence of the third age*, London: Weidenfeld & Nicholson.

Latimer, J. (2011) 'Home, care and frail older people: relational extension and the art of dwelling', in C. Ceci, M.E. Purkis and K. Björnsdottir (eds) *Homecare: international and comparative perspectives*, London: Routledge, pp 35-61.

Latimer, J., Davis, T., Bagley, M.C. and Kipling, D. (2011) 'Ageing science, health care and social inclusion of older people', *Quality in Ageing and Older Adults*, vol 12, pp 11-16.

Laukka, P. (2007) 'Uses of music and psychological well-being among the elderly', *J Happiness Studies*, vol 8, no 2, pp 215-41.

Lee, C.E., Folsom, A. and Blair, S. (2003) 'Physical activity and stroke risk: a meta-analysis', *Stroke*, vol 34, no 10, pp 2475-81.

Lee, C.E., Mcardle, A. and Griffiths, R.D. (2007) 'The role of hormones, cytokines and heat shock proteins during age-related muscle loss', *Clin Nutr*, vol 26, pp 524-34.

Lee, N. (2001) *Childhood and society: growing up in an age of uncertainty*, Buckingham: Open University Press.

Lee, S.J., Yook, J.S., Han, S.M. and Koo, H.S. (2004) 'A Werner syndrome protein homolog affects C. elegans development, growth rate, life span and sensitivity to DNA damage by acting at a DNA damage checkpoint', *Development*, vol 131, pp 2565-75.

Le Mesurier, N. (2003) *The hidden store: older people's contributions to rural communities*, London: Age Concern.

Leri, A., Franco, S., Zacheo, A., Barlucchi, L., Chimenti, S., Limana, F., Nadal-Ginard, B., Kajstura, J., Anversa, P. and Blasco, M.A. (2003) 'Ablation of telomerase and telomere loss leads to cardiac dilatation and heart failure associated with p53 upregulation', *EMBO J*, vol 22, pp 131-9.

Lesta, B. and Petocz, P. (2006) 'Familiar group singing: addressing mood and social behaviour of residents with dementia displaying sundowning', *Austral J Music Therapy*, vol 17, pp 2-17.

Livesley, N. (2011) *The future ageing of ethnic minority populations England and Wales*, London: Centre for Policy on Ageing (www.cpa.org.uk/policy/briefings/ageing_ethnic_minority_population.pdf).

Lizardo, O. (2006) 'How cultural tastes shape personal networks', *American Sociological Review*, vol 71, no 5, pp 778-807.

Llewellyn, M. (2004) 'Designed by women and designing women: gender, planning and the geographies of the kitchen in Britain, 1917-1946', *Cultural Geographies*, vol 11, pp 42-60.

Lloyd, L., Calnan, M., Cameron, A., Seymour, J. and Smith, R. (2014) 'Identity in the fourth age: perseverance, adaptation and maintaining dignity', *Ageing and Society*, vol 34, no 1, pp 1-19.

Lloyd-Sherlock, P., Barrientos, A. and Mase, J. (2012) 'Social inclusion of older people in developing countries: relations and resources', in T. Scharf and N. Keating (eds) *From exclusion to inclusion in old age: a global challenge*, Bristol: Policy Press, pp 51-69.

Loch, C.H., Sting, F.J., Bauer, N. and Mauermann, H. (2010) 'How BMW is defusing the demographic time bomb', *Harvard Business Review*, March, pp 99-102.

Lucia, A.D. and Lepsinger, R. (1999) *The art and science of competency models*, San Francisco, CA: Jossey-Bass/Pfeiffer.

Lung, F.W., Chen, N.C. and Shu, B.C. (2007) 'Genetic pathway of major depressive disorder in shortening telomeric length', *Psychiatr Genet*, vol 17, pp 195-9.

Luyckx, K., Goossens, L., Soenens, B. and Beyers, W. (2006) 'Unpacking commitment and exploration: Preliminary validation of an integrative model of late adolescent identity formation', *Journal of Adolescence*, vol 29, pp 361-78.

Macdonald, A.S., Teal, G., Bamford, C. and Moynihan, P.J. (2012) 'Hospitalfoodie: an inter-professional case study of the redesign of the nutritional management and monitoring system for vulnerable older hospital patients', *Quality in Primary Care*, vol 20, no 3, pp 169-77.

McCarthy, K., Heneghan, F., Ondaatje, E., Zakaras, L. and Brooks, A. (2004) *Gifts of the muse reframing the debate about the benefits of the arts*, Santa Monica, CA: Rand Corporation.

McEwen, B.S. (2000) 'Allostasis and allostatic load: implications for neuropsychopharmacology', *Neuropsychopharmacology*, vol 22, pp 108-24.

McKenna, S.P., Doward, L.C., Alonso, J., Kohlmann, T., Niero, M., Prieto, L. and Wiren, L. (1999) 'The QoL-AGHDA: an instrument for the assessment of quality of life in adults with growth hormone deficiency', *Quality of Life Research*, vol 8, no 4, pp 373-83.

McKie, L. (1999) 'Older people and food: independence, locality and diet', *British Food Journal*, vol 101, pp 528-36.

McShane, R. and Skelt, L. (2009) 'GPS tracking for people with dementia', *Working with Older People*, vol 13, no 3, pp 34-7.

MAG (Malnutrition Action Group) (2003) *The 'MUST' report: nutritional screening of adults: a multidisciplinary responsibility*, Redditch: BAPEN (www.bapen.org.uk/professionals/publications-and-resources/bapen-reports).

MAG (2011) *The 'MUST' explanatory booklet. A guide to the Malnutrition Universal Screening Tool' ('MUST') for adults*, edited by V. Todorovic, C. Russell and M. Elia, Redditch: BAPEN (www.bapen.org.uk/pdfs/must/must_explan.pdf).

Maglione, J.E. and Ancoli-Israel, S. (2012) 'Sleep disorders in the elderly', in C.M. Morin and C.A. Espie (eds) *The Oxford handbook of sleep disorders*, Oxford: Oxford University Press, pp 769-86.

Malley, J., Hancock, R., Murphy, M., Adams, J., Wittenberg, R., Comas-Herrera, A., Curry, C., King, D., James, S., Morciano, M. and Pickard, L. (2011) 'The effect of lengthening Life Expectancy on future pension and Long-Term Care expenditure in England, 2007 to 2032', *Health Statistics Quarterly*, vol 52, Winter 2011, pp 33-61 (www.ons.gov.uk/ons/rel/hsq/health-statistics-quarterly/no--52---winter-2011/index.html)

Marcia, J.E. (1980) 'Identity in adolescence', in J. Adelson (ed) *Handbook of adolescent psychology*, New York: Wiley, pp 159-87.

Marcia, J.E. (2002) 'Identity and psychosocial development in adulthood', *Identity*, vol 2, no 1, pp 7-28.

Marcus, B., Simkin, L., Rossi, J. and Pinto, B. (1996) 'Longitudinal shifts in employees' stages and processes of exercise behavior change', *Am J Health Promotion*, vol 10, no 3, pp 195-200.

Markus, H. and Nurius, P. (1986) 'Possible selves', *Am Psychologist*, vol 41, no 9, pp 954-69.

Marshall, T.H. (1950) *Citizenship and social class*, Cambridge: Cambridge University Press.

Martin, G.M., Oshima, J., Gray, M.D. and Poot, M. (1999) 'What geriatricians should know about the Werner syndrome', *J Am Geriatr Soc*, vol 47, pp 1136-44.

Maslow, A. (1954) *Motivation and personality*, New York: Harper & Row.

Mason, P.A., Boubriak, I., Robbins, T., Lasala, R., Saunders, R. and Cox, L.S. (2012) 'The Drosophila orthologue of progeroid human WRN exonuclease, DmWRNexo, cleaves replication substrates but is inhibited by uracil or abasic sites: analysis of DmWRNexo activity in vitro', *Age (Dordr)*, vol 35, pp 793-806.

Mather, K.A., Jorm, A.F., Parslow, R.A. and Christensen, H. (2011) 'Is telomere length a biomarker of aging? A review', *J Gerontol A Biol Sci Med Sci*, vol 66, pp 202-13.

Matsumoto, M. and Inoue, K. (2007) 'Predictors of institutionalisation in elderly people living at home: the impact of incontinence and commode use in rural Japan', *J Cross-Cult Gerontol*, vol 22, pp 421-32.

Mattison, J.A., Roth, G.S., Beasley, T.M., Tilmont, E.M., Handy, A.M., Herbert, R.L., Longo, D.L., Allison, D.B., Young, J.E., Bryant, M., Barnard, D., Ward, W.F., Qi, W., Imgram, D.K. and de Cabo, R. (2012) 'Impact of caloric restriction on health and survival in rhesus monkeys from the NIA study', *Nature*, vol 489, pp 318-21.

Mayhew, L., Karlsson, M. and Rickayzen, B. (2010) 'The role of private finance in paying for long term care', *The Economic Journal*, vol 120, no 548, F478–F504.

Medawar, P.B. (1952) *An unsolved problem of biology*, London: H.K. Lewis.

Mehta, I.S., Bridger, J.M. and Kill, I.R. (2010) 'Progeria, the nucleolus and farnesyltransferase inhibitors', *Biochem Soc Trans*, vol 38, pp 287-91.

Melzer, D., Lan, T. and Guralnik, J.M. (2003) 'The predictive value for mortality of the index of mobility-related limitation – results from the EPESE study', *Age and Ageing*, vol 32, pp 619-25.

Menec, V. (2002) 'The relation between everyday activities and successful aging: a 6-year longitudinal study', *The Journals of Gerontology*, Series B, vol 58, issue 2, S74-S82.

Meyer, T.E., Kovacs, S.J., Ehsani, A.A., Klein, S., Holloszy, J.O. and Fontana, L. (2006) 'Long-term caloric restriction ameliorates the decline in diastolic function in humans', *J Am Coll Cardiol*, vol 47, pp 398-402.

Middling, S., Bailey, J., Maslin-Prothero, S. and Scharf, T. (2011) 'Gardening and the social engagement of older people', *Working with Older People*, vol 15, pp 112-20.

Milbourne, P. and Doheny, S. (2012) 'Older people and poverty in rural Britain: material hardships, cultural denials and social inclusions', *Journal of Rural Studies*, vol 28, no 4, pp 389-97.

Millar, A. (1988) 'Following nature', *Philos Quart*, vol 38, pp 165-85.

Miller, R.A. (2004) '"Accelerated aging": a primrose path to insight?', *Aging Cell*, vol 3, pp 47-51.

Miller, R.A. and Brown, W. (2004) 'Steps and sitting in a working population', *Int J Behav Med*, vol 11, no 4, pp 219-24.

Minamino, T., Miyauchi, H., Yoshida, T., Ishida, Y., Yoshida, H. and Komuro, I. (2002) 'Endothelial cell senescence in human atherosclerosis: role of telomere in endothelial dysfunction', *Circulation*, vol 105, pp 1541-4.

Miskelly, F. (2005) 'Electronic tracking of patients with dementia and wandering using mobile phone technology', *Age and Ageing*, vol 34, pp 497-9.

Mohren, D.C., Jansen, N.W., Kant, I., Galama, J.M., van den Brandt, P.A. and Swaen, G.M. (2002) 'Prevalence of common infections among employees in different work schedules', *Journal of Occupational and Environmental Medicine*, vol 44, no 11, pp 1003-11.

Mollenkopf, H., Marcellini, F., Ruoppila, I., Szeman, Z., Tacken, M. and Wahl, H.W. (2004) 'Social and behavioural science perspectives on out-of-home mobility in later life: findings from the European project MOBILATE', *Eur J Ageing*, vol 1, pp 45-53.

Morgan, J. (1986) 'Unpaid productive activity over the lifecourse', in Committee on Aging Society (ed) *Productive roles in an older society*, Washington, DC: National Academy Press, pp 73-110.

Morgan K., Kucharczyk, E. and Gregory, P. (2011) 'Insomnia: evidence-based approaches to assessment and management', *Clin Med*, vol 11, no 3, pp 278-81.

Morgan, K., Gregory, P., Tomeny, M., David, B.M. and Gascoigne, C. (2012) 'Self-help treatment for insomnia symptoms associated with chronic conditions in older adults: a randomised controlled trial', *J Am Ger Soc*, vol 60, no 10, pp 1803-10.

Morris, J. and Hardman, A. (1997) 'Walking to health', *Sports Med*, vol 23, no 5, pp 306-32.

Morris, J. and Heady, J. (1953) 'Mortality in relation to the physical activity of work', *Br J Indust Med*, vol 10, no 1, pp 245-54.

Morris, M., Lundell, J. and Dishman, E. (2004) 'Catalyzing social interaction with ubiquitous computing: a needs assessment of elders coping with cognitive decline', Paper presented at CHI '04 'Extended Abstracts on Human Factors in Computing Systems', 24-29 April, Vienna.

Morrow-Howell, N., Hinterlong, J., Rozario, P. and Tang, F. (2003) 'The effects of volunteering on the well-being of older adults', *The Journals of Gerontology*, Series B, vol 58, no 3, S137-S145.

Morsink, L.F., Vogelzanks, N., Nicklas, B.J., Beekman, A.T., Satterfield, S., Rubin, S.M., Yaffe, K., Simonsick, E., Newman, A.B., Kritchevsky, S.B. and Penninx, B.W. (2007) 'Associations between sex steroid hormone levels and depressive symptoms in elderly men and women: results from the Health ABC study', *Psychoneuroendocrinology*, vol 32, pp 874-83.

Moscovici, S. (2000) *Social representations. Explorations in social psychology*, Cambridge: Polity Press.

Murphy, M.J. (2009) 'The "golden generations" in historical context', *British Actuarial Journal*, vol 15 (Suppl.), pp 151-84, ISSN 1357-3217.

Murphy, M.J. and Di Cesare, M. (2012) 'Use of an age–period–cohort model to reveal the impact of cigarette smoking on trends in twentieth-century adult cohort mortality in England and Wales', *Population Studies*, vol 66, no 3, pp 259-77, ISSN 0032-4728.

Murray, M. (2002) 'Connecting narrative and social representation theory in health research', *Social Science Information*, vol 41, pp 653-73.

Murray, M. and Crummett, A. (2010) '"I don't think they knew we could do these sorts of things": social representations of community and participation in community arts by older people', *Journal of Health Psychology*, vol 15, no 5, pp 777-85.

Naegele, G. and Walker, A. (2006) *A guide to good practice in age management*, Dublin: European Foundation for the Improvement of Living and Working Conditions.

Naegele, G. and Walker, A. (eds) (2009) *Ageing and social policy: Britain and Germany compared*, Houndmills: Palgrave.

Navarro, C.L., Cau, P. and Levy, N. (2006) 'Molecular bases of progeroid syndromes', *Hum Mol Genet*, 15 spec no 2, R151-61.

NCEA (National Center on Elder Abuse) (1998) *The national elder abuse incidence study*, Orange, CA: NCEA (www.aoa.gov/AoARoot/AoA_Programs/Elder_Rights/Elder_Abuse/docs/ABuseReport_Full.pdf).

Nelson, G., Wordsworth, J., Wang, C., Jurk, D., Lawless, C., Martin-Ruiz, C. and von Zglinicki, T. (2012) 'A senescent cell bystander effect: senescence-induced senescence', *Aging Cell*, vol 11, pp 345-9.

Neugarten, B.L. (1974) 'Age groups in American society and the rise of the young-old', *Ann Am Acad Pol Soc Sci*, vol 415, pp 187-98.

Newman, A.B., Simonsick, E.M., Naydeck, B.L., Boudreau, R.M. Kritchevsky, S.B., Nevitt, M.C. et al (2006) 'Association of long-distance corridor walk performance with mortality, cardiovascular disease, mobility limitation, and disability', *Journal of the American Medical Association*, vol 295, no 17, pp 2018-26.

Newman, A., Goulding, A. and Whitehead, C. (2013) 'How cultural capital, habitus and class influence the responses of older adults to the field of contemporary visual art', *Poetics*, vol 41, no 5, pp 456-80.

Ng, T.W.H. and Feldman, D.C. (2008) 'The relationship of age to ten dimensions of job performance', *J Appl Psychol*, vol 93, no 2, pp 392-423.

Nilsson, C.J., Avlund, K. and Lund, R. (2011) 'Onset of mobility limitations in old age: the combined effect of socioeconomic position and social relations', *Age and Ageing*, vol 40, pp 607-14.

Nordmark, G., Bengtsson, C., Larsson, A., Karlsson, F.A., Sturfelt, G. and Ronnblom, L. (2005) 'Effects of dehydroepiandrosterone supplement on health-related quality of life in glucocorticoid treated female patients with systemic lupus erythematosus', *Autoimmunity*, vol 38, pp 531-40.

Nyunoya, T., Monick, M.M., Klingelhutz, A., Yarovinsky, T.O., Cagley, J.R. and Hunninghake, G.W. (2006) 'Cigarette smoke induces cellular senescence', *Am J Respir Cell Mol Biol*, vol 35, pp 681-8.

ODPM (Office of the Deputy Prime Minister) (2006) *A Sure Start to later life*, London: The Stationery Office.

OECD (Organisation for Economic Co-operation and Development) (1988a) *Reforming public pensions*, Paris: OECD.

OECD (1988b) *Ageing populations – the social policy implications*, Paris: OECD.

OECD (1998) *Maintaining prosperity in an ageing society*, Paris: OECD.

Oeppen, J. and Vaupel, J.W. (2002) 'Broken limits to life expectancy', *Science*, vol 296, pp 1029-31.

Ogami, M., Ikura, Y., Ohsawa, M., Matsuo, T., Kayo, S., Yoshimi, N., Hai, E., Shirai, N., Ehara, S., Komasu, R., Naruko, T. and Ueda, M. (2004) 'Telomere shortening in human coronary artery diseases', *Arterioscler Thromb Vasc Biol*, vol 24, pp 546-50.

Ogilvie, D., Foster, C., Rothnie, H., Cavill, N., Hamilton, V., Fitzsimons, C. and Mutrie, N. (2007) 'Interventions to promote walking: systematic review', *BMJ*, vol 334, no 7605, pp 1204-14.

Oh, H., Wang, S.C., Prahash, A., Sano, M., Moravec, C.S., Taffet, G.E., Michael, L.H., Youker, K.A., Entman, M.L. and Schneider, M.D. (2003) 'Telomere attrition and Chk2 activation in human heart failure', *Proc Natl Acad Sci USA*, vol 100, pp 5378-83.

Oliver, D. (2008) '"Acopia" and "social admission" are not diagnoses: why older people deserve better', *J R Soc Med*, vol 101, pp 168-74.

Olivetti, G., Giordano, G., Corradi, D., Melissari, M., Lagrasta, C., Gambert, S.R. and Anversa, P. (1995) 'Gender differences and aging: effects on the human heart', *J Am Coll Cardiol*, vol 26, pp 1068-79.

Olovnikov, A.M. (1973) 'A theory of marginotomy. The incomplete copying of template margin in enzymic synthesis of polynucleotides and biological significance of the phenomenon', *J Theor Biol*, vol 41, pp 181-90.

Olshansky, S.J. and Carnes, B.A. (2001) *The quest for immortality: science at the frontiers of ageing*, New York: W.W. Norton & Co.

Olshansky, S.J., Passaro, D.J., Hershow, R.C., Layden, J., Carnes, B.A., Brody, J., Hayflick, L., Butler, R., Allison, D. and Ludwig, D. (2005) 'A potential decline in life expectancy in the United States in the 21st century. A special report', *New England Journal of Medicine*, vol 352, no 11, pp 1138-45.

ONS (Office for National Statistics) (2000) *Self-reported health problems: by gender and age, 1996-97: social trends dataset* (www.ons.gov.uk/ons/rel/social-trends-rd/social-trends/no--30--2000-edition/index.html).

ONS (2005) *Focus on older people*, London: Department for Work and Pensions (www.ons.gov.uk/ons/rel/mortality-ageing/focus-on-older-people/2005-edition/index.html).

ONS (2010) *Statistical bulletin: internet access 2010*, pp 1-18, London: HMSO (www.ons.gov.uk/ons/rel/rdit2/internet-access---households-and-individuals/2010/stb-internet-access---households-and-individuals--2010.pdf).

ONS (2011a) 'Population estimates for UK, England and Wales, Scotland and Northern Ireland, Population Estimates Timeseries 1971 to current year' (www.ons.gov.uk/ons/rel/pop-estimate/population-estimates-for-uk--england-and-wales--scotland-and-northern-ireland/population-estimates-timeseries-1971-to-current-year/index.html).

ONS (2011b) 'Life expectancy at birth and at age 65 by local areas in the United Kingdom, 2004-06 to 2008-10' (www.ons.gov.uk/ons/rel/subnational-health4/life-expec-at-birth-age-65/2004-06-to-2008-10/index.html).

ONS (2012a) 'Statistical bulletin. Deaths registered in England and Wales (Series DR), 2011' (www.ons.gov.uk/ons/rel/vsob1/mortality-statistics--deaths-registered-in-england-and-wales--series-dr-/2011/stb-deaths-registered-in-england-and-wales-in-2011-by-cause.html).

ONS (2012b) 'National population projections, 2010-based projections' (www.ons.gov.uk/ons/rel/npp/national-population-projections/2010-based-projections/index.html).

Orentreich, N., Brind, J.L., Rizer, R.L. and Vogelman, J.H. (1984) 'Age changes and sex differences in serum dehydroepiandrosterone sulfate concentrations throughout adulthood', *J Clin Endocrinol Metab*, vol 59, pp 551-5.

Ostler, E.L., Wallis, C.V., Aboalchamat, B. and Faragher, R.G. (2000) 'Telomerase and the cellular lifespan: implications of the aging process', *J Pediatr Endocrinol Metab*, vol 13, suppl 6, pp 1467-76.

Oswald, F., Wahl, H.-S., Voss, E., Schilling, O., Freytag, T., Auslander, G., Shoval, N., Heinik, J. and Landau, R. (2010) 'The use of tracking technologies for the analysis of outdoor mobility in the face of dementia: first steps into a project and some illustrative findings from Germany', *J Housing Elderly*, vol 24, pp 55-73.

Owen, N., Bauman, A. and Brown, W. (2009) 'Too much sitting: a novel and important predictor of chronic disease risk?', *Br J Sports Med*, vol 43, no 2, pp 81-3.

Pahl, R. and Spencer, E. (2003) 'Capturing personal communities', in C. Phillipson, G. Allen and D. Morgan (eds) *Social networks and social exclusion*, Aldershot: Ashgate, pp 72-96.

Paine, T. (2011) *The age of reason*, ed. Kerry Walters, Peterborough: Broadview Press.

Papia, G., McLellan, B.A., El-Helou, P., Louie, M., Rachlis, A., Szalai, J.P. and Simor, A.E. (1999) 'Infection in hospitalized trauma patients: incidence, risk factors, and complications', *J Trauma*, vol 47, pp 923-7.

Park, E.J., Lee, J.H., Chae, J.H., Lee, K.H., Han, S.I. and Jeon, Y.W. (2006) 'Natural killer T cells in patients with major depressive disorder', *Psychiatry Res*, vol 144, pp 237-9.

Park-Lee, E. and Caffrey, C. (2009) 'Pressure ulcers among nursing home residents: United States, 2004', *NCHS Data Brief*, pp 1-8.

Passos, J.F., Nelson, G., Wang, C., Richter, T., Simillion, C., Proctor, C.J., Miwa, S., Olijslagers, S., Hallinan, J., Wipat, A., Sarektzki, G., Rudolph, K.L., Kirkwood, T.B. and von Zglinicki, T. (2010) 'Feedback between p21 and reactive oxygen production is necessary for cell senescence', *Mol Syst Biol*, vol 6, p 347.

Pate, R., Pratt, M., Blair, S., Haskell, W., Macera, C., Bouchard, C., Buchner, D., Ettinger, W., Heath, G., King, A., Kriska, A., Leon, A., Marcus, B., Morris, J., Paffenbarger, R., Patrick, K., Pollock, M., Rippe, J., Sallis, J. and Wilmore, J. (1995) 'Physical activity and public health. A recommendation from the Centers for Disease and Prevention and the American College of Sports Medicine', *JAMA*, vol 273, no 5, pp 402-7.

Peace, S., Holland, C. and Kellaher, L. (2006) *Environment and identity in later life*, Maidenhead: Open University Press and McGraw-Hill Education.

Peace, S., Wahl, H.-V., Oswald, F. and Mollenkoph, G. (2007) 'Environment and ageing', in J. Bond, S. Peace, F. Dittmann-Kohli and G.J. Westerhof (eds) *Ageing in society: European perspectives in gerontology*, London: Sage Publications, pp 209-34.

Pensions Policy Institute (2011) *An assessment of the Government's options for state pension reform: A discussion paper by Daniela Silcock, NikiCleal, Chris Curry, Daniel Redwood and John Adams*, London: Pensions Policy Institute (www.pensionspolicyinstitute.org.uk/publications/reports/an-assessment-of-the-governments-options-for-state-pension-reform).

Pfeiffer, E. (ed) (1974) *Successful aging: a conference report*, Durham, NC: Duke University.

Phillips, J.E., Walford, N.S. and Hockey, A.E. (2012) 'How do unfamiliar environments convey meaning to older people? Urban dimensions of placelessness and attachment', *International Journal of Ageing and Later Life*, vol 6, no 2, pp 73-102.

Phillipson, C. (1982) *Capitalism and the construction of old age*, London: Macmillan.

Phillipson, C. (1998) *Reconstructing old age: new agendas in social theory and practice*, London: Sage Publications.

Phillipson, C., Ahmed, N. and Latimer, J. (2003) *Women in transition. A study of the experiences of Bangladeshi women living in Tower Hamlets*, Bristol: Policy Press.

Phoenix, C. (2010) 'Auto-photography in aging studies: exploring issues of identity construction in mature bodybuilders', *Journal of Aging Studies*, vol 24, no 3, pp 167-80.

Pierson, P. (2000) *The new politics of the welfare state*, Oxford: Oxford University Press.

Pirkl, J. (1994) *Transgenerational design: products for an aging population*, New York, NY: Van Nostrand Reinhold.

Polefka, T.G., Meyer, T.A., Agin, P.P. and Bianchini, R.J. (2012) 'Effects of solar radiation on the skin', *J Cosmet Dermatol*, vol 11, pp 134-43.

Porter, K., Fischer, J. and Johnson, M. (2011) 'Improved physical function and physical activity in older adults following a community-based intervention: relationships with a history of depression', *Maturitas*, vol 70, no 3, pp 290-4.

Portrait, F., Teeuwiszrn, E. and Deeg, D. (2011) 'Early life undernutrition and chronic diseases at older ages: the effects of the Dutch famine on cardiovascular diseases and diabetes', *Soc Sci Med*, vol 73, pp 711-18.

Potratz, W., Gross, T. and Hilbert, J. (2009) 'Silver economy: purchasing power and the quest for quality of life', in G. Naegele and A. Walker (eds) *Ageing and social policy: Britain and Germany compared*, Houndmills: Palgrave, pp 82-105.

Postman, N. (1994) *The disappearance of childhood*, New York: Random House Inc (Vantage Press).

Power, M., Quinn, K., Schmidt, S. (2005) 'Development of the WHOQoL – old module', *Qual Life Research*, December, vol 14, no 10, pp 2197-214.

Pransky, G.S., Benjamin, K.L., Savageau, J.A., Currivan, D. and Fletcher, K. (2005) 'Outcomes in work-related injuries: a comparison of older and younger workers', *Am J Indust Med*, vol 47, no 2, pp 104-12.

Preto, A., Singhrao, S.K., Haughton, M.F., Kipling, D., Wynford-Thomas, D. and Jones, C.J. (2004) 'Telomere erosion triggers growth arrest but not cell death in human cancer cells retaining wild-type p53: implications for antitelomerase therapy', *Oncogene*, vol 23, pp 4136-45.

Probert, A., Tremblay, M. and Gorber, S. (2008) 'Desk potatoes: the importance of occupational physical activity on health', *Can J Public Health*, vol 99, no 4, pp 311-18.

Prochaska, J. and DiClemente, C. (1983) 'Stages and processes of self-change of smoking: toward an integrative model of change', *J Consulting Clinical Psychol*, vol 51, no 3, pp 390-5.

Prochaska, J., DiClemente, C. and Norcross, J. (1992) 'In search of how people change: applications to addictive behaviors', *Am Psychologist*, vol 47, no 9, pp 1102-14.

Pruitt, L.A., Glynn, N.W., King, A.C., Guralnik, J.M., Aiken, E.K., Miller, G. and Haskell, W.L. (2008) 'Use of accelerometry to measure physical activity in older adults at risk for mobility disability', *J Aging Physical Activity*, vol 16, pp 416-34.

Quadagno, J. (1989) 'Generational equity and the politics of the welfare state', *Politics & Society*, vol 17, pp 353-76.

Radford, D.J., Wang, K., McNelis, J.C., Taylor, A.E., Hechenberger, G., Hofmann, J., Chahal H., Arlt, W. and Lord, J.M. (2010) 'Dehydroepiandrosterone sulfate directly activates protein kinase C-⊠ to increase human neutrophil superoxide generation', *Mol Endocrinol*, vol 24, pp 813-21.

Rajpathak, S.N., Liu,Y., Ben-David, O., Reddy, S., Atzmon, G., Crandall, J. and Barzilai, N. (2011) 'Lifestyle factors of people with exceptional longevity', *J Am Geriatr Soc*, vol 59, pp 1509-12.

Rasquin, S.M.C., Willems, C., de Vlieger, S., Geers, R.P.J. and Soede, M. (2007) 'The use of technical devices to support outdoor mobility of dementia patients', *Technology and Disability*, vol 19, pp 113-20.

Rees-Jones, I., Hyde, M., Victor, C.E., Wiggins, R.D., Gilleard, C. and Higgs, P. (2008) 'The historical evolution of the third age', in I. Rees-Jones, M. Hyde, C.E. Victor, R.D. Wiggins, C. Gilleard and P. Higgs (eds) *Ageing in a consumer society: from passive to active consumption in Britain*, Bristol: Policy Press, pp 13-28.

Revell, V. and Skene, D.J. (2010) 'Impact of age on human non-visual responses to light', *Sleep and Biological Rhythms*, vol 8, pp 84-94.

Reynolds, F. (2010) '"Colour and communion": exploring the influences of visual art-making as a leisure activity on older women's subjective well-being', *Journal of Aging Studies*, vol 24, pp 135-43.

Riach, P.A. and Rich, J. (2007) *An experimental investigation of age discrimination in the English labor market*, Discussion paper no 3029, Bonn: Institute for the Study of Labor, IZA.

Richards, N., Warren, L. and Gott, M. (2012) 'The challenge of creating "alternative" images of ageing: lessons from a project with older women', *Journal of Aging Studies*, vol 26, no 1, pp 65-78.

Riley, K.P. and Snowden, D.A. (2000) 'The challenges and successes of aging: findings from the Nun Study', *Advances in Medical Psychotherapy*, vol 10, pp 1-12.

Riley, M. (1992) 'Cohort perspectives', in E. Borgatta and M. Borgatta (eds) *The encyclopedia of social sciences*, New York: Macmillan, pp 52-65.

Rioux, L. (2005) 'The well-being of aging people living in their own homes', *Journal of Environmental Psychology*, vol 25, pp 231-43.

Robinson, L., Brittain, K., Lindsay, S., Jackson, D. and Olivier, P. (2009) 'Keeping In Touch Everyday (KITE) project: developing assistive technologies with people with dementia and their carers to promote independence', *International Psychogeriatrics*, vol 21, no 3, pp 494-502.

Rose, M. (2011) 'The end of ageing: why life begins at 90', *New Scientist*, issue 2824, p 42.

Ross, R., Wight, T.N., Strandness, E. and Thiele, B. (1984) 'Human atherosclerosis. I. Cell constitution and characteristics of advanced lesions of the superficial femoral artery', *Am J Pathol*, vol 114, pp 79-93.

Rowe, J. and Kahn, R. (1987) 'Human aging: usual and successful', *Science*, vol 237, pp 143-9.

Rowles, G.D. (1983) 'Place and personal identity in old age: observations from Appalachia', *Journal of Environmental Psychology*, vol 3, pp 299-313.

Royal College of Art (2012) 'i-design – knowledge and tools for inclusive design' (www.hhc.rca.ac.uk/961/all/1/i-design.aspx).

Royal College of Physicians Edinburgh (2005) 'Memorandum in response to House of Lords Select Committee on Science and Technology's *Inquiry to Examine the Scientific Aspects of Ageing*', London: House of Lords (www.publications.parliament.uk/pa/ld200506/ldselect/ldsctech/20/20we24.htm).

Royal Commission on Long-term Care (1999) *With respect to old age: Long term care – rights and responsibilities*, Cm 4192–I, London: The Stationery Office (http://collections.europarchive.org/tna/20081023125241/http:/www.archive.official-documents.co.uk/document/cm41/4192/4192.htm).

Rubinstein, R.L. (2002) 'The qualitative interview with older informants: some key questions', in G.D. Rowles and N.E. Schoenberg (eds) *Qualitative gerontology: a contemporary perspective*, New York: Springer, pp 137-53.

Rubenstein, R.L. and de Medeiros, K. (2004) 'Ecology and the ageing self', in H.-W. Wahl, R.J. Scheidt and P.G. Windley (eds) *Annual review of gerontology and geriatrics*, vol 23, New York: Springer Publishing Company, Inc, pp 59-84.

Rutter, M. (2008) 'Developing concepts in developmental psychopathology', in J.J. Hudziak (ed) *Developmental psychopathology and wellness: genetic and environmental influences*, Washington, DC: American Psychiatric Publishing, pp 3-22.

Saarikallio, S. (2010) 'Music as emotional self-regulation throughout adulthood', *Psychology of Music* (http://pom.sagepub.com/content/early/2010/09/30/0305735610374894).

Sahin, E. and Depinho, R.A. (2012) 'Axis of ageing: telomeres, p53 and mitochondria', *Nat Rev Mol Cell Biol*, vol 13, pp 397-404.

Salles, A.S. and Gyi, D.E. (2012) 'The specification of personalised insoles using additive manufacturing', *Work: A Journal of Prevention, Assessment and Rehabilitation*, vol 41, no 1, pp 1771-4.

Sapolsky, R.M., Krey, L.C. and Mcewen, B.S. (1986) 'The neuroendocrinology of stress and aging: the glucocorticoid cascade hypothesis', *Endocr Rev*, vol 7, pp 284-301.

Scaffidi, P. and Misteli, T. (2005) 'Reversal of the cellular phenotype in the premature aging disease Hutchinson-Gilford progeria syndrome', *Nat Med*, vol 11, pp 440-5.

Scase, R. and Scales, J. (2000) *Fit and fifty?*, Swindon: Economic and Social Research Council.

Scharpf, F. and Schmidt, V. (eds) (2000) *Welfare and work in open economies*, Oxford: Oxford University Press.

Scherger, S. (2009) 'Cultural practices and the life course', *Cultural Trends*, vol 18, no 1, pp 23-45.

Schmidt, P.J., Daly, R.C., Bloch, M., Smith, M.J., Danaceau, M.A., St Clair, L.S., Murphy, J.H., Haq, N. and Rubinow, D.R. (2005) 'Dehydroepiandrosterone monotherapy in midlife-onset major and minor depression', *Arch Gen Psychiatry*, vol 62, pp 154-62.

Schuller, T. and Watson, D. (2009) *Learning through life: inquiry into the future for lifelong learning*, Leicester: NIACE.

Science and Technology Committee, House of Lords (2005) *Ageing: scientific aspects*, London: The Stationery Office.

Selbin, E. (2010) *Revolution, rebellion, resistance: the power of story*, London: Zed Books.

Selwyn, N. (2002) 'Establishing an inclusive society? Technology, social exclusion and UK government policy making', *Journal of Social Policy*, vol 31, issue 1, pp 1-20.

Selye, H. and Fortier, C. (1949) 'Adaptive reactions to stress', *Res Publ Assoc Res Nerv Ment Dis*, vol 29, pp 3-18.

Sen, A. (1992) *Inequality re-examined,* Oxford: Clarendon Press.

Settersten, R.A., Jr (2005) 'Linking the two ends of life: what gerontology can learn from childhood studies', *The Journals of Gerontology Series B: Psychological Sciences and Social Sciences*, vol 60, S173-S180.

Shaw, A.C., Joshi, S., Greenwood, H., Panda, A. and Lord, J.M. (2010) 'Aging of the innate immune system', *Current Opinion Immunol*, vol 22, pp 507-13.

Shephard, R. (1997) 'What is the optimal type of physical activity to enhance health?', *Br J Sports Med*, vol 31, no 4, pp 277-84.

Shergold, I. and Parkhurst, G. (2012) 'Transport-related social exclusion amongst older people in rural Southwest England and Wales', *Journal of Rural Studies*, vol 28, no 4, pp 412-21.

Sherrington, C., Whitney, J.C., Lord, S.R., Hherbert, R.D., Cumming, R.G. and Close, J.C. (2008) 'Effective exercise for the prevention of falls: a systematic review and meta-analysis', *J Am Geriatr Soc*, vol 56, pp 2234-43.

Sherwood, N. and Jeffery, R. (2000) 'The behavioral determinants of exercise: implications for physical activity interventions', *Ann Rev Nutr*, vol 20, no 1, pp 21-44.

Shiels, P.G. (2010) 'Improving precision in investigating aging: why telomeres can cause problems', *J Gerontol A Biol Sci Med Sci*, vol 65, pp 789-91.

Shiogai, Y., Stefanovska, A. and McClintock, P.V.E. (2010) 'Nonlinear dynamics of cardiovascular ageing', *Physics Rep*, vol 488, pp 51-110.

Shoval, N., Auslander, G., Cohen-Shalom, K., Isaacson, M., Landau, R. and Heinik, J. (2010) 'What can we learn about the mobility of the elderly in the GPS era?', *J Transport Geography*, vol 18, pp 603-12.

Shoval, N., Auslander, G., Freytag, T., Landau, R., Oswald, F., Seidl, U. et al (2008) 'The use of advanced tracking technologies for the analysis of mobility in Alzheimer's disease and related cognitive diseases', *BMC Geriatrics*, vol 8, no 1, p 7.

Shoval, N., Wahl, H.-W., Auslander, G., Isaacson, M., Oswald, F., Edry, T., Landau, R. and Heinik, J. (2011) 'Use of global positioning system to measure the out-of-home mobility of older adults with different cognitive functioning', *Ageing Soc*, vol 31, pp 849-69.

Silva, E.B. (2000) 'The cook, the cooker and the gendering of the kitchen', *The Sociological Review*, vol 48, no 4, pp 612-28.

Silva, E. (2008) 'Cultural capital and visual art in the contemporary UK', Special Issue on 'The consequences of instrumental museum and gallery policy', *Cultural Trends*, vol 17, no 4, pp 267-87.

Simon, N.M., Smoller, J.W., Mcnamara, K.L., Maser, R.S., Zalta, A.K., Pollack, M.H., Nierenberg, A.A., Fava, M. and Wong, K.K. (2006) 'Telomere shortening and mood disorders: preliminary support for a chronic stress model of accelerated aging', *Biol Psychiatry*, vol 60, pp 432-5.

Skene, D.J. (2009) 'Testing blue light with the elderly', *Lighting J*, vol 74, no 3, pp 15-18.

Smith, A.E. (2000) 'Quality of Life: A review', *Education and Ageing*, vol 15, no 3, pp 419-35.

Smith, J. and Freund, A.M. (2002) 'The dynamics of possible selves in old age', *J Gerontol Series B: Psychol Sci Social Sci*, vol 57, no 6, pp 492-500.

Smith, N.R., Kelly, Y.J. and Nazroo, J.Y. (2009) 'Intergenerational continuities of ethnic inequalities in general health in England', *Journal of Epidemiology and Community Health*, vol 63, pp 253-8.

Snowdon, D.A., Tully, C.L., Smith, C.D., Riley, K.P. and Markesbery, W.R. (2007) 'Serum folate and the severity of atrophy of the neocortex in Alzheimer disease: findings from the Nun Study', *American Journal of Clinical Nutrition*, vol 71, no 4, pp 993-8.

Snowdon, D.A., Kemper, S.J., Mortimer, J.A., Greiner, L.H., Wekstein, D.R. and Markesbery, W.R. (1996) 'Linguistic ability in early life and cognitive function and Alzheimer's disease in late life: findings from the Nun Study', *Journal of the American Medical Association*, vol 275, no 7, pp 528-32.

Soden, S. (2011) 'Redefining cultural roles in older age: grandmothering as an extension of motherhood', in V. Ylänne (ed) *Representing ageing: images and identities*, Basingstoke: Palgrave, pp 84-99.

Spilman, P., Podlutskaya, N., Hart, M.J., Debnath, J., Gorostiza, O., Bredesen, D., Richardson, A., Strong, R. and Galvan, V. (2010) 'Inhibition of mTOR by rapamycin abolishes cognitive deficits and reduces amyloid-beta levels in a mouse model of Alzheimer's disease', *PLoS One*, vol 5, e9979.

Stamatakis, E., Ekelund, U. and Wareham, N. (2007) 'Temporal trends in physical activity in England: the Health Survey for England 1991 to 2004', *Preventive Med*, vol 45, no 6, pp 416-23.

Stehbens, W.E., Delahunt, B., Shozawa, T. and Gilbert-Barness, E. (2001) 'Smooth muscle cell depletion and collagen types in progeric arteries', *Cardiovasc Pathol*, vol 10, pp 133-6.

Stein, P.S., Desrosiers, M., Donegan, S.J., Yepes, J.F. and Kryscio, R.J. (2007) 'Tooth loss, dementia and neuropathology in the Nun Study', *Journal of the American Dental Association*, vol 138, no 10, pp 1314-22.

Strehler, B.L. (1959) 'Origin and comparison of the effects of time and high-energy radiations on living systems', *Q Rev Biol*, vol 34, pp 117-42.

Ströhle, A. (2009) 'Physical activity, exercise, depression and anxiety disorders', *J Neural Transmission*, vol 116, no 6, pp 777-84.

Studenski, S., Perera, S., Patel, K., Rosano, C., Faulkner, K., Inzitari, M., Brach, J., Chandler, J., Cawthon, P., Barrett Connor, E., Nevitt, M., Visser, M., Kritchevsky, S., Badinelli, S., Harris, T., Newman, A.B., Cauley, J., Ferrucci, L. and Guralnik, J. (2011) 'Gait speed and survival in older adults', *JAMA*, vol 305, no 1, pp 50-8.

Sun, D., Muthukumar, A.R., Lawrence, R.A. and Fernandes, G. (2001) 'Effects of calorie restriction on polymicrobial peritonitis induced by cecum ligation and puncture in young C57BL/6 mice', *Clin Diagn Lab Immunol*, vol 8, pp 1003-11.

Svansdottir, H.B. and Snaedal, J. (2006) 'Music therapy in moderate and severe dementia of Alzheimer's type: a case-control study', *Int Psychogeriatrics*, vol 18, no 4, pp 613-21.

Tadd, W. and Calnan, M. (2009) 'Caring for older people: why dignity matters – the European experience', in L. Nordenfelt (ed), *Dignity in care for older people*, Oxford: Wiley-Blackwell, pp 119-45.

Tait, J. and Lyall, C. (2001) *Investigation into ESRC funded interdisciplinary research, Final Report*, Edinburgh: Scottish Universities Policy Research and Advice Network.

Taylor, A. and Hallam, S. (2008) 'Understanding what it means for older students to learn basic musical skills on a keyboard instrument', *Music Education Res*, vol 10, no 2, pp 285-306.

Taylor, C. (1991) 'The dialogical self', in D.R. Hiley, J.F. Bohman and R. Shusterman (eds) *The interpretive turn: philosophy, science, culture*, Ithaca, NY: Cornell University Press, pp 304-14.

Taylor, D. (2011) 'Developing a visual language to enhance knowledge transfer in the design of smart clothes and wearable technology for the active ageing', *Design Principles and Practices*, vol 5, no 6, pp 369-88.

Taylor, D.H., Jr, Ezell, M., Kuchibhatla, M., Ostbye, T. and Clipp, E.C. (2008) 'Identifying trajectories of depressive symptoms for women caring for their husbands with dementia', *J Am Geriatr Soc*, vol 56, pp 322-7.

Taylor, P. and Walker, A. (1998) 'Employers and older workers: attitudes and employment practices', *Ageing Soc*, vol 18, no 6, pp 641-58.

Thompson, J.L., Bentley, G., Davis, M., Coulson, J., Stathi, A. and Fox, K.R. (2011) 'Food shopping habits, physical activity and health-related indicators among adults aged ≥70 years', *Public Health Nutrition*, vol 14, pp 1640-9.

Thomson, F. and Caighead, M. (2008) 'Innovative approaches for the treatment of depression: targeting the HPA axis', *Neurochem Res*, vol 33, pp 691-707.

Thune, I., Brenn, T., Lund, E. and Gaard, M. (1997) 'Physical activity and the risk of breast cancer', *New Eng J Med*, vol 336, no 18, pp 1269-75.

Tilt, J., Unfried, T. and Roca, B. (2007) 'Using objective and subjective measures of neighbourhood greenness and accessible destinations for understanding walking trips and BMI in Seattle, Washington', *A J Health Promot*, Mar-Apr, vol 21, no 4, pp 371-9.

Tinsley, M. (2012) *Too much to lose: understanding and supporting Britain's older workers*, London: Policy Exchange, pp 1-64 (www. policyexchange.org.uk/images/publications/too much to lose.pdf).

Tomiyama, A.J., O'Donovan, A., Lin, J., Puterman, E., lazaro, A., Chan, J., Dhabhar, F.S., Wolkowitz, O., Kirschbaum, C., Blackburn, E. and Epel, E. (2012) 'Does cellular aging relate to patterns of allostasis? An examination of basal and stress reactive HPA axis activity and telomere length', *Physiol Behav*, vol 106, pp 40-5.

Townsend, P. (1981) 'The structured dependency of the elderly: the creation of social policy in the twentieth century', *Ageing & Society*, vol 1, no 1, pp 5-28.

Townsend, P. (1986) 'Ageism and social policy', in C. Phillipson and A. Walker (eds) *Ageing and social policy*, Aldershot: Gower, pp 15-44.

Twigg, J. (2004) 'The body, gender, and age: Feminist insights in social gerontology', *Journal of Ageing Studies*, vol 18, pp 59-73.

Tyrka, A.R., Price, L.H., Kao, H.T., Porton, B., Marsella, S.A. and Carpenter, L.L. (2010) 'Childhood maltreatment and telomere shortening: preliminary support for an effect of early stress on cellular aging', *Biol Psychiatry*, vol 67, pp 531-4.

UN (United Nations) (2002) *Report of the Second World Assembly on Ageing*, New York: UN.

Utsuyama, M. and Hirokawa, K. (1987) 'Age-related changes of splenic T cells in mice – a flow cytometric analysis', *Mech Ageing Dev*, vol 40, pp 89-102.

Varvarigou, M., Creech, A., Hallam, S. and McQueen, H. (2012a) 'Bringing different generations together in music-making – an intergenerational music project in East London', *Int J Community Music*, vol 4, no 3, pp 207-20.

Varvarigou, M., Hallam, S., Creech, A. and McQueen, H. (2012b) 'Benefits experienced by older people who participated in group music-making activities', *Journal of Applied Arts and Health*, vol 3, no 2, pp 183-98.

Vedhara, K., Mcdermott, M.P., Evans, T.G., Treanor, J.J., Plummer, S., Tallon, D., Cruttenden, K.A. and Schifitto, G. (2002) 'Chronic stress in non-elderly caregivers: psychological, endocrine and immune implications', *J Psychosom Res*, vol 53, pp 1153-61.

Veenhoven, R. (2000) 'The four qualities of life', *J Happiness Studies*, vol 1, no 1, pp 1-39.

Venn, S. and Arber, S. (2011) 'Daytime sleep and active ageing in later life', *Ageing Soc*, vol 31, no 2, pp 197-216.

Venn, S. and Arber, S. (2012) 'Understanding older people's decisions about the use of sleeping medication: issues of control and autonomy', *Sociology of Health and Illness*, vol 34, no 8.

Vera-Sanso, P. (2012) 'Gender, poverty and old-age livelihoods in urban South India in an era of globalisation', *Oxford Development Studies*, vol 40, issue 3, pp 324-40.

Victor, C.R., Martin, W. and Zubair, M. (2012) 'Families and caring amongst older people in South Asian communities in the UK: a pilot study', *European Journal of Social Work*, vol 15, issue 1, pp 81-96.

Villar, F., Celdrán, M., Pinazo, S. and Triadó, C. (2010) 'The teacher's perspective in older education: The experience of teaching in a university for older people in Spain', *Educational Gerontology*, vol 36, no 10, pp 951-67.

Vincent, J. (1996) 'Who's afraid of an ageing population? Nationalism, the free market and the construction of old age as an issue', *Critical Social Policy*, vol 16, pp 3-26.

Vincent, J. (2006) 'Ageing contested: anti-ageing science and the cultural construction of old age', *Sociology*, vol 40, pp 681-98.

von Zglinicki, T. and Martin-Ruiz, C.M. (2005) 'Telomeres as biomarkers for ageing and age-related diseases', *Curr Mol Med*, vol 5, pp 197-203.

Voorbij, A.I.M. and Steenbekkers, L.P.A. (1998) 'Physical variables: exertion of force', in L.P.A. Steebekkers and C.E.M. van Beijsterveldt (eds) *Design-relevant characteristics of ageing users*, Delft: Delft University Press, pp 48-59.

WAG (Welsh Assembly Government) (2007) *Fulfilled lives, supportive communities: a strategy for social services in Wales over the next decade*, Cardiff: WAG (http://wales.gov.uk/topics/health/publications/socialcare/strategies/lives/?lang=en).

WAG (2008) *The strategy for older people in Wales 2008-2013: living longer, living better*, Cardiff: WAG (http://wales.gov.uk/topics/olderpeople/publications/strategy2008-2013/?lang=en).

WAG and Food Standards Agency Wales (2003) *Food and well being: reducing inequalities through a nutrition strategy for Wales*, Cardiff: WAG (http://wales.gov.uk/about/cabinet/cabinetstatements/2003/26.02.2003foodandwellbeing?lang=en).

Wahl, H.-W. and Iwarsson, S. (2007) 'Person–environment relations in old age', in R. Fernandez- Ballesteros (ed) *Geropsychology – European perspectives for an ageing world*, Göttingen: Hogrefe, pp 49-66.

Walford, N.S., Samarasundera, E., Phillips, J.E., Hockey, A.E. and Foreman, N. (2011) 'Producing a navigational index from measures of built environment quality using oral narratives and virtual routes', *Landscape and Urban Planning*, vol 100, no 1-2, pp 163-8.

Walker, A. (1980) 'The social creation of poverty and dependency in old age', *Journal of Social Policy*, vol 9, no 1, pp 49-75.

Walker, A. (1990) 'The economic "burden" of ageing and the prospect of intergenerational conflict', *Ageing & Society*, vol 10, no 4, pp 377-96.

Walker, A. (1993) *Age and attitudes*, Brussels: European Commission.

Walker, A. (1994) 'Work and income in the third age – an EU perspective', *The Geneva Papers on Risk and Insurance*, vol 19, no 73, pp 397-407.

Walker, A. (1999a) 'The principles and potential of active ageing', Introductory Report for the European Commission Conference on Active Ageing, Brussels, 15-16 November.

Walker, A. (1999b) *Managing an ageing workforce: a guide to good practice*, Dublin: European Foundation for the Improvement of Living and Working Conditions.

Walker, A. (2002) 'A strategy for active ageing', *International Social Security Review*, vol 55, no 1, pp 121-40.

Walker, A. (2003) 'Securing the future of old age in Europe', *Journal of Societal and Social Policy*, vol 2, no 1, pp 13-32.

Walker, A. (2006) 'Aging and politics – an international perspective', in R. Binstock and L. George (eds) *Handbook of aging and the social sciences*, Burlington, VA: Elsevier Academic Press, pp 339-59.

Walker, A. (2007) 'Why involve older people in research?', *Age & Ageing*, vol 36, pp 481-3.

Walker, A. (2009) 'The emergence and application of active ageing in Europe', *Journal of Aging & Social Policy*, vol 21, pp 75-93.

Walker, A. (2013) 'Multi-disciplinarity, user engagement and the design of special programmes of ageing research in the United Kingdom – a response to Lansley', *Ageing and Society*, vol 33, no 5, p 762.

Walker, A. and Deacon, B. (2003) 'Economic globalisation and policies on ageing', *Journal of Societal and Social Policy*, vol 2, no 2, pp 1-18.

Walker, A. and Hennessy, C.H. (2002) 'The UK national collaboration on ageing research', *Lifespan: The Journal of the British Society for Research on Ageing*, vol 11, no 1.

Walker, A. and Maltby, T. (2012) 'Active ageing: a strategic policy solution to demographic ageing in the European Union', *International Journal of Social Welfare*, vol 21, suppl 1, pp 117-30.

Walker, A. and Naegele, G. (eds) (1999) *The politics of old age in Europe*, Buckingham: Open University Press.

Wang, W., Chen, J.X., Liao, R., Deng, Q., Zhou, J.J., Huang, S. and Sun, P. (2002) 'Sequential activation of the MEK-extracellular signal-regulated kinase and MKK3/6-p38 mitogen-activated protein kinase pathways mediates oncogenic ras-induced premature senescence', *Mol Cell Biol*, vol 22, pp 3389-403.

Wanless, D. (2006) *Securing good care for older people. Taking a long-term view*, London: King's Fund, (www.kingsfund.org.uk/publications/securing-good-care-older-people)

Warburton, D.E., Nicol, C. and Bredin, S.S. (2006) 'Health benefits of physical activity: the evidence', *Can Med Assoc J*, vol 174, no 6, pp 801-9.

Ward, R.A. (1979) 'The meaning of voluntary association participation to older people', *Journal of Gerontology*, vol 34, no 3, pp 438-45.

Warren, L. and Richards, N. (2012) '"I don't see many images of myself coming back at myself": representations of women and ageing', in V. Ylänne (ed) *Representing ageing: images and identities*, Basingstoke: Palgrave, pp 149-68.

Wegman, D.H. (1999) 'Older workers', *Occup Med*, vol 14, pp 537-57.

Westendrop, R.G. and Kirkwood, T.B.L. (2007) 'The biology of human ageing', in J. Bond, S. Peace, F.-D. Kohli and G. Westerhoff (eds) *Ageing in society*, London: Sage Publications, pp 15-37.

Weuve, J., Kang, J., Manson, J., Breteler, M.M., Ware, J. and Grodstein, F. (2004) 'Physical activity, including walking, and cognitive function in older women', *JAMA*, vol 292, no 12, pp 1454-61.

WHO (World Health Organization) (1994) *Health for all: updated targets*, Copenhagen: WHO.

WHO (2001a) *Health and ageing: a discussion paper*, Geneva: WHO.

WHO (2001b) *Active ageing: from evidence to action*, Geneva: WHO.

WHO (2002) *Active ageing: a policy framework*, Geneva: WHO (http://whqlibdoc.who.int/hq/2002/WHO_NMH_NPH_02.8.pdf).

WHO (2012) *Demographic trends, statistics and data on ageing. Healthy ageing. Facts and figures*, Geneva: WHO (www.euro.who.int/en/what-we-do/health-topics/Life-stages/healthy-ageing/facts-and-figures/demographic-trends-and-data-on-ageing).

WHO Expert Consultation (2004) 'Appropriate body-mass index for Asian populations and its implications for policy and intervention strategies', *The Lancet*, vol 363, pp 157-63.

Whysall, Z., Haslam, C. and Haslam, R. (2007) 'Developing the stage of change approach for the reduction of work-related musculoskeletal disorders', *J Health Psychol*, vol 12, no 1, pp 184-97.

Wikgren, M., Maripuu, M., Karlsson, T., Nordfjall, K., Bergdahl, J., Hultdin, J., Del-Favero, J., Roos, G., Nilsson, L.G., Adolfsson, R. and Norrback, K.F. (2012) 'Short telomeres in depression and the general population are associated with a hypocortisolemic state', *Biol Psychiatry*, vol 71, pp 294-300.

Willcox, D.C., Willcox, B.J., Wang, N.C., He, Q., Rosenbaum, M. and Suzuki, M. (2008) 'Life at the extreme limit: phenotypic characteristics of supercentenarians in Okinawa', *J Gerontol A Biol Sci Med Sci*, vol 63, pp 1201-8.

Williams, E.Y., Gibb, A., Gyi, D.E. and Haslam, R. (2012a) 'Building healthy construction workers', in M. Anderson (ed) *Contemporary ergonomics and human factors 2012: proceedings of the International Conference on Ergonomics & Human Factors 2012*, 16-19 April, Blackpool, London: Taylor & Francis, pp 69-70.

Williams, E.Y., Gyi, D.E., Gibb, A. and Haslam, R. (2012b) 'Facilitating good ergonomics: workplace design and wellbeing for the ageing population', *Proceedings of the XXIVth Annual International Occupational Ergonomics and Safety Conference*, 7-8 June, Ft Lauderdale, FL: International Society for Occupational Ergonomics and Safety (CD ROM).

Williams, G. (1957) 'Pleiotropy, natural selection, and the evolution of senescence', *Evolution*, vol 11, pp 389-411.

Williams, S.J., Meadows, R. and Arber, S. (2010) 'Sociology of sleep', in F. Cappaccio, M. Miller and S. Lockley (eds) *Sleep epidemiology*, Oxford: Oxford University Press, pp 275-99.

Winterson, J. (2012) *Why be happy when you could be normal?*, London: Vintage.

Withnall, A. (2010) *Improving learning in later life*, Abingdon: Routledge.

Withnall, A., McGivney, V. and Soulsby, J. (2004) *Older people learning: myths and realities*, Leicester: Niace with the UK Department for Education and Skills.

Wittenberg, R., Hu, B., Hancock, R., Morciano, M., Comas-Herrera, A., Malley, J. and King, D. (2011) *Projections of demand for and costs of social care for older people in England 2010-2030, under current and alternative funding systems. Report of research for the commission on funding of care and support*, Personal Social Services Research Unit (PSSRU) Discussion paper 2811/2 University of Kent and LSE (http://eprints.lse.ac.uk/40720/1/2811-2.pdf).

Wolfe, D.B. and Snyder, R. (2003) *Ageless marketing: strategies for reaching the hearts and minds of the new customer majority*, Chicago, IL: Dearborn Trade Publishing.

Wolkowitz, O.M., Mellon, S.H., Epel, E.S., Lin, J., Dhabhar, F.S., Su, Y., Reus, V.I., Rosser, R., Burke, H.M., Kupferman, E., Compagnone, M., Nelson, J.C. and Blackburn, E.H. (2011) 'Leukocyte telomere length in major depression: correlations with chronicity, inflammation and oxidative stress – preliminary findings', *PLoS One*, vol 6, e17837.

Wong, M., Koh, D. and Lee, M. (1998) 'Assess workers' needs and preferences first before planning a physical fitness programme: findings from a polytechnic institute in Singapore', *Occupational Med*, vol 48, no 1, pp 37-44.

Wood, D.J., Ions, G.K., Quinby, J.M., Gale, D.W. and Stevens, J. (1992) 'Factors which influence mortality after subcapital hip fracture', *J Bone Joint Surg*, vol 74, pp 199-202.

Woodward, K.M. (ed) (1999) *Figuring women: Women, bodies, generations*, Bloomington, IN: Indiana University Press.

Woodward, K. (2006) 'Performing age, performing gender', *Feminist Formations*, vol 18, no 1, pp 162-89.

World Bank, The (1994) *Averting the old age crisis*, New York: Oxford University Press.

Wylie, C., Copeman, J. and Kirk, S.F.L. (1999) 'Health and social factors affecting the food choice and nutritional intake of elderly people with restricted mobility', *J Human Nutr Dietetics*, vol 12, no 5, pp 375-80.

Ylänne, V. (2012) 'Introduction', in V. Ylänne (ed) *Representing Ageing: Images and Identities*, Basingstoke and New York: Palgrave Macmillan, pp 1-16.

Yokote, K. and Saito, Y. (2008) 'Extension of the life span in patients with Werner syndrome', *J Am Geriatr Soc*, vol 56, pp 1770-1.

Zalot, M. (2001) 'Wall calendars: structured time, mundane memories and disposable images', *Journal of Mundane Behavior*, vol 3, no 2 (www.mundanebehavior.org/issues/v2n3/zalot.htm).

Zhang, Y.B., Harwood, J., Williams, A., Ylänne-McEwan, V., Wadleigh, P.M. and Thimm, C. (2006) 'The portrayal of older adults in advertising: a cross-national review', *Journal of Language and Social Psychology*, vol 25, pp 264-80.

Znaimer, M. (2013) 'Zoomer nation' (http://zoomernation.com).

Zubair, M., Martin, W. and Victor, C.R. (2012a) 'Embodying gender, age, ethnicity and power in "the field": reflections on dress and the presentation of the self in research with older Pakistani Muslims', *Sociological Research Online*, vol 21.

Zubair, M., Martin, W. and Victor, C.R. (2012b) 'Doing Pakistani ethnicity, the female way: issues of identity, trust and recruitment when researching older Pakistani Muslims in the UK', in M. Leontowitsch (ed) *Researching later life and ageing: expanding qualitative research agendas and methods*, Basingstoke: Palgrave, pp 63-83.

Appendix: NDA Programme project team members

A combined genetic and small molecule approach to studying the role of the p38/MK2 stress signalling pathway in a human premature ageing syndrome:
Mark Bagley, University of Sussex; Terry Davis, David Kipling and Joanna Latimer, Cardiff University.

Ages and Stages: the place of theatre in representations and recollections of ageing:
Miriam Bernard, David Amigoni, Lucy Munro, and Michael Murray, Keele University; Jill Rezzano, New Vic Theatre; Michelle Rickett; Ruth Basten; Tracy Harrison.

Ageing, poverty and neo-liberalism in urban South India:
Penny Vera-Sanso, Birkbeck College; V. Suresh, M. Hussein, K. Saravanan and S.Henry, Centre for Law, Policy and Human Rights Studies, Chennai, India; Barbara-Harris White, HelpAge International.

Ageing, wellbeing and development: a comparative study of Brazil and South Africa:
Armando Barrientos, Julia Mase, University of Manchester; Peter Lloyd Sherlock, University of East Anglia; Joao Saboia, Federal University of Rio de Janeiro; Valerie Moller, Rhodes University; Astrid Walker-Bourne, HelpAge International.

Biomechanical and sensory constraints of step and stair negotiation in old age:
Costas Maganaris, Liverpool John Moores University; Vasilios Baltzopoulos, Brunel University.
   With I. Di Giulio, University College London; D.A. Jones, E. Kingdon, and N. Reeves, Manchester Metropolitan University; G. Spiropuolos, University of Thessaly; J. Gavin, A. Ewen, G.S. King and T. Underdown, Liverpool John Moores University; and M Royes, Building Research Establishment.

CALL-ME: Promoting independence and social engagement among older people in disadvantaged communities:

Michael Murray, Roger Beech, Sian Maslin-Prothero, Tom Scharf, Frederika Ziegler, Keele University: Amanda Crummett, Jan Bailey, Sharon Middling, Amy Bennion, Tracey Harrison and Kim Rawlinson.

Contemporary visual art and identity construction – wellbeing amongst older people:

Andrew Newman, Anna Goulding, Newcastle University.

Partners and collaborators included Arts Council England; Equal Arts (a charity facilitating access to the arts for older people); Age Concern Gateshead; BALTIC Centre for Contemporary Art; Northern Gallery for Contemporary Art; and the Institute for Ageing and Health, Newcastle University.

Decision making in detecting and preventing financial abuse of older adults:

Mary Gilhooley, Priscilla Harris, Brunel University; Ken Gilhooley, University of Hertfordshire; Catherine Hennessy and Tony Gilbert, University of Plymouth; David Stanley, Northumbria University; Bridget Penhale, University of East Anglia; Deborah Cairns, Miranda Davies and Libby Notley, Brunel Institute of Ageing Studies.

Design for Ageing Well: improving the quality of life for the ageing population using a technology enabled garment system:

Jane McCann, Dr Katy Stevens, David Taylor, Jeni Bougourd, Juliette Smith, Jeanette East and Molly Price, University of Wales; Chris Nugent, Professor Bryan Scotney, Dr Paul McCullagh, Dr Dewar Findlay, Professor Sally MacClean, Dr Eric Wallace, Liam Burns and Ian Cleland, University of Ulster; Professor Stephen Benton and Boris Altemeyer, University of Westminster; Dr Tracey Williamson, Dr Julia Ryan and Laura Seppala, University of Salford; and Dr Victoria Haffenden, University of Brighton.

Plus a range of industrial collaborators including clothing producers and providers of technology and fabrics.

Dynamics of cardiovascular ageing:

Aneta Stefanovska, Peter V.E. McClintock, P. Jane Owen-Lynch, Dmytro Latsenko, Lancaster University; Dr Peter Clarkson, NHS Highland; Dr Alan Bernjak, University of Sheffield.

Families and caring in South Asian communities:

Christina Victor, Brunel University; Wendy Martin, Brunel University; Maria Zubair, University of Reading; Dr Subrata Saha, University of Reading.

Fiction and the cultural mediation of ageing: the importance of controlling the narrative of ageing:

Professor Philip Tew, Dr Nick Hubble, Dr Jago Morrison, Brunel University.

With Demos, the mass observation Archive at Sussex University and the London District U3A.

Grey and Pleasant Land? An interdisciplinary exploration of the connectivity of older people in rural civic society:

Catherine Hennessy, Ray Jones, Andrew Phippen, Innocento Maramba, George Giarchi, Gloria Lankshear, Plymouth University; Robin Means, Nigel Curry, Graham Parkhurst, Charles Musselwhite, Ian Shergold, Ian Biggs, Sinon Evans, Jane Bailey, Dan Buzzo, University of the West of England; Kip Jones, Kathleen Galvin, Les Todres, Yvette Staelens, Lee-Ann Fenge, Rosie Read, Marilyn Cash, Bournemouth University; Vanessa Burholt, Judith Phillips, Swansea University; Janet Smithson, Exeter University; Rhiannon Fisher, University of Gloucestershire.

HALCyon: Healthy ageing across the life course: capitalising on the value of UK life course cohorts:

Diana Kuh; Avan Aihie; Yoav Ben Schlomo; Rachel Cooper; Ian Day; Ian Deary; Jane Elliot; Catherine Gale; James Goodwin; Rebecca Hardy; Alison Lennox; Marcus Richards; Thomas von Zglinicki; Tamuno Alfred; Paula Aucott; Sean Clouston; Mike Gardner; Zeinab Mulla; Emily Murray; Sam Parsons; Vicky Tsipouri.

With Cyrus Cooper; Leone Craig; Dorly Deeg; Panos Demakakos; John Gallacher; Scott Hofer; Richard Martin; Carmen Martin-Ruiz; Geraldine McNeill; Gita Mishra; Chris Power; Paul Shiels; Humphrey Southall; John Starr; Andrew Steptoe; Kate Tilling; Lawrence Whalley, Stephanie Pilling.

Innovation in envisioning dynamic biomechanical data to inform healthcare and design guidelines and strategy:

Alastair Macdonald, Glasgow School of Art; Catherine Docherty, Research Consultant, Journey; David Loudon, Glasgow School of Art.

Landscapes of cross-generational engagement:

Peter Wright, University of Newcastle; William Gaver, Goldsmith University of London; Mark Blythe, Northumbria University; Andy Boucher; John Bowers; David Cameron; Nadine Jarvis; Toby Kerridge; Robert Phillips; Alex Wilkie.

Maintaining dignity in later life: a longitudinal qualitative study of older people's experiences in support and care:

Dr Liz Lloyd, Ailsa Cameron, Professor Randall Smith, Dr Kate White, University of Bristol; Professor Michael Calnan, University of Kent; Professor Jane Seymour, University of Nottingham.

Mappmal: a multidisciplinary approach to developing a prototype for food provision and nutritional management of older hospital patients.

Paula Moynihan, Newcastle University, Alastair Macdonald, Glasgow School of Art; Lisa Methven, Margot Gosney, University of Reading; Patrick Oliver, Carl May, University of Newcastle; with Clare Bamford, Gemma Teal, Ben Heaven, Roussa Tsikritzi, Clare Payne, Yiannis Mavrommattis, Robert Coomber, Jack Weedon; Alan Bell, Carol Fairfield (all from one of the three universities above) and Martin Maguire (University of Loughborough).

Migration, nutrition and ageing across the lifecourse in Bangladeshi families: a transnational perspective (MNA)

Janice Thompson, University of Bristol; Barry Bogin, Loughborough University; Vanja Garaj, Brunel University; Michael Heinrich, University of London School of Pharmacy; Petra Meier, University of Sheffield; Joy Merrill, Swansea University; with Fateha Ahmed; Nabila Ahmed; Jusna Begum; Runa Begum; Shelina Hurt; Sofina Khatun; Farida Khatun-Miah; Rehana Miah; Bablin Molik, Shaheena Nahar Omar. Consultants: Katy Gardner, Sussex University; Christina Victor, Brunel University.

Modelling ageing populations to 2030 (MAP2030):

M. Murphy, London School of Economics; E. Grundy, University of Cambridge; R. Hancock, University of East Anglia; R.D. Wittenberg, A. Comas-Herrera, L.M. Pickard, London School of Economics; J.E.B. Lindesay, University of Leicester; C. Curry, Pensions Policy Institute, J.N. Malley, London School of Economics.

Music for Life project: the role of participation in community music activities in promoting social engagement and well-being in older people:

Susan Hallam , Institute of Education, University of London; Andrea Creech; Helena Gaunt; Anita Pincas; Maria Varvarigou; Hilary McQueen.

Novel assessment of nutrition and ageing: NANA project:

Arlene Astell, University of St Andrews; Liz Williams, Sheffield University; Tim Adlam, University of Bath; Faustina Hwang, Reading University.

New metrics for exploring the relationship between mobility and successful ageing:

Lynn McInnes, Pamela Briggs, Linda Little, Northumbria University; Lynn Rochester, Newcastle University.

Older people's use of unfamiliar space:

Judith Phillips, Swansea University; Nigel Walford, Kingston University; Nigel Forman, Middlesex University; Ann Hockey, Anglia Ruskin University; Mike Leis, Swansea University; Edgar Samarasundra and Mark del Aguila.

Quality of life in older age: psychometric testing of the multidimensional Older People's Quality of Life (OPQOL) questionnaire and the causal model underpinning it:

Anne Bowling, D. Banister, P. Stenner, H. Titheridge, K. Sproston, T. McFarquhar, University College London.

Representing self – representing ageing. Look at me! Images of women and ageing:

Lorna Warren, University of Sheffield; Merryn Gott, University of Auckland; Susan Hogan, University of Derby; Naomi Richards, University of Sheffield; Eventus; Rosy Martin.

Somnia – Optimising quality of sleep among older people in the community and care homes: an integrated approach:

Sara Arber, University of Surrey; David Armstrong, King's College London; Ingrid Ayres, University of Surrey/University of Vechta, Germany; Kevin Morgan, Loughborough University, Roger Opwood, Bath University; Debra J. Skene, University of Surrey.

Sustaining IT use by older people to promote autonomy and independence (Sus-IT):

Leela Damodaran, Wendy Olphert, Matthew Atkinson, Stephan Bandelow, Matt Bell, Terri Gilbertson, Penny Harrison, Melanie Heeley, Eef Hogervorst, Cilin Machin, Nga Nguyen, Jatinder Sandhu, Marian Smith, Veronica van der Wardt, Loughborough University; Amr Ahmed, University of Lincoln; Peter Gregor, Paula Forbes, David Sloan, University of Dundee; David Frohlich, Chris Lim, University of Surrey; Irene Hardill, Northumbria University; Suzette Keith, Middlesex University; Leonie Ramondt, Anglia Ruskin University; Mark Shelbourn, Nottingham Trent University; Hannah Beardon, Steve Thompson.

Synergistic effects of physical and psychological stress upon immunesenescence:

Janet Lord, University of Birmingham; Anna Phillips, University of Birmingham.

Tackling ageing continence through theory, tools and technology (TACT3):

Eleanor van der Heuvel, Mary Gilhooley, Ian Sutherland, Felicity Jowitt, Kevin McKee, Lena Dahlberg, Stuart Parker, Patrick Gaydecki, Norman Ratcliffe, Jo-Anne Bichard, Adele Long, Nikki Cotterill, Susie Orme.

Towards understanding the biological drivers of cell ageing:
Dr Lynne Cox, Dr Penelope Mason, University of Oxford.

Trajectories of senescence through Markov models:
David Steinsaltz, University of Oxford; Professor Jim Carey, University of California at Davis; Dr Martin Kolb, University of Oxford; Dr Habib Saadi, Dr Viani Djeundje Biatat, Dr Andrey Pavlov, Gurjinder Mohan.

Transitions, choices and health in early old age: analyses of longitudinal data:
David Blane, Imperial College; Bola Akinwale, Imperial College and DWP; Melanie Bartley, UCL; Paul Boyle, University of St Andrews; Giuseppe Costa, University of Turin; Seeromanie Harding, University of Glasgow; Teresa Lefort, Older People's Reference Group; Kevin Lynch, ONS; Caroline Needham, Help the Aged; Pekka Martikainen, University of Helsinki; Richard Wiggins, Institute of Education.

Transitions in kitchen living:
Sheila Peace, John Percival, The Open University; Martin Maguire, Colette Nicolle, Russ Marshall, Ruth Sims, Clara Lawton, Loughborough University Design School.

Working late: strategies to enhance productive and healthy environments for the older workforce:
Cheryl Haslam, Loughborough University; Stacy Clemes, Loughborough University; Joanne Crawford, Institute for Occupational Medicine; Alistair Gibb, Diane Gyi, Roger Haslam, Martin Maguire, Hilary McDermott, Kevin Morgan and Colette Nicolle, Loughborough University.

Index

Notes

vs. indicates a comparison.

To save space in the index, the following abbreviations have been used:

DFAW project - Design for Ageing Well project

FCAMP - Fiction and Cultural Mediation of Ageing Project

mappmal project - 'Multidisciplinary approaches to develop a prototype for the prevention of malnutrition in older people' project

MINA project - 'Migration, nutrition and ageing across the life course in Bangladeshi families. A transitional perspective'

NANA project - 'Novel assessment of nutrition and ageing' project

NDA programme - New Dynamics of Ageing Programme

OPUS project - Older People's Use of Unfamiliar Space project

SOS project - Safety on Stairs project

SUS-IT project - Sustaining IT use by older people to promote autonomy and independence project

TACT3 project - Tackling Ageing Continence through Theory, Tools and Technology project

TiKL project - Transitions in Kitchen Living project

A

absolute poverty, 190
accelerometers, 127
access, 183–90
  digital access, 185–6
    see also SUS-IT (Sustaining IT use by older people to promote autonomy and independence) project
  institutional access, 187–8
    see also 'Decision making in detecting and preventing financial abuse of older adults' study
  social and political organisations, 188–90, 207
    see also 'Ageing, Well-being and Development' project
  spatial access, 183–5
    see also OPUS (Older People's Use of Unfamiliar Space) project
  unfamiliar places, 183
  well-known places, 183
accomplishments, subjective well-being, 120–1
active ageing, 242–4

Belgium, 254
citizen/society partnership, 256–7
compromised immunity, 123–5
definition, 183, 254–5
empowerment, 256
genesis of, 248–50
grass-roots initiatives, 257–8
heterogeneity concerns, 256
inclusivity, 252–8, 255
inequality concerns, 256
intergenerational solidarity, 255
life course perspective, 253
local community, 257–8
mobility effects *see* mobility
modern concepts, 249–50
music making, 143–6
national variations, 256
obligations, 255–6
participation, 256
as policy paradigm, 242–3
as preventative concept, 255
productive ageing, change from, 248–9
productive ageing *vs.*, 254
research, importance in, 242
rights, 255–6

strategies for, 255–8
visual arts, 146–9
  see also The Contemporary visual
    art and identity construction -
    Well-being amongst older people
    project
well-being, 253
WHO concept, 182, 252–3, 257
active citizenship, development of,
  243–8
activity
  definition, 255
  moderate intensity activity, 133–4
acute care, nutrition, 175
adaptive immune system, 59
adrenocortical steroid hormones
  compromised immunity, 124
  depression, 62
adult daughters, MINA project, 196–7
The Advisory Group on Malnutrition
  (2009), 155
ageing
  active *see* active ageing
  biological *see* biological ageing
  cells *see* cell ageing
  deficit models, 150–1
  definitions of *see* definition of ageing
  genetics of *see* genetics of ageing
  healthy *see* healthy ageing
  ill health with, 115–16
  interventions in *see* interventions in
    ageing
  longitudinal, 37
  measurement of *see* measurement of
    ageing
  mechanisms of, 26–7
  modulation of *see* modulating ageing
  political economy, 250–2
  population *see* population ageing
  productive *see* productive ageing
  public representation of, 101
  skin, 50–1
  social constructs *see* social constructs
    of ageing
  society's definition of, 26–7
  theories of *see* theories of ageing
  tissues *see* tissue ageing
  understanding of, 9
Ageing and biology project, 4
Ageing and fiction project, 5
'Ageing, poverty and neoliberalism in
  urban South India' project, 193–5
  conclusions, 194–5
  family businesses, 194
  methods, 193
  paid work, 193–4
  poverty, 194
  unpaid work, 193–4
'Ageing, Well-being and Development'
  project, 4, 189–90, 207
  format, 189

methods, 189
results, 189–90
Age Net (1997-2000), 13, 15
age-related conditions
  telomeres, 45
  see also chronic diseases; *specific
    diseases/disorders*
Ages and stages, 4, 96–102, 111
  archival material, 96–9
  bereavement feelings, 100
  documentary performances, 96–7,
    101–2
  interviews, 96–7, 98–101
  participation, 101
  public representation of ageing, 101
  repertoire, 96–7
  retirement, 100
  sense of belonging, 99–100
  sense of continuity, 99
  social networks, 100
  social roles, 100–1
  tape recordings, 98
  venue, 96
Age UK, nutrition concerns, 176
agility, nutrition problems, 171
AHRC (Arts and Humanities Research
  Council), 2
AIGA (American Institute for Graphic
  Arts), 225
Alzheimer's disease, 58
  animal models, 66–7
Ambient Kitchen (Newcastle
  University), 235
American Institute for Graphic Arts
  (AIGA), 225
animal models
  Alzheimer's disease, 66–7
  caloric restriction, 65
antagonistic pleiotropy, 33
anthropometry, MINA project, 159
anti-cancer mechanisms, cell ageing, 47
anti-diabetic drugs, 67–8
appreciation of life, 117
Arber, Sara, 3
Arcadia (Crace), 82–3
archives, Ages and stages, 96–9
Art and identity project, 5
art galleries, 91–6, 110–11
  community arts project, 85–6
  see also The Contemporary visual art
    and identity construction - Well-
    being amongst older people project
Arts and Humanities Research Council
  (AHRC), 2
Astell, Arlene, 3, 8
attitude
  competencies, 224, 225
  designer competencies, 225–6
*Attitude, Skill and Knowledge (ASK):
  a new model for design education*
  (Bakarman), 225–6

authorship, 204–6
  see also Fiction and Cultural
    Mediation of Ageing Project
    (FCMAP)
autonomy, 156
  'Music for Life' project, 145

B

Bagley, Mark C, 4
Bakarman, A A, *Attitude, Skill and
  Knowledge (ASK): a new model for
  design education,* 225–6
BALTIC Centre for Contemporary Art
  (Gateshead), 91, 147, 197–8
Baltimore Longitudinal Study of
  Ageing, 37
Bangladesh
  social interaction *vs.* UK, 196
  see also 'Migration, nutrition and
    ageing across the life course in
    Bangladeshi families. A transitional
    perspective' (MINA)
BAPEN, nutrition concerns, 176
Barrientos, Armando, 4
barriers, 'Grey and pleasant land?'
  project, 192
Basic Needs Satisfaction at Work Scale,
  145
Basic Psychological Needs Scale, 145
BBSRC (Biotechnology and Biological
  Sciences Research Council), 1–2
  initiatives on ageing, 14 (Table)
B cells, 59
Beckett, Samuel, 96
behaviour, sedentary *see* sedentary
  behaviour
Belgium, active ageing, 254
belonging, sense of, 99–100
Belsay Hall, Castle and Gardens
  (Northumberland), 92, 147
bereavement feelings, Ages and stages,
  100
Berlin Ageing Study, 151
Bernard, Miriam, 4, 7
bi-annual Programme meetings, NDA
  Programme multi-disciplinarity,
  17–18
biological ageing, 31–2, 43–60
  associated diseases, 32, 32 (Fig.)
    see also specific diseases
  cell ageing *see* cell ageing
  common cause, 64
  CUPID (Cumulative, Universal,
    Progressive, Inherent, Deleterious),
    31
  definition, 26
  environment, 37
  genetics *see* genetics of ageing
  importance in care approaches, 74
  inevitable processes *vs.* effects, 30–1
  longitudinal ageing, 37

pathways, 40
physical systems, 51–60
  see also specific organs
premature human ageing diseases,
  41–3
  see also specific diseases/disorders
study of, 37–43
tissue ageing *see* tissue ageing; *specific
  tissues*
  see also theories of ageing
Biology and ageing study, 30
*The biology of ageing: observations and
  principles* (Arking), 33
Biotechnology and Biological Sciences
  Research Council *see* BBSRC
  (Biotechnology and Biological
  Sciences Research Council)
Blane, David, 4
blood
  amount pumped, 53
  low oxygen, 52–3
blood pressure, 52
blood vessels
  brain, 58
  wall elasticity, 55
  wall thickening, 52
B lymphocytes, 59
body scanning
  DFAW project, 217–18
  see also specific methods
body shape changes, 211
body trauma, stress, 62–3
bone density, mobility, 126
Bowling, Ann, 4
brain
  ageing changes, 56–7
  blood vessels, 58
  grey matter, 56–8, 57 (Fig.)
  white matter, 56–8, 57 (Fig.)
Brazil *see* 'Ageing, Well-being and
  Development' project
British Society of Gerontology's Early
  Career Researchers in Ageing, 18
bystander intervention, 188

C

calcium supplements, 70
calenders, 104
CALL-ME project, 5, 84–91, 202–4
  action design, 85
  community arts projects *see*
    community arts project
  community exercise projects, 85
  employment, 203
  gardening projects, 85
  group activity organisation, 203–4
  local group activities, 203–4
  methods, 202–3
  neighbourhood identification, 203
  neighbourhood importance, 203
  public house importance, 203

surveys, 203
caloric restriction (CR), 65–6
Canada, NDA Programme, 7–8
Canadian Institutes of Health Research (CIHR), 7–8
cancer, 34
  caloric restriction, 66
  control by immune system, 58–9
capacity building, NDA Programme multi-disciplinarity, 17–18
Cardiovascular ageing project, 5
cardiovascular system, 51–5, 51 (Fig.)
  amount of blood pumped, 53
  homeostasis, 52
  see also specific organs
care
  biological ageing importance, 74
  expenditure, 122–3
  long-term, nutrition, 175
care homes, nutrition, 173–6
Care Quality Commission (CQC)
  Dignity and Nutrition Inspection Programme, 174
  nutrition concerns, 176
carers
  design projects, 215
  stress, 63–4
CARESIM, 132
Caring for our future: progress report on funding reform (HM Government 2012), 122
CASP-12, 145
CASP-19, 119
castles, 184
CBT-1 (Cognitive Behavioural Therapy for Insomnia), 138, 139
cell ageing, 44–8, 49 (Fig.), 64
  anti-cancer mechanism, 45, 47
  detection of, 47
  heart disease, 55–6
  immune system, 47
  myocytes, 55–6
  physical changes, 47
  stress-induced, 46
  telomere loss, 44–6
Cell ageing project, 4
chair design, hospital nutrition, 175
Cheesman, Peter, 96–7
chemicals, cell ageing, 46
chickenpox (varicella-zoster), 60
Chief Medical Officer, exercise guidelines, 133
childhood-onset progeria, 42–3
chronic diseases, 9–10
  biological ageing, 32, 32 (Fig.)
  exercise effects, 133
  mobility, 125–6
  poor sleep, 139
  see also specific diseases/disorders
chronological age, 27–8

churches
  access effects, 184
  groups, 189
CIHR (Canadian Institutes of Health Research), 7–8
civic activities, 192
clothes, sizes of see garments
CMV (cytomegalovirus) infections, 60
COACH prompting system project, 8
co-design
  DFAW project, 231–2
  teams in NDA Programme, 227
cognitive assessments, 166
Cognitive Behavioural Therapy for Insomnia (CBT-I), 138, 139
cognitive function
  in design, 212
  deterioration, 150
  'Music for Life' project benefits, 146
cognitive function project, Canadian NDA Programme, 8
cold weather, MINA project, 195
collaborative research projects, 3–4, 6
  see also specific projects
communal kitchens, 162
communication with older people, 230–1 (Fig.)
community, local, 257–8
community arts
  definition, 84
  see also specific arts types; specific projects
community arts project, 85–91, 110
  artwork exhibitions, 85–6
  community building, 90
  craftwork, 87
  friendships, 89–90
  local primary schools, 86–7
  media, 90
  officialdom, 90–1
  organisation, 85
  participatory nature, 90–1
  pottery, 87–8
  silk-screen printing, 88
  social interactions, 89–90
  talent discovery, 88–9
  see also CALL-ME project; The Contemporary visual art and identity construction - Well-being amongst older people project
community building, 90
community exercise projects, 85
comparative wealth, 190
competencies
  attitude, 224, 225
  definition, 223–4
  design projects, 238
  knowledge, 224
  skills, 224
compression of morbidity, 38, 39 (Fig.)
compromised immunity, 123–5
  hip fractures, 123–4

stress, 124–5
computer use, 185–6
concentric circle social network maps, 199
concept maps, DFAW project, 228
conceptualising of old age, 116–17
confidence improvement, SOS project, 218
Connect programme, Guildhall School of Music, 144
The Contemporary visual art and identity construction - Well-being amongst older people project, 91–6, 110–11, 147–9, 197–8
analysis methods, 148
art lovers, 149
baseline data, 92
benefits, 147
cultural engagement, 94–5
decline, 92–3
ethical approval, 91
exclusion in, 198
groups, 147
learning importance, 94
mental activity, 94
methods, 147, 197
middle-class participants, 198
narrative construction, 95–6, 111
negative social representation, 93–4
organisation, 91
provision changes, 95
recruitment, 91
response differences, 197
self-identity interpretation, 148–9
social exclusion, 92–3
transport needs, 95
variation of opinion, 148–9
venues, 91–2, 147–8
working-class participants, 197
continence control project, Canadian NDA Programme, 8
continence issues, design importance, 212–13
continuity, sense of, 99
core components, quality of life, 118
cortisol
depression, 62
stress, 60
counter-narratives, 84–91
see also specific projects
counter stories, 102
couples, NANA project, 167
Cox, Lynne, 4
CQC *see* Care Quality Commission (CQC)
Crace, Jim, 82–3
craftwork, 87
critical narrativity, 79
critical reflection, 206
Cross-Council Coordination Committee on Ageing Research, 15

cultural barriers, multi-disciplinary research, 11
cultural beliefs, MINA project, 160
cultural capital, social class, 197–8
see also The Contemporary visual art and identity construction - Well-being amongst older people project
cultural changes, social constructs of ageing, 28
cultural engagement
authorship, 204–6
see also Fiction and Cultural Mediation of Ageing Project (FCMAP)
The Contemporary visual art and identity construction - Well-being amongst older people project, 94–5
cultural influences, MINA project, 165
cultural narratives, 80–4
Cumulative, Universal, Progressive, Inherent, Deleterious (CUPID), biological ageing, 31
CUPID (Cumulative, Universal, Progressive, Inherent, Deleterious), biological ageing, 31
cytomegalovirus (CMV) infections, 60

D
Damodaran, Leela, 3, 8
data collection, 'Working Late' project, 141–2
daughters, adult, 196–7
daytime sleep, 129, 138–9
DB (defined benefit) pensions, 123
DCMS (Department for Culture, Media and Sport), 131
DC (defined contribution) pensions, 123
Deaf Sentence (Lodge), 82
'Decision making in detecting and preventing financial abuse of older adults' study, 187–8
decline, The Contemporary visual art and identity construction - Well-being amongst older people project, 92–3
deficit models of ageing, 150–1
defined benefit (DB) pensions, 123
defined contribution (DC) pensions, 123
definition of ageing
biological, 26
society's definition, 26–7
sole definition of individuals, 181–2
definition of science of ageing, 11
dementia
incidence of, 150
increase in, 116
music making, 143
Dementia Services Development Centre, 212

demographic changes
  healthy ageing, 113–15
  social constructs of ageing, 28
Department for Culture, Media and
  Sport (DCMS), 131
dependency ratios, 71–2
depression
  immune system effects, 61–2
  poor sleep, 128
descriptive knowledge, designer
  competencies, 226
designers
  competency, 225–7
  design projects, 215
  topics, 223
Design for Ageing Well (DFAW) project
  see DFAW project
design projects
  answering desire/want, 217
  answering need, 216–17
  aspect analysis, 214–23, 214 (Table)
  clarity, 221–2
  competency, 238
  confidence/competence
    improvement, 218–19
  empowerment, 220
  end user involvement, 228–33, 233
    (Table)
  feeling connected, 219
    see also DFAW project; Envision
      project; SOS project; TACT3
      (Tackling Ageing Continence
      through Theory, Tools and
      Technology) project; TiKL
      (Transitions in Kitchen Living)
      project; 'Working Late' - Ageing
      productively through design'
      project
  identifiable outputs, 234
  image improvement, 219–20
  importance of, 211
  inclusive for all, 217–18
  independence, 222–3
  staying active, 215–16
  synergy, 234–7, 238
  usability, 220–1
  younger end users, 236–7
DFAW project, 3, 214 (Table)
  body scanning, 217–18
  clarity, 221
  co-design process, 231–2
  concept maps, 228
  confidence/competence
    improvement, 218, 219
  connection, feeling of, 219
  design of, 215
  desires/wants, 217
  empowerment, 220
  end users, 236, 237
  image improvement, 220
  inclusivity, 217–18

independence, 222
initial surveys, 229
need, answering of, 216–17
OPUS project synergy, 236
outcomes, 237
staying active, 216
subject specialists, 228
TACT3 project synergy, 234
TiKL project synergy, 236
usability, 221
user groups, 231
user involvement, 229–32
vial signs monitoring, 216
'Working Late' project synergy, 235
DHEA
  compromised immunity, 124
  as nutritional supplement, 69–70
  stress, 60
DHEAS
  compromised immunity, 124–5
  depression, 62
  stress, 60–1
diaphragm, 52
diaries, 205
  mass observation, FCAMP, 83
dietary interventions, 70
digital access, 185–6
Dignity and Nutrition Inspection
  Programme, 174
Dignity in care project, 4
Dilnot Commission on Funding of
  Care and Support, 121–2
direct political participation, 246
disability
  affecting factors, 115
  nutrition, 172
disadvantaged neighbourhoods
  loneliness, 84–5
  social engagements, 202–4
    see also CALL-ME project
  social isolation, 84–5
disposable soma theory, 33–4
DNA structure, 44
documentary performances, Ages and
  stages, 96–7, 101–2
domestic equipment, 172
domestic kitchens, 162
Douglas, Mary, 30
drama *see* Ages and stages
drinking habit changes, 166

E

eating habit changes, 166
eating out, nutrition, 173–6
Economic and Social Research Council
  (ESRC)
  Growing Older Programme, 117
  initiatives on ageing, 14 (Table)
  NDA Programme organisation, 1

economics
  'Ageing, Well-being and Development'
    project, 190
  cross-generational ramifications,
    195–7
    see also 'Migration, nutrition and
      ageing across the life course in
      Bangladeshi families. A transitional
      perspective' (MINA)
  'Families and caring in South Asian
    communities' project, 201
  financial austerity, 149
  financial interventions, 131–3
  funding *see* funding
  healthcare costs, 71–2
  low income groups, 192
  macro-political economy of ageing,
    247–8
  negative stereotypes, challenging of,
    193–5
    see also 'Ageing, poverty and
      neoliberalism in urban South
      India' project
  political economy of ageing, 250–2
  social constructs of ageing, 29–30
  see also poverty
employment
  barriers to, 129–30
  CALL-ME project, 203
  extension to, 140–2
    see also 'Working Late' – Ageing
      productively through design'
      project
  paid, 210
  physical capacity for work, 130
  unpaid, 193–4, 210
Employment Equality (Age)
  Regulations (2006), 129
empowerment
  active ageing, 256
  SOS project, 220
endothelium (blood vessels), 54–5
end users
  design projects, 215
  involvement in design projects,
    228–33, 233 (Tab.)
Engineering and Physical Sciences
  Research Council (EPSRC)
  design research, 209–10
  initiatives on ageing, 14 (Table)
  NDA Programme organisation, 2
English Longitudinal Study of Ageing, 9
environment
  biological ageing, 37
  FCAMP, 81–2
Envision project, 4, 214 (Table)
  clarity, 221–2
  design of, 215
  end users, 236
  end users, additional, 237
  independence, 222

outcomes, 237
  SOS project synergy, 235
  synergy, 235
  usability, 221
  'Working Late' project synergy, 236
  younger end users, 237
epistemological barriers to multi-
  disciplinary research, 11
EPSRC *see* Engineering and Physical
  Sciences Research Council
  (EPSRC)
Epstein Barr virus (EBV) infections, 60
EQUAL (Extend Quality Life) Initiative
  (1995), 13, 14 (Table)
  NDA Programme multi-disciplinarity,
    18–19
  Research Council distribution, 19–20,
    19 (Table)
Equality Act (2010), 129
ERA (The Experimental Research on
  Ageing), 14 (Table)
ERA-AGE (European Research Area
  on Ageing), 15
error catastrophe, 34
ESRC *see* Economic and Social
  Research Council (ESRC) Growing
  Older Programme
ethnicity, social connectivity, 198–201
  see also 'Families and caring in South
    Asian communities' project
ethnography, mappmal project, 161
EU *see* European Union (EU)
European collaboration, NCAR
  objectives, 15
The European Nutrition for Health
  Alliance (2011), 156
European Research Area on Ageing
  (ERA-AGE) project (2004-09), 15
European Union (EU)
  employment guidelines, 250–1
  political economy of ageing, 250–2
evolutionary theories of ageing, 33–4
exercise, 133–7, 210
  benefits, 134–5
  chronic illness effects, 133
  disincentives, 137
  fall prevention, 134–5
  guidelines, 133
  increase in, 70
  MINA project, 170–1
  moderate intensity activity, 133–4
  muscle strength, 134
  occupation-based, 135
  sleep improvement, 138
  time spent, 134
  types, 137
  vigorous intensive activity, 133–4
  see also 'Working Late' – Ageing
    productively through design' project
exhibitions, Representing self –
  representing ageing project, 104–5

expectations of decline, 37
experience misrepresentation, FCAMP, 205–6
The Experimental Research on Ageing (ERA) Programme (2001-07), 14 (Table)
Extend Quality of Life Initiative *see* EQUAL (Extend Quality Life) Initiative (1995)

F

fall(s), associated risks, 116
fall prevention, 212
  exercise, 134–5
'Families and caring in South Asian communities' project, 199–201, 207–8
  challenges, 199, 201
  economic structures, 201
  friends, 201
  important relationships, 201
  problem-focused orientation, 199
  social network maps, 199, 200 (Fig.)
  social structures, 201
family businesses, 'Ageing, poverty and neoliberalism in urban South India' project, 194
family structure, MINA project, 168
Fast, Jane, 7
FCAMP *see* Fiction and Cultural Mediation of Ageing Project (FCMAP)
fear, barriers to healthy ageing, 131
feedback, unprompted, 104
fiction, 80–4
Fiction and Cultural Mediation of Ageing Project (FCMAP), 80–4, 204–6
  critical reflection, 206
  diaries, 205
  environment, 81–2
  experience misrepresentation, 205–6
  methods, 204–5
  novels, 82–3, 110, 112
  reading groups, 204–5
  resistance to, 206
  self-reflection, 83–4
  structure, 205
The fight for Shelton Bar, 97
finances
  austerity, 149
  interventions, 131–3
  see also economics
Financial abuse project, 4
fluid intelligence, 150
focus groups, NDA Programme, 227
food environments, 162–76
  historical, 162–5
  lifestyle effects, 165–71
  transition, 177

food ethnobotanical knowledge, MINA project, 159
food restrictions, Dutch famine study, 37–8
food routines, NANA project, 167
foods, healthy, 168–9
Food Standards Agency Wales (2003), 176
food types, MINA project, 168
fourth age, 116
fried foods, MINA project, 169
friends, 'Families and caring in South Asian communities' project, 201
friendships, community arts project, 89–90
Fülöp, Tamàs, 7
funding
  collaboration, NCAR objectives, 15
  multi-disciplinary research barriers, 12, 16–17
  NDA Programme, 6
FUTURAGE (Road Map for the Future of Ageing Research), 242, 256
Future Bathroom (Sheffield University), 235
future-oriented self-image, 153

G

gadgets, nutrition, 172
gait speed, 127–8
gardening, 137
  CALL-ME project, 85
garments
  size of, 211
  sport-related, 231
genetics of ageing, 37, 38–41
  compression of morbidity, 38, 39 (Fig.)
  see also specific genes
geography, ageing effects, 36
Gien, Lan, 7
Gilhooly, Mary, 4
glitazones, 67–8
globalisation, 245–6
Global Position Satellites (GPS), 126–7
goal-directed activities, subjective well-being, 121
golden generation, 114
good health retention, 72–3
government cut campaigns, 250
GPS (Global Position Satellites), 126–7
grandmother effect, 33–4
grass-roots initiatives, active ageing, 257–8
Great British Public Toilet Map, TACT3 project, 216, 221, 222
Great North Museum (Newcastle-upon-Tyne), 92, 147
'Grey and pleasant land?' project, 3, 191–3

barriers identified, 192
civic activities, 192
informal activities, 192
low income groups, 192
methods, 191–2
minority groups, 192
grey matter of brain, 56–8, 57 (Fig.)
group activity organisation, CALL-ME
   project, 203–4
group singing, 143–4
The Growing Older Programme (1999-
   2005), 14 (Table)
Guildhall School of Music, 144

H

HALCyon Project, 3
Hallam, Susan, 4
Hancock, Ruth, 121–2
Handbook of theories of ageing (Bengtson),
   33
Haslam, Cheryl, 3, 7
Hatton Gallery (Newcastle-upon-Tyne),
   92, 147
health, social barriers to, 153
Health and creative ageing project,
   Canadian NDA Programme, 7
health barriers, 190
healthcare costs, 71–2
health promotion, long-term care, 153
healthy ageing, 113–21
   barriers to, 121–31
      see also individual barriers
   demographic changes, 113–15
   economic barriers, 121–3
   employment barriers, 129–30
   employment extension, 140–2
      see also 'Working Late' - Ageing
      productively through design'
      project
   exercise *see* exercise
   financial interventions, 131–3
   interventions, 131–49
      see also specific interventions
   loss of work, 129–30
   poor sleep, 128–9
   psychosocial barriers, 130–1
   quality of life *see* quality of life (QoL)
   sleep improvement, 137–40
   subjective well-being, 120–1
health years, 117
healthy foods, MINA project, 168–9
hearing changes, 211–12
heart, 52
heart disease, 55–6
heart rate (HR), 53
   monitoring devices, 212
   variability of, 53–4, 54 (Fig.)
heart rate variability (HRV), 53
height distribution, 211
Hennessey, Catherine, 3, 8
heterogeneity

active ageing concerns, 256
   WHO active ageing, 254
HGPS *see* Hutchinson–Gilford progeria
   syndrome (HGPS)
high-income countries, participation
   and social connectivity, 182–3
high-street shops, access to, 184
hip fractures, 123–4
   stress, 62–3
historic buildings, access to, 184
Hofer, Scott, 7
homeostasis, cardiovascular system, 52
'hospitalfoodie' concept, 161–2, 174–5
   family communication, 175
hospitals, nutrition in, 174
HR *see* heart rate (HR)
HRV (heart rate variability), 53
human help, computer use, 186
Hutchinson–Gilford progeria syndrome
   (HGPS), 42–3
   progerin accumulation prevention,
   68–9
   rapamycin therapy, 67
hypnotic drugs, sleep improvement, 138
hypoxia, 52–3

I

IDEAS Factory, 6
identity, 151–3
   social constructs of ageing, 29
ideological differences, multi-
   disciplinary research barriers, 12
IGOs (international government
   organisations), 245–6
ill health with ageing, 115–16
image diversity, 107–8
immune response project, Canadian
   NDA Programme, 7
immune system, 58–60, 61 (Fig.)
   cancer control, 58–9
   cell ageing, 47
   cell types, 59
   compromised *see* compromised
      immunity
   depression, 61–2
   infections, 59–60
   inflammation, 59
   memory cells, 60
   modulation of, 69–70
   physical barriers, 59
   thymus, 60
immunological challenge, 34
immunosenescence *see* compromised
   immunity
important relationships, 'Families and
   caring in South Asian communities'
   project, 201
inactivity *see* sedentary behaviour
inclusivity
   active ageing, 255
   designs in access effects, 184–5

independence, 156
industrialisation, retirement, 191
industry participation, 'Working Late'
    project, 141
inequality
    active ageing, 256
    WHO active ageing, 254
infections
    depression effects, 61–2
    immune response, 59–60
    persistent, 60
    see also specific infections
inflammation, immune system, 59
influenza, 58
informal activities, 'Grey and pleasant
    land?' project, 192
information collection, NANA project,
    160
information technology project,
    Canadian NDA Programme, 8
'in-home' mobility, 127
initial surveys, DFAW, 229
innate immune system, 59
institutional access, 187–8
    see also 'Decision making in detecting
    and preventing financial abuse of
    older adults' study
insulin/insulin-like signalling pathway,
    39
Integrated Approaches to Healthy
    Ageing Programme, MRC, 14
    (Table)
Interactive analysis of functional and
    cognitive change across the IALSA,
    Canadian NDA Programme, 7
intergenerational solidarity, 255
international government organisations
    (IGOs), 245–6
intervention development, 'Working
    Late' project, 136–7
interventions in ageing
    age-related disease increase, 71
    ethics of, 70–3
    good health retention, 72–3
    healthcare costs, 71–2
    social care costs, 71–2
    societal structure, 71
    'un-naturalness,' 71
    see also modulating ageing; specific
    interventions
interviews
    Ages and stages, 96–7, 98–101
    'Music for Life' project, 146
    NDA Programme, 227
    professional, 187–8
    Representing self - representing
    ageing project, 103
    TiKL project, 158
isolation, MINA project, 195

J
The jolly potters, 97
Jutai, Jeffrey W, 8

K
Keating, Nora, 8
kitchen(s)
    communal, 162
    design, 213
    domestic, 162
Kitchen living project, 5
The Knotty, 97, 98
knowledge
    competencies, 224
    designer competencies, 226
    multi-disciplinary research barriers, 11
KT-EQUAL, 18
Kuh, Diana, 3, 7

L
labels, clarity, 222
lack of interest, 192
Landscapes project, 5
Latimer, J, 30
laziness see sedentary behaviour
learning, importance of, 94
leisure pursuits, NANA project, 166–7
life-ability, quality of life, 117
life course interventions, 'Working Late'
    project, 136
life course perspective, active ageing,
    253
life expectancy changes, 9, 113–14
Lifelong Health and Wellbeing (LLHW)
    Programme, 14 (Table)
    NDA Programme collaborative
    research programmes, 6
    Research Council distribution, 19–20,
    19 (Table)
lifestyle, food environments, 165–71
Lifetime homes, lifetime neighbourhoods,
    178
light/lighting
    nutrition problems, 172
    sleep, 139–40
literature review, mappmal project, 161
liveability, quality of life, 117
LLHW see Lifelong Health and
    Wellbeing (LLHW) Programme
Lloyd, Liz, 4
LMNA gene, 43
local community, 257–8
local group activities, 203–4
local primary schools, 86–7
location-based tracking, 126–7
Lodge, David, 82
London Olympics (2012), 184–5
loneliness
    disadvantaged neighbourhoods, 84–5
    MINA project, 195
The Longevity Genes Project, 38

longitudinal ageing, 37
Longitudinal ageing project, 5
Longitudinal data project, 4
long-term care, nutrition, 175
Look at me! project, 5
Lord, Janet, 4, 7
loss of function, 9
loss of work *see* unemployment
low income groups, 'Grey and pleasant
  land?' project, 192
lungs, 52

M
Macdonald, Alistair, 4
macro-political economy of ageing,
  247–8
Madrid International Plan on Action on
  Ageing (MIPAA) (2002), 253
Maganaris, Constantinos, 5, 8
magnetic resonance imaging (MRI),
  56–7, 57 (Fig.)
'Maintaining dignity in later life'
  project, 152–3
major depressive disorder (MDD), 62
malnutrition
  consequences, 156
  definition, 155
  prevalence, 155
  recovery delay, 175
  risks for, 156
  wound healing, 175–6
  see also nutrition
Malnutrition matter (BAPEN), 176
MAP2030, 3
  financial interventions to support
    healthy ageing, 131
  healthy ageing economic barriers,
    121–2
mappmal project, 3, 161–2, 174
  family communication, 175
  rationale, 175–6
mass observation diary keeping,
  FCAMP, 83
McCann, Jane, 3
McFadyen, Bradford J, 8
McInnes, Lynn, 5
McKay, Ian, 86
MDD (major depressive disorder), 62
meals, MINA project definition, 169
measurement of ageing, 34–7
  mortality rates, 35–6, 35 (Fig.)
  susceptibility to death, 34
mechanisms of ageing, 26–7
mechanistic theories of ageing, 34
Medawar, Peter, 33
media, 90
  representation of ageing, 102
  visual, 79
Medical Research Council (MRC), 2
  initiatives on ageing, 14 (Table)

Integrated Approaches to Healthy
  Ageing Programme, 14 (Table)
Meeting nutritional needs, 178–9
meetings, NDA Programme, 227
memory cells, immune system, 60
mental activity, 94
metformin, 67
methodological barriers to multi-
  disciplinary research, 11
microwaves, 219–20
migration history, MINA project, 165
'Migration, nutrition and ageing across
  the life course in Bangladeshi
  families. A transitional perspective'
  (MINA), 3, 158–60, 195–7
  adult daughters, 196–7
  anthropometry, 159
  conclusions, 177
  cultural beliefs, 160
  experts, 159
  family structure, 168
  food environment, 164–5
  food ethnobotanical knowledge, 159
  food types, 168–9
  fried foods, 169
  healthy foods, 168–9
  inter-generational component, 159
  lifestyle, 167–9, 170–1
  meal definition, 169
  member types, 167–8
  mixed-method approach, 159
  older roles, 158–9
  physical activity, 170–1
  questionnaires, 159–60
  results, 195–6
  salt, 169
  self-exclusion, 196–7
  structure, 195
  study design, 159
  transnational component, 159
Mihaildis, Alex, 8
MINA project *see* 'Migration, nutrition
  and ageing across the life course in
  Bangladeshi families. A transitional
  perspective' (MINA)
minority groups, 'Grey and pleasant
  land?' project, 192
MIPAA (Madrid International Plan on
  Action on Ageing) (2002), 253
mobile phone use, 185
  SUS-IT, 185
mobility, 125–8
  assessment, 126–7
  barriers to community involvement,
    192
  bone density, 126
  chronic illness, 125–6
  design issues, 213
  improvement interventions, 126
  'in-home,' 127
  interventions, 127–8

mortality predictor, 126
'out-of-home,' 125, 127
predictors of, 127–8
problem incidence, 125
self-respect, 128
social life restriction, 125
Mobility and ageing project, 5
moderate intensity activity, 133–4
modulating ageing, 64–70
   caloric restriction, 65–6
   disease reduction, 64
   progerin accumulation prevention,
      68–9
   stress kinase signalling inhibition, 67–8
   telomere reactivation, 68
   TOR complex regulation, 66–7
   see also interventions in ageing
morbidity
   compression of, 38, 39 (Fig.)
   obesity, 114
morbid period, 73–4
mortality rates
   measurement of ageing, 35–6, 35
      (Fig.)
   mobility as predictor, 126
   participation and social connectivity,
      182
   premature, reduction of, 9
Moynihan, Paula, 3
MRC *see* Medical Research Council
   (MRC)
MRI (magnetic resonance imaging),
   56–7, 57 (Fig.)
mTORC, 39, 41
'Multidisciplinary approaches to
   develop a prototype for the
   prevention of malnutrition in older
   people' (mappmal) *see* mappmal
   project
multi-disciplinary research, 10, 11–20
   barriers to, 11–12
   case for, 12–13
   NCAR objectives, 15
   NDA Programme, 16–18
   UK initiatives, 13–16
   see also specific projects
Murphy, Michael, 3
Murray, Michael, 5
muscle strength, exercise, 134
muscle wasting *see* sarcopenia
'Music for Life' project, 4, 144–6
   cognitive benefits, 146
   interviews, 146
   perceived benefits, 146
   research methods, 144–5
   results, 145–6
   sample characteristics, 145
   venues, 144
music making, active ageing, 143–6
   see also 'Music for Life' project
mutations in telomeres, 45–6

myelin sheaths, 56
myocytes, cell ageing, 55–6

N

NANA (Novel Assessment of Nutrition
   and Ageing) project, 3, 160–1
   cognitive assessment, 166
   conclusions, 176–7
   couples, 167
   exercise, 171
   food routines, 167
   leisure pursuits, 166–7
   lifestyle effects, 166, 170
   obesity, 173
   overweight members, 173
   Scottish background, 164
   solitary people, 167
narratives, 77–8, 111
   construction, 95–6, 111
   critical, 79
   cultural, 80–4
   cultural differences, 78–9
   exchange of, 77–8
   foreclosure, 78
   functions, 78
National Collaboration on Ageing
   Research (NCAR) (2001-04),
   11–12, 14 (Table), 15
National Institute of Clinical Excellence
   (NICE), nutrition concerns, 176
national variations, active ageing, 256
navigation studies, OPUS project,
   183–4
NCAR (National Collaboration on
   Ageing Research), 11–12
NCAR (National Collaboration on
   Ageing Research) (2001-04), 14
   (Table), 15
NDA Programme (New Dynamics of
   Ageing), 1–8, 14 (Table)
   ageing effects, 241
   Canada, 7–8
   collaborative research projects, 6
   see also specific projects
   commissioning of, 5–7
   disciplines, 210
   funding, 6
   inter-disciplinary communication,
      227–8
   multi-disciplinary research, 16–18
   objectives, 2
   programme projects, 4–5
   projects, 2–3
   see also specific projects
   Research Council distribution, 19–20,
      19 (Table)
   research councils, 1–2
   research themes, 2
   subject specialists, 228
   subthemes, 2
needs, SOS project, 216

negative social representation, 93–4
negative stereotypes, challenging of,
    190–5
  economic contribution, 193–5
    see also 'Ageing, poverty and
      neoliberalism in urban South
      India' project
  rural community capital, 191–3
    see also 'Grey and pleasant land?'
      project
neighbourhoods
  disadvantages *see* disadvantaged
    neighbourhoods
  identification, CALL-ME project, 203
  importance of, CALL-ME project,
    203
neoliberalism, 245
nerve cells, 57 (Fig.)
nervous system, 56–8
  cell structure, 57 (Fig.)
neutrophils, hip fractures, 124
New Dynamics of Ageing Programme
    see NDA Programme (New
    Dynamics of Ageing)
New Dynamics of Nutrition, 6
Newman, Andrew, 5
newsletters, NDA Programme, 227
New Victoria Theatre, 96
NICE, nutrition concerns, 176
Nice girls, 97
nighttime awakening, 128–9
nocturia, 129
normative knowledge, designer
    competencies, 226
Northern Gallery for Contemporary
    Art (Sunderland), 91, 148
Novel Assessment of Nutrition and
    Ageing project *see* NANA (Novel
    Assessment of Nutrition and
    Ageing) project
novel preparatory networks initiative, 17
novels, FCAMP, 82–3, 110, 112
nuclear lamins, 43
Nun Study on ageing and Alzheimer's
    disease, 13
nutrition, 155–79
  health and well-being, 171–3
  healthy foods, 168–9
  independence loss, 173–6
  poor intrauterine nutrition, 36
  projects *see* mappmal project;
    'Migration, nutrition and ageing
    across the life course in Bangladeshi
    families. A transitional perspective'
    (MINA); NANA (Novel Assessment
    of Nutrition and Ageing) project;
    TiKL (Transitions in Kitchen
    Living) project
  see also food environments;
    malnutrition; obesity

O
obesity, 173
  morbidity effects, 114
  NANA project, 173
  prevalence, 155
  sedentary behaviour, 135
obligations, active ageing, 255–6
occupation-based exercise, 135
odour detection, TACT3 project, 216
OECD (Organisation for Economic
    Co-operation and Development),
    246
oestrogen, skin ageing, 50–1
Office for National Statistics (ONS),
    114–15
officialdom, community arts project,
    90–1
Older People's quality of life (OPQoL),
    118–19
Older People's Reference Group
    (OPRG), 10
Older People's Use of Unfamiliar Space
    project *see* OPUS (Older People's
    Use of Unfamiliar Space) project
ONS (Office for National Statistics),
    114–15
OPEN DATA, 220
Open Method of Coordination, 250–1
operational knowledge, designers, 226
Opportunity age (DWP, 2005), 251–2
OPQoL (Older People's quality of life),
    118–19
OPRG (Older People's Reference
    Group), 10
OPUS (Older People's Use of
    Unfamiliar Space) project, 5, 183–4
  DFAW project synergy, 236
  findings, 184
  navigation studies, 183–4
  study methods, 183–4
  wayfinding, 183–4
oral history
  food environment interviews, 162–3
  TiKL project, 158
Organisation for Economic Co-
    operation and Development
    (OECD), 246
Organiser for Working Late (OWL),
    140–1
  development, 142
Our age, our stage, 101–2
'out-of-home' mobility, 125, 127
OWL *see* Organiser for Working Late
    (OWL)
oxygen, cell ageing, 46

P
p38 MAP kinase, 46
  drug inhibition, 67
paid employment, 210

paid work, 'Ageing, poverty and
    neoliberalism in urban South India'
    project, 193–4
Parr, Martin, 95
Parrworld (Parr), 95
participation and social connectivity,
    181–208
  access see access
  active ageing, 256
  Ages and stages, 101
  difficulties in, 207
  generation of meaningful process,
    202–6
    see also CALL-ME project; Fiction
      and Cultural Mediation of Ageing
      Project (FCMAP)
  high-income countries, 182–3
  historical aspects, 182–3
  main thoughts behind, 181
  positive impact on mortality, 182
  structural factors, 195–201
    see also The Contemporary visual
      art and identity construction -
      Well-being amongst older people
      project; 'Families and caring
      in South Asian communities'
      project; 'Migration, nutrition and
      ageing across the life course in
      Bangladeshi families. A transitional
      perspective' (MINA)
participatory community arts project,
    90–1
Pearce, Sheila, 5
peer review system, multi-disciplinary
    research barriers, 12
pensionable age, 28
pensions
  healthy ageing economic barriers, 123
  private pensions, 123
  public pensions, 245–6
  state see state pensions
  types, 123
perceived benefits, 'Music for Life'
    project, 146
performance see Ages and stages
persistent infections, 60
Personal Social Services Research Unit
    (PSSRU), 132
Phillips, Judith, OPUS project, 5
physical activity see exercise
physical barriers, immune system, 59
physical body trauma, stress, 62–3
physical capacity for work, 130
physical disability, nutrition, 172
physiological barriers to good health,
    153
pleiotropy, antagonistic, 33
pneumonia, 58
  hip fractures, 124
policy and practice links, NCAR
  objectives, 15

political economy of ageing, 250–2
political organisations, 188–90
  see also 'Ageing, Well-being and
    Development' project
political participation, 252
  direct, 246
poor intrauterine nutrition, 36
poor sleep, healthy ageing, 128–9
population ageing
  cost of, 245
  implications, 114
positive image of ageing, 212
post-modernism, 247
pottery, 87–8
poverty
  absolute, 190
  'Ageing, poverty and neoliberalism in
    urban South India' project, 194
  low income groups, 192
  see also economics
Poverty in India, 5
premature human ageing diseases, 41–3
  childhood-onset progeria, 42–3
  Werner syndrome, 41–2
premature mortality reduction, 9
primary schools, local, 86–7
private pensions, 123
productive ageing
  active ageing vs., 254
  change to active ageing, 248–9
professional interviews, 187–8
progerias see premature human ageing
  diseases
progerin, 42–3
  accumulation prevention, 68–9
projects
  NDA Programme, 2–3, 4–5
  see also specific projects
providers of design projects, 215
PSSRU (Personal Social Services
  Research Unit), 132
psychological barriers
  good health, 153
  multi-disciplinary research, 11
public houses (pubs), 203
public pensions, 245–6
public representation of ageing, 101

Q

quality of life (QoL), 117–19
  core components, 118
  definitions, 117
  definitions by aged, 117–18
  Schedule for Self-Evaluation of
    Quality of Life, 118
  WHO, 119
Quality of life project, 4
questionnaires
  MINA project, 159–60
  NDA Programme, 227

Representing self - representing
  ageing project, 104
'Working Late' project, 141–2

R

racial stereotyping, 106
RAE (Research Assessment Exercise),
  12
rapamycin, 66–7
reactive oxygen species (ROS), 46
reading groups, FCAMP, 83–4, 204–5
reception barriers, multi-disciplinary
  research, 11
recovery delay, malnutrition, 175
relationships, 'Families and caring in
  South Asian communities' project,
  201
repertoire, Ages and stages, 96–7
replicative senescence *see* cell ageing
Representing self - representing ageing
  project, 102–9
  calenders, 104
  counter stories, 102
  difficulties, 103–4
  exhibition success, 104–5
  image diversity, 107–8
  interviews, 103
  media representation of ageing, 102
  organisation, 103
  questionnaires, 104
  racial stereotyping, 106
  stereotype resistance, 105–6
  unprompted feedback, 104
  women, 103
research, 10
  impact on society, 10
  paradigm shift, 10–11
  themes in NDA Programme, 2
Research Assessment Exercise (RAE),
  12
Research Councils, initiatives on ageing,
  14 (Table)
resilience, 151–3
respiration rate, 53
retirement
  age of, 28
  Ages and stages, 100
  careers, 116–17
  industrialisation, 191
  negative aspects, 191
retirement housing, nutrition, 173–6
Rhesus monkeys, caloric restriction
  models, 65
rights, active ageing, 255–6
risk exposure, employment, 140
Road Map for the Future of Ageing
  Research (FUTURAGE), 242, 256
role expectations, MINA project, 165
ROS (reactive oxygen species), 46
Royal Commission on Long-term Care
  (1999), 132

rural communities
  Canadian NDA Programme project, 8
  capital, 191–3

S

Safety on Stairs (SOS) project *see* SOS
  project
The Sage (Gateshead), 144
SAGE (The Science of Ageing)
  Programme (1998–2001), 14 (Table)
salt, MINA project, 169
sarcopenia, 50
  prevention benefits, 72
Schedule for Self-Evaluation of Quality
  of Life (SEIQoL), 118
schools, local primary, 86–7
The Science of Ageing (SAGE)
  Programme (1998-2001), 14 (Table)
Second World Assembly on Ageing
  (2002), 102
sedentary behaviour, 134
  health risks, 135
  obesity, 135
SEIQoL (Schedule for Self-Evaluation
  of Quality of Life), 118
self-exclusion, MINA project, 196–7
self-image, 151–3
self-reflection, 80–4
  FCAMP, 83–4
self-respect, mobility, 128
sense of belonging, 99–100
sense of continuity, 99
senses
  changes in, 211–12
  nutrition problems, 171
sensory neurons, 56
seven ages of man speech (Shakespeare),
  31–2, 79, 96
Shakespeare's "seven ages of man"
  speech, 31–2, 79, 96
shingles, 60
Shipley Art Gallery (Gateshead), 91–2,
  148
signage, access effects, 184–5
signalling incoherence, 34
silk-screen printing, 88
silver economy, 247
singing, groups, 143–4
sitting, 134
  'Working Late' project, 136
skills, 224
  designer competencies, 226
skin ageing, 50–1
sleep
  daytime, 129, 138–9
  initiation, 128–9
  interventions, 137–40
  light, 139–40
  poor, 128–9

'Sleep in Ageing' collaboration
  see SomIA ('Sleep in Ageing')
    collaboration
sleeping medication, 139
social barriers to good health, 153
social capital, 182
  see also participation and social
    connectivity
social care costs, 116
  interventions in ageing, 71–2
social class, cultural capital, 197–8
  see also The Contemporary visual art
    and identity construction - Well-
    being amongst older people project
social clubs, 189
social connectivity
  ethnicity, 198–201
    see also 'Families and caring in South
      Asian communities' project
    see also participation and social
      connectivity
social constructs of ageing, 27–31, 36–7
  chronological age, 27–8
  cultural changes, 28
  demographic changes, 28
  economics, 29–30
  effects on individuals, 28
  identity relationship, 29
  negative aspects, 28–9
  pensionable age, 28
  retirement age, 28
social engagements, 202–4
  see also CALL-ME project
social environment variables, ageing
    effects, 36–7
social etiquette, TiKL project, 163–4
social exclusion, The Contemporary
    visual art and identity construction
    - Well-being amongst older people
    project, 92–3
social exclusion/isolation, 244
  disadvantaged neighbourhoods, 84–5
  mobility, 125
  tissue ageing, 48, 50
social inclusion, 74
  digital inclusion effects, 186
social interactions
  community arts project, 89–90
  TiKL project, 166
social network(s)
  Ages and stages, 100
  music making, 143
social network maps
  concentric circle, 199
  'Families and caring in South Asian
    communities' project, 199, 200 (Fig.)
social organisations, access to, 188–90
  see also 'Ageing, Well-being and
    Development' project
social participation, 251

social relationships
  'Music for Life' project, 145
  subjective well-being, 121
social roles, 210
  Ages and stages, 100–1
social structures
  'Families and caring in South Asian
    communities' project, 201
  interventions in ageing, 71
society's definition of ageing, 26–7
solidarity, intergenerational, 255
solitary people, NANA project, 167
SomIA ('Sleep in Ageing')
    collaboration, 3, 138–40
  daytime sleep, 138–9
SOS project, 5, 214 (Table)
  additional end users, 237
  answering desire/want, 217
  answering need, 216
  confidence/competence
    improvement, 218
  empowerment, 220
  Envision project synergy, 235
  image improvement, 220
  inclusive for all, 218
  independence, 222
  new end users, 236
  outcomes, 237
  staying active, 216
  TiKL project synergy, 234–5
  younger end users, 237
South Africa *see* 'Ageing, Well-being and
    Development' project
South Asian project, 5
SPARC (Strategic Promotion of Ageing
    Research Capacity) (2005-09), 14
    (Table)
spatial access, 183–5
sport-related garments, 231
stairs *see* SOS project
stakeholders, design projects, 215
state pensions
  healthy ageing economic barriers,
    122–3
  welfare regime effect, 244
staying active, design projects, 215–16
Stefanovska, Aneta, 5
Steinsaltz, David, 5
stereotype resistance, 105–6
Strategic Promotion of Ageing
    Research Capacity (SPARC) (2005-
    09), 14 (Table)
strength, changes in, 211
stress, 60–4
  carer stress, 63–4
  cell ageing, 46
  cortisol, 60
  DHEA, 60
  DHEAS, 60–1
  hip fractures, 62–3
  management of, 63, 70

physical body trauma, 62–3
Stress and immunity project, 4
stress kinase signalling inhibition, 67–8
structural barriers, multi-disciplinary research, 11
subject specialists, NDA Programme, 228
superannuation, 244
surveys
  CALL-ME project, 203
  initial in DFAW, 229
  NDA Programme, 227
susceptibility to death, measurement of ageing, 34
SUS-IT (Sustaining IT use by older people to promote autonomy and independence) project, 3, 185–6
  computer use, 185–6
  mobile phone use, 185
Sustaining IT use by older people to promote autonomy and independence project *see* SUS-IT (Sustaining IT use by older people to promote autonomy and independence) project
synergy, design projects, 238

Y

Tackling Ageing Continence through Theory, Tools and Technology project *see* TACT3 (Tackling Ageing Continence through Theory, Tools and Technology) project
TACT3 (Tackling Ageing Continence through Theory, Tools and Technology) project, 4, 214 (Table)
  additional end users, 237
  answering desire/want, 217
  confidence/competence improvement, 218
  design of, 215
  DFAW project synergy, 234
  empowerment, 220
  feeling connected, 219
  Great British Public Toilet Map, 216, 221, 222
  image improvement, 220
  inclusive for all, 218
  independence, 222
  new end users, 236
  odour detection, 216
  outcomes, 237
  staying active, 216
  subject specialists, 228
  usability, 221
'Taking Part' project, 131
talents, community arts project, 88–9
Tannenbaum, Cara, 8
tape recordings, 98
T cells, 59

Technology Foresight Initiative (1994/5), 13
telomeres
  age-related conditions, 45
  definition, 44
  loss, 44–6
  mutations in, 45–6
  reactivation, 68
telomere shortening
  carer stress, 63
  depression, 62
  in endothelial cells, 55
temperature control (thermoregulation), 52–3
Tew, Philip, 5
theatres *see* Ages and stages
theories of ageing, 32–4
  evolutionary theories, 33–4
  mechanistic theories, 34
  'wear-and-tear' theory, 33
thermoregulation (temperature control), 52–3
third age definition, 116
Thompson, Janice, 3
thymus, 60
TiKL (Transitions in Kitchen Living) project, 157–8, 214 (Table)
  additional end users, 237
  aims, 157–8
  answering desire/want, 217
  answering need, 216
  clarity, 222
  conclusions, 177–9
  confidence/competence improvement, 218, 219
  design, 157
  DFAW project synergy, 236
  empowerment, 220
  Envision project synergy, 235
  feeling connected, 219
  health and well-being, 171–3
  height concerns, 211
  image improvement, 220
  inclusive for all, 218
  independence, 222
  lifestyle effects, 165
  new end users, 236
  outcomes, 237
  quotations, 163–4
  social etiquette, 163–4
  social interactions, 166
  SOS project synergy, 234–5
  staying active, 216
  usability, 221
  user involvement, 232
  younger end users, 237
time spent, exercise, 134
tissue ageing, 48–51
  sarcopenia, 50
  skin ageing, 50–1

social isolation, 48, 50
see also specific tissues
T lymphocytes (T cells), 59
TOR complex regulation, 66–7
tracking, location-based, 126–7
Transitions in Kitchen Living project
    see TiKL (Transitions in Kitchen
    Living) project
transport needs, 95
trauma, stress, 62–3
trip hazards, removal of, 70
TSB COBALT (Foundation for
    Assistive Technology), 235

U

ultraviolet (UV) radiation, cell ageing,
    46
understanding of ageing, 9
unemployment, healthy ageing, 129–30
unfamiliar places, access, 183
United Nations (UN), 253
universal needs, subjective well-being,
    120
University of the Third Age, 150
'un-naturalness,' interventions in ageing,
    71
unpaid employment, 193–4, 210
unprompted feedback, 104
unusual structures, access effects, 184
user groups, DFAW project, 231
US National Institute on Ageing, 72
utility of life, quality of life, 117

V

van den Heuvel, Eleanor, 4, 8
varicella-zoster, 60
vasomotion, 52
venous insufficiency, skin ageing, 50
Vera-Sanko, Penny, 5
vial signs monitoring, DFAW project,
    216
Victor, Christina, 5
vigorous intensive activity, 133–4
vision, changes in, 211–12
visual arts, 146–9
    see also The Contemporary visual art
    and identity construction - Well-
    being amongst older people project
visual media, 79
visual representations, 102–9, 111
vitamin B supplements, 70
vitamin D supplements, 70

W

WAG, nutrition concerns, 176
waking at night, 128–9
walking, 137
Walking Works Wonders initiative, 235
Warren, Lorna, 5
wayfinding, OPUS project, 183–4
wealth, comparative, 190

'wear-and-tear' theory of ageing, 191
websites
    clarity, 221
    NDA Programme, 227
welfare state
    ageing *vs.*, 246–7
    effects of, 243
well-being, active ageing, 253
well-known places, access, 183
Werner syndrome (WS), 41–2
    therapy, 67
Westminster Adult education Service,
    144
white matter of brain, 56–8, 57 (Fig.)
WHO *see* World Health Organization
    (WHO)
WHOQoL-OLD, 119
Winterson, Jeanette, 109–10
Wittenberg, Raphael, 121–2
'@ work cards,' 142, 143 (Fig.)
working-class participants, 197
'Working Late' - Ageing productively
    through design' project, 3, 135–7,
    140–2, 214 (Table)
    answering desire/want, 217
    answering need, 216
    Canadian NDA Programme, 7
    data collection, 141–2
    DFAW project synergy, 235
    Envision project synergy, 235
    feeling connected, 219
    inclusive for all, 218
    industry participation, 141
    intervention development, 136–7
    life course interventions, 136
    new end users, 236
    outcomes, 237
    questionnaires, 141–2
    sitting time data, 136
    '@ work cards,' 142, 143 (Fig.)
    working place design, 141
    younger end users, 237
working place design, 141
work loss *see* unemployment
World Health Organization (WHO)
    active ageing, 249–50, 252–3, 257
    active ageing concept, 182
    quality of life, 119
wound healing, malnutrition, 175–6
Wright, Peter, 5
WRN gene, 42
WS *see* Werner syndrome (WS)

Y

Year of Older People (1993), 253
Young, Wendy, 8

Z

Zoomer nation, 72